City, State

OXFORD COMPARATIVE CONSTITUTIONALISM

Series Editors
Richard Albert, William Stamps Farish Professor of Law,
The University of Texas at Austin School of Law
Robert Schütze, Professor of European and Global Law,
Durham University and College of Europe

Comparative constitutional law has a long and distinguished history in intellectual thought and in the construction of public law. As political actors and the people who create or modify their constitutional orders, they often wish to learn from the experience and learning of others. This cross-fertilization and mutual interaction has only accelerated with the onset of globalization, which has transformed the world into an interconnected web that facilitates dialogue and linkages across international and regional structures. Oxford Comparative Constitutionalism seeks to publish scholarship of the highest quality in constitutional law that deepens our knowledge of local, national, regional, and global phenomena through the lens of comparative public law.

Advisory Board
Denis Baranger, Professor of Public Law, Université Paris II Panthéon-Assas
Wen-Chen Chang, Professor of Law, National Taiwan University
Roberto Gargarella, Professor of Law, Universidad Torcuato di Tella
Vicki C. Jackson, Thurgood Marshall Professor of Constitutional Law,
Harvard Law School
Christoph Möllers, Professor of Public Law and Jurisprudence,
Humboldt-Universität zu Berlin
Cheryl Saunders A.O., Laureate Professor Emeritus, Melbourne Law School

ALSO PUBLISHED IN THIS SERIES
Poland's Constitutional Breakdown
Wojciech Sadurski

City, State

Constitutionalism and the Megacity

RAN HIRSCHL

OXFORD
UNIVERSITY PRESS

OXFORD
UNIVERSITY PRESS

Oxford University Press is a department of the University of Oxford. It furthers the University's objective of excellence in research, scholarship, and education by publishing worldwide. Oxford is a registered trademark of Oxford University Press in the UK and certain other countries.

Published in the United States of America by Oxford University Press
198 Madison Avenue, New York, NY 10016, United States of America.

© Ran Hirschl 2020

Library of Congress Cataloging-in-Publication Data
Names: Hirschl, Ran, author.
Title: City, state : constitutionalism and the megacity / Ran Hirschl.
Description: New York : Oxford University Press, 2020. | Includes bibliographical references and index.
Identifiers: LCCN 2020005411 (print) | LCCN 2020005412 (ebook) | ISBN 9780190922771 (hardback) | ISBN 9780190922795 (epub) | ISBN 9780190922801 (online) | ISBN 9780190922788 (updf)
Subjects: LCSH: Municipal corporations. | Constitutional law, | Municipal government.
Classification: LCC K3431.H57 2020 (print) | LCC K3431 (ebook) | DDC 342/.09—dc23
LC record available at https://lccn.loc.gov/2020005411
LC ebook record available at https://lccn.loc.gov/2020005412

1 3 5 7 9 8 6 4 2
Printed by Sheridan Books, Inc., United States of America

Note to Readers
This publication is designed to provide accurate and authoritative information in regard to the subject matter covered. It is based upon sources believed to be accurate and reliable and is intended to be current as of the time it was written. It is sold with the understanding that the publisher is not engaged in rendering legal, accounting, or other professional services. If legal advice or other expert assistance is required, the services of a competent professional person should be sought. Also, to confirm that the information has not been affected or changed by recent developments, traditional legal research techniques should be used, including checking primary sources where appropriate.

(Based on the Declaration of Principles jointly adopted by a Committee of the American Bar Association and a Committee of Publishers and Associations.)

You may order this or any other Oxford University Press publication
by visiting the Oxford University Press website at www.oup.com.

Contents

Introduction

An Urban Era

This book addresses a fundamental void. Contemporary constitutional thought and constitutional practice have failed to address one of the major challenges of modern governance: urban agglomeration and the rise of the megacity. Cities are both ubiquitous and crucial to today's society, culture, economics, and politics. Indeed, the twenty-first century has been hailed the "century of the city."[1] Major demographic, economic, and political trends point to the increasing centrality of cities, and extensive urbanization more generally. The current figures are mind-boggling. Research clearly establishes that the ever-expanding urbanization trend—arguably the most significant demographic trend of our time—is set to continue. The forecasts for 2030 or 2050, let alone for 2100, range from disturbing to near dystopian. Projections suggest that megacities of 50 million or even 100 million inhabitants are set to emerge by the end of the century, mostly in the Global South. Nonetheless, cities have remained virtually absent from constitutional law, and from comparative constitutional studies generally. In the face of such unequivocal scientific evidence of a mounting urban challenge, the silence of constitutional law and scholarship is deafening. Accordingly, I argue in this book that we desperately need new thinking about constitutionalism and urbanization.

A century ago, only 1 in 10 people lived in an urban area; today, for the first time in recorded human history, the majority of the world's population lives in cities. This shift marks a major and unprecedented transformation of the organization of society, both spatially and geopolitically. The majority of the growth is in the Global South, but the Global North has seen its fair share of change, too, at accelerating rates. In 1800, 3% of the world's population lived in cities. In 1950, less than 30% did; by 1990, 43% of us were city dwellers. By 2019, this proportion had grown to 56%. This trend becomes even more significant when we consider that, during this time (see Figure I.1), the world's population has increased from 2.6 billion (1950) to 5.3 billion (1990) to 7.6 billion in 2019, bringing the urban population from 750 million in 1950 to 2.2 billion in 1990 and 4.3 billion in 2019.

---

[1] Report: *Century of the City* (Rockefeller Foundation, 2006); online: https://www.rockefellerfoundation.org/report/century-of-the-city/.

City, State. Ran Hirschl, Oxford University Press (2020). © Ran Hirschl.
DOI: 10.1093/oso/9780190922771.001.0001

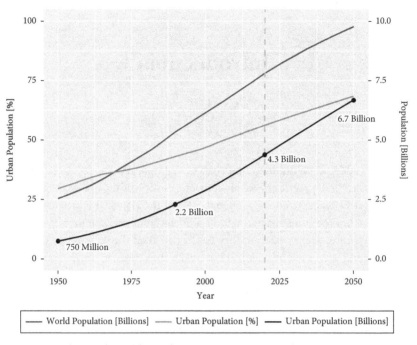

Figure I.1   Urban and World Population 1950–2050

In other words, from 1950 to 1990 alone, the number of city dwellers worldwide tripled. What is more, within a quarter of a century from the 1990s to the present day—a single generation—the number of city dwellers has increased by a further 95%, nearly double. By 2050, an additional 2.5 billion people are expected to live in urban settings. In other words, approximately 70% of the world population (projected at 10 billion) will reside in cities (85% within OECD countries). This represents an unprecedented human agglomeration in urban areas, with ever-widening density gaps between cities and hinterlands, as well as among megacity neighborhoods.[2]

Continent-by-continent demographic data (presented in Table I.1 and in Figure I.2 below) reflects the massive scope of urbanization in the developing world. From 1960 to 2018, North America's urban population grew from 143 million to 299 million and is projected to grow to 387 million by 2050. Europe's urban population grew from 348 million in 1960 to 553 million in 2018, and is projected to grow to 599 million in 2050. During the same period (1960–2018), the urban population in Asia grew from 360 million to approximately 2.26 billion

---

[2] For recent data, *see World Urbanization Prospects: The 2018 Revision* (Population Division of the UN Department of Economic and Social Affairs [UN DESA], 2019).

Table I.1 Urban Population by Continent over Time

Continent	Proportion of urban population (%)						Actual size of urban population (millions)					
	1960	1980	2000	2018	2030	2050	1960	1980	2000	2018	2030	2050
Europe	57.4	67.6	71.1	74.5	77.5	83.7	348	469	517	553	573	599
North America	69.9	73.9	79.1	82.2	84.7	89.0	143	188	247	299	335	387
Latin America and Caribbean	49.4	64.6	75.5	80.7	83.6	87.8	109	235	397	526	600	685
Asia	21.2	27.1	37.5	49.9	56.7	66.2	360	717	1400	2266	2802	3479
Africa	18.6	26.8	35.0	42.5	48.4	58.9	53	129	286	548	824	1489

Data source: "World Urbanization Prospects: The 2018 Revision, Online Edition" (UN Department of Economic and Social Affairs, Population Division, 2019).

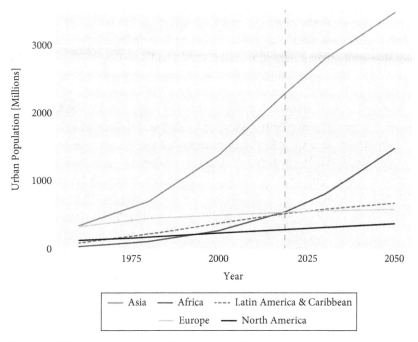

Figure I.2 Urban Population by Continent over Time

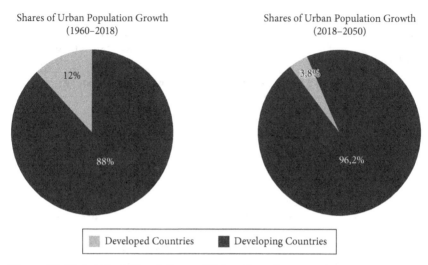

Shares of Urban Population Growth (1960–2018)

Shares of Urban Population Growth (2018–2050)

Figure I.3 Global North/South Share of Urban Growth

(a more than sixfold increase) and is projected to further grow to 3.47 billion in 2050. Thus, in the course of less than a century (1960–2050), urban populations in Asia will have grown nearly tenfold with an addition of approximately 3 billion urban dwellers in Asia alone (compared to roughly half a billion in Europe and North America combined). In Africa, urban growth is equally staggering. Africa's urban population increased from 53 million in 1960 to 548 million in 2018—more than a tenfold increase within half a century. It is projected to further increase to 1.34 billion by 2050—a growth of nearly 1.3 billion urban dwellers within less than a century.[3]

Slicing the data another way (see Figure I.3), approximately 88% of urban population growth since 1960 has taken place in the developing world, meaning that about 9 of every 10 new urban dwellers since 1960 reside in Asia, Africa, or Latin America. While North America and Europe saw an additional 361 million people living in cities from 1960 to 2018 (about 156 million in North America, 205 million in Europe), Africa, Asia, and Latin America have witnessed an increase of more than 2.8 billion in their combined urban population over the same time frame (about 495 million in Africa; 1.9 billion in Asia; 417 million in Latin America). In Asia alone, mass migration expands city populations by 120,000 per day, or about 900,000 people every week. As shown in Figure I.3, the urbanization forecasts for the next three decades indicate that the developing world's share of the global urban population is set to increase to over 96% by 2050, while North America and Europe will contribute less than 4%. Demographic

[3] *Id.*

projections for the next three decades further suggest that more than one-third of the growth of the world's urban population between 2018 and 2050 will emanate from a small number of lower- to upper-middle income countries, notably India (where more than 400 million additional urban dwellers are projected), China (more than 250 million), and Nigeria (190 million).[4]

The extensive urbanization trend in the developing world puts tremendous demands on cities to provide suitable resources, infrastructure, and services to accommodate the groundswells of new and existing urban dwellers. This ever-increasing pressure manifests itself in other major policy challenges facing twenty-first-century government worldwide, including environmental protection, public health, and extreme poverty.

Critically, as rural areas shrink in population, the fight against poverty rapidly shifts to major urban centers and their vast suburbs.[5] Slums and shantytowns become an inevitable feature of most African and South East Asian megacities.[6] Despite roughly stagnant income levels among the world's poorest countries, urbanization rates in these countries have grown exponentially over the last half century.[7] Over 60% of the world's refugees live within the jurisdictional boundaries of large cities. Over 80% of internally displaced people worldwide live in major urban areas. Consequently, approximately one billion of the world's poor now reside in slums at the outskirts of megacities such as Manilla, Jakarta, Mumbai, and Kinshasa.[8] The GDP per capita in the Democratic Republic of Congo, to pick one example, stood at approximately $220 in 1960; in 2018, it stood at $560. During that time, the country's population increased more than fivefold (from 16 million to 85 million), and the population of Kinshasa, the

---

[4] Id.

[5] See, e.g., Diana Mitlin and David Satterthwaite, Urban Poverty in the Global South: Scale and Nature (Routledge, 2013); Paula Lucci and Tanvi Bhatkal, "Monitoring Progress on Urban Poverty: Are the Indicators Fit for Purpose?" (ODI, 2014); Marie Ruel et al., "Food Security and Nutrition: Growing Cities, New Challenges," Global Food Policy Report (2017); Elizabeth Kneebone and Alan Berube, Confronting Suburban Poverty in America (Brookings Institute Press, 2017). While rural poverty is still very high, in particular in Sub-Saharan Africa, the Middle East, and North Africa, rural areas were found to have reduced poverty more quickly over time than urban areas. See Sabina Alkire et al., "Poverty in Rural and Urban Areas: Direct Comparison Using the Global MPI 2014" (Oxford Poverty & Human Development Initiative, 2014).

[6] For a classic, mid-1990s account of burgeoning Global South slums that are regarded as uncontainable and inadequate, see Jeremy Seabrook, In the Cities of the South: Scenes from a Developing World (Verso, 1996).

[7] See Edward L. Glaeser, "A World of Cities: The Causes and Consequences of Urbanization in Poorer Countries," Journal of the European Economic Association 12 (2014): 1154–1199. Addressing the prospects for reducing poverty in developing world megacities, Glaeser concludes that "[F]or large cities with weak governments, draconian policies may be the only way to curb negative externalities, suggesting a painful trade-off between dictatorship and disorder."

[8] One frequently cited article suggests that the urbanization of poverty emanates from better access to public transportation in urban centers. See Edward L. Glaeser, Matthew E. Kahn, and Jordan Rappaport, "Why the Poor Live in Cities? The Role of Public Transportation," Journal of Urban Economics 63 (2008): 1–24.

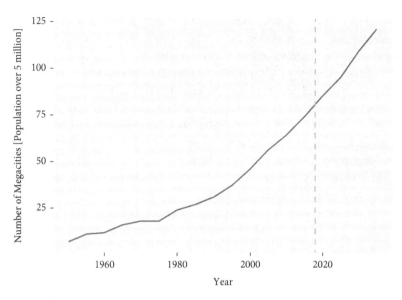

Figure I.4 Megacities over Time

country's capital, grew from 400,000 in 1960 to 13 million in 2018, a staggering 32-fold increase.

In 1900, there were only 12 cities in the world with one million residents or more.[9] Today, the number has passed 550. An immediate byproduct of the extensive urbanization of the last century is the emergence of megacities and megacity regions.[10] The term "megacities" has been applied, sometimes to cities with 5 million people or more, sometimes to cities whose limits or metropolitan areas house at least 10 million people. Wherever we draw the line, the number of megacities has skyrocketed. Between 1990 and 2018 alone (see Figure I.4), the number of cities worldwide with at least 5 million inhabitants living within the boundaries of a single urban authority (i.e., excluding metro area population) more than tripled, from 26 to 81.[11] That number is expected to further increase to 109 cities by 2030.[12] In 1950, only one city (New York) had a population of more

---

[9] In the late eighteenth century, Beijing was the first city in history to have reached a population of one million. London reached that milestone circa 1825.

[10] In her book *The Global City: New York, London, Tokyo* (Princeton University Press, 2001), Saskia Sassen argues that while globalization has resulted in the dispersion of numerous day-to-day services, it has not been accompanied by any corresponding decentralization of (state) control. Instead, Sassen argues, control has become even more centralized. "The more globalized the economy becomes, the higher the agglomeration of central function in few sites, that is, the global cities" (p. 5).

[11] *See, The World's Cities in 2018—Data Booklet* (Population Division of the UN Department of Economic and Social Affairs [UN DESA], 2018).

[12] *Id.*

than 10 million.[13] In 2018, 33 megacities had a city-proper population greater than 10 million; of those, the most-populated megacity outside of Asia, Latin America, and Africa is Moscow, ranked 21st, with a population of over 12.5 million. At least 15 other large cities in the developing world were on the brink of cracking the 10 million league, including Dar es Salaam, Teheran, Hyderabad, Kuala Lumpur, and Ho Chi Minh City. When metro area population is taken into account, as of 2018, 47 urban centers had populations of at least 10 million; of those, only six are in North America or Europe, while the other 41 are in Asia (32), Latin America (6), or Africa (3).[14] The numbers are stunning: as of 2018, Tokyo's population stands at 38 million; Shanghai at 34 million; Jakarta at 32 million; Delhi at 28 million; Seoul at 26 million; Beijing, Manila, and Mumbai at 25 million each; while the populations of metro São Paulo, Mexico City, Karachi, and Lagos stand at 22 million each. New York—the paradigmatic example of a Western megacity—is ranked 10th in the world in terms of its metro area population with approximately 24 million. Cairo, Los Angeles, and Dhaka, each with a metro area population of 19 million, do not crack the top 15 most-populated cities list. Megacities such as Bangkok, Rio de Janeiro, and Bangalore, each with a metro area population of between 13 to 15 million, are ranked between 20th and 30th. When another criterion is applied—the concentration of people in a given city relative to the overall population of the entire country—the list of megacities becomes even longer. Santiago de Chile (6.5 million people) and the Taipei-Keelung metropolitan area (8 million people) do not meet the 10 million standard, but are home to well over one-third of their respective nations' overall populations.

The extensive urban agglomeration and population growth in megacities is expected to continue in the coming decades. Demographic models suggest that by 2030, Delhi's population will reach 36 million (30% more than its current population), Karachi's population will reach 30 million (30% increase over 2018), while Dhaka's population will stand at 28 million (a 32% increase over 2018). Some projections suggest that megacities of 50 million or even 100 million inhabitants (dubbed "metapolis") are likely to emerge within the next century, while density and geographic concentration will continue to rise, with the percentage of land area occupied by human settlement remaining well below 10%.[15] New research further suggests that by 2100, approximately one-quarter

---

[13] *See* Richard Stren, "Cities and Politics in the Developing World: Why Decentralization Matters," *in* Karren Mossberger et al. eds., *The Oxford Handbook of Urban Politics* (Oxford University Press, 2012), 567–589.

[14] *See City Mayors Statistics 2017*; online: http://www.citymayors.com/statistics/largest-cities-mayors-1.html.

[15] *See, e.g.*, Robert H. Samet, "Complexity, the Science of Cities, and Long-Range Futures," *Futures* 47 (2013): 49–58.

of the world's population will reside in the world's 101 largest cities, with an overall megacity population between 1.6 and 2.3 billion. Should current urbanization patterns in Africa continue, studies suggest, the populations of Lagos and Kinshasa could both reach 85 million by 2100, while the population of Dar es Salaam will reach 75 million. Meanwhile, the population of several megacities in the Indian subcontinent (Mumbai, Delhi, Kolkata, Karachi, and Dhaka) will have reached 50 to 70 million each by the turn of the twenty-first century.[16]

A stark contrast exists between the conventional image of world cities such as New York and London and the harsher reality experienced by most residents of huge metropolises in the developing world. Anyone who has visited Mumbai, Dhaka, Manila, Jakarta, or Lagos has seen the sights. (The overall population density in Dhaka and Manila, to pick one pertinent metric, is approximately 45,000 people per square kilometer [116,550 per square mile]; this is a qualitatively different universe than New York City, America's densest metropolis, with 11,000 people per square kilometer [28,500 per square mile]). The day-to-day existence in these and other similarly situated megacities in the Global South is marred by inadequate and dilapidated infrastructure, insufficient housing and sanitation, hastily designed "development" projects that are often closely aligned with business interests, vast socioeconomic gaps, a prevalent informal economy, and loose law-and-order standards. These problems are further exacerbated by the constant influx of people migrating to the outskirts of large cities. In fact, in most developing world megacities, the gap between the successful metro region image and the grim reality is even starker as the concentration of affluent populations in the urban core stands in sharp contrast to the segregation and hopelessness of many millions of displaced, unskilled, or disadvantaged populations outside of it. To truly encompass the megacity challenge, we must therefore look beyond the popular portrayal of the city as either glitzy or dystopian, and turn our gaze to the far more realistic, outer fringes of the urbanization swell. No wonder recent UN (United Nations) reports declare the management of urbanization, especially in low-income and lower-middle-income countries, one of the greatest challenges of our times.[17]

When the lens is broadened to encompass entire metropolitan regions, contemporary agglomeration numbers suggest that the futuristic metapolis projection has already begun to materialize. The so-called Northeast megalopolis (the Boston to Washington corridor or "Bosneywash") is home to over 50 million people; the Pearl River delta metropolitan area (sometimes referred to as the Guangdong-Hong Kong-Macau Greater Bay Area) is home to approximately

---

[16] See Daniel Hoornweg and Kevin Pope, "Population Predictions for the World's Largest Cities in the 21st Century," *Environment and Urbanization* 29 (2017): 195–216.

[17] See *World Urbanization Prospects: The 2018 Revision.*

70 million people; while 85 million people reside in Japan's Taiheiyo Belt, stretching from Tokyo to Fukuoka.[18] This remarkable shift touches on some of the core elements of political public life: how we conceive and govern the relationship between territory, people, and political organization—the building blocks of political sovereignty and constitutional law. The normative problems that emerge from cities' constitutional non-status are obvious, including deficiencies in democracy, subsidiarity, and stakeholding. What sociologists term "super-diversity" (intersectional or multidimensional diversity that transcends customary ethnic, religious, linguistic, educational, socioeconomic, gender, or sexual orientation lines) is the reality of metropolitan demographics and the essence of everyday urban life.[19] And yet, constitutions continue to treat cities, the main sites of multiculturalism, where diversity manifests itself most fully, as mere policy delivery agents, without constitutional voice or meaningful capacity to generate revenue independently. At the very least, our current urban era exposes a critical gap within constitutions between the rights they guarantee (social, economic, and other equity-enhancing rights) and their power to make good on these guarantees.

Surprisingly, however, our constitutional institutions and constitutional imagination have not even begun to catch up with the new reality. Though we live in the century of the city, we are still captives of constitutional structures, doctrines, perceptions, and expectations that were conceived along with the modern nation-state and germinated through the age of revolution, a historical process that saw the subjugation of the sovereign city.[20] Any attempt to put urban government at the center of the constitutional order will therefore require against-the-grain constitutional thought combined with strong political will, a combination that has generally not yet emerged in politics or scholarship. Cities feature centrally in canonical political theory texts (e.g., Plato's *Republic*, Machiavelli's *The Prince*, and Marx and Engels's *The German Ideology*) as well as in utopian and avant-garde social thought (e.g., Campanella's *The City of the Sun*, Charles Fourier's imagined community of *Phalanstère*, the Paris Commune (1871), or Walter Benjamin's *The Paris Arcades Project*). Novel thinking about urbanization and cities is prevalent throughout the human sciences; Henri Lefebvre's *Le droit*

[18] Geographers and economists have identified even broader, multi-jurisdictional regions or urban condensation, notably Western Europe's "Blue Banana" (London-Amsterdam-Paris-Frankfurt-Milan) with its 110 million inhabitants; or the Ganges River agglomeration, which is home to over 400 million people, over 5% of the world's population. While these regions are referred to in academic and some international policy-making conversations, they lack any features of public law entities.

[19] *See* Steven Vertovec, "Super-Diversity and Its Implications," *Ethnic and Racial Studies* 30 (2007): 1024–1054.

[20] *See, e.g.,* Maarten Prak, *Citizens without Nations: Urban Citizenship in Europe and the World, c. 1000–1789* (Cambridge University Press, 2018).

à la ville, Saskia Sassen's work on global cities, Paul Krugman's theorization of megacities as economies of scale, Richard Florida's ideas about cities as magnets for the creative classes, and Benjamin Barber's *If Mayors Ruled the World* are merely a few examples of this scholarly richness. By stark contrast, very little of this intellectual flurry has penetrated constitutional law, let alone comparative constitutional law, where the city is virtually nonexistent. Despite extensive urbanization worldwide and the tremendous surge of the megacity as a demographic, economic, cultural, and service-providing entity, we currently lack the basic conceptual language and constitutional categories to capture and address this new reality, one of the most important developments in the world today.

But the problem runs much deeper than a scholarly void, stark as it is. Most constitutional orders currently in existence, and virtually all of those adopted prior to the great urbanization of the last few decades, treat cities, including some of the world's most significant urban centers, as "creatures of the state," fully submerged within a Westphalian constitutional framework, and assigned limited administrative local governance authority. Their *constitutional* statuses range anywhere from secondary to nonexistent. Whereas approximately 60% of the national constitutions currently in effect designate their respective country's "national capital," only a small handful of these constitutions (not to mention the other 40% of national constitutions) address these cities, let alone other large cities within their territorial jurisdiction, as metropolitan centers per se. Scattered examples of non-capital city-provinces are precious few exceptions to this reality, and virtually none is predicated on a deep, across-the-board constitutional recognition of the metropolis as an autonomous or distinct order of government.

In many settings worldwide, hardwired constitutional arrangements reflect outdated concepts of spatial governance featuring constitutional division of competences adopted in a pre-megacity era and increasingly detached from twenty-first-century realities. Consequently, cities—home to the majority of mankind, ubiquitous and crucial to every aspect of twenty-first-century society, culture, economics, and politics—do not exist constitutionally, and with few exceptions, remain subjugated by a Westphalian sovereigntist order and by the state's innate inclination to maintain jurisdictional primacy over its territory.[21] National constitutions' entrenched nature and innately statist outlook render the city systemically weak and to a large degree underrepresented. As extensive urbanization marches on, an ever-widening gap emerges between what is expected of a modern metropolis, and what cities can actually deliver in the absence of adequate standing, representation, taxation powers, or robust policy-making authority. The Coronavirus pandemic of 2020 further accentuates the disparity

---

[21] For an elaboration of this logic, *see* Ran Hirschl and Ayelet Shachar, "Foreword: Spatial Statism," *International Journal of Constitutional Law* 17 (2019): 387–438.

between the tremendous pressures, threats, and challenges that evermore populous urban centers face, and cities' limited independent capacity to provide services and support for their residents.

In this book—to my knowledge the first of its kind in comparative constitutional studies—I pursue a five-part inquiry into the scope, origins, and shaky
normative grounds of the great constitutional silence concerning one of the most
significant phenomena of our time: urban agglomeration and the rise of megacities. Taken together, the comparative investigation in these five chapters aims to
provide answers to five interrelated questions: First, what is the status of cities in
national constitutions worldwide? Second, how are we to explain the continued
silence of constitutions, constitutional jurisprudence, and constitutional thought
with respect to urban agglomeration and the consequent rise of megacities?
Third, given national constitutions' general antagonism toward autonomous city
power, how can we explain those instances where constitutional empowerment
of cities does occur? Fourth, what is the constitutional status and prospect of city
self-emancipation initiatives pursued through international intercity collaboration, city-based human rights charters, or experiments with urban citizenship?
Finally, from jurisprudential, normative, and practical standpoints, what may
justify a transformation in the constitutional status of—and more broadly in the
constitutional discourse about—megacities?

The discussion advances in several steps. In Chapter 1 ("The Sound of
Constitutional Silence"), I highlight the bewildering silence of contemporary
constitutional discourse with respect to cities and urbanization, as well as the
strong statist outlook embedded in national constitutional orders, effectively
rendering the metropolis a constitutional nonentity. I contrast the human sciences' intellectual fascination with the urban domain with the meager attention
cities get in constitutional scholarship. I go on to survey the (non)status of large
metropolitan centers in national constitutions worldwide.

National constitutions naturally reflect a Westphalian understanding of
the modern state, its institutions and competences, its sovereignty, jurisdictional boundaries, and mode of territorial governance. This state-centered
conceptualization of territorial sovereignty may regard large cities as potential
competitors of state authority, or at the very least as sites of potential mass mobilization and popular political resistance, and not without reason. The threat
of urban uprising, usually latent, can rapidly turn explosive. From the French
Revolution (think of the storming of the Bastille) to the Arab Spring (think of
the massive demonstrations in Cairo's Tahrir Square), and to recent uprisings
in Hong Kong and Santiago, large cities have a long tradition as sites of popular
resistance, radicalization, and revolution. Moreover, large cities' diverse composition and relatively progressive profile (one would be hard-pressed to think of a
large city anywhere whose populace has been consistently less diverse or more

conservative than the rest of the polity) position the city as a spring of alternative ideas, values, and worldviews. The urban domain thus becomes not only a potential site of popular resistance to state hegemony—a spatial threat—but also an ideational threat to exclusionary national meta-narratives of collective identity, and to conservative ideals of distributive justice.

Most large cities strive, *ceteris paribus*, for greater policy-making autonomy, enhanced taxation authority, and for improved status on the national political and constitutional scene. In most settings, they don't get it. For a host of reasons I discuss in Chapter 1, the standard constitutional treatment of cities, and of urban agglomeration, ranges from neglect to subjugation. Given the relative difficulty to amend long-standing constitutional structures, let alone what we know about political incentive structures and constitutional change, the reluctance of the wielders of constitutional power to relinquish it volitionally to potential competitors is anything but surprising. But, given national constitutional orders' innate antagonism toward autonomous city power, how are we to explain the instances in which constitutional empowerment of cities does occur? Such a reorientation away from constitutional subjugation and toward city empowerment requires a constellation of strong political incentives. As I show in Chapters 2 and 3, these incentives are more likely to present themselves in Global South constitutional settings. All things considered, the mind-boggling scope of urbanization in the Global South, combined with greater constitutional flexibility; and, for better or worse, governments' tendency to use this flexibility in service of strategic goals and political interests, makes the "new world" of constitutionalism a more fertile terrain for experimentation with the constitutional empowerment of megacities.

In Chapter 2 ("The Metropolis in 'Old World' Constitutional Law"), I examine the constitutional subjugation of the metropolis throughout much of the Global North in constitutional orders adopted over a two-century span between the late eighteenth century and the 1970s, from the United States and Canada to the UK, Western Europe, and Australia. I illustrate how constitutional stalemate has emerged in these countries as a result of hardwired city-subverting constitutional frameworks, rigid amendment rules, a lack of political incentives to empower cities, and oftentimes proactive resistance to city power. In Chapter 3 ("Constitutional Innovation in Governing the Metropolis: Law, Economics, Politics"), I contrast the status of metropolises in old-world constitutional orders with their status in "new world" constitutional orders—largely in the Global South—where new ideas about the constitutional governance of the metropolis are more likely to emerge. From Asia (e.g., China, South Korea, Japan, Vietnam) to Africa (e.g., South Africa), innovative, sometimes radical, constitutional measures have been introduced, some with more success than others, to address the metropolis issue. I show how South Africa's constitutionalization of city power as part of its 1996 constitutional transformation is arguably the most effective of these attempts to date. In other Global South settings—notably India and Brazil—constitutional experimentation with city emancipation has succumbed to deeply engrained intergovernmental hierarchies. And in yet other settings, strategic behavior and colliding incentive structures have driven attempts to either strengthen (e.g., Buenos Aires, Mexico City), or weaken (e.g., Nairobi, Cairo, Dhaka) megacities.

Taken as a whole, the comparative inquiry I pursue in Chapters 2 and 3 helps identify three factors, the confluence of which facilitates innovation (or conversely, stagnation) in the constitutional governance of megacities: (i) a *necessity* factor—an acute need to think creatively about urban agglomeration in large, densely populated countries where much of the world's urban expansion worldwide has taken place; (ii) a *constitutional* factor—a constitutional order's amenability, whether formal or informal, to change in response to the astonishing rise of megacities; and (iii) a *political* factor—the interplay of power holders' incentives alongside national and sub-national governments' interests in enabling or subverting megacity emancipation. My comparative examination of the constitutional (non)treatment of the urban challenge in "old world" and in "new world" constitutional settings suggests that the truly cutting-edge constitutional thought and innovation in this area has taken place in Asia, Latin America, and Africa, rather than the handful of "usual suspect" jurisdictions from which the informal canon of comparative constitutionalism has emanated (e.g., United States, Canada, UK, Australia, Germany).[22]

In Chapter 4 ("Attempts at City Self-Empowerment"), I turn to examine efforts by constitutionally voiceless cities and mayors to expand cities' quasi-constitutional powers through urban citizenship schemes or, more frequently, through international networking and collaboration based on notions such as "the right to the city," "sustainable cities," "solidarity cities," and "human rights cities." For the most part, such initiatives have a socially progressive undercurrent to them, addressing policy areas such as air quality and energy efficient construction, "smart cities" (cities that implement new technologies), affordable housing, enhanced community representation, or accommodating policies toward refugees and asylum seekers. Such experimentation with city self-emancipation is increasing in popularity and possesses significant potential in policy areas *not directly addressed or hermetically foreclosed by statist constitutional law* (notably, environmental protection). It may also positively affect the lives of undocumented immigrants who must rely on city-based identification and services to survive.

---

[22] For a critique of this "usual suspect"-based "canon," *see* Ran Hirschl, *Comparative Matters: The Renaissance of Comparative Constitutional Law* (Oxford University Press, 2014), 4, 244.

However, meaningful as these projects may be at the practical or symbolic level, their constitutional bite is seriously limited in a state-dominated constitutional universe. With few exceptions, these initiatives live *beside* the formal constitutional or international law frameworks that govern national jurisdictions, rather than existing as a part within (let alone as a viable alternative to) these prevalent legal frameworks. I go on to suggest that of the three main types of city self-emancipation—urban citizenship, human right city charters, and international city networks—the former may be seen as the most "offensive" to the constitutional order as it challenges the state's exclusive monopoly in defining the status, rights, and duties of its members, as well as the boundaries of membership itself.

Finally, in Chapter 5 ("Rethinking City Constitutional Status"), I devote considerable attention to exploring some key arguments for assigning greater constitutional status and standing to cities. Arguments based on anti-discrimination, equal representation, and inclusion of historically disenfranchised minority groups are particularly relevant to city life, given the diverse demographic composition and challenging socioeconomic reality in many large cities. Other arguments for city autonomy invoke economic and social rights, often calling for core minimum guarantees in order to address the challenges of poverty or homelessness in cities. Within this group of rights, the right to housing is particularly relevant to urban life. However, all these arguments, significant as they are to everyday city life, are general in nature. In principle, they apply to any social setting, urban or not.

Other arguments for city power emanate directly from the urban condition itself, treating the urban domain as a distinct setting. Such arguments may have powerful intuitive appeal but little concrete constitutional purchase. In this category, two bold ideas stand out: Henri Lefebvre's intriguing yet fuzzy notion of a "right to the city"; and pragmatic calls for local government to have a more prominent political voice, such as Benjamin Barber's proposal for mayors "to rule the world." However, even these daring arguments for enhanced city power do not seem to acknowledge or appreciate the full scope of urban centers' *constitutional* powerlessness. Taken together, existing threads of argument are either general and non-city specific, overly abstract and hard to operationalize, or are lacking in crucial constitutional particulars. It is also not always clear whether these arguments refer to the rights of city dwellers, or to the standing and status of cities as an order of government. Additionally, such arguments tend to overlook crucial aspects of urban agglomeration ranging from extreme density and the limited economic leverage of cities to systemic political underrepresentation and a structural constitutional bias in favor of a statist constitutional order. What is more, common arguments for city power seldom acknowledge the unique challenges that megacities in low-income and lower-middle-income countries face. Put simply, extant arguments seem to fall short of capturing the full scale of the urban challenge to contemporary constitutional thought.

To address this gap, I introduce several fresh lines of thought in support of constitutionalizing city power, illuminating dimensions of the city problem that have been addressed either scantly or not at all to date. These considerations range from cities' structural dependence on corporate capital and the systemic electoral political underrepresentation of large urban centers (what I term "one person, half a vote"), to democratic stakeholding norms that may justify devolution of authority to cities, as well as pragmatic arguments linking megacities' constitutional empowerment to their capacity to address key challenges such as climate change, economic inequality, extreme density, and social integration in increasingly diverse settings. En route, I explore several constitutional designs that may remedy the systemic underrepresentation of urban voters while providing suitable voice to rural area constituencies. Taken together, these various lines of argumentation form a strong and timely case in favor of extending enhanced constitutional standing to cities and their residents.

Importantly, I argue that taking the megacity seriously means shaking up the rather stagnant constitutional thought of spatial governance, fixated as it is on state- or province-based federalism, regions, and electoral districts, failing to address the urban agglomeration that the world is now seeing on a massive, unprecedented scale. Specifically, I highlight the acute need to consider a new place for large cities as constituent units in the theory and practice of federalism and other multilayered spatial governance structures, as well as in electoral systems of unitary states. In the current "age of the city," large cities are not only the chief service providers for, and home to the majority of each country's members, but are also distinguished within the polity by their function as hubs of diversity and close human interaction. Their unmatched diversity (let alone their sheer population size, in many cases much larger than dozens of sovereign nation-states) is more conducive to cultural openness, ideational pluralism, and to competitive democracy, than considerably less diverse or far smaller settings.

By corollary, I suggest that notions of subsidiarity, commonly deployed with respect to the status of constituent units in transnational constitutional orders, have considerable theoretical purchase in the current urban age, and thus should be routinely invoked in discussions concerning enhancement of urban centers' constitutional power. Taking subsidiarity seriously in this context may open the door for granting qualified autonomy to large urban centers in interpreting constitutional norms that are pertinent to the urban context, emphasizing a more pluralistic and spatially-consciousness view of public law. This and other, closely related concepts discussed in this book, can be thought of as embryonic pathways towards a constitutional realization of the "right to the city." And even more importantly, such transformed constitutional discourse would address a key aspect of city underrepresentation, namely the *constitutional nonexistence of cities qua order of government*, and more generally, the great constitutional silence surrounding today's extensive urbanization and the consequent rise of megacities.

The premise of this book is that a polity's constitutional order is more than mere law; in principle, it reflects that polity's core identity, commitments, priorities and aspirations, and serves as a compass guiding its political and public life. Granted, from a functionalist standpoint, constitutional law is commonly defined as the law that establishes the role, powers, and structure of the essential governing entities within the state. In this view, constitutional law also determines the spatial boundaries of authority, as well as listing polity members' basic rights and duties. Even from this angle alone, cities—the places that serve as home, and affect the lives of the clear majority of human kind—deserve recognition in any modern constitutional order. However, it is a deeper symbolic facet of constitutions that makes the constitutionalization of city power essential. From a normative and poetic standpoint, constitutions, constitutional institutions, and constitutional jurisprudence do more than allocating competences, powers, and rights. Taken together, they define and signal who we are as a political community, what moral and political ideals we cherish and strive for, and how we wish for others to reflect upon our polity. Neither administrative law, nor municipal law—two domains of public law that are commonly drawn upon to govern cities—can lay claim to such elevated legal *and* symbolic status in a given polity's legal hierarchy.[23] Thus, akin to any other instances of major constitutional void—large-scale underrepresentation and democracy deficit, inadequate government institutions, or outdated hierarchies—a principled remedy to cities' constitutional nonexistence is not to address the matter via legal byroads, but rather through public law's main highway: constitutional law.

---

[23] On the complex distinction between constitutional law and administrative law, *see* John Gardner, "Can There Be A Written Constitution?," *in Law as a Leap of Faith* (Oxford University Press, 2012), 89–124; Luc Heuschling, "The Complex Relationship Between Administrative and Constitutional Law: A Comparative and Historical Analysis," *The Max Planck Handbooks in European Public Law, Volume I: The Administrative State* (Oxford University Press, 2017), 493–556; Tom Ginsburg, "Written Constitutions and the Administrative State: On the Constitutional Character of Administrative Law," *in* Susan Rose-Ackerman, Peter Lindseth, and Blake Emerson, eds., *Comparative Administrative Law* (Edward Elgar, 2017), 117–127.

1

The Sound of Constitutional Silence

The heyday of localism is upon us. Supermarkets and restaurants boast of their locally grown foods. National governments wage tariff wars to protect "our workers." From Trump to Brexit, a resurgent "us first" rhetoric characterizes virtually all variants of political populism, left and right. Nationalist political leaders talk openly about protecting their people from "the other," whether it be the immigrant or the international tribunal that threatens to spoil the authentic, national identity. Cosmopolitan constitutional values have limited or no place in this "us versus them" discourse, which privileges narratives of national purity and leaders who profess allegiance to "the ordinary person," a denizen of the cultural, economic, and political hinterlands. The nationalistic zeitgeist behind this trend is captured in Trump's famous lines: "There is no global anthem, no global currency, no certificate of global citizenship. From now on, it's going to be 'America First' ";[1] and "I was elected to represent the citizens of Pittsburgh, not Paris."[2] Similar "us first" sentiments echo through the rhetoric of nationalist-populist voices worldwide, from the German extreme-right AfD party to the French *Rassemblement national* (National Rally). In the colorful words of Matteo Salvini, leader of the Italian right party *Lega Nord* (North League), "Matteo Renzi [former center-left prime minister] can give his own kids wine made without grapes, Tunisian oil, Moroccan oranges, Canadian wheat and Polish milk. We prefer products from our own land."[3]

Meanwhile, in highbrow discussions on the perils of globalization, pernicious international corporations, and the "democracy deficit" implicit in supranational governance, politicians and intellectuals are united in calling for better representation of local interests, worldviews, and policy preferences in an increasingly globalized world. An "us first" backlash drives threats of withdrawal from reputable international fora in the name of protecting national identity and culture. To maintain their legitimacy, supranational tribunals develop subsidiarity and "margin of appreciation" doctrines aimed at accommodating domestic

---

[1] *Cited in* Greg Ip, "We Are Not the World," *Wall Street Journal*, January 7, 2017.

[2] Donald Trump when announcing that the United States would be withdrawing from the Paris Climate Agreement (Reported in *The Guardian*, June 1, 2017).

[3] *Cited in* James Politi, "Fiery Salvini Forces Anti-Immigrant Tone on Italy Poll Debate," *Financial Times*, March 2, 2018.

City, State. Ran Hirschl, Oxford University Press (2020). © Ran Hirschl.
DOI: 10.1093/oso/9780190922771.001.0001

traditions and policy preferences while maintaining a one-rule-fits-all jurisprudential umbrella.

This neo-secessionist "opting out" trend, with nations leaving supranational
governance agreements and sub-national units struggling against nation-states,
has largely passed over the urban sphere (we see a notable exception to this rule
in the sporadic sanctuary city litigation in the United States, which I discuss in
some detail in Chapter 2). As the modern state has effectively eliminated the
city as a formal political entity, constitutional representation of the urban—the
habitat of over half of the world's population—is minimal. Age-old federalism
doctrines predicated on regions or on states as the relevant subunits remain the
main, and perhaps even the only, constitutional response to spatial grievances.

As cities lack constitutional standing to advance their agendas, their ability to
influence constitutional power structures through "exit" threats, or even through
credible "voice" tactics (to borrow Albert Hirschman's famous terminology) is
virtually nonexistent. Cities, unlike capital, are fixed in place. This anchoring
spatial factor plays a key role in delineating, and frequently constraining, their
bargaining power. Shrewd players who are not anchored to a single location
may engage in "forum shopping"—essentially choosing the jurisdiction or
legal forum that is likely to benefit them the most. Companies commonly register their businesses in overseas jurisdictions that offer favorable taxation
and banking rules. Mass producers of goods tend to gravitate to jurisdictions
with lower wages, reduced safety standards, and/or poorly protected workers'
rights. Companies invoke "capital flight" talk to extract greater concessions from
governments, essentially threatening to move operations elsewhere where costs
are lower if their demands are not accepted. These threats can be extremely effective in acquiring tax cuts, investment in infrastructure, and favorable trade
platforms. A city, by contrast, is not going anywhere. Lacking any territorial exit
options, and able to exercise only limited "voice" channels, many cities must
align themselves either with big business or with broader political interests at the
national or sub-national levels, and think creatively about how to operate within
the regulatory niches in policy areas that permit limited city autonomy.

Amid unprecedented levels of urbanization worldwide, the near-absolute
silence of constitutions and constitutional thinkers on city power points to a
statist outlook embedded in modern constitutionalism, which in turn informs
the methodological nationalism that still characterizes much of the literature.[4]
National constitutions reflect a "seeing like a state" vision of the territories they
govern and, more often than not, a dated conceptualization of the territory's

---

[4] Exception to this tendency is found in the literature on constitutional pluralism, which is preoccupied with the coexistence of national and supranational constitutional orders. However, even
within that body of literature, no attention is given to urbanization or to cities.

geographical organization and demographic composition. Modern states—conquerors of the city—will not entertain the possibility of emancipating cities unless doing so would benefit the states themselves. The state's latent trepidation of the big city as a site of political volatility, of potential challenge to central authority, and also even of possibly revolutionary mass mobilization that threatens to topple the regime also plays into the statist reluctance to empower urban centers. The sheer number of megacity dwellers has long surpassed that of many nation-states. The proximity of the "haves" and the "have nots" is potentially explosive. Other spatial factors that characterize cities (e.g., human density and connectivity, the rapid spread of ideas, large strategically located public congregation spaces, the visibility of government buildings and symbolic monuments and squares), further mark the metropolis as a source of potential threat to state hegemony. (Little wonder that one of the first measures taken by besieged regimes when attempting to calm popular uprisings is to enforce curfew in big cities.) Accordingly, constitutional orders continue to subordinate the local and disregard the imperative of urban autonomy.

In this chapter, I set the stage for the chapters that follow by examining four introductory dimensions of the political and constitutional discourse around cities: (i) the tremendous interest in cities throughout much of the human sciences as contrasted with the silence of public law in general, and of comparative constitutional law in particular; (ii) the dominant statist stance embedded in constitutional law, in particular as it addresses sovereignty and spatial governance of the polity; (iii) a brief account of what national constitutions actually say about cities, and more significantly what they do not; and (iv) the tendency in political discourse on collective identity to understand the "local" almost exclusively at the national or regional levels, rather than distinguishing urban interests from those of the state. Taken together, the four angles of city constitutional (non)status I examine in this chapter highlight the bewildering silence of contemporary constitutional discourse with respect to cities and urbanization, as well as the strong statist outlook embedded in national constitutional orders, effectively rendering the metropolis a constitutionally non-tenable entity.

I. State Dominance, Constitutional Silence

The Italian city-states (e.g., Florence, Genoa, Venice) are common landmarks in the history of Western civilization. Studies have also shown the significance of city-based religious toleration and refugee acceptance policies in explaining Frankfurt's late-medieval prominence and the ascendancy of Amsterdam during the Dutch Golden Age. The Northern European Hanseatic League is often mentioned as a medieval example of intercity collaboration that had significant economic benefits for its members. More recently, however, the triumph of the modern state has subjected cities and regions to the statist constitutional project. As the US Supreme Court noted in *Hunter v. Pittsburgh*, "municipal corporations are subdivisions of the state, created as convenient agencies for exercising such of the governmental powers of the state as may be intrusted [sic] to them ... The number, nature, and duration of the powers conferred upon these corporations and the territory over which they shall be exercised rests in the absolute discretion of the state."[5]

While mostly absent from core constitutional discussions, the city has attracted much attention from philosophers and political theorists. Classical works of political theory, from Plato's *Republic* to Niccolò Machiavelli's *The Prince* and Marx and Engels's *The German Ideology*, address the city and the tension between town and country. Jean-Jacques Rousseau, Johann Gottfried Herder, and Ralph Waldo Emerson despised the city and glorified the pastoral countryside. Walter Benjamin's unfinished *The Paris Arcades Project*, about the connection between cities and nature, is considered a milestone in critical social thought. Concern with demographic imbalances brought the Athenians to think of a strategy to link urban and rural areas together in "tribes" in order for the city and the hinterlands to balance each other out. Likewise, one of Thomas More's explanations for the stability of the fictitious *Utopia* (1515) was the fact that its 54 cities were all the same size, suggesting an implied critique of the already very large city of London, which in the early sixteenth century overpowered the rest of the country. Tommaso Campanella's *The City of the Sun* (1602), Francis Bacon's *New Atlantis* (1622), and later Charles Fourier's imagined community of *Phalanstère* (revived by Le Corbusier in his *Unité d'habitation* project in Marseille) further envisioned utopian cities with rational purpose, equality, and common spaces. Debates about the ideal size of a democratic community subsequently ensued.

Contemporary political theory has generated renewed discussion on the urban space as a site of dense social interaction and as an alternative to state- or ethnicity-based political community, and on the city as a potential source for its dwellers' rights and entitlements to renewed urban life.[6] Rainer Bauböck has revived the discussion about urban citizenship (dubbed "city-zens").[7] Other political theorists (e.g., Avner de-Shalit) have written about cities as political communities and as potential identity bases;[8] and further exploring the possibility of

---

[5] *Hunter v. City of Pittsburgh*, 207 U.S. 161 (1907), 178–179.
[6] *See, e.g.*, Margaret Kohn, *The Death and Life of the Urban Commonwealth* (Oxford University Press, 2016).
[7] Rainer Bauböck, "Reinventing Urban Citizenship," *Citizenship Studies* 7 (2003): 139–160; Avner de-Shalit, *Cities and Immigration* (Oxford University Press, 2018).
[8] *See, e.g.*, Daniel A. Bell and Avner de-Shalit, *The Spirit of Cities: Why the Identity of a City Matters in a Global Age* (Princeton University Press, 2011).

drawing on *jus domicile* (a place-based membership criterion) as an alternative to current state-based membership models, in particular in the context of immigrant rights.[9] Arguably the most important conceptual innovation of the last half century concerning the normative foundations of city dwellers' rights is the right to the city, first introduced in the late 1960s by French philosopher Henri Lefebvre in his groundbreaking book *Le droit à la ville* (1968).

Not only has Lefebvre conceptualized the urban space as a political field or sphere of power, he also offers normative grounds for restructuring the power relations that underlie urban space, and calls for a transfer of control from capital and the state to urban inhabitants.[10] Conceptually, he argues that the right to the city is the right to "urban life, to renewed centrality, to places of encounter and exchange, to life rhythms and time uses, enabling the full and complete usage of . . . moments and places."[11] The context for Lefebvre's formulation was his vision—in the spirit of the neo-Marxist tradition of the late 1960s—of city inhabitants incrementally reclaiming space in the city through enhanced communal interface, so that a web of social interactions could form between people and ultimately trump the social atomism and alienation brought about by advanced capitalism.

Yet Lefebvre never fully elaborated on the concrete meaning of the right to the city. Over the last half century, philosophers and political theorists have been offering various interpretations of Lefebvre's abstract formulation. As my University of Toronto colleague Peggy Kohn astutely observes, the exact meaning of the term nevertheless remains hard to pin down, due in part to the broad interpretive literature itself, the evolution in Lefebvre's own formulation of the concept, and the tension between Lefebvre's historical-materialist critique of urban power relations and his utopian vision of urban renewal.[12] Kohn offers a compelling conceptualization of the city as a commonwealth based on solidarism, which collectively produces social good available equally to all who live in it and contribute to its vibrancy. Building on the notion of rights "as protecting fundamental interests that are recognized by, and entail obligations for, others," Kohn attempts to concretize the right to the city as a right that "protects access, enjoyment, and co-determination of the commonwealth of the city."[13] Such a

---

[9] *See, e.g.*, Harald Bauder, "*Jus Domicile*: In Pursuit of a Citizenship of Equality and Social Justice," *Journal of International Political Theory* 8 (2012): 184–196.

[10] Mark Purcell, "Globalization, Urban Enfranchisement, and the Right to the City: Towards an Urban Politics of the Inhabitant," *cited in* "Urban Policies and the Right to the City" (UN Habitat discussion paper, March 18, 2005).

[11] Henri Lefebvre, *The Right to the City, in* Eleonore Kofman and Elizabeth Lebas, eds., *Writings on Cities* (Blackwell, 1996), 63–184, at 178.

[12] *See, e.g.*, Margaret Kohn, *The Death and Life of the Urban Commonwealth* (Oxford University Press, 2016), 177–178.

[13] *Id.* at 3.

conceptualization of the right to the city, she argues, has radical implications for urban politics, in particular with respect to housing, public transit, and governance of public space.[14]

In a closely related line of thought, inspired by Elinor Ostrom's Nobel prize-winning work on governing common pool resources, Sheila Foster and Christian Iaione suggest that the city's open spaces—and perhaps even the city itself—may be conceptualized as a commons that ought to be governed by urban communities as a collective, or shared, resource pool.[15] Such a conceptualization, they argue, calls for a departure from the privatization of common resources or monopolistic public regulatory control over them, and a move toward what they see as pluralistic "urban collaborative governance." This collaborative governance model would foster increased cooperation among social innovators, civil society organizations, public authorities, business, and knowledge institutions (e.g., universities, museums, cultural centers, etc.). The normative starting point here seems to echo elements of Lefebvre's right to the city, in that the city possesses "shared resources that belong to all inhabitants" and is aligned with their "right to be a part of the creation of the city, the right to be a part of the decision-making processes shaping the lives of the city inhabitants, and the power of inhabitants to shape decisions about the collective resources in which we all have a stake."[16]

Political activists, international organizations, and city networks have invoked the right to the city in arguing for enhanced city autonomy as well as for various rights and entitlements of city dwellers as polity members. Neo-Marxist accounts have characterized the right to the city as a collective right, and have invoked it to assert public ownership of the city's territory and opposition to the privatization of urban space.[17] This right has been brought up liberally in debates concerning housing, transit, governance of public space, and meaningful political participation.[18]

A related argument raised by radical democracy theorists posits that city power offers an appealing alternative to exclusive state power, or at least a challenge to the "nationalization of politics." In his book *Urbanization without Cities*, for example, Murray Bookchin argues that fully empowered members of a body

[14] *Id.* at 9.

[15] Sheila Foster and Christian Iaione, "The City as a Commons," *Yale Law and Policy Review* 34 (2016): 281–349.

[16] Foster and Iaione, "The City as a Commons," 288.

[17] *See, e.g.*, Don Mitchell, *The Right to the City: Social Justice and the Fight for Public Space* (Guilford Press, 2003); David Harvey, *Rebel Cities: From the Right to the City to the Urban Revolution* (Verso, 2012).

[18] Kohn, *The Death and Life of the Urban Commonwealth*, 177. *See also* Mark Purcell, "Possible Worlds: Henri Lefebvre and the Right to the City," *Journal of Urban Affairs* 36 (2014): 141–154; Peter Marcuse, "From Critical Urban Theory to the Right to the City," *City* 13 (2009): 185–197; David Harvey, "The Right to the City," *International Journal of Urban and Regional Research* 27 (2003): 939–941.

politic are much closer to the true meaning and ultimate fulfillment of democratic ideals when exercised on a city scale rather than on a nation-state scale.[19]
Predictably, national politics is captured by national meta-narratives, struggles
over control of state institutions, and large-scale resource allocation processes.
Such a system is aimed at establishing the state as the main pillar of solidarity,
loyalty and collective identification, en route weakening alternative collective
identity bases, notably the urban or the local. Against the nationalization of politics, Bookchin advocates the creation of a worldwide parliament of cities as a
counterbalance to the state-based political scheme.

However, as Margit Mayer notes, the revolutionary edge of the right to the city
has been replaced with identity-based claims for inclusion. The maxim was originally formulated in the 1960s as a radical answer to the crisis of Fordism and as
part of the antiwar movement. The concept was later reformulated as a response
to austerity and the political shift toward neoliberalism in the 1980s, and then to
the globalization of markets in the 1990s and 2000s. In recent years, however, the
right to the city has taken a different form, and is now often invoked to demand
full, inclusive, and equal membership within existing political systems, and to
promote the progressive realization of such values within and by cities.[20]

To some extent, this transformation reflects contemporary liberal rights jurisprudence, heavily occupied with what has been termed "claims of culture" or
(less favorably) "identity politics." This trend is part of a general shift from redistribution to recognition in contemporary political discourse, accurately captured
in the debate between Nancy Frazer and Axel Honneth, as well as other critical
social theorists.[21] Admittedly, identity- or culture-based claims often intersect
with socioeconomic status. However, they seldom address head-on concepts
such as economic inequality, class or even human development (HDI), or real
purchasing power. In many cases, the politics of identity/identities is driven by
a quest for recognition, cultural self-determination, or formal legal status. The
"politics of recognition" in its prevalent constitutional form deals with ethnicity,
race, religious creed, or sexual identities, not with economic inequality as an independent (i.e., not identity-related) source of concern. In such identity-based
discourse, "recognition" precedes, and oftentimes wipes out, "redistribution."

The city also features prominently in the social sciences. Historians and
economists have extensively debated the role of medieval Europe's city-state in

[19] Murray Bookchin, *Urbanization Without Cities: The Rise and Decline of Citizenship* (Black Rose Book, 1987).
[20] Margit Mayer, "The 'Right to the City' in the Context of Shifting Mottos of Urban Social Movements," *City* 13 (2009): 362–374.
[21] Nancy Frazer and Axel Honneth, *Redistribution or Recognition?: A Political-Philosophical Exchange* (Verso, 2004); Nancy Fraser, "Social Justice in the Age of Identity Politics: Redistribution, Recognition, and Participation," *The Tanner Lectures on Human Values* (Stanford University Press, 1996).

laying the foundations for the emergence of early-modern Europe's economic supremacy, warfare power, and technological advancements. Early sociologists, most notably Georg Simmel and Max Weber, wrote about the modern city's psychological and societal functions. Weber's *The City*—and later *Economy and Society*—also laid the foundations for the argument famously developed by institutional economists, such as Douglass North, about the importance of secured property rights for economic growth.[22] The ability of autonomous cities—a distinct feature of medieval and early-modern European political development—to safeguard property rights against rulers' arbitrary power was an important catalyst in Europe's economic ascent.[23] In the 1950s, C. Wright Mills, Floyd Hunter, and Robert Dahl drew on the American city as a laboratory for studying power and distribution of authority within political communities. Roger Gould's study of the Paris Commune—a revolutionary government that ruled Paris for a couple of months in 1871—introduced a community-based (as opposed to class-based) understanding of that famous episode of urban resurgence and brief autonomy.[24] In a similar vein, Manuel Castells's early work focused on "urban social movements" that in addition to advancing their cause, help shape local identity.[25] Meanwhile, social historians such as Mike Rapport have highlighted the centrality of the city as a locus of social and political unrest during the late eighteenth-century Age of Revolution.[26] Modern political sociologists, from Shmuel N. Eisenstadt and Peter Hall to Charles Tilly and Saskia Sassen, have examined the political and economic roots of the evolution, decline, and re-emergence of the city and, later, the world city. Sassen's influential book *The Global City: New York, London, Tokyo* (2001) is a prime example of this line of inquiry, suggesting that global cities have emerged as key command points of

---

[22] Max Weber, *The City* (Free Press, 1966); Max Weber, *Economy and Society* (University of California Press, 1922).

[23] *See, e.g.,* Douglass C. North and Robert Paul Thomas, *The Rise of the Western World* (Cambridge University Press, 1973); Douglass C. North and Barry Weingast, "Constitutions and Commitment: The Evolution of Institutions Governing Public Choice in Seventeenth-Century England," *Journal of Economic History* 49 (1989): 803–832. Counterarguments suggest that in striving to maintain their monopolies, professional guilds in autonomous city-states erected barriers to entry into professions, thereby inhibiting innovation and competition. *See* David Stasavage, "Was Weber Right? The Role of Urban Autonomy in Europe's Rise," *American Political Science Review* 10 (2014): 337–354.

[24] Roger Gould, *Insurgent Identities: Class, Community and Protest in Paris from 1848 to the Commune* (University of Chicago Press, 1995).

[25] *See, e.g.,* Manuel Castells, *The City and the Grassroots: A Cross-Cultural Theory of Urban Social Movements* (University of California Press, 1983). For a recent account of such long-term effects of grassroots activism in Global South megacities such as Mumbai or Shanghai, *see* Mark Frazier, *The Power of Place: Contentious Politics in Twentieth-Century Shanghai and Bombai* (Cambridge University Press, 2019).

[26] *See, e.g.,* Mike Rapport, *The Unruly City: Paris, London and New York in the Age of Revolution* (Basic Books, 2017).

the world economy and as focal points of financial services and innovation.[27] More recent accounts portray global cities as inscriptions of the ideals of an international market society in space, "embody[ing] the ascendance of a set of neoliberal principles at a certain moment in history," with all the familiar tendencies, good or bad, that come with such ideological hegemony.[28]

Within political science, scholars have described contemporary local governments as components of complex multilevel governance structures, "having a host of vertical and horizontal relationships with a large range of other governmental, private and voluntary bodies."[29] By these accounts, local government is part of a system of continuous negotiations among nested governments at several territorial tiers, all woven together in a complex policy network.[30] Other writers have focused on the spatial dimension of political preferences, emphasizing the tendency of like-minded or similarly situated people to concentrate in certain localities (neighborhoods, towns, cities), and the increasing divides in voting patterns along urban/rural lines.[31] Several political scientists have extended this argument to suggest that, in first-past-the-post electoral systems, urban centers tend to be underrepresented compared to rural areas, mainly as a result of the historic concentration of left-leaning voters in cities and the aggregative wide margin of progressive candidate wins in urban electoral districts compared to more moderate right-leaning candidate wins in rural districts.[32] Others have suggested that, at least in the United States, the relative unification and better organization of city leaders throughout the twentieth century helped form a cohesive, well-represented, and often effective political force in shaping national policy-making.[33] Literature on progressive grassroots social movements in America's distressed communities points to new mobilization and policy tools available to activists at the city and neighborhood levels.[34]

---

[27] Saskia Sassen, *The Global City: New York, London, Tokyo* (Princeton University Press, 2001). Sassen lists additional cities as "global," notably Frankfurt and Paris. For a survey of the earlier literature on the subject, *see* John Friedmann, "The World City Hypothesis," *Development and Change* 17 (1986): 69–83.

[28] Simon Curtis, *Global Cities and Global Order* (Oxford University Press, 2016).

[29] Michael Goldsmith, "Cities in Intergovernmental Systems," *in* Peter John, Karen Mossberger, and Susan E. Clarke, eds., *Oxford Handbook of Urban Politics* (Oxford University Press, 2012), 133–151, 134.

[30] *See* Liesbet Hooghe and Gary Marks, *Multi-Level Governance and European Integration* (Rowman & Littlefield, 2001).

[31] *See, e.g.,* Bill Bishop, *The Big Sort: Why the Clustering of Like-Minded America Is Tearing Us Apart* (Houghton Mifflin, 2008); Jonathan Rodden, "The Geographic Distribution of Political Preferences," *Annual Review of Political Science* 13 (2010): 321–340.

[32] *See* Jonathan Rodden, *Why Cities Lose: The Deep Roots of the Urban-Rural Divide* (Basic Books, 2019).

[33] *See* Thomas Ogorzalek, *The Cities on the Hill: How Urban Institutions Transformed National Politics* (Oxford University Press, 2018).

[34] *See, e.g.,* Clarence Stone and Robert Stoker, eds., *Urban Neighborhoods in a New Era: Revitalizing Politics in the Post-industrial City* (University of Chicago Press, 2015).

Meanwhile, scholars of urban planning and innovation studies have paid considerable attention to the city as an engine of economic growth, a magnet for the creative classes, and a potential catalyst of regional cooperation. In the 1960s, believing that opportunities arising from close human interaction drove economic development, Jane Jacobs famously criticized the supposedly "rational" mode of urban planning (residential districts, business centers, etc.) as lethal for spontaneous innovation.[35] In another stream of thought, heavily influenced by economic theory, cities are commonly conceptualized as firm-like collective agents operating in a competitive field, attempting to position themselves favorably by discouraging settlement by costly, welfare-dependent populations,[36] instead luring in the "productive classes" with attractive housing, employment, demographic composition, culture and recreation, public safety and cleanliness, high-quality education, and other similar enticements.[37] Scholars of innovation, such as Richard Florida, have spoken about the competitiveness of cities, urban regions, and city clusters in attracting the "creative class" as a key driving force of urban economic development.[38] Against this thread, prominent critics of competitive economic models of urban development (e.g., Neil Brenner), point to the neoliberal foundations of such models and to the outright subjection of urban development to hegemonic neoliberal worldviews, and to the needs and interests of advanced capitalism more generally.[39] Meanwhile, leading economists (e.g., Paul Krugman) have connected ideas about economies of scale with population agglomeration and urban region density, thereby elucidating the economic logic behind the rise of megacities and of urban clustering more generally.[40] Others have emphasized the lack of attention to communities as a "third pillar" in canonical economic theory long dominated by attention to states and markets.[41]

---

[35] Jane Jacobs, *The Death and Life of Great American Cities* (Random House, 1961).

[36] *See, e.g.,* Paul E. Peterson, *City Limits* (University of Chicago Press, 1981).

[37] *See generally* Arthur O'Sullivan, *Urban Economics* (9th ed., McGraw Hill, 2018); David Audretsch, Albert Link, and Mary Walshok, *The Oxford Handbook of Local Competitiveness* (Oxford University Press, 2015).

[38] Richard Florida, *The Rise of the Creative Class* (Basic Books, 2002). At the same time, cities that have been successful in their ability to attract the creative classes have more often than not witnessed increasing gentrification, unaffordability, segregation, and inequality. *See, e.g.,* Richard Florida, *The New Urban Crisis: How Our Cities Are Increasing Inequality, Deepening Segregation, and Failing the Middle Class, and What We Can Do About It* (Basic Books, 2017).

[39] *See, e.g.,* Neil Brenner and Nikolas Theodore, eds., *Spaces of Neoliberalism: Urban Restructuring in North America and Western Europe* (Blackwell, 2002).

[40] By such accounts, small cities face an uphill battle unless they develop a unique specialty. All contingencies aside, Krugman argues, "if you back up enough, it makes sense to think of urban destinies as a random process of wins and losses in which small cities face a relatively high likelihood of experiencing gambler's ruin." *See* Paul Krugman, "The Gambler's Ruin of Small Cities (Wonkish)," *New York Times,* December 30, 2017; Emily Badger, "What Happens When the Richest U.S. Cities Turn to the World?," *New York Times,* December 22, 2017.

[41] Raghuram Rajan, *The Third Pillar: How Markets and the State Leave the Community Behind* (Penguin Press, 2019).

Scholarly accounts of urban politics, of cities as sites of technological innovation and social integration, and of intercity collaboration on transportation or environmental issues, to name but a few research foci, have been flourishing in the social sciences.

Reputable journalism, too, has discovered urban agglomeration. Outlets such as *Forbes Magazine* ("A New Era for the City-State," 2010), *Foreign Policy* ("Metropolis Now," 2010), *The Boston Globe* ("The City-State Returns," 2015), and *Aeon* ("Return of the City-State," 2017) have addressed the promise of city-states such as Singapore or Monaco to provide effective, problem-solving governance. The major thrust is that "the 21st century will not be dominated by America or China, Brazil or India, but by the city. . . the age of the nation-state is over. The new urban era has begun."[42] *The Guardian*, one of the world's leading newspapers, runs a section on cities that is supported by the Rockefeller Foundation. Prominent public intellectuals have penned bestselling popular science books, such as *A Country for Cities*, *The Metropolitan Revolution*, *Global Cities* and *Triumph of the City*, and most famously Benjamin Barber's *If Mayors Ruled the World*, all pointing to the rising significance of cities, and perhaps also to the desirability of urban power as an alternative means of "getting things done" compared to bureaucracy- and politics-heavy national governments.[43] Echoing a similar sentiment, Rahm Emanuel (former mayor of Chicago) argues in a recent book, *The Nation City*, that cities stand at the center of innovation and effective governance in a variety of areas from education to environmental policies, and may therefore be successful drivers of change in an "age of dysfunction" in American politics.[44]

This line of thought follows a pragmatist outlook: cities are good at solving problems. City governance, due to its relatively manageable scale, practical experience, and "hands-on" approach, may serve as an alternative to state apparatuses that are comparatively unwieldly, detached, and burdened by bureaucracy and politics. Pragmatist proponents argue that cities should seize the current zeitgeist of "new localism" and take control over policies targeting social and economic problems within their ambits.[45] Benjamin Barber's *If Mayors Ruled the*

---

[42] Parag Khanna, "Beyond City Limits," *Foreign Policy* 181 (September/October 2010): 120–128, 122.

[43] Benjamin R. Barber, *If Mayors Ruled the World: Dysfunctional Nations, Rising Cities* (Yale University Press, 2013); Vishaan Chakrabarti, *A Country of Cities: A Manifesto for an Urban America* (Metropolis Books, 2013); Bruce Katz and Jennifer Bradley, *The Metropolitan Revolution: How Cities and Metros Are Fixing Our Broken Politics and Fragile Economy* (Reprint ed., Brookings Institution Press, 2013); Greg Clark, *Global Cities* (Brookings Institution Press, 2016); Edward Glaeser, *Triumph of the City: How Our Greatest Invention Makes Us Richer, Smarter, Greener, Healthier, and Happier* (Penguin Press, 2011).

[44] Rahm Emanuel, *The Nation City: Why Mayors are Now Running the World* (Knopf, 2020).

[45] Bruce Katz and Jeremy Nowak, *The New Localism: How Cities Can Thrive in the Age of Populism* (Brookings Institution Press, 2018).

World makes what is arguably the boldest argument for giving more power to cities. His reasoning is practical: cities can deliver where big government can't. He suggests that cities' tendency to find practicable solutions to big policy challenges, as well as their unique combination of local engagements and cosmopolitan inclinations, make cities better suited than states to deal with major contemporary governance problems in areas including housing, jobs, transportation, and education. But while cities are ideally situated to deal with these issues, national and sub-national near-monopolies in these policy areas stand in the way of their ability to do so. If mayors ruled the world, Barber writes, "the more than 3.5 billion people (over half the world's population) who are urban dwellers and the many more in the exurban neighborhoods beyond could participate locally and cooperate globally at the same time—a miracle of civic 'glocality' promising pragmatism instead of politics, innovation rather than ideology and solutions in place of sovereignty."[46]

Within legal academia, scholars of international and global law have identified the interconnectivity of the urban with national and international governance levels,[47] and more specifically the increasing involvement of cities in international policy-making, particularly in environmental protection and global climate change regimes, but also in areas such as anti-poverty, international migration, and refugee policies.[48] While lacking formal standing in international law, international city and mayoral networks have formed around an array of common goals, from joining the UN-Habitat program to vowing to implement the Paris Agreement, to demanding representation at the global and pan-European policy-making fora concerning the refugee crisis. In fact, some observers have gone as far as suggesting that today's cities "are more involved in international policy-making, more savvy at navigating the international halls of power, more ambitious about voicing their opinions at the global level, and more influential in shaping global initiatives than perhaps at any time since Italy's city-states dominated during the Renaissance."[49] In short, the last few decades have seen a burst of interest in novel thinking about urbanization and cities through the human sciences.

By stark contrast, very little of this intellectual richness has extended into the world of constitutional law. Here, the city remains a nonentity and a non-subject. The existing conversation, be it academic or jurisprudential, about all matters

---

[46] Barber, *If Mayors Ruled the World*, 5.

[47] Yishai Blank, "The City and the World," *Columbia Journal of Transnational Law* 44 (2006): 875–939.

[48] *See, e.g.*, Helmut Aust, "The Shifting Role of Cities in the Global Climate Change Regime: From Paris to Pittsburgh and Back?," *Review of European, Comparative and International Environmental Law* 28 (2019): 57–66.

[49] Chrystie Flournoy Swiney and Sheila Foster, "Cities Are Rising in Influence and Power on the Global Stage," *City Lab*, April 15, 2019.

sub-national—regions, states, provinces, etc.—is limited to centuries-old ideas about the supposedly proper units of federalism and subsidiarity; there are precious few exceptions to this reality. Excuses abound. The world may well see cities of 50 or 100 million people in the foreseeable future . . . but this need not concern contemporary constitutional jurisprudence. More than 95% of urban population growth before 2050 will take place in the developing world . . . but oh well, we live in New York. Evidence clearly shows that the rural/urban divide is a major factor in explaining political, cultural, and economic differences . . . but this is a matter for social scientists, not for public law. And so on and so forth.

The gap is even more glaring when it comes to comparative constitutionalism. Despite the tremendous renaissance of comparative constitutional law, not a single comparative study considers constitutional innovation and stalemate from the standpoint of city-state relations. In fact, the metropolis is virtually nonexistent in comparative constitutional law, constitutional design, and constitutional thought. With the partial exception of a few American legal academics (e.g., Gerlad Frug, Hendrik Hartog, Richard Schragger) whose work focuses on American cities' legal and constitutional status,[50] there are no book-length comparative accounts of the challenges to constitutional governance posed by extensive urbanization, the rise of the metropolis, or by consequent tensions along a center/periphery demographic and geopolitical axis. In comparative constitutional thought, the city continues to be nonexistent, quietly accepted as something fully subsumed within existing federalism and "separation of powers" doctrinal schemes. *The Oxford Handbook of Comparative Constitutional Law*, for example, is a major state-of-the-field collection that includes over 50 chapters spread over a thousand pages.[51] Not a single chapter addresses the urban challenge in passing, let alone in significant detail. A similar silence resounds in virtually all other definitive handbooks, companions, and textbooks on comparative constitutional law.[52]

Predictably, even the recent resurgence of a periphery/center divide in economic and political discourse has not generated much novel legal or constitutional thinking about cities or spatial dimensions of constitutionalism more generally. The rapidly expanding constitutional literature that addresses the rise

[50] Gerald Frug, "The City as a Legal Concept," *Harvard Law Review* 93 (1980): 1057–1154; Hendrik Hartog, *Public Property and Private Power: The Corporation of the City of New York in American Law 1730–1870* (University of North Carolina Press, 1983); Richard C. Schragger, *City Power* (Oxford University Press, 2016).
[51] Michel Rosenfeld and András Sajó, eds., *The Oxford Handbook of Comparative Constitutional Law* (Oxford University Press, 2012).
[52] *See, e.g.,* Mark Tushnet, Thomas Fleiner, and Cheryl Saunders, eds., *Routledge Handbook of Constitutional Law* (Routledge, 2013); Vicki Jackson and Mark Tushnet, *Comparative Constitutional Law*, 3rd edition (Foundation Press, 2014); Roger Masterman and Robert Schütze, eds., *The Cambridge Companion to Comparative Constitutional Law* (Cambridge University Press, 2019).

of various populist, illiberal, or authoritarian threats to constitutional democracy tends to overlook the political geography dimensions of these trends.[53] Consequently, little or no intellectual energy is invested by this otherwise bold and innovative body of scholarship in developing constitutional designs that would aim to remedy or mitigate the spatial shortcomings of the contemporary constitutional canon. In the European legal academy—preoccupied as it is with questions of national constitutional sovereignty vis-à-vis the emerging pan-European constitutional order—urban agglomeration is not really on anyone's radar. Merely a couple of books written by public law scholars focus on the constitutional status of cities in Asia—the continent that has experienced and is projected to see the most significant level or urbanization worldwide.[54] Meanwhile, in the United States, a handful of legal scholars have suggested that a more decentralized, region-based notion of federalism may be required in order for the concentration of power in Washington to be diffused.[55] Others analyze the rise of so-called human rights cities (discussed later), or federal and state legal assaults on city power (discussed in detail in Chapter 2).[56] However, as timely and intellectually refreshing as these accounts are, they represent merely a drop when compared to the ocean of constitutional law literature focused on the state as the spatial and conceptual epicenter of the constitutional universe.

II. Spatial Statism

This stark gap in constitutional scholarship on cities, amid ever-expanding urban agglomeration worldwide, reflects a long-standing state-centered vision of the constitutional order. As Nick Barber observes in his recent treatise on the principles of constitutionalism, "[C]onstitutionalism is a doctrine that is derived from, or at least tightly connected to, the state. It applies to those creating

---

[53] See, e.g., Tom Ginsburg and Aziz Z. Huq, How to Save a Constitutional Democracy (University of Chicago Press, 2018); Kim Lane Scheppele, "Autocratic Legalism," University of Chicago Law Review 85 (2018): 545–584; and David Landau, "Abusive Constitutionalism," U.C. Davis Law Review 47 (2013): 189–260.

[54] See, e.g., Andrew Harding and Mark Sidel, eds., Central-Local Relations in Asian Constitutional Systems (Hart Publishing, 2015).

[55] See, e.g., Yishai Blank and Issachar Rosen-Zvi, "Reviving Federal Regions," Stanford Law Review 70 (2018): 1895–1993; David Fontana, "Federal Decentralization," Virginia Law Review 104 (2017): 727–795.

[56] Martha Davis, "Design Challenges for Human Rights Cities," Columbia Human Rights Law Review 49 (2017): 28–66; Erin Scharff, "Hyper Preemption: A Reordering of the State-Local Relationship?," Georgetown Law Journal 106 (2018): 1469–1522; Kenneth Stahl, "Preemption, Federalism and Local Democracy," Fordham Urban Law Journal 44 (2017): 133–179; Erin Scharff, "Powerful Cities? Limits on Municipal Taxing Authority and What to Do about Them," New York University Law Review 91 (2016): 292–343; Richard C. Schragger, "The Attack on American Cities," Texas Law Review 96 (2018): 1163–1233.

states and, also, to those who act within and upon the structures of the state."[57] Why does this statist project, whether principled or pragmatic, ignore urban agglomeration?

Of interest here are historical accounts of the rise of the modern state and the corresponding demise of city and sub-national autonomy. It is well-known that the process of state formation in Europe involved the subjugation of the medieval city. Medieval and early-modern city-states' and autonomous communities' powers were gradually yet effectively subordinated to the growing authority of the early-modern state, with its quest for full control over its territory and people.[58] New, state-based citizenship and equivalent political membership regimes gradually replaced city-based ones.[59] In some cases, the subjugation of city powers by the state-led leviathan-building project was swift—either as a result of clear power imbalances, or because pooling military or economic resources of several smaller units to create a more potent, larger one served the interests of weakened city-states. In other instances, emerging states had to resort to active disciplining and open confrontation with recalcitrant, self-asserting cities, adamant on maintaining their sovereignty and authority over their territory, people, capital, and knowledge. Given the considerable variance in how city-states were incorporated into the modern state, it is clear that a range of historical and regional contingencies influenced this evolution alongside broader geographical, cultural, and economic factors. Sooner or later, however, the vast majority of hitherto autonomous cities (at least in Europe) were "nationalized," enveloped by the early-modern state, their power giving way to the state-centered conception of sovereignty and spatiality. Whereas in 1500, the city-state in all its varieties was the dominant political unit in Europe, by 1800 it had given way to the early-modern state and its overseas colonies.

Subsequent political paths converged, with few exceptions, upon a single form of a medium-sized, centralized state, with the later addition of federalism as a joint-governance pact between sub-national administration and a national government. It was during this phase of the evolution of city-state relations that substantial urban communities lost much of their previous autonomy and status. As states sought to establish their monopoly over the legitimate exercise of physical force and authority; enhance their influence on economic and social life; and, most importantly, control "who gets what, when and how" within their respective territories, they also laid stronger and stronger claims to primacy as the

---

[57] N. W. Barber, *The Principles of Constitutionalism* (Oxford University Press, 2018), 11.

[58] *See, e.g.*, Patrick Le Galès, *European Cities: Social Conflicts and Governance* (Oxford University Press, 2002); Hendrik Spruyt, *The Sovereign State and Its Competitors* (Princeton University Press, 1996).

[59] *See generally* Maarten Prak, *Citizens without Nations: Urban Citizenship in Europe and the World, c. 1000–1789* (Cambridge University Press, 2018).

focus of popular loyalty and collective identity.[60] As cities became nationalized, state-centered bureaucracies and governance structures emerged. Cities were increasingly perceived as mere components, however important, of nation-states; and as cogs, however central, in national economies.[61] As Gerald Frug has shown in his seminal *Harvard Law Review* article written in 1980, the legal conceptualization of the city during that grand transformation was consistently narrowed to a powerless "creature of the state" and to an entity authorized by the state to solve purely local problems. In that process, Frug argues, "it is not simply that cities have become totally subject to state control—although that itself demonstrates their powerlessness—but also that cities have lost the elements of association and economic strength that had formally enabled them to play an important part in the development of Western society."[62] As the statist project of national constitutions, both centrist and federalist, achieved prominence, the effect on the constitutional imagination with respect to political geography and spatial autonomy was immediate and complete, leading to a dearth of creative thinking concerning city governance.

One prominent consequence of this political atrophy is the exclusion of cities from the purview of contemporary federalism, both in theory and in practice. Historically, federalism has been developed and deployed in response to pooling factors, including military interests (both defensive and offensive) and economic welfare.[63] A group of interested units join together into one of several types of confederated entities—multi-tribe (e.g., the ancient Israelites), multination (e.g., the Iroquois Confederacy), multi-republic (e.g., the Helvetic Confederation), and multi-city-state (e.g., the Hellenic Achaean League, the Lombard League

---

[60]   *See* Charles Tilly, *Coercion, Capital and European States, AD 990–1992* (Blackwell, 1992); Peter J. Taylor, *World City Network: A Global Urban Analysis* (Routledge, 2004). Holding the monopoly over the legitimate use of physical force by a government in a well-defined territory is, according to Max Weber, one of the defining features of the state. *See generally Weber's Rationalism and Modern Society: New Translations on Politics, Bureaucracy, and Social Stratification* (Tony Waters and Dagmar Waters, trans. and eds., Palgrave, 2015), 129–198.

[61]   Taylor, *World City Network*, 15.

[62]   Gerald Frug, "The City as a Legal Concept," 1119–1120.

[63]   Francesco Palermo and Karl Kössler, *Comparative Federalism: Constitutional Arrangements and Case Law* (Hart Publishing, 2017), 68. For useful surveys of the leading accounts for why federalism forms, why it may be beneficial, and why it is a justifiable mode of governance under certain circumstances, *see, e.g.,* Jaroslaw Kantorowicz, "Federalism," in Roger Congleton, Bernard Grofman, and Stefan Voigt, eds., *The Oxford Handbook of Public Choice* (Oxford University Press, 2019), 72–93; Michael Burgess, *In Search of the Federal Spirit: New Comparative Empirical and Theoretical Perspectives* (Oxford University Press, 2012); Pablo Beramenda, "Federalism," in Carles Boix, Susan Stokes, and Pablo Beramendi, eds., *The Oxford Handbook of Comparative Politics* (Oxford University Press, 2009), 752–781; Brian Galligan, "Comparative Federalism," Sarah Binder et al., eds., *The Oxford Handbook of Political Institutions* (Oxford University Press, 2008), 261–280; Jonathan Rodden, "Federalism," in Donald Wittman and Barry Weingast, eds., *The Oxford Handbook of Political Economy* (Oxford University Press, 2006), 357–370.

in Northern Italy, or the Northern European Hanseatic League).[64] In modern federations, however, and in the field of contemporary constitutional studies, the near-exclusively applied "unit" of federalism is the state and its equivalents (provinces, Länder, cantons, regions, emirates, etc.). As Heather Gerken writes of the American context, "[f]ederalism scholars have typically confined themselves to states, the only subnational institutions that possess sovereignty."[65] The same is true in other federalist settings around the world, with the few exceptions I discuss in Chapter 3. Worldwide, the Westphalian model continues to dominate the theory and practice of federalism, with its notion of sovereign territorial states divided along ethnic, religious, and linguistic cleavages and reflecting conventional notions of nationhood, peoplehood, and/or historical patterns of conquest and settlement. In this universe, cities, home to the majority of mankind, ubiquitous and crucial to every aspect of twenty-first-century society, culture, economics, and politics are virtually absent, "the forgotten stepchildren of both federal politics and scholarship."[66]

The beginning of modern federalism can be attributed to the worldwide "federalist revolution" that coincided with the emergence of nation-states encompassing large territories and populations.[67] According to Elazar, the American *Federalist Papers* represent the "classic formulation of the principles of modern federalism."[68] Indeed, its basic features—the separation of powers, exclusive authority over certain matters for constituent units, and legislative representation for constituent units—have served as a blueprint for subsequent federations.[69] The states comprising the United States, legitimized by their "settled existence over generations," have each become gradually differentiated in respect of their internal cultural, social, and political patterns.[70] Other innovations of modern federalism were introduced by Switzerland's Constitution (1848), which introduced direct democracy at the national level; the orientation of federal arrangements toward "the purpose of managing diversity" rather than checking political power; and an "administrative federalism" that assigns the canton's broad discretion to implement federal laws.[71] The German federal

---

[64] *See, e.g.*, S. Rufus Davis, *The Federal Principle: A Journey Through Time in Quest of a Meaning* (University of California Press, 1978); Daniel J. Elazar, *Exploring Federalism* (University of Alabama Press, 1987).

[65] Heather Gerken, "Foreword: Federalism All the Way Down," *Harvard Law Review* 124 (2010): 6–74, 21.

[66] Loren King, "Cities, Subsidiarity, and Federalism," *in* James Fleming and Jacob Levy, eds., *Federalism and Subsidiarity: NOMOS LV* (New York University Press, 2014), 295.

[67] Elazar, *Exploring Federalism*, 109–110.

[68] Elazar, *Exploring Federalism*, 143.

[69] Thomas Hueglin and Alan Fenna, *Comparative Federalism: A Systematic Inquiry*, 2nd ed. (University of Toronto Press, 2015), 92.

[70] Daniel J. Elazar, *American Federalism: A View from the States*, 2nd ed. (Crowell, 1972), 11, 14–25.

[71] Palermo and Kössler, *Comparative Federalism*, 77–79.

constitutions of 1867 and 1871 introduced highly asymmetrical power relations between Prussia and the other constituent units.[72] Many variations on the federalist theme have emerged over the last 150 years; however, state-sized entities are the common building blocks of virtually all of them.

Very little attention has been devoted in political theory, let alone in constitutional theory, to federalism's "unit" question. This gap is particularly troubling, as Jacob Levy observes, considering the prevalence of federalism and the dominant status of state-sized, sub-national units in contemporary federalism.[73] For Levy, one of the few authors to have addressed the unit size issue, "federations are made of provinces that are too few, too large, too rigid, too constitutionally entrenched, and too tied up to ethnocultural identity to match theories based on competitive federalism, Tiebout sorting [supposed optimization of public service provision based on competition across local jurisdictions], democratic self-government, or subsidiarity."[74]

The exclusion of cities from modern federalism, like the constitutional silence on urban agglomeration, reflects a confluence of factors, including institutional and intellectual path dependence, amendment difficulty, and lack of political will, at times proactive resistance, to empowering cities. Above all, however, it may reflect and perpetuate an embedded tendency in public law that Ayelet Shachar and I have termed *spatial statism*—the notion that public law, through its spatial ordering, partakes in sustaining the centrality of a state-oriented locus and focus of sovereign control of its territory in the face of competing forces, real or perceived.[75] Of course, a range of economic forces transcend the power of the state, knowing no borders: investment, trade, capital mobility, knowledge transfer, tax evasion, etc. Politically, too, international organizations are proliferating and transnational standard setting is on the rise. Nonetheless, core aspects of "classical" public law remain largely statist, especially those focused on territoriality, a vital dimension of sovereignty.[76] There remains a strong statist grip

---

[72] Palermo and Kössler, *Comparative Federalism*, 79–82.

[73] Jacob T. Levy, "Federalism, Liberalism, and the Separation of Loyalties," *American Political Science Review* 101 (2007): 459–477. *See, more generally*, Stephen Tierney, "Federalism and Constitutional Theory," *in* Gary Jacobsohn and Miguel Schor, eds., *Comparative Constitutional Theory* (Edward Elgar, 2018), 45–65.

[74] If the leading theories of federalism are to be taken seriously, Levy argues ("Federalism, Liberalism, and the Separation of Loyalties," 460–463), they warrant a much more flexible, decentralized model of federalism, composed of smaller constituent units than the typical state- or province-sized ones.

[75] Ran Hirschl and Ayelet Shachar, "Foreword: Spatial Statism," *International Journal of Constitutional Law* 17 (2019): 387–438.

[76] Definitions of sovereignty may vary, but legally there are three enduring constituent features: people, territory, and political authority exercised over that territory and its people. In international law, Article 1 of the Montevideo Convention on the Rights and Duties of the State (1933), echoes the traditional Westphalian view, stating that "The State as a person of international law should possess the following qualifications: (a) a permanent population; (b) a defined territory; (c) government; and (d) capacity to enter into relation with other States."

over zoning and land policy, takings, public works and infrastructure investment, social welfare, and control over intergenerational wealth transfer through
inheritance and property taxation, to say nothing of the intensely government-
controlled military, policing intelligence and surveillance domains. Statist concern with territorial sovereignty also manifests in less obvious arenas, from the
growing anxiety over immigration, borders, and "uncontrolled" entry to the
doctrine of permanent sovereignty over natural wealth and resources, from state
control of religious sites and attire in the public sphere to the rise of statist neo-
secessionism driven by nationalist-populist trends. Taken in conjunction, these
ongoing statist projects suggest that the state is alive and well as a potent actor in
the public law arena. Global markets have weakened the state's fiscal autonomy,
but have fallen short of dismantling a core element of the Westphalian order: the
state's legal grip over its territory. Facing existential threats to its long-standing
dominance, the state has modified and reinvented itself to remain a key player in
the struggle for spatial control. A similar statist impulse, I argue, also drives the
state's innate concern from the rise of large, densely populated, politically significant, and economically potent cities.

This, in turn, points to the continued relevance, albeit in a new configuration,
of classical works in political sociology and state theory, from Weberian accounts
to James Scott's *Seeing Like a State*, which emphasize the ability to consolidate
and enforce laws over a defined territory as one of the constitutive factors for
the rise and endurance of the modern state. As several public law theorists have
pointed out, the state is a core building block, indeed a sine qua non concept, in
public law;[77] it has never abandoned its claim "to be the center of the legal universe."[78] At least when it comes to constitutional control of cities, where the state
remains the master of the domain, that claim certainly holds true.

The state's existential fear of large cities is also driven by a more immediate
concern. Large cities can serve as nurseries for potentially unruly radicalization, leading to an undermining of state power, possibly even to political revolution. By their very nature, megacities are densely populated and are home
to critical masses of people. They facilitate close human interaction and feature
public spaces where large crowds can easily congregate, thereby allowing for a
rapid spread of ideas, including potentially socially and politically destabilizing

---

[77] Martin Loughlin, "The State: Conditio Sine Qua Non," *International Journal of Constitutional
Law* 16 (2018): 1156–1163. Loughlin argues that in linking territory, authority, and people in an in-
telligible scheme, the state is "the foundational concept that enables lawyers coherently to engage
with the issue of political authority." For an overview of pertinent patterns of change and continuity
in public law-related statehood theory, *see, e.g.*, Neil Walker, Cormac Mac Amhlaigh, and Claudio
Michelon, "Law, Polity and the Legacy of Statehood: An Introduction," *International Journal of
Constitutional Law* 16 (2018): 1148–1155.
[78] Barbo Fassbender, "The State's Unabandoned Claim to Be the Center of the Legal Universe,"
International Journal of Constitutional Law 16 (2018): 1207–1214.

ones. Cities, in particular capital cities, are home to important government buildings, national monuments, and media outlets that provide concrete targets for protestors; the popular capture of these emblems of power has both practical and symbolic meaning. The Occupy Wall Street movement in New York or the massive, at times veering-out-of-hand demonstrations that took place in Toronto or Hamburg against G-20 leaders and their pro-globalization and pro-corporations plans may ultimately be controllable. But as the street warfare in Hong Kong, mass demonstrations in Tahrir Square, or the wide protests in the streets of Santiago suggest, the megacity features a potentially explosive combination of people, ideas, and spatial conditions that from a statist point of view is better kept under check.

III. What Do National Constitutions Say about Cities?

As creatures of the modern state, national constitutions generally say little about cities as autonomous political communities. To the extent that these constitutions acknowledge cities, they almost always do so in the context of administrative assignment of local government competences; of the 195 national constitutions in effect at the end of 2019, 150 constitutions include reference to "municipal government" while 82 constitutions refer to "local government." Some of these constitutions introduce hierarchies of municipalities by their population size, often without differentiation between cities of 100,000 or 200,000 people and multimillion person megacities. Only 9 constitutions refer to "self-governing municipalities"; 23 constitutions assign to municipalities the power to levy local taxes.

Most "old world" constitutions (constitutional orders adopted over a two-century span, between the late eighteenth century and the 1970s), whether federal (e.g., United States, Canada, Australia, Mexico, Germany), unitary (e.g., France, the Netherlands, Sweden), or somewhere in between (e.g., UK, Spain, Italy), covering North America, Western Europe, and many former colonies elsewhere, treat cities, including some of the world's most significant urban centers, as creatures of the state, fully submerged within a Westphalian constitutional framework, and assigned limited administrative local governance authority.

While large cities in North America and Western Europe are considered business hubs, corporate centers, or "global cities," their *constitutional* statuses range anywhere from secondary to nonexistent. American cities, some of which are among the world's largest, lack constitutional personality, and are principally at the mercy of state governments, constitutionally speaking. Doctrines such as "Dillon's Rule" and home rule (the "Cooley Doctrine") formulated in the mid-nineteenth century and endorsed by the US Supreme Court in the early twentieth century (see detailed discussion in Chapter 2) continue to govern the constitutional status of American megacities today. Large Canadian cities, essentially the front-line delivery agents of Canadian multiculturalism and social integration, are governed by a constitutional order that dates back to 1867 (at which time metro Toronto's population was less than 50,000; today it is 7.5 million). In this reckoning, "municipal institutions" are creatures of provincial governments, and are controlled exclusively by provincial authority, alongside "charities," "eleemosynary institutions," "shops," and "saloons and taverns." Australia's constitutional order too allows for near-complete state domination of cities and metropolitan governance more generally. Meanwhile, the Rhine-Ruhr metropolitan region (Germany's largest urban agglomeration with over 11 million people) lacks any autonomous constitutional standing or personality; in fact, it is not even mentioned in the state constitution of North Rhine-Westphalia, within the boundaries of which it exists. The same is true of Frankfurt, described in Saskia Sassen's seminal work as a "global city" alongside New York, London, and Tokyo—yet not even a whisper about Frankfurt in the Hessian state constitution. As I show in Chapter 3, the dynamics of megacity constitutional empowerment in "new world" constitutional settings, mainly Asia and Latin America, is somewhat different, reflecting a confluence of varying demographic, political, and constitutional factors. However, even in those parts of the constitutional cosmos, the starting point and basic assumption of statist constitutional orders is that the city is just a component—and a largely dependent one at that—of the nation-state and its statist constitutional framework.

A clear indication of the national outlook embedded in the constitutional treatment of cities is the fact that, of the 195 constitutions in effect by the end of 2019, no fewer than 119 designate their respective country's "national capital": the constitution of Belarus (1994) states that "[T]he capital of the Republic of Belarus is Minsk"[79]; the constitution of Paraguay (1992) states that "[T]he city of Asunción is the capital of the republic and seat to the powers of the State."[80] Several constitutions designate the capital city as governed by a separate law; the constitution of Serbia (2006), for example, states that "[T]he status of the City of Belgrade, the capital of the Republic of Serbia, shall be regulated by the Law on the Capital and the Statute of the City of Belgrade. The City of Belgrade shall have competences delegated to the municipality and city by the Constitution and the Law, and other competences may be delegated to it in accordance with the Law on the Capital."[81] The constitution of Moldova (1994) states that "[T]he status of the capital of the Republic of Moldova—the city of

---

[79] Constitution of Belarus (1994; rev. 2004), Art. 20.
[80] Constitution of Paraguay (1992; rev. 2011), Art. 157.
[81] Constitution of Serbia (2006), Art. 189.

Chisinau—shall be regulated by organic law."[82] The constitution of Venezuela (1999) states that "[T]he city of Caracas is the capital of the Republic and the seat of the organs of national power."[83] In other countries, a similar outcome is achieved via quasi-constitutional decrees; the Philippines's Presidential Decree 940 (1976) establishes Manila as the capital; section 1 reads: "The capital of the Philippines is hereby designated to be Manila and the area prescribed as Metro Manila under Presidential Decree No. 824 shall be the permanent seat of national government." In other national constitutions (e.g., Czech Republic [Prague], Tajikistan [Dushanbe], Uzbekistan [Tashkent]), capital cities are granted formal status similar to that of sub-national units (e.g., provinces, oblasts).[84] The Republic of North Macedonia's constitution extends local self-government powers to Skopje, that country's capital.[85] One of Israel's 14 Basic Laws (which taken together serve as that country's de facto constitution), known as "Basic Law: Jerusalem, Capital of Israel" (1980), states that Jerusalem, complete and united, is the capital of Israel and seat of the president, the parliament (Knesset), the government, and the Supreme Court. Virtually all these national constitutions assign special status to capital cities as the nation's symbolic pillar and the contemporary seat of government; virtually none address these cities as large metropolitan centers per se. Scattered examples of non-capital city-provinces (e.g., Bremen or Hamburg in Germany or Basel-Stadt in Switzerland) are precious few exceptions to this reality, and virtually none is predicated on a deep, across-the-board constitutional recognition of the metropolis as an autonomous or distinct order of government.

Several constitutional orders, all of them outside North America and Western Europe (a point that I examine in considerable detail in Chapter 3) acknowledge the new reality of megacity prominence and extend fiscal autonomy and policy-making authority to such cities. Here, population size, governance complexity, and centrality to the country's economic and geopolitical well-being matter. Tokyo, the world's largest metropolis, enjoys recognition as both a "city" and a "prefecture," owing to a mix of primary legislation, constitutional provisions, and political traditions that evolved from the 1940s onward. Both the Chinese and the Russian constitutions assign special status to key cities—Beijing, Shanghai,

[82]   Constitution of Moldova (1994; rev. 2016), Art. 110.
[83]   Constitution of Venezuela (1999; rev. 2009), Art. 18.
[84]   *See, e.g.*, Constitution of the Czech Republic (1993; rev. 2013), Art. 1, Art. 3.
[85]   Constitution of the Republic of Macedonia (1991; rev. 2011), Art. 117: "[T]he City of Skopje is a particular unit of local self-government the organization of which is regulated by law. In the City of Skopje, citizens directly and through representatives participate in decision-making on issues of relevance for the City of Skopje particularly in the field of urban planning, communal activities, culture, sport, social security and child care, preschool education, primary education, basic health care and other fields determined by law . . . The City is autonomous in the execution of its constitutionally and legally determined spheres of competence; supervision of the legality of its work is carried out by the Republic."

Tianjin, and Chongqing in China; Moscow and St. Petersburg in Russia—which are viewed as engines of economic growth and as centers of national importance. These constitutional designations entrust megacity authorities with considerably more policy-making tools than those available to other cities.[86] A similar notion finds expression in the constitution of Vietnam, where a constitutional division was established in 1992 and further reinforced in 2013 between provinces and "cities directly under the central authority," or "centrally run cities," referring to Hanoi and Ho Chi Minh City.[87] The constitution of South Korea, as well, establishes 17 sub-national units, of which 8 are designated "first-level" cities (including Busan, Gwangju, Incheon, and Seoul), and Sejong as a special self-governing city.[88] The Hong Kong Basic Law (1997) establishes a unique joint-governance model between China and Hong Kong, with the latter operating as a special autonomous region within China. In many of these settings, constitutional support of megacities reflects astute, long-term central government planning aimed at fostering megacity power as the engine of regional or national economic growth.

In other instances—for example, as with recent constitutional reforms concerning urban affairs in India and Brazil—constitutional treatment of megacities is part of an overhaul of federalism. In India, the 73rd and 74th constitutional amendments (1992) were aimed at enhancing the constitutional autonomy of local government and articulated a vision of decentralized power and responsibility through the provision of constitutional status to urban centers. And in Brazil, the City Statute (2001), alongside Articles 182 and 183 of the constitution (1988), address matters of urban development and self-governance. (As I show in Chapter 3, in both countries, the long-standing reality of sub-national control over cities and politically-driven intergovernmental affairs have brought about mixed results.) Arguably, the most expansive constitutional protection of cities on offer today is featured in the South African constitution (1996), where a nexus of constitutional provisions, notably Chapter 7 (ss. 151–164) of the constitution, guarantee municipal standing and empower cities' planning and fiscal autonomy. Certain capital cities that have grown into some of the world's largest

[86] In 2014, the Crimean city of Sevastopol was granted a constitutional status similar to that of Moscow and St. Petersburg, as Crimea was officially annexed to the Russian Federation and subjected to its constitution. Ukraine reacted in 2016 by enshrining Sevastopol as city of national significance in its own constitution. See discussion in Chapter 3.

[87] Constitution of the Socialist Republic of Vietnam (2013), Art. 110.

[88] In 2004, the Korean Constitutional Court famously blocked an attempt to establish Sejong as the new national capital. In a nutshell, the court ruled that as a matter of constitutional convention, Seoul was the nation's capital. Hence, the Constitutional Court ruled the government's decision to relocate the nation's capital was unconstitutional as the project required an explicit revision of the constitution to that extent, a step the government was not prepared to take. *See* KCCR 2004Hun-Ma554 *Relocation of Capital City Case* (decision released October 21, 2004) [South Korea Constitutional Court].

urban centers enjoy a self-governing "national territory" status (e.g., Delhi), or have been elevated from a "federal district" status to a full-fledged state or sub-national unit constitutional status (e.g., Mexico City, Buenos Aires), have acquired a full state-like status, on par, constitutionally speaking, with other recognized sub-national units/states/provinces. These and other innovative constitutional mechanisms represent ways of addressing some of the challenges faced by the modern metropolis while the state maintains central constitutional control. However, in Canada, Australia, Germany, France, and the United States—all "old world" constitutional settings—these innovations remain beyond the purview of viable constitutional renewal discourse, let alone practice.

IV. The Boundaries of the "Local" and "Us"

Contrary to what many globalists and post-nationalists may have predicted or wished, separatist impulses, rather than disappearing into the currents of history, have instead gained renewed momentum worldwide. The Catalonia bid for independence is perhaps the most obvious, recent example of secessionist sentiment at the sub-national level. After government officials in Madrid turned to the Spanish Constitutional Court to successfully prevent a plebiscite on separation in Catalonia from taking place (the court ruled in 2014 that the referendum would be unconstitutional as only the federal government may launch a referendum on such matters), the government of Catalonia, in an explicit act of defiance, proceeded with a non-binding referendum.[89] A year later, the separatist "Together for Yes" (JxSí) coalition won the Catalan regional elections, garnering approximately 40% of the popular vote, and setting in motion a well-orchestrated secessionist campaign. A political showdown ensued between pro-independence forces in Catalonia and the Spanish government, backed by the EU and its anti-secessionist line. The Spanish Constitutional Court reiterated that a Catalan secession referendum would not be constitutional, let alone a declaration of independence.[90] Eventually, the Spanish government invoked Article 155 of the Spanish Constitution to impose direct rule in Catalonia.

In 2014, nearly half of Scottish voters expressed their desire for independence in a widely publicized referendum. Nicola Sturgeon, the First Minister of Scotland, has recently indicated that a second referendum on Scottish independence is imminent. Following the trend, in 2016, a referendum was held in the Republika Srpska—a semiautonomous entity within Bosnia and Herzegovina—on having its own, separate independence day in defiance of an explicit BiH

---

[89] Constitutional Court Judgment 42/2014 (March 25, 2014).
[90] Constitutional Court Judgment 259/2015 (December 2, 2015).

Constitutional Court ruling that declared the introduction of such an independence day or the holding of a referendum to approve it to be unconstitutional.[91] Constitutional disobedience aside, an overwhelming 99% of the votes casted supported the creation of an independent "Day of Republika Srpska." A year later, Republika Srpska leaders vowed to ignore another BiH Constitutional Court ruling holding that military bases within Republika Srpska's territory are under the exclusive jurisdiction of the BiH government (and thus expandable to NATO troops).[92] And in Puerto Rico—a US territory—a "full statehood" movement has been gaining momentum. In a referendum held in June 2017, 97% of the ballots cast favored statehood. Advocates of Puerto Rican statehood cite a long list of slights they attribute to their "second-class" membership in the American Federation—their fettered access to suffrage being at the top.[93] Meanwhile, in California, the secessionist Yes California movement (dubbed Calexit) has been picking up steam, with polls suggesting that approximately one-third of Californians support the idea.[94] From Kashmir to Kurdistan to Flanders, older quests for ethnicity-, religion-, or linguistic-based sub-national political autonomy remain active. In the Russian Federation, secessionist movements routinely take up arms against the central government (e.g., in Chechnya, Dagestan) while others outside the country are supported by the same central government (e.g., Georgia's Abkhazia and South Ossetia, Ukraine's Crimea). Meanwhile, "resource regionalism" thrives in the oil-rich provinces of Venezuela, Bolivia, and Nigeria, to name a few examples. In short, rumors of secession's demise in the age of global convergence have been greatly exaggerated; the list of secessionist movements and autonomy-aspiring regions and movements is as long today as it has ever been.

In recent years, a new trend—*neo-secessionism*—has arisen as an explicitly counter-convergent mode of response to various globalization trends, constitutional or otherwise. The rhetoric invoked by its proponents directly and explicitly targets elements of new constitutionalism and thrives on voters' intuitive resentment toward externally imposed, rigid sets of rules and norms, and the consequent limitations on national and local policy choices. The explicit target

---

[91] See "Bosnian Serb Referendum Backs Disputed 9 January Holiday," *BBC News* (September 25, 2016); online: http://www.bbc.com/news/world-europe-37465653.

[92] See "Court Rejects Bosnian Serb Claim to Army Facilities," *Balkan Insight* (August 16, 2017); online: http://www.balkaninsight.com/en/article/court-rejects-bosnian-serb-claim-to-army-facilities-08-16-2017.

[93] The federal government, however, is unlikely to accept that wish; as observers point out, "Puerto Rico would bring with it a massive, unpayable debt, and the potential to swing the current balance of power in Congress." See Joseph Blocher and Mitu Gulati, "Puerto Rico and the Right of Accession," *Yale Journal of International Law* 43 (2018): 229–271.

[94] See "Plans for California to Secede from the US Picking Up Steam," *ABC News* (January 27, 2017); online: http://abc7news.com/politics/plan-for-california-to-secede-from-us-picking-up-steam/1725013/.

of this neo-secessionist trend is global constitutionalism in its various ideological and institutional guises. The 2016 Brexit referendum—an unprecedented,
popular rejection of supranational political and constitutional convergence—is
a prime example. Populist-nationalist opposition groups in other EU member
states, from the Nordic countries to the Netherlands, and from Austria to Greece,
have also voiced grave concerns about the presumed threat to national sovereignty posed by the pan-European constitutional project. The financial crisis of
2008, in particular, boosted public support for separatist parties that questioned
the logic and future of the "ever closer union" project.[95] In Greece, the Golden
Dawn party has turned from a fringe, neo-Nazi pariah party that received less
than 5,000 votes in 1996, into the third largest party there, while the *Syriza* party
has advanced from being a small radical left party to the governing party (2015
through 2019), and currently the second largest, and main opposition party.
While these parties advance very different agendas, they share a core "Greece
first" line. In Spain, the leftist *Podemos* ("We Can") party promotes an outspoken
antiglobalization and antiestablishment agenda that seeks to curtail the Treaty of
Lisbon and its pan-European constitutionalization agenda; from the other side
of the political spectrum, the populist right-wing *Vox* party advocates ultranat-
ionalism, with a vision of a unified Spain with little or no regional autonomy.
In Finland, at the other end of Europe, the Finns Party (formerly known as
True Finns)—a populist-nationalist party advancing a clear, anti-EU, "Finland
first" agenda—has emerged as the second largest political party in that country.
In neighboring Sweden, a traditional bastion of social democracy, the Sweden
Democrats—a far-right party evolving in the late 1980s from the *Bevara Sverige
Svenskt* ("Keep Sweden Swedish") movement—has also become a significant po-
litical force.[96]

In recent electoral campaigns, parties representing various local variants of
the right-wing, "us first" agenda received unprecedented popular support: Fidesz
(Hungarian Civic Alliance) and its KDNP satellite party received 48.5% of the
votes in the 2018 general elections (translated into an overwhelming majority
of 134 seats in the 199-seat parliament); Poland's Law and Justice (PiS) received
37.6% of the vote in 2015 and a whopping 43.6% in the 2019 parliamentary
elections (the far-right Confederation Party received an additional 6.8% of the
vote); and the Austrian Freedom Party (FPÖ) received 26% in 2017 and 16% in
2019. Meanwhile, the anti-immigration Danish People's Party (*Dansk Folkeparti*)
emerged over the part decade as a considerable political force; in its peak (2015),

---

[95] *See* Francesco Nicoli, "Hard-line Euroscepticism and the Eurocrisis: Evidence from a Panel
Study of 108 Elections Across Europe," *Journal of Common Market Studies* 55 (2017): 312–331.
[96] The party received 17.6% of the popular vote in the 2018 election, which translated into a record
high of 62 seats in the Swedish parliament.

it received 21.1% of the popular vote in the 2015 general elections. The Sweden Democrats party received 17.6% of the popular vote in the 2018 election, translated into a record high of 62 seats in the Swedish parliament. Italy's ultranationalist (and formerly northern secessionist) Lega Nord received 17.4% of the votes in the 2018 general election (compared to a mere 4.1% in 2013). The far-right Party for Freedom (PVV) in the Netherlands garnered 13.1% of the popular vote in the 2017 general elections (compared to 10% in 2013), translated into 20 seats in the 150-seat parliament. And in France, the National Front (FN, renamed National Rally in 2018), led by Marine Le Pen, received 13.2% of the popular vote in the 2017 elections for the French National Assembly, while Le Pen herself attracted 21.3% of the vote in the first round of the 2017 presidential elections, and nearly 34% in the second round runoff. In Germany, the controversial right to far-right Alternative for Germany (AfD) party attracted an unprecedented 12.6% of the popular vote in the federal elections held in October 2017 (translated into 94 seats in the Bundestag—the first time the AfD had won any Bundestag seats at all).

Virtually all of these parties profess to represent authentic popular voices diametrically opposed to an unrepresentative yet all-encompassing international order. On similar lines, President Trump repeatedly professes to protect the interests of "ordinary people," who are framed as victims of corrupt, mostly invisible elites that supposedly rule the country and the world. According to that narrative, the American political institutions have been captured by a small, unrepresentative social stratum—mostly urban, educated, and economically well-off—that draws upon the constitutional order to advance liberal, neoliberal, cosmopolitan, and/or business friendly worldviews and policy preferences. There is also a complementary "us vs. them" sentiment, constructed on a sharp distinction between hardworking Americans (often depicted as white and Christian) and everything else (often framed as a hodgepodge of international economic forces, China, Europe, Muslims, illegal immigrants, and others who are not the real "us").

President Trump drew upon such rhetoric in his reaction to the Coronavirus crisis, repeatedly blaming foreign countries and foreign subjects for the spread of the virus in the United States. In a similar fashion, President Trump's 2017 announcement that the United States would withdraw from the Paris Climate Agreement, he espoused a "protect the ordinary people" rationale by suggesting that US compliance with the Paris Agreement could "cost America as much as 2.7 million lost jobs by 2025, according to the National Economic Research Associates." Turning to an explicit "us vs. them" sentiment, Trump stated: "I was elected to represent the citizens of Pittsburgh, not Paris."[97] He went on to suggest

---

[97] Donald Trump when announcing that the United States would be withdrawing from the Paris Climate Agreement (Reported in *The Guardian*, June 1, 2017).

that participation would require the United States to pay a significant sum to the Green Climate Fund that was set up by the Accord. "So we're going to be paying billions and billions and billions of dollars and we're already way ahead of anybody else," he said, "Many of the other countries haven't spent anything. And many of them will never pay one dime."[98] (In November 2019, the US government notified the UN of its intent to withdraw from the Paris Agreement; the withdrawal takes effect one year from delivery of that notification, i.e., in November 2020). Of course, absent from this rhetoric is the similar gap between America's major cities (18 of 21 having voted Democrat), which are major contributors to the federal tax collection; and America's typically Republican countryside, which, tends by and large, to be on the receiving end of federal money. Moreover, as this "us first" rhetoric gains prevalence, the Trump administration has been fighting municipalities that refuse to play along with the federal government's anti-Muslim and anti-immigrant stance.

American constitutional discourse, too, has witnessed a surge in nationalist exclusionary sentiment, exemplified in the fierce and ongoing debate over the role of foreign precedents in constitutional interpretation—a controversy described by one astute commentator as "an episode in America's culture wars."[99] Conservative members of the Supreme Court—Chief Justice Roberts and Justices Alito, Thomas, and the late Antonin Scalia—have opposed the citation of foreign law in constitutional cases on several grounds, most notably with regards to American constitutional sovereignty, constituent autonomy, and America's particularist constitutional legacy. In Judge Richard Posner's words, "no thanks, we already have our own laws."[100]

The notion of popular constitutionalism (essentially suggesting that people should play an active role in constitutional interpretation and "retain authority in day-to-day administration of fundamental law") is not foreign to American constitutional thought.[101] This body of literature suggests that the US Constitution

---

[98] The White House, "Statement by President Trump on the Paris Climate Accord, June 1, 2017" (Washington, DC: Office of the Press Secretary, June 1, 2017); online: https://www.whitehouse.gov/the-press-office/2017/06/01/statement-president-trump-paris-climate-accord.

[99] Mark Tushnet, "Referring to Foreign Law in Constitutional Interpretation: An Episode in the Culture Wars," *University of Baltimore Law Review* 3 (2006): 299–312. *See also* Norman Dorsen, "The Relevance of Foreign Legal Materials in U.S. Constitutional Cases: A Conversation between Justice Antonin Scalia and Justice Stephen Breyer," *International Journal of Constitutional Law* 3 (2005): 519–541; Martha Minow, "The Controversial Status of International and Comparative Law in the United States," *Harvard International Law Journal Online*, August 27, 2010.

[100] Richard Posner, "No Thanks, We Already Have Our Own Laws," *Legal Affairs* (July–August 2004); online: http://www.legalaffairs.org/issues/July-August-2004/feature_posner_julaug04.msp.

[101] Larry D. Kramer, "Popular Constitutionalism, circa 2004," *California Law Review* 92 (2004): 959, 961 n. 3, *cited in* Aziz Z. Huq, "The People Against the Constitution," *Michigan Law Review* 116 (2018): 1123–1144.

belongs to the people at least as much as it belongs to politicians, courts, and jurists, and should therefore be more commonly engaged within people's lives. However, the "ordinary people" Trump and other populist neo-secessionists purport to speak for do not reflect the entire American citizenry.[102] These populist voices are not in the business of proactive constitutional citizenship along the lines suggested by popular constitutionalists such as Larry Kramer or Mark Tushnet.[103]

Other prominent proponents of neo-secessionism commonly invoke anti-constitutional convergence rhetoric in the name of protecting "our" values against external impositions. Former British Prime Minister Theresa May, for one, has on multiple occasions expressed her support for the UK's opting out of the European Convention on Human Rights (ECHR), suggesting that the convention "can bind the hands of parliament, adds nothing to our prosperity, makes us less secure by preventing the deportation of dangerous foreign nationals—and does nothing to change the attitudes of governments like Russia's when it comes to human rights . . . so regardless of the EU referendum, if we want to reform human rights laws in this country, it isn't the EU we should leave but the ECHR and the jurisdiction of its court."[104]

Direct attacks against constitutional actors with apparently cosmopolitan outlooks in the name of "our" identity, culture, or values have taken place in an increasing number of countries, from Hungary, Poland, Russia, Turkey, and Israel to the Philippines, India, Malaysia, Brazil, and Venezuela. Yet, in virtually none of these settings has the "us first" rhetoric or emphasis on particularism over universalism been translated into national leaders' support for city empowerment vis-à-vis the dominant state apparatus. In the Philippines, to pick one example, President Duterte has declared on multiple occasions his disregard for international human rights norms, supposedly because of their irrelevance to the country's situation. In 2018, Duterte went on to declare that the Philippines would withdraw from the International Criminal Court treaty (the withdrawal materialized in 2019), and called upon other countries to follow suit.[105] Meanwhile, Manila continues to be one of the densest cities in the world; has the highest homeless population in the world relative to city size; and struggles with

[102] *See* Huq, "The People Against the Constitution."

[103] Larry D. Kramer, *The People Themselves: Popular Constitutionalism and Judicial Review* (Oxford University Press, 2004); Mark Tushnet, *Taking the Constitution Away from the Court* (Princeton University Press, 1999).

[104] Theresa May, *Home Secretary's Speech on the UK, EU and Our Place in the World*, Address to the Institute of Mechanical Engineers, London, April 25, 2016; online: https://www.gov.uk/government/speeches/home-secretarys-speech-on-the-uk-eu-and-our-place-in-the-world.

[105] *See* "Philippine's Rodrigo Duterte Urges Nations to Abandon International Criminal Court," *Deutsche Welle* (March 18, 2018); online: http://www.dw.com/en/philippines-rodrigo-duterte-urges-nations-to-abandon-international-criminal-court/a-43028013.

crime, corruption, and pollution, but no constitutional empowerment of the city is in sight.

A similar localist backlash against the "outer world" emanates from the other end of the political spectrum. Antiestablishment, antiglobalization activists, resenting the so-called Washington Consensus, have lashed out against the authority of international tribunals, which they see as indifferent to the concerns of the economically vulnerable.[106] These activists oppose what they term "new constitutionalism"—the unheralded diffusion of a set of quasi-constitutional supranational treaties and institutions that place global economic governance beyond democratic reach and promote uneven development by privileging transnational corporations at the expense of the world's economic hinterlands.[107] Cities from Toronto to Hamburg have seen grassroots movements and massive, sometimes violent demonstrations against G-20 leaders and their supposedly pro-globalization, pro-corporate agendas.

Little of this energy has been channeled to enhance true local autonomy. The closest is Wallonia's adamant objection to the Canada-EU Comprehensive Economic and Trade Agreement (CETA).[108] Even EU member-state constitutional courts occasionally defy convergence by maintaining national constitutional sovereignty vis-à-vis the emerging pan-European constitutional order, all while remaining silent on sub-national, let alone municipal autonomy. In December 2016, the Supreme Court of Denmark decided in the *Ajos Case* that the judge-made principles of EU law concerning non-discrimination on the grounds of age developed after the *Danish Accession Act* (2008), were not binding.[109] The court went on to decide that it would exceed its own mandate within the Danish constitutional framework if it gave priority to EU law over Danish law in such situations.[110] A few months earlier, the Russian Constitutional Court had reached a similar decision with respect to the European Court of

---

[106] *See generally* Mikael Rask Madsen, Pola Cebulak, and Micha Wiebusch, "Backlash against International Courts: Explaining the Forms and Patterns of Resistance to International Courts," *International Journal of Law in Context* 14 (2018): 197–220.

[107] *See, e.g.*, Stephen Gill and A. Claire Cutler, eds., *New Constitutionalism and World Order* (Cambridge University Press, 2014).

[108] Using the constitutional instruments available to them—Articles 207 and 208 of the Treaty on the Functioning of the European Union (requiring unanimity in the negotiation and conclusion of trade agreements); and Articles 127, 128, and 167 of the Belgian Constitution (requiring cooperation between the parliaments of the Flemish and French communities in negotiating and ratifying international treaties; these treaties take effect only after they have received the approval of the parliament of each of the two communities)—regional autonomy activists were able to temporarily prevent settlement of the treaty in the face of trans-Atlantic concordance.

[109] Mikael Madsen, Henrik Palmer Olsen, and Urška Šadl, "Competing Supremacies and Clashing Institutional Rationalities: The Danish Supreme Court's Decision in the Ajos Case and the National Limits of Judicial Cooperation," *European Law Journal* 23 (2017): 140–150.

[110] SCDK Case No. 15/2014 *Dansk Industry (DI) acting for Ajos A/S v. The Estate left by A* (Dec. 6, 2016).

Human Rights' (ECtHR) 2013 ruling on prisoners' voting rights in *Anchugov and Gladkov v. Russia*.[111] The court held that, in this case, the ECtHR ruling could not be implemented in Russia as it contradicts the Russian Constitution.[112]

As discussed earlier, resentment toward the emerging pan-European constitutional framework has been on the rise in several European countries. In fact, the very multilayered, fragmented European constitutional framework and the corresponding eminence of the pan-European rights regime has given rise to the theoretical posture known as constitutional pluralism. Building on the German Federal Constitutional Court's *Maastricht Case* articulation of dual (EU and German) constitutional authority, proponents of this view describe a reality of, and provide normative justification for, a post-national, multifocal constitutional order (at least with respect to the distribution of constitutional authority in Europe) in which there is no single legal center or hierarchy, and "where there is a plurality of institutional normative orders, each with its functioning constitution."[113] So plurality of orders is a good thing, it seems, but even here the potential constitutional standing of cities is not considered.[114] Interestingly, the subjugation of megacities and local government in Europe's national and supranational constitutional discourse continues, while governments in Europe have spent tremendous energy to extend principles of subsidiarity in the emerging pan-European constitutional order. The jurisprudence of the ECtHR reflects this approach, treading between fostering a robust pan-European human rights regime and averting backlashes against its rulings, which most often stem from perceptions that such rulings encroach too heavily on established local traditions. In several leading rulings concerning freedom of and from religion, the ECtHR deferred to national preferences in allowing the crucifix in Italy's classrooms (*Lautsi v. Italy*, 2011) and in allowing the French ban on religious face covering (*S.A.S. v. France*, 2014).[115] A key concept that guides such rulings is the "margin of appreciation."[116] The Council of

---

[111] Applications Nos. 11157/04 and 15162/05 Eur. Ct. H.R. (Grand Chamber, July 4, 2013).

[112] See Constitutional Court of the Russian Federation, Judgment of 19 April 2016 No. 12-P/2016.

[113] Neil MacCormick, *Questioning Sovereignty: Law, State, and Nation in the European Commonwealth* (Oxford University Press, 1999); Nico Krisch, *Beyond Constitutionalism: The Pluralist Structure of Postnational Law* (Oxford University Press, 2010); but *see* Joseph H. H. Weiler, "Prologue: Global and Pluralist Constitutionalism: Some Doubts," *in* Gráinne de Búrca and Joseph H. H. Weiler, eds., *The World of European Constitutionalism* (Cambridge University Press, 2012); Martin Loughlin, "Constitutional Pluralism: An Oxymoron?," *Global Constitutionalism* 3 (2014): 9–30.

[114] Few exceptions exist. See, *e.g.*, Michèle Finck, *Subnational Authorities and EU Law* (Oxford University Press, 2017).

[115] *Lautsi v. Italy*, App. No. 30814/06, 2011, Eur. Ct. H.R. (Grand Chamber, March 18, 2011); *S.A.S. v. France*, App. No. 43835/11, Eur. Ct. H.R. (Grand Chamber, July 1, 2014).

[116] Alastair Mowbray, "Subsidiarity and the European Convention on Human Rights," *Human Rights Law Review* 15 (2015): 313–341; Samantha Besson, "Subsidiarity in International Human Rights Law—What Is Subsidiary about Human Rights?" *American Journal of Jurisprudence* 61 (2016): 69–107; Robert Spano, "Universality or Diversity of Human Rights? Strasbourg in the Age of Subsidiarity," *Human Rights Law Review* 14 (2014): 487–502.

Europe defines the "margin of appreciation" as the space for maneuvering that the Strasbourg organs are willing to grant national authorities in fulfilling their obligations under the ECHR.[117] From a jurisprudential standpoint, the margin of appreciation allows states to have a measure of diversity in their interpretation of human rights treaty obligations, based on local traditions, heritage, and context. Essentially a concept of qualified and reasoned deference, the margin of appreciation is at the core of some of the most important rulings of the ECtHR, and has become increasingly central to the viability and future of the entire ECHR system. This trend toward deference was given the formal stamp of approval in 2013 when the Committee of Ministers of the Council of Europe adopted Protocol 15 to the ECHR, which seeks to encourage the incorporation of subsidiarity and margin of appreciation within the ECHR and ECtHR system. It has been further strengthened in the intergovernmental 2015 Brussels Declaration, which "reiterates the subsidiary nature of the supervisory mechanism established by the Convention and in particular the primary role played by national authorities, namely governments, courts and parliaments, and their margin of appreciation in guaranteeing and protecting human rights at national level, while involving National Human Rights Institutions and civil society where appropriate."[118] As of 2019, 45 out of 47 member countries in the Council of Europe have ratified the protocol, thereby consolidating principles of subsidiarity within the Council of Europe.

As we have seen, however, the localist talk aimed at enhancing these countries' constitutional sovereignty vis-à-vis the European supranational constitutional order seems to go quiet when the conversation turns to enhanced urban or regional autonomy within those very same national constitutional orders. On the one hand, there has been a resounding "yes" to the idea of returning power to the people and to enhanced national constitutional sovereignty pitted against the outside world. On the other, there has been an absolute "no" to local autonomy vis-à-vis the national constitutional order.

While calls for greater deference to and representation of the local have been vocally advanced by national, sub-national, and regional leaders and ideologues, the "local" within such dissenting rhetoric seldom if ever means the urban. From a constitutional governance standpoint, the localization trend stops well before the city level. Why? The answer may be painfully simple: because cities lack the constitutional power to bring their own local interests to the fore. Corporations can advance credible capital flight threat. Member states in regional and transnational regimes regulating trade, climate change, or human rights can opt out

[117] Andrew Legg, *The Margin of Appreciation in International Human Rights Law* (Oxford University Press, 2012).
[118] Besson, "Subsidiarity in International Human Rights Law," 71.

of these agreements. And in federal systems, sub-national units enjoy constitutional standing and are considered major building blocks of the national political pact. Such sub-national units may invoke state rights, nullification, secession, and other exit options. Economically viable individual members of a given polity, or a given city for that matter, often exercise their right to leave that polity and relocate when conditions become less than favorable. Cities, by contrast, have none of these options available to them: no relocation threats, no capital flight option, and no viable exit. As their bargaining power is systemically limited, their constitutional voice is seldom heard.

In the world of increased localist resentment, states are much better positioned than cities to express their grievances. The ability of countries such as Hungary and Venezuela to have their voices heard, let alone exit their constitutional environs, is not enjoyed by any megacity with a far larger population or with considerably greater economic or political significance than these countries. Withdrawal of cities from the constitutional order within which they operate is simply not an option. In most instances, the "us" in the "us/them" divide or the "local" in the local/global" divide refer to collective identity (vis-à-vis others who do not share it and often pose a threat to it), to the nation-state (vis-à-vis the international or global community), or to a supposedly authentic subnational affiliation constructed as an antidote to a detached or morally corrupt "center." However, as we shall see in the next chapter, when it comes to actually empowering local government, the entire "us first" discourse vanishes, as it is seldom if ever considered relevant or applicable to cities qua autonomous political communities.

Conclusion

The world is urbanizing at an extraordinary rate. The majority of humanity now lives in cities. Megacities of 50 million or urban regions of 100 million are no longer considered mere science fiction. Consequently, cities draw tremendous attention in public policy circles and throughout the human sciences as more and more officials, researchers, and public intellectuals point to cities' crucial significance in promoting innovation, effectively addressing core policy challenges, and in reviving democratic participation. Yet in public law, and in particular in constitutional law, this intellectual renaissance is nowhere to be seen. The silence is deafening, considering the unprecedented urbanization trends worldwide, never mind the countless studies that point to cities as centers of innovation or as effective problem-solving entities. The muteness is even more striking in comparative constitutional law—constitutional law's supposedly cosmopolitan intellectual sibling. As we have seen, 90% of urban swelling over the last half century has taken place in the developing world. Yet, very few major comparative accounts of the constitutional status of megacities have been published to date.

Extensive urbanization processes notwithstanding, the state dominates the city politically and legally. This domination affects public discourse. While the local/global and us/them distinctions feature prominently in early twenty-first-century political discourse, the "local" and the "us" in such rhetorical configurations mostly refer to the national (versus the global), the sub-national (as in region, state, or province), or to a supposedly authentic ethnic or religious identity that defines "us" (versus diverse, multicultural society). It seldom, if ever, refers to the urban as a meaningful affiliation category. If anything, this kind of rhetoric serves to ignite or fuel anti-city impulses in favor of a supposedly "unrefined" yet "authentic" periphery with purportedly uncorrupt moral and cultural preferences.

Even as influential cities emerge, the state and its accompanying statist constitutional vision are reluctant to give away governance power, reflecting *spatial statism*, as well as their innate fear of potential competition and loss of sovereignty. Constitutional law—in its capacity as the legal foundation for the state's institutions and their prerogatives—creates and reflects a statist understanding of the polity's legal order. Consequently, national constitutions, constitutional jurisprudence, and constitutional scholarship overlook the city and urban agglomeration more generally. Constitutional concepts such as subsidiarity or margin of appreciation are confined to constitutionally recognized polities. Cities or urban regions rarely qualify even when they are far larger than certain countries, account for a major part of their country's economic viability, or are home to a significant portion of a given country's populace. Ultimately, the key features of national constitutions as being both firmly entrenched and innately statist render the city systemically weak and to a large degree underrepresented.

2

The Metropolis in "Old World" Constitutional Law

Urban agglomeration is among the most burning policy challenges of the twenty-first century. This much has been acknowledged by virtually all the most reputable international, regional, and national research bodies, whether their interests are demographic, economic, environmental, or sociological. The current figures are mind-boggling, and the research clearly establishes that this issue is set to gain even greater prominence as ever-expanding urbanization processes march on. The forecasts for 2030 or 2050, let alone for the twenty-second century, range from the futuristic to the near dystopian. In the face of such unified scientific evidence, the silence of comparative constitutional studies with respect to the mounting urban challenge, and political geography more generally, is striking.

In this chapter and the next, I examine the constitutional treatment of megacities across a range of polities, loosely divided into "old" (largely in the Global North) and "new" (largely in the Global South) constitutional orders. In this chapter, I consider the general tendency of national constitutions throughout the Global North—from the United States and Canada to the UK, Western Europe, and Australia—to subjugate city power, whether due to dated yet hardwired city-subverting constitutional frameworks, rigid amendment rules, or a lack of political incentives among national or sub-national power holders to constitutionally emancipate cities. In Chapter 3, I turn my focus to the exceptions to this general trend and consider the few settings—virtually all of them in Asia, Latin American, and Africa—where governments have allowed for meaningful constitutional empowerment of megacities and large urban centers. By comparing these two groups of polities—the hardwired, city-constraining "old-world" constitutional orders on the one hand with several "new world" constitutional orders that allow for some city-empowering constitutional reform on the other—I identify some of the concrete vectors that have proven conducive to constitutional transformation in this realm.

A comprehensive, polity-by-polity analysis of the many constitutional responses to urban agglomeration worldwide would take a group of researchers several years of work and would result in multiple thick volumes of material. Such an account falls well beyond the scope, means, and purpose of this book.

City, State. Ran Hirschl, Oxford University Press (2020). © Ran Hirschl.
DOI: 10.1093/oso/9780190922771.001.0001

Nevertheless, even a cursory survey reveals how cities in general, and megacities in particular, have been overlooked, mistreated, and systematically constrained in the constitutional domain, both by the formal textual contents of constitutions and by the jurisprudence that interpret these texts. The status of urban centers varies from one constitutional setting to another, reflecting different constitutional structures and traditions. Yet, with the few, intriguing exceptions I discuss in the next chapter, even in the most ambitious urban governance renewal projects, the high-flying political talk has seldom been accompanied by any real constitutional walk. The masters of the statist constitutional domain approach questions of urban governance from a "seeing like state" point of view, locked within inherited structures and reluctant to hand their authority over to entities without real bargaining power or exit options. Consequently, real constitutional empowerment of cities is only likely to happen within constitutional structures that are either recent enough to have taken the megacity phenomenon into account, or flexible enough to be capable of change in response to it. And even in a constitutional order amenable to change, reform is only possible under a constellation of exceptional economic and political circumstances sufficient to transform major stakeholders' incentive structures. Generally, then, an overarching statist outlook, rigid constitutional frameworks and a lack of political incentive make the constitutional empowerment of megacities highly unlikely.

I. The United States

There can be no disputing that certain "hardwired" structural elements of America's constitutional order are to blame for many of the country's contemporary political woes.[1] The obsolescence of the American Constitution, compounded by the distortions it has undergone to serve certain policy outcomes over the years, has given rise to many pressing political problems, not the least of which is the oppression of the modern city. For obvious reasons, a constitutional order adopted in the late eighteenth century and designed to resist change may be deficient in its ability to sustain effective, rational government for a twenty-first-century powerhouse democracy, let alone to address new challenges like the

---

[1] *See, e.g.,* Robert Dahl, *How Democratic Is the American Constitution?,* 2nd ed. (Yale University Press, 2002), 91–118 ("[C]ompared with other democratic countries our performance appears, on balance, to be mediocre at best. How much does our performance have to do with our constitutional system? To tease out the extent of that connection would be extraordinarily difficult. . . ." *Id.* at 118); Sanford Levinson, *Our Undemocratic Constitution: Where the Constitution Goes Wrong (and How We the People Can Correct It)* (Oxford University Press, 2006). In one of our conversations, Levinson pointed out that the Electoral College structure, to pick one obvious example, generates presidential candidates' selective interest in urban centers located in swing states; cities located in other settings seldom feature equivalent interest, policy ideas, or campaign trail time.

megacity. But while the twenty-first-century urban agenda has become a casualty of a late eighteenth-century-federalism framework, it has failed, by and large, to attract the interest it deserves among American legal thinkers.

The good news is that, meager as the constitutional and especially comparative constitutional thought has been on cities in America and elsewhere, the United States is in fact one of the few countries that has shown any signs of intellectual life in this area, alongside a tradition of successful city-based social activism. Several observers point out that progressive municipal agendas in San Francisco (with respect to LGBT marriage equality), Portland (with respect to corporate tax surcharge), or New York (with respect to universal prekindergarten) have led the way in planting the seeds of social change.[2] Others argue that despite their lack of sovereignty, localities' relative autonomy with respect to schooling and education has created a bifurcated approach to citizenship, whereby people who lack legal status by national citizenship criteria, enjoy some membership-based public goods at the local level.[3]

Within American legal academia, a few scholars have critiqued American cities' constitutional powerlessness and lack of representation in the country's old and inflexible federalism meta-structure. The common denominator in most of these accounts is that legal institutions, at both the state and the federal levels, limit the power of cities to pursue substantive policy goals other than economic development.[4] As Gerald Frug and David Baron—pioneering scholars of American municipal law—have shown, state laws restrict the power of American cities to raise revenue and tax new forms of income, control land use, grant privileges to their residents, or develop services that compete with state governments or prominent elements of the private sector. Legal-theoretical developments have further limited city power, such as the rise of the public/private distinction in nineteenth-century-American legal thought, which helped to curtail municipalities' corporate rights according to notable legal historian Hendrik Hartog.[5] Whereas the business corporation was designated by law as a private entity and thus awarded various legal and constitutional protections that enable it to assert rights against state encroachment, cities, as public corporations, were wholly beholden to state power.[6] Other scholars have pointed

---

[2] *See, e.g.,* Heather Gerken and Joshua Revesz, "Progressive Federalism: A User's Guide," *Democracy* 44 (2017); online: https://democracyjournal.org/magazine/44/progressive-federalism-a-users-guide/.

[3] *See, e.g.,* Kenneth Stahl, *Local Citizenship in a Global Age* (Cambridge University Press, 2020).

[4] *See* Richard C. Schragger, *City Power:Urban Governance in a Global Age* (Oxford University Press, 2016).

[5] *See id.;* Gerald Frug and David J. Barron, *City Bound: How States Stifle Urban Innovation* (Cornell University Press, 2008); Wendell E. Pritchett, "City Power in a New Era of Localism," *Fordham Urban Law Journal* 44 (2017): 1449–1461.

[6] Richard C. Schragger, "When White Supremacists Invade a City," *Virginia Law Review Online* 104 (2018): 58–73, 67–68.

out that the subjection of American cities' authority to state and federal legislative powers was also driven by efforts "to limit the scope and impact of local
governments exactly at the time that immigrants were taking control of those
governments. . . ."[7] As African Americans, Latinos and other persons of color
have gained greater influence over local governments, "cities continue to be
chastised as "ungovernable and inherently corrupt."[8] Some scholars have even
gone so far as to suggest that the federalist ideology of the 1780s was itself a reaction against an earlier, more diffuse conception of sovereignty, and an attempt to
subordinate competing claims to authority made by local institutions, including
cities, as well as by indigenous nations and separatist movements.[9]

American constitutional jurisprudence on city power represents a very small
fraction of that country's federalism case law. From a formal constitutional standpoint, American states divide into two groups, each with its own fundamental
rule for municipal constitutional power. Forty states follow some version of what
scholars call "Dillon's Rule." Formulated by jurist John Dillon in the 1860s, the
rule requires that all exercise of city power be traced back to a specific legislative
grant of authority. The presumption is that cities do not have legislative authority
unless it is explicitly granted to them through a concrete, identifiable piece of legislation. In other words, municipal corporations owe their origin to, and derive
their powers and rights wholly from, the state legislature. In Dillon's own words,
municipal corporations "derive their powers and rights wholly from the legislature. It breathes into them the breath of life, without which they cannot exist. As
it creates, so it may destroy. If it may destroy, so it may abridge and control."[10] The
US Supreme Court endorsed Dillon's Rule in *Atkin v. Kansas* (1903), stating that
municipal corporations are "the creatures—mere political subdivisions—of the
state" and "only auxiliaries of the state for the purposes of local government."[11]
Hunter v. City of Pittsburgh, a major US Supreme Court ruling rendered in 1907,
stands out as the most authoritative, landmark articulation of Dillon's Rule.[12] In
the words of that decision, "municipal corporations are subdivisions of the state,
created as convenient agencies for exercising such of the governmental powers of
the state as may be intrusted [sic] to them . . . The number, nature, and duration
of the powers conferred upon these corporations and the territory over which
they shall be exercised rests in the absolute discretion of the state."[13]

---

[7] Pritchett, "City Power in a New Era of Localism," 1455.

[8] *Id.*

[9] *See, e.g.,* Gregory Ablavsky, "Empire States: The Coming of Dual Federalism," *Yale Law Journal*
128 (2019): 1794–1868.

[10] *Clinton (City of) v. Cedar Rapids and Missouri River Railroad Co.,* 24 Iowa 455 (1868).

[11] *Atkin v. Kansas,* 191 U.S. 207 (1903).

[12] For an overview of the *Hunter* ruling, its evolution and legacy, *see* Josh Bendor, "Municipal
Constitutional Rights: A New Approach," *Yale Law & Policy Review* 31 (2012): 390–431.

[13] *Hunter v. City of Pittsburgh,* 207 U.S. 161 (1907), 178–179.

On the other side of the divide are the 10 states that are considered "home rule" (so-called Cooley Doctrine) jurisdictions. Here, cities enjoy a broader initial grant of authority and are able to act without specific authorization. In these states, an article of amendment in the state constitution grants cities and municipalities lawmaking power to govern themselves as they see fit, provided they comply with state and US constitutions. The "Cooley Doctrine" upon which "home rule" jurisdiction is based reflects the notion of an inherent right to local self-determination. In practice, however, even in states that follow the "home rule" principle, legislatures can (and often do) override municipal laws with ordinary legislation.

In some home rule states—New York being a prime example—an intricate system of joint governance has evolved whereby the state may legislate in certain policy areas only upon approval of affected localities, whereas in other policy areas, counties may pass laws only upon the approval of the state.[14] In several major cities that account for a significant portion of their respective states' populations—notably Chicago (Illinois), and New York City (New York)—state legislatures allow for what has been termed "integrated governance" of the school system whereby the mayor controls public schools in the city and directly appoints the head of the school system. In 2002, the New York State legislature granted then-mayor of New York City, Michael Bloomberg, full control over the New York City Department of Education. This deferential policy, which was one of Mayor Bloomberg's major accomplishments in transforming New York, has continued ever since, with a few brief lapses due to legislative negotiations between the city and state authorities. By contrast, a plan put forward in 2006 by Los Angeles Mayor Antonio Villaraigosa to bring the Los Angeles Unified School District—the second largest public school district in the United States, after NYC—under city management was found by a court to be in violation of the California Constitution.[15]

Even as powerful a city as NYC too often finds itself bound by limiting, preemptive state legislation that prevents the city from implementing policy changes in key areas. Consider gun control. A few years ago, NYC passed a local legislation that made it illegal for gun owners with a city firearm license to carry their firearms outside the city.[16] The law drew on a distinction between a "premise

---

[14] Section 2 of Article IX of the New York State Constitution, for example, gives local governments the power to pass laws relating to matters such as "the acquisition, care, management and use of its highways, roads, streets, avenues and property"; and the "safety, health and well-being of persons or property" who live within the locality as long as these laws aren't inconsistent with the constitution or general state statutes. The state can involve itself in these matters only if it obtains prior approval from an affected locality or enacts a law that applies to an entire category of localities (for example, every county in the state). This relationship is reversed for matters of taxation, where counties require state approval before enacting new statutes.

[15] *Mendoza v. State of California*, 149 Cal.App.4th 1034 (2007).

[16] *See* Title 38, Rules of the City of New York, Chaps. 5 and 16.

license" (allowing owners to register a firearm for use in a particular location, e.g., their home) and a "carry license"; this allowed some limitations on the transportation of weapons. As expected, the gun lobby was quick to react. In contesting the constitutional validity of the NYC law, a group of gun owners sued the city, arguing that the city legislation was premised on a view of the Second Amendment's right to bear arms as a home-bound right "with any ability to venture beyond the curtilage with a firearm, even locked and unloaded, a matter of government grace."[17] Such a view, they argued, is inconsistent with text, history, tradition, and with pertinent US Supreme Court's rulings. They further argued that the law prevented gun owners from taking their guns to locations where they had a right to bring them (e.g., second homes or firing ranges outside city limits). The Federal District Court and the US Court of Appeals for the Second Circuit upheld the law. However, in 2018, the New York State legislature passed legislation preempting the NYC law, and preventing its implementation. The city was left with no choice but to repeal the law. In a follow-up legislation, New York State further adopted a law that forbids NYC from ever reviving that legislation.[18] This case is by no means an outlier. In 2014, for example, New York State Governor Andrew Cuomo effectively tamed New York City Mayor Bill de Blasio's plan to tax high-income earners in the city to fund universal, city-wide pre-K program, and opposed Mayor de Blasio's attempts to raise the minimum wage within the city and to limit the expansion of charter schools.[19] Even the fact that both leaders are members of the same party (Democrats) could not overcome the state's innate inclination to limit city-based policy initiatives.

American jurisprudence shows a similar resistance to city empowerment. In *Mayor of the City of New York v. Council of City of New York* (2013), for example, the Supreme Court of New York invalidated a city ordinance requiring prevailing wage rather than the New York State's minimum wage to be paid to building service workers employed by entities receiving one million dollars or more annually from the city.[20] The court followed *Wholesale Laundry Bd. of Trade v. City of New York* (1962) in finding that the state minimum wage law preempted the local minimum wage regulation even when the local minimum wage regulation mandated a higher minimum wage than the state minimum wage.[21]

---

[17] Quoted in Garrett Epps, "The Age of the 'Dead Parrot' Supreme Court Case," *The Atlantic*, December 9, 2019.

[18] Even though the NYC law has been repealed, the US Supreme Court has granted review of the lower rulings in favor of the city legislation. The oral hearing in *New York State Rifle and Pistol Association v. City of New York* took place in December 2019, and revolved around the question of whether the court should make a decision on the constitutional validity of a law that is no longer on the books.

[19] *See* Richard C. Schragger, "The Political Economy of City Power," *Fordham Urban Law Journal* 44 (2017): 99–132, 100.

[20] *Mayor of the City of New York v. Council of City of New York*, 2013 N.Y. Slip Op. 31802(U), 1–2.

[21] *Id.* at 6.

And lest we forget the general "freedom of commercial speech" jurisprudence, which consistently limits the utility of city ordinances that aim to inform the public about health hazards associated with certain products. In 2019, to pick one example, the Ninth Circuit Court of Appeals in an 11-judge unanimous ruling, granted a preliminary injunction against a San Francisco ordinance requiring health warnings on advertisements for soda and other sugary drinks.[22] In accepting the beverage industry's claims, the court ruled that such a requirement would "offend the plaintiffs' [the corporations'] First Amendment rights by chilling protected speech." The public corporation—the city—responsible for the well-being of its residents, was inhibited from acting.

In California, state law takes precedent over "home rule" if the policy field in question is of statewide rather than strictly local interest. Based on that rationale, in *Fiscal v. City and County of San Francisco* (2008), the California Court of Appeal affirmed the trial court's decision ruling that state penal code law preempted a San Francisco ordinance that prohibited city residents from possessing, selling, distributing, and manufacturing firearms and ammunition.[23] The court found state law to comprehensively govern firearms possession, sale, licensing, and registration, thereby preempting city-specific ordinances on the matter.[24] It noted that the state law's statewide application reflects the legislature's balancing of the general public's interest in being protected from criminal misuse of firearms and the interests of law-abiding citizens in using guns.[25]

Meanwhile in a recent ruling concerning Chicago, the third largest city in America, the Supreme Court of Illinois struck down, under the Illinois Constitution Home Rule provision, a city decision to hold some suburban car rental agencies outside the city's borders responsible for paying city property lease tax on vehicles leased to Chicago residents. The impugned bylaw, Ruling 11 by the Chicago Department of Revenue, captured agencies within three miles of city limits based on the presumption that Chicago residents would use the leased vehicles primarily in the city. Ruling 11 therefore extended tax liability unless the agency could prove that the cars would not be so used.[26] The court found that Ruling 11 amounted to a tax on transactions outside the city's borders because the vehicle may or may not actually be used within the city, regardless of

---

[22] *American Beverage Association v. City & County of San Francisco*, 916 F.3d 749 (2019). The ordinance passed by San Francisco in June 2015 required advertisements on billboards and posters within city limits to include a warning that drinking high-sugar beverages contributes to obesity, diabetes, and tooth decay.

[23] *Fiscal v. City and County of San Francisco*, 158 Cal.App.4th 895, 900 (2008).

[24] *Id.* at 902.

[25] In a similar vein, the Supreme Court of Arizona ruled in *State ex rel. Brnovich v. City of Tucson* (2017) that the State of Arizona may constitutionally prohibit a city's local ordinance mandating the destruction of firearms that the city obtains through forfeiture or as unclaimed property because the matter involved state concern. *See State ex rel. Brnovich v. City of Tucson*, 242 Ariz. 588, 591 (2017).

[26] *Hertz Corp. v. City of Chicago*, 2017 IL 119945 (2017).

the underlying presumption of use.[27] In other words, a rather formalistic view based on a narrow interpretation of the home rule principle prevented the City of Chicago from closing a loophole in tax regulations resulting in large part from extensive urban sprawl.

Adding to the constitutional animosity between states and cities are the ideological differences that often separate the generally more cosmopolitan and deeply diverse cities from the more conservative and often less-diverse surrounding rural areas. The urban/rural divide in contemporary America is well-documented. Consider the results of the 2016 presidential elections: Hillary Clinton garnered 48.2% of the total vote (nearly 66 million); while Donald Trump, the eventual winner, received 46.1% (nearly 63 million) of votes. However, because Hilary Clinton voters were generally concentrated in dense urban areas, the combined land area of all electoral districts won by Clinton was 530,000 square miles or 15% of the entire US territory, whereas the combined land area of "Trump country" was about 3 million square miles, or a whopping 85% of the entire US territory.

Chicago and Illinois provide a prime example of this divide. The City of Chicago has had Democrat mayors consecutively since 1931. In 2011 and again in 2015, the City of Chicago elected Rahm Emanuel—a former White House chief of staff and avid Obama supporter—as mayor. In 2019, Chicago voters elected Lori Lightfoot—an African American and an openly gay woman—as mayor, making Chicago the largest city in US history to have an openly LGBTQ mayor. By contrast, oscillating between Republican and Democrat governors (Republicans governed the state from 1977 to 2003 and again from 2015 to 2019), the State of Illinois is a considerably less socially progressive polity.

Despite the activism and creativity of cities, discussed in Chapter 1, several states have enacted laws that prohibit cities from joining international city networks.[28] Recent reports further suggest that states override municipal legislation with increasing regularity. According to the National League of Cities' 2018 report on *City Rights in an Era of Preemption: A State by State Analysis*, "state legislatures have stricken down laws passed by city leaders in four crucial areas of local governance: economics, social policy, health and safety."[29] Leading

---

[27] *Id.*, para. 30.

[28] For instance, between 2013 and 2015, a movement to oppose environmental protection under the UN Agenda 21 agreement and to protect private property rights led state representatives in Arizona, Georgia, Mississippi, Texas, New Hampshire, and Alabama to introduce legislation to ban municipalities from entering into agreements with intergovernmental organizations participating in Agenda 21. The bills passed in Alabama, New Hampshire, and Texas. *See* Elwood Earl Jr Sanders, "Is It Constitutional for an American Municipality to Join ICLEI?," *Appalachian Journal of Law* 13 (2014): 127–146; John Celock, "New Hampshire Lawmakers Kill Agenda 21 Ban," *Huffington Post* (February 6, 2013); online: https://www.huffingtonpost.com/2013/02/06/new-hampshire-agenda-21_n_2633364.html?guccounter=1.

[29] https://www.nlc.org/resource/city-rights-in-an-era-of-preemption-a-state-by-state-analysis (April 2, 2018).

experts on American cities' constitutional status (e.g., Richard Briffault, Richard Schragger, Martha Davis) note that there are various ways in which states could frustrate cities' efforts to address the welfare of urban residents by implementing redistricting and rezoning to dilute local power to the suburbs. Instances of pre-emption have expanded considerably in the last decade, with states preempting or overriding city ordinances concerning issues as diverse as local living wage regulations, gun control, municipal civil rights law, tobacco regulations, LGBTQ anti-discrimination rights, posting nutritional information in restaurants, anti-plastic and environmental protection legislation, and sanctuary city policies.[30] A recent article suggests that in contrast to classical preemption aimed at har-monizing the policies of different levels of government, the "new preemption" involves "sweeping state laws that clearly, intentionally, extensively, and at times punitively bar local efforts to address a host of local problems."[31] Another recent study finds that "politically conservative states are the most likely to use preemp-tion, although institutional features like Home Rule and legislative profession-alism also contribute to this activity."[32] These states use preemption "to rein in local authority that may be challenging traditional political norms."[33] The scope of such preemption measures is staggering. In a recent comprehensive study, Schragger notes that such anti-city preemption legislation often results from specific industries' successful lobbying to avoid local regulation.[34] For example, states with rich oil resources, such as Oklahoma and Texas, have preempted the local regulation of hydraulic fracturing after lobbying efforts from the oil in-dustry. The National Rifle Association has aggressively lobbied at the state level. Forty-three states have enacted preemption statutes that specifically address firearms and ammunitions. Eleven of these states have adopted absolute preemp-tion of municipal firearm regulations. Over 30 states have state preemption laws

[30] Martha Davis, "Design Challenges for Human Rights Cities," *Columbia Human Rights Law Review* 49 (2017): 28–66, at 29–30. *See also* Erin Scharff, "Hyper Preemption: A Reordering of the State-Local Relationship?," *Georgetown Law Journal* 106 (2018): 1469–1522; Lori Riverstone-Newell, "The Rise of State Preemption Laws in Response to Local Policy Innovation," *Publius: The Journal of Federalism* 47 (2017): 403–425; Kenneth Stahl, "Preemption, Federalism and Local Democracy," *Fordham Urban Law Journal* 44 (2017): 133–179; Erin Scharff, "Powerful Cities? Limits on Municipal Taxing Authority and What to Do about Them," *New York University Law Review* 91 (2016): 292–343; Richard C. Schragger, "The Attack on American Cities," *Texas Law Review* 96 (2018): 1163–1233. Schragger further notes that "these legal challenges to municipal regulation have been accompa-nied by an increasingly shrill anti-city politics, emanating from state and federal officials." *See gener-ally* Gerald Frug, *City-Making: Building Communities without Building Walls* (Princeton University Press, 1999).
[31] Richard Briffault, "The Challenge of the New Preemption," *Stanford Law Review* 70 (2018): 1995–2027, 1997.
[32] Luke Fowler and Stephanie L. Witt, "State Preemption of Local Authority: Explaining Patterns of State Adoption of Preemption Measures," *Publius: The Journal of Federalism* 49 (2019): 540–559, 552.
[33] *Id.* at 552–553.
[34] Schragger, "The Attack on American Cities," 1170. The data on preemptive state legislation cited in this paragraph and the next draws on Schragger, "The Attack on American Cities," 1170–1175.

relating to tobacco. Ten states preempt licensing of vending machines containing tobacco products. At least 7 states preempt the local regulation of e-cigarettes. Oklahoma amended the state's tobacco preemption statutes to explicitly preempt the regulation of e-cigarettes and related vapor products. Several states have even invoked the preemption strategy to prevent local government from removing Confederate statues and other Confederate symbols.[35]

Amid this aggressive preemption wave, several American cities have won some key battles. The "Fight for $15" movement (emanating in 2012 from New York City) in support of a higher minimum wage is a prime example. A recent report estimates that more than 40 cities and counties have adopted their own minimum wage laws; it suggests that as of late 2018, an estimated 22 million workers have won $68 billion in raises since the Fight for $15 began.[36] In New York City, for example, the minimum wage for employers with 11 workers or more was set at $15 as of January 2019 and was applied to smaller businesses commencing in January 2020. Rates are lower in other parts of New York State. In San Francisco, minimum wage hourly rate was set at $15.59 as of July 2019. In Seattle, minimum wage is at $16 for large employers, and $15 for all other employers. However, no fewer than 25 states adopted legislation that prohibits minimum wage laws at the local level.

Preemptive state legislation designed to tame city power is also common in the realm of labor, employment, and anti-discrimination. In late 2018, to pick one recent example, courts in Texas have declared unconstitutional a city ordinance in Austin (and by extension similar legislation in San Antonio) that required employers to provide extended paid sick leave to their employees. The Texas Court of Appeals ruled in November 2018 that the ordinance violated the Texas Constitution because it was effectively preempted by the Texas Minimum Wage Act (2009).[37] This episode is not an outlier. At least 25 states have passed statutes, many of them passed within the last five years, preempting local authorities from mandating differing minimum wages for private employers. The State of Alabama, to provide an example, reacted swiftly to the Birmingham City Council vote to increase minimum wage in the city incrementally by fast tracking a bill that would prevent cities enacting their own minimum wage regulations. As the state legislature was deliberating the preemptive bill, the city sought to introduce a higher minimum wage immediately. The next day, Alabama's governor

[35] Richard C. Schragger and C. Alex Retzloff, "Confederate Monuments and Punitive Preemption: The Latest Assault on Local Democracy," White Paper, Local Solutions Support Center, June 2019; Virginia Public Law and Legal Theory Research Paper No. 2019-54, University of Virginia School of Law, October 2019. Available at SSRN: https://ssrn.com/abstract=3462746.

[36] Laura Huizar and Yannet Lathrop, "How Workers Have Lost Billions in Wages and How We Can Restore Local Democracy," *NELP Report* (July 3, 2019); online: https://www.nelp.org/publication/fighting-wage-preemption/.

[37] *Texas Association of Business and Others v. City of Austin*, 565 S.W. 3d 425 (2018).

signed the bill into law, negating the city's minimum wage. In December 2019, the Court of Appeals of the Eleventh Circuit dismissed an equal protection suit filed against the Alabama Attorney General by two Birmingham workers who earned less than the minimum as the suit did not meet standing requirements.[38]

In a similar vein, at least 12 states have enacted laws that preempt local authority from regulating the benefits that private employers provide to their employees. At least 15 states have enacted laws that preempt local authority from regulating the amount of paid or unpaid leave that private employers provide their employees. Nineteen states have preempted local governments from passing laws requiring companies in their jurisdictions to provide paid family leave. As well, states have preempted areas that are traditionally areas of local authority, such as land use and schools. At least 11 states have preempted affordable housing requirements or inclusionary zoning measures. And the list goes on and on. As Schragger observes, "it is unclear how a system overtly dedicated to the principles of devolution can be so hostile to the exercise of municipal power."[39]

Schragger's perspicacious answer is that a "structural anti-urbanism" remains "an enduring feature of American federalism."[40] He goes on to argue that "[C]ities qua cities are not represented in state or national legislatures. So too, the equal representation of states in the Senate privileges rural voters over urban ones. And the mere existence of states competing for power limits the possibilities for decentralizing power to cities."[41] In a similar vein, Paul Diller suggests that structural malapportionment in Senate seats (consider that Wyoming, Vermont, or South Dakota, each with less than a million inhabitants, enjoy similar representation to California, with 40 million) is heavily skewed in favor of rural area policy preferences (e.g., investment in highways as opposed to public transit).[42] In rejecting equal state suffrage arguments in defense of current Senate structure, Diller quotes Chief Justice Warren's opinion in *Reynolds v. Sims* (1964): "[L]egislators represent people, not trees or acres."[43] With respect to urban underrepresentation in Congress, Diller begins to advance the

---

[38] *See Lewis v Governor of Alabama*, 914 F.3d 1291 (2019). Initially, a three-judge panel of the 11th Circuit Court of Appeals held (July 2018) that the state's actions were "rushed, reactionary, and racially polarized," and that the preempting law violated the Equal Protection Clause. However, in January 2019, the full 11th Circuit Court of Appeals agreed to rehear the decision en banc. The court released its ruling on December 13, 2019, in a nutshell holding that the plaintiffs did not have Article III standing to sue the Attorney General, because they could not demonstrate that their alleged injuries were fairly traceable to his conduct, or that those injuries would be redressed by the declaratory and injunctive relief they have requested. Because the employees lacked standing to sue, the court did not consider the merits of their equal protection claim.

[39] Schragger, "The Attack on American Cities," 1163.

[40] *Id.* at 1167.

[41] *Id.*

[42] Paul A. Diller "Reorienting Home Rule: Part 1—the Urban Disadvantage in National and State Lawmaking," *Louisiana Law Review* 77 (2016): 287–358.

[43] *Id.* at 287.

claim (later theorized and empirically substantiated in Jonathan Rodden's work, which I discuss in detail in Chapter 5) that due to uneven spatial concentration of Democrats and Republican voters, Democrat candidates (more often than not favored by urban voters) require larger support than Republican candidates to get elected; consequently urban policy preferences are underrepresented in the House relative to the actual popular support it garners.[44] At any rate, states are largely free to (and oftentimes actually do) draw congressional districts in a way that disrespects local jurisdictional lines.[45] (I return to this point in Chapter 5.) Kenneth Stahl further speculates that cities have become overwhelmingly democratic while state legislatures are dominated by representatives of rural areas, which are largely Republican.[46] As a result, the vertical relationship between states and local government has become an outlet for partisan conflict. Stahl suggests that gerrymandering of state electoral districts often results in electoral districts that are misaligned with municipal boundaries. Consequently, municipalities' representation in state legislatures is weakened.

Since President Trump assumed office, there has been a frenzy of litigation and heated political rhetoric on "sanctuary cities" that resist the Trump administration's policies on immigration or the environment. The federal government and many Republican states, deploying "us vs. them" rhetoric and touting their commitment to "America first" policies, have taken an aggressive, punitive line against cities refusing to acquiesce to exclusionary government policies on immigration and refugees. Cities whose residents and governments disagree with these policies have come up against legislative preemption and political coercion at the federal and state levels, with mixed success.

As of 2019, at least 11 states have adopted preemption legislation against sanctuary cities, forbidding local governments from adopting policies that limit cooperation with federal immigration authorities.[47] Texas's Senate Bill 4 (SB4) is a glaring example of such state preemption in immigration policy. Adopted in early 2017, SB4 barred local sanctuary city policies and threatened civil penalties and removal of local officials who adopt or even "endorse" such policies. The bill was passed after Texas Governor Greg Abbott expressly stated that he favored a "broad-based law by the state of Texas that says across the board, the state is going to preempt local legislation."[48] The City of El Cenizo, Texas (a small, largely Spanish-speaking immigrant town, located 20 miles south of Laredo, right on

---

[44]   *Id.* at 322–335.

[45]   *Id.* at 345.

[46]   Stahl, "Preemption, Federalism and Local Democracy."

[47]   Catherine E. Shoichet, "Florida Is about to Ban Sanctuary Cities. At Least 11 Other States Have, Too," *CNN* (May 9, 2019); online: https://edition.cnn.com/2019/05/09/politics/sanctuary-city-bans-states/index.html.

[48]   Richard C. Schragger, "Forum Response: Cities on a Hill," *Boston Review* (February 14, 2018).

the US-Mexico border) brought a pre-enforcement action against SB4, challenging provisions that prohibited noncompliance with Immigration Customs Enforcement detainer requests and provisions that prohibited local policies that would limit cooperation with federal immigration enforcement.[49] Following a year of lower court battles, the Fifth Circuit Court ruled in May 2018 that, with the exception of the prohibition on endorsing sanctuary city policies, SB4 did not violate the constitution.[50] Justice Jones excised the term "endorse" from the rest of the bill after finding the restriction "proscribes core political speech when such 'endorsement' is uttered by elected officials," and was thus contrary to the First Amendment.[51] Notably, the court found that the Texas bill had not been preempted by federal legislation in the area, distinguishing it by commenting that the existing federal legislation "regulates *how* local entities may cooperate in immigration; SB4 specifies *whether* they cooperate."[52] The federal laws of immigration did not evince a sufficient intention from Congress to preclude complementary state legislation on the subject.

At the Fifth Circuit, the City of El Cenizo accused the state of unlawfully "commandeering" the municipality. Although the court waived the argument because it had not been raised properly below, Justice Jones held that, even if it had not been waived, the argument would not have been successful.[53] "Texas law is clear," the court held; "the Texas Constitution prohibits a city from acting in a manner inconsistent with the general laws of the state. Thus, the legislation may, by general law, withdraw a particular subject from a home rule city's domain."[54] "For better or for worse," the court concluded, "Texas can 'commandeer' its municipalities in this way."[55] Enough said.[56]

---

[49] *City of El Cenizo, Texas v State,* 264 F.Supp.3d 744. Interestingly, El Cenizo drew on constitutional arguments typically used by states vis-a-vis the federal government, including, inter alia, the US Supreme Court ruling in *Printz v. United States* (521 US 898, 1997) to argue that akin to federal government in its relation to states, the *state* cannot commandeer its cities to enforce federal immigration laws, as the sovereignty of states pursuant to the 10th Amendment, also applies to political subdivisions of the state.

[50] A prior opinion (*City of El Cenizo, Texas v. Texas,* 885 F.3d 332 (5th Cir. 2018)) was originally released on March 13, but was withdrawn and substituted by the May 8 opinion (*City of El Cenizo, Texas v. Texas,* 890 F.3d 164 (5th Cir. 2018)). This was done to eliminate reference to *United States v. Gonzalex-Longoria,* 831 F.3d 670 (5th Cir. 2016) following the Supreme Court's striking down of that decision in *Sessions v. Dimaya,* 138 S.Ct. 1204, L.Ed.2d (2018).

[51] *City of El Cenizo, Texas v. Texas,* 890 F.3d 164, 184 (5th Cir. 2018).

[52] *Id.* at 177.

[53] *Id.* at 191.

[54] *Id.*

[55] *Id.*

[56] Consequently, Texas proceeded to sue the City of San Antonio in the first enforcement action under SB4, for failing to involve Department of Homeland Security's Immigration and Customs Enforcement's (ICE) agents when police found a truck trailer full of undocumented migrants. In July 2019, the Texas District Court granted a partial dismissal of the claim, ruling that several provisions of the law could not be enforced at the relevant times due to a temporary injunction from a federal court in unrelated litigation. Emma Platoff, "Judge Dismisses Part of Texas' 'Sanctuary City' Lawsuit

American sanctuary cities have, by and large, had greater success challenging the constitutionality of the federal government's withholding of grants from cities that refuse to enforce or collaborate on federal immigration regulations.[57] In early 2020, The US Court of Appeals for the Second Circuit ruled in a case involving New York City, among other plaintiffs, that the Trump administration may withhold federal grants to pressure sanctuary jurisdictions into cooperating with federal immigration enforcement policies.[58] However, that ruling stood in direct contrast to a string of earlier and later rulings by the First, Third, Seventh and Ninth Circuit Courts striking down the very same policy. In a series of cases involving Chicago, Philadelphia, and San Francisco, among other cities, courts have taken the line that federal law and the Constitution did not allow the federal executive, specifically the Department of Justice, to make Edward Byrne Memorial Justice Assistance Grants (JAGs) conditional on compliance with immigration policies.[59] Courts have taken a similar approach in litigation involving state and joint state-city challenges to federal policy. Specifically, the three immigration-enforcement conditions that former Attorney General Jeff Sessions (in the case of Chicago and Philadelphia), Attorney General William Barr (in a recent case involving the City of Providence), and President Trump (in the case involving San Francisco) imposed on sanctuary cities unduly encroached upon Congress's prerogatives in that area. Essentially, the courts in all these cases have ruled that neither the president nor the attorney general can unilaterally withhold federal grants from sanctuary jurisdictions without Congress's

---

against San Antonio," *Texas Tribune* (July 11, 2019); online: https://www.texastribune.org/2019/07/11/judge-dismisses-texas-lawsuit-sanctuary-city-san-antonio-paxton/.

[57] *See, e.g., City of Chicago v. Sessions*, 264 F.Supp.3d 933 (decided April 18, 2018); *City of Philadelphia v. Sessions,* 309 F.Supp.3d 289 (decided June 6, 2018), affirmed in *City of Philadelphia v. Attorney General of the United States of America*, 916 F.Supp.3d 276 (decided on February 15, 2019); *City and County of San Francisco v. Trump,* 2018 WL 3637911 (decided August 1, 2018); *City and County of San Francisco v. Sessions*, 2019 WL 1024404 (decided March 4, 2019, overturning three further conditions that Attorney General Jeff Sessions imposed following the previous decision); *City of Los Angeles v. Sessions*, 2018 WL 6071072. In the case involving Philadelphia, for example, the City of Philadelphia challenged the three conditions that AG Sessions unilaterally imposed on sanctuary cities in exchange for federal JAG grant money: (1) the requirement that local jurisdictions provide ICE officials access to local prisons, (2) the requirement that local jurisdictions notify ICE when they release aliens from local prisons, and (3) the requirement that local jurisdictions certify compliance with 8 U.S.C. Sec. 1373 (stipulating that a local government may not restrict its officers from communicating with ICE about the citizenship or immigration status of a person).

[58] 19-267 (L) *New York et al. v. United States Dep't of Justice et al.* (Second Circuit; ruling released Feb. 26, 2020). But see *City of Providence v. United States Department of Justice, No. 19-1802* (First Circuit; ruling released on March 24th, 2020), decided merely four weeks later. As of March 2020, the Second Circuit's ruling stands as the sole, anomalous pro-government decision in this particular context.

[59] JAG is a mandatory federal grant representing the largest annual source of federal funding for local law enforcement.

say-so.[60] However, the main question in these cases has been whether the federal government's punitive withholding of the grants was ultra vires. None of these cases has dealt with foundational questions concerning the city's constitutional status in an era of unprecedented urban agglomeration.

It seems clear, then, that constitutional empowerment of cities is not currently a priority in the American legal discourse, either in the sanctuary city debate or otherwise. In order for this to change, and for the question of cities' constitutional status to gain the attention it deserves, considerably more radical thinking is required on the part of scholars and lawmakers alike. As the starting point for this rethinking of city power, we might take Robert Dahl's or Sanford Levinson's criticism of the present rigid, outmoded, and hardwired constitutional order.

II. Canada

American proponents of enhancing city power—an uphill battle, as we have seen—may find solace in the fact that, disempowered as American cities are, Canadian cities easily win the title of constitutionally weakest in North America. In fact, few countries in the world have witnessed Canada's level of resistance by senior levels of government to loosening restraint and regulation on cities.[61] As a primer on Canadian politics describes it, "Canadian cities have been, without a doubt, the outcasts of Canadian federalism."[62] Lacking any direct constitutional powers, cities and municipalities in Canada exist only as bodies of delegated provincial authority, entirely dependent on provincial legislation for their power and sources of revenue. Given that 85% of Canada's population lives in cities,

---

[60] See, e.g., California ex rel. Becerra v. Sessions, 2018 WL 6069940 (N.D. Cal. November 20, 2018); United States v. California, 921 F.3d 865 (9th Cir. 2019); New York v. United States Department of Justice, 343 F.Supp.3d. 213 (S.D.N.Y. November 30, 2018). The case involved the States of New York, Connecticut, New Jersey, Rhode Island, and Washington; the Commonwealths of Massachusetts and Virginia; and the City of New York. These jurisdictions sued the administration to halt its unilateral anti-sanctuary conditions on their JAG/Byrne grants. The District Court (Southern District of New York) ruled that the Department of Justice lacked statutory authority to impose the conditions, and thus acted ultra vires and in violation of the separation of powers in imposing them unilaterally (that is, without specific congressional authority). Additionally, in Oregon v. Trump, 2019 WL 3716932 (August 7, 2019), the State of Oregon and City of Portland brought a successful claim in the district court over restrictions on their JAG funding. In City of Los Angeles v. Barr, 2019 WL 5608846 (October 31, 2019), the 9th Circuit Court held that the DOJ lacked authority to require JAG recipients to comply with DHS requests with respect to immigrants in their cities. In an earlier case decided by the 9th Circuit Court (City of Los Angeles v. Barr, 2019 WL 3049129), the court upheld the DOJ's inclusion of LA's identity as a sanctuary city in compiling a "score" for allocating competitive funding under the Public Safety Partnership and Policing Act (not an example of JAG).
[61] See Alison Smith and Zachary Spicer, "The Local Autonomy of Canada's Largest Cities," Urban Affairs Review 54 (2018): 931–961, 932. See generally Alan Broadbent, Urban Nation (Harper Collins, 2008).
[62] Luc Turgeon, "Cities within the Canadian Intergovernmental System," in Alain Gagnon, ed., Contemporary Canadian Federalism (University of Toronto Press, 2009), 367.

and that over 50% of the nation's population is concentrated in six metro areas, be something of an understatement to say that the constitutional non-status of cities in 21st century Canada—purportedly one of the world's leading constitutional democracies—reflects serious constitutional datedness and creates a major democracy deficit, possibly in violation of some of the country's major constitutional pillars, as defined by the Supreme Court of Canada.[63]

The British North America Act, 1867 (renamed Constitution Act, 1867) established the constitutional (and by extension, political) landscape for current federal and provincial relationships with municipalities. In that mid-nineteenth-century document, cities are virtually nonexistent, with no residual authority of their own. Section 91 of the Constitution Act, 1867 lists the main legislative areas reserved to the federal government, while section 92 sets out the legislative areas reserved for the provincial governments. There are two key provisions in section 92: section 92(8), which gives the provinces exclusive control over municipalities; and section 92(16), which gives the provinces authority over all matters of a local or private nature. Other provincial powers include jurisdiction over "hospitals, asylums, charities, and eleemosynary institutions" (s. 92(7)) as well as "shop, saloon, tavern and auctioneer licenses" (s. 92(9)). In a long string of rulings stretching back to the late 1930s, courts have given interpreted section 92(8) as giving broad powers to provincial legislatures to regulate and control "municipal institutions" including the power to restructure, amalgamate, or abolish municipalities.[64] In short, Toronto, the metropolis that is home to approximately 20% of Canada's population and over 50% of Ontario's population, is as constitutionally subject to provincial control as any charity, shop, or bar. Such is the impact in 2020 of Canada's foundational constitutional document, now 153 years old.

Initially, most provinces (with the exceptions of Nova Scotia and PEI) enacted pan-municipal legislation that provided municipalities with a general statutory framework. Each of these acts outlined the varying levels of political authority, autonomy, and fiscal capacity that each province gave to its municipalities. These general municipal acts were traditionally treated as "laundry list" legislations, granting municipalities only those powers which the provinces explicitly spelled out. In other words, as creatures of statute, cities could only make laws to the extent that their enabling statutes permitted them to do so. This approach is

---

[63] As is well-known, in its decision in the *Quebec Secession Reference* case (1998), the Supreme Court of Canada stated that the Canadian Constitution is based on four equally significant underlying principles: (1) federalism, (2) democracy, (3) constitutionalism and the rule of law, and (4) the protection of minorities. None of these principles trumps any of the others. See *Reference re Secession of Quebec*, [1998] 2 S.C.R. 217.

[64] *Ladore v. Bennett* (1939) is often considered the first major ruling of that string; *Ladore v. Bennett*, [1939] A.Ç. 468, [1939] 13 D.L.R. 1, [1939] 12 W.W.R. 566 (P.C.).

commonly attributed to the legacy of the American Dillon's Rule, with no concept of home rule in Canadian constitutional discourse.[65] The provinces continued to carry full responsibility for land-use planning and enjoy full autonomy to create their own framework legislation to structure their land planning systems.[66] The federal government could also affect land-use planning at the provincial and municipal levels through the financial support of targeted projects, such as urban development and infrastructure programs. Lacking even minimal legislative powers and funding sources, Canadian cities' autonomous voice in this constitutional matrix has been very limited.

Gradually trending away from the legacy of Dillon's Rule, most provinces have, over the past 25 years, introduced new or extensively reformed municipal frameworks that have expanded the autonomy and scope of municipal powers.[67] In general, provinces have extended city powers through the introduction of new statutes for cities (e.g., Saskatchewan's Cities Act, 2002); through the broad expansion of powers for all municipalities within the province (e.g., Alberta); and through the use of so-called charters tailored specifically to selected cities (e.g., Vancouver, Winnipeg, Montreal)[68] or similarly enabling provincial legislation (e.g., The City of Toronto Act, 2006).[69] But while the provinces' reforms have responded to the need for more flexible governance structures in Canada's larger cities, they have done so without giving away any "final word" authority.[70]

Although city charters have been used throughout Canada's history, and extensively in Quebec, the modern city charter has generally been used in response to the unique administrative responsibilities and challenges that face large Canadian cities.[71] However, as Andrew Sancton observes, such city charters are considered ordinary pieces of provincial legislation without special constitutional significance, and are therefore not protected from provincial amendment

---

[65] Ron Levi and Mariana Valverde, "Freedom of the City: Canadian Cities and the Quest for Governmental Status," *Osgoode Hall Law Journal* 44 (2006): 415–418.

[66] The federal government controls land use for lands under its direct control, for example, national parks and waterways, areas of the national capital, etc.).

[67] Joseph Garcea, "The Empowerment of Canadian Cities: Classic Canadian Compromise," *International Journal of Canadian Studies* 49 (2014): 86–89.

[68] The term "charter city" generally refers to cities whose powers are not governed by a general municipal statute, but are instead subject to specifically tailored provincial legislation. Such legislation differentiates that city from other municipalities in the same provincial jurisdiction and is aimed to provide it with flexibility in terms of reform, spending responsibilities, and access to revenue. The impact in practice, in particular with respect to revenue generation, has been considerably more modest. *See* Harry Kitchen, "Is 'Charter-City Status' a Solution for Financing City Services in Canada—or Is That a Myth?," *University of Calgary School of Public Policy Research Papers* 9, no. 2 (January 2016); Michael Dewing and William Young, *Municipalities, the Constitution, and the Canadian Federal System* ([Ottawa]: Parliamentary Information and Research Service, 2006), 18.

[69] City of Toronto Act, *2006,* SO 2006, c 11, Schedule A. The *act* came into effect on January 1, 2007.

[70] Joseph Garcea, "The Empowerment of Canadian Cities: Classic Canadian Compromise," 87.

[71] Ron Levi, "Freedom of Canadian Cities," 447.

or repeal, like all legislation relating to municipal powers in Canada.[72] It is generally agreed that, although there are no immediate negative effects to a large city by its designation as a charter city, neither does a charter offer more than modest positive effects in the form of concrete powers of revenue generation. These benefits vary depending on the political culture of each province. For example, the province of British Columbia has historically been hesitant to exercise direct authority over municipalities, while the Ontario government does not tend to show the same restraint.[73]

To help mitigate these variances, federal governments driven by changing ideational preferences and strategic electoral considerations have occasionally committed themselves to urban renewal through multilevel funding schemes. A recent illustration is the Trudeau government's 12-year Investing in Canada plan, which commits 180 billion Canadian dollars in cost-sharing platforms for addressing Canada's "infrastructure gap."[74] The government's broad definition of infrastructure, including anything from subway and light-rail projects to social inclusion programs, make big cities the obvious benefactors of such joint federal-provincial funding schemes. However, none of these programs involves even a rudimentary plan, let alone a fully developed one, for constitutional renewal that would transfer meaningful legislative, tax collection or policy-making prerogatives to cities. Provincial governments, often with the tacit or explicit support of the federal government, continue exclusively to call the shots, constitutionally speaking.

Let us zoom in on Ontario, Canada's most populous province. Ontario's capital city, Toronto, is Canada's largest metro area and the fourth largest city in North America (after Mexico City, Los Angeles, and New York), consistently ranked among the world's top financial centers.[75] Metropolitan Toronto's population has passed 7 million with a growth rate of approximately 18% over the last decade—nearly double that of Canada or Ontario. The City of Toronto itself, home to 3 million people, has far more people than five of Canada's provinces. And yet, the city has none of the constitutional or self-government prerogatives that the provinces possess. It is estimated that every second immigrant to Canada settles in the Greater Toronto Area; consequently, over 48% of the city's population is

---

[72] According to Andrew Sancton, one of Canada's leading scholars of municipal law and local government, city charters are "nothing more" than "ordinary statutes," subject to provincial subjugation at any time. *See* Andrew Sancton, *Canadian Local Government: An Urban Perspective*, 2nd ed. (Oxford University Press, 2015), 30.

[73] Andrew Sancton, "The False Panacea of City Charters? A Political Perspective on the Case of Toronto," *University of Calgary School of Public Policy Research Papers* 9, no. 3 (January 2016): 2.

[74] *See* Neil Bradford, "A National Urban Policy for Canada? The Implicit Federal Agenda," *IRPP Insight* 24 (2018): 9.

[75] The City of Toronto itself is home to approximately 3.5 million people. The Greater Toronto Area (GTA) or the Greater Toronto and Hamilton Area (GTHA) are home to approximately 7.5 million people.

foreign born.[76] On a practical level, given its size and unique demographic composition, the city carries much of the day-to-day brunt and responsibility of sustaining viable multiculturalism in the public sphere. At the same time, for every household tax dollar paid in Ontario, municipalities (including Toronto) collect only 9 cents.[77]

Moreover, the same constitutional order creates dense electoral districts (ridings) in several major urban centers alongside sparsely populated ones in largely rural areas. The result is a blatant departure from the "one person, one vote" principle to the detriment of voters in urban centers, in particular underrepresented minorities who congregate in cities. In the *Saskatchewan Reference* ruling (1991)—arguably one the most politically consequential decisions of the Supreme Court of Canada (SCC) in the last few decades—the Supreme Court of Canada considered the validity of Saskatchewan's Representation Act, 1989, which established provincial ridings with variances in population across constituencies, each riding containing a population within 25% of the provincial quotient.[78] The case turned on whether the dilution in relative voting power for the electorate in higher-population (mostly urban) ridings ran counter to the right to vote, guaranteed by section 3 of the Canadian Charter of Rights and Freedoms. Justice McLachlin, writing for the majority, found that section 3 was not a guarantee for absolute parity of voting power across electoral districts, but rather a guarantee for "effective representation" generally.[79] In rejecting a plain "one person one vote" in favor of an "effective representation" approach, she considered factors such as community history, minority representation, geography, and how spread out the riding population is. These factors may be accommodated "within a variance of 25 percent above and below the average constituency population (the electoral quotient), except in undefined 'extraordinary' circumstances."[80] The court held that "[p]roceeding from the initial premise of equality, the commission should, in determining constituency boundaries and

---

[76] According to the Statistics Canada 2011 National Household Survey (NHS), as of 2011, 48.6% of the population of Toronto was foreign born. A similar challenge is evident in Vancouver, Canada's third largest city, where approximately 41% of the city's population are first-generation immigrants.

[77] *See* Sunil Johal et al., "Rethinking Municipal Finance for the New Economy" (Mowat Centre, 2019).

[78] *Reference re Provincial Electoral Boundaries (Saskatchewan)*, [1991] S.C.R. 158, [*Saskatchewan Reference*]. For an overview of relevant jurisprudence in the decade following the *Saskatchewan Reference, see* Ronald E. Fritz, "Challenging Electoral Boundaries under the Charter: Judicial Deference and Burden of Proof," *Review of Constitutional Studies* 5, no. 1 (January 1999) [*Electoral Boundaries under the Charter*].

[79] *Saskatchewan Reference*, para. 26.

[80] *See* Jennifer Smith, "Community of Interest and Minority Representation: The Dilemma Facing Electoral Boundaries Commissions," *Electoral Insight—Readjustment of Federal Electoral Boundaries* (October 2002); online: http://www.elections.ca/content.aspx?section=res&dir=eim/issue6&document=p5&lang=e.

allocating ridings between urban and rural areas, be free to consider such factors as geography, demography and communities of interest."[81]

While the court's decision in the *Saskatchewan* Reference has drawn considerable criticism (some scholars have referred to the ruling as one "of the most unfortunate episodes in Canada's legal history" or as "antiquated and highly problematic"),[82] it has been closely adhered to in lower court rulings concerning challenges to electoral boundaries. In 1994, the Alberta Civil Liberties Association (ACLA) challenged newly-drawn provincial electoral boundaries, arguing that the resulting underrepresentation of inner-city voters constituted systemic discrimination against certain minority groups.[83] The relevant legislation allowed for the McLachlin-approved 25% population deviation.[84] The ACLA did not argue against *Saskatchewan*, but asserted that the dilution of the urban vote was nonetheless contrary to the Charter of Rights and Freedoms' section 3 and section 15(1) ("equality rights").[85] The court rejected this challenge and upheld the legislation. In 1998, the PEI Court of Appeal expressly declined to depart from McLachlin's *Saskatchewan* holding in *Charlottetown (City) v. Prince Edward Island*. The City of Charlottetown mounted an unsuccessful section 3 ("right to vote") challenge to provisions in the provincial Election Act allowing electoral districts to vary in population by ±25% of the average, as allowed in *Saskatchewan*. Charlottetown challenged the *Saskatchewan* holding, asserting that departures from parity between districts should only be justifiable under section 1 of the Canadian Charter of Rights and Freedoms.[86] The court disagreed.

The dilution of the urban vote in Canada following the *Saskatchewan Reference* decision has been significant. Even within Ontario, federal electoral districts vary in population from less than 60,000 (e.g., rural Kenora, in Northwest Ontario) to over 100,000 (e.g., Toronto-Danforth, in the heart of Toronto) per riding. In some cases, the population rises to over 110,000 per riding, such as Brampton, Markham, Richmond Hill, or Thornhill—neighborhoods that are home to extensive first-generation Canadian citizen populations. And these stark differences do not reflect the concentration of nonvoting, yet-to-naturalize immigrant populations in major urban centers, an issue that further exacerbates

---

[81] *Saskatchewan Reference*, para. 90.

[82] *See, e.g.*, David Johnson, "Canadian Electoral Boundaries and the Courts: Practices, Principles and Problems," *McGill Law Journal* 39 (1994): 224–247; Mark Carter, "Reconsidering the Charter and Electoral Boundaries," *Dalhousie Law Journal* 22 (1999): 53–92; Brian Studniberg, "Politics Masquerading as Principles: Representation by Population in Canada," *Queen's Law Journal* 34 (2009): 611–668.

[83] *Reference re: Order in Council 215/93 Respecting the Electoral Divisions Statutes Amendment Act*, 1994 ABCA 342 at para. 35 [*Alberta Reference*].

[84] Keith Hamilton and Brian Wallace, "Drawing Electoral Boundaries in British Columbia," *Journal of Parliamentary and Political Law* 2 (2008): 27–62, 38.

[85] *Alberta Reference*, paras. 37–38.

[86] *Charlottetown (City) v. Prince Edward Island*, 142 DLR (4th) 343, 362 (PE SCTD 1996).

the relative underrepresentation of ridings in big cities.[87] The unfortunate outcome has been a chronic underrepresentation of major urban centers in key national decision-making fora.[88] As Michael Pal and Sujit Choudhry point out, it is rather ironic that a systemic constitutional underrepresentation of Canadian urban centers with large minority populations hinges, at least in part, on the *Saskatchewan Reference*'s rationale of community interest and minority protection as justifying large variances across electoral districts.[89]

And there is more. Canada's smallest province, Prince Edward Island (PEI) (with a population of 150,000) has a constitutionally guaranteed representation of four House of Commons seats—that is, one parliament member per less than 35,000 residents.[90] Ontario (with a population of nearly 14 million) has 121 guaranteed House of Commons seats (106 prior to 2015)[91]—that is, one parliament member per approximately 115,000 residents. In other words, an average Ontarian is about three times less represented than an average resident of PEI. To add to the constitutional datedness and systemic city underrepresentation, the federal and provincial governments lack strong incentive to reshuffle the pertinent constitutional cards. Such a reshuffle would result not only in a major loss of their respective revenue and planning control but—perhaps most importantly— would not result in any immediate political gain for either of the major parties. Predictably, a pre-election commitment by Justin Trudeau and the Liberal Party in 2015 to revise the electoral system in order to veer closer to a fully democratic "one person, one vote" principle was abandoned by the Trudeau government in early 2017, citing "lack of consensus on the matter."

---

[87] Michael Pal and Sujit Choudhry, "Is Every Ballot Equal: Visible-Minority Vote Dilution in Canada," *IRPP Choices* 13, no. 1 (January 2007).

[88] *Id.* at 6.

[89] *Id.* at 4. In a 2014 follow-up article, Pal and Choudhry find that minority groups in urban centers continued to suffer from vote dilution. Such underrepresentation, they argue, runs counter to the "effective representation" standard, and may therefore infringe section 3 even under *Saskatchewan*. See Michael Pal and Sujit Choudhry, "Still Not Equal?: Visible Minority Vote Dilution in Canada," *Canadian Political Science Review* 8 (2014): 85–101.

[90] The constitutional source for this anomaly is section 51a of the Constitution Act, 1867, which establishes a "Senate floor" rule (adopted in 1915) whereby "a province shall always be entitled to a number of members in the House of Commons not less than the number of senators representing such province." Constitution Act, 1867, Art. IV, § 51A, 30 & 31 Vict., c. 3 (UK). When PEI joined the confederation in 1873, it was guaranteed four seats in the appointed Senate. With respect to House of Commons seats, PEI was allotted six seats. Section 51 of the Constitution Act, 1867, stated that the number of seats allocated to each province would be recalculated after each 10-year census, starting with the 1871 census. Due to population decline in the late nineteenth and early twentieth centuries, PEI and other maritime provinces begun to lose House of Common seats. Following pressure from PEI (Charlottetown, PEI hosted the confederation talks in 1864 and is often regarded as the birthplace of Canada), the "senatorial clause" was adopted in 1915. It remains in effect today.

[91] The Fair Representation Act, 2011, implemented in the 2015 elections, added 30 seats to the House of Commons in an attempt to address this problem; consequently, the province of Ontario's number of House of Commons representatives increased from 106 to 121. However the quotient riding population in Ontario (as well as in British Columbia and Alberta), has remained significantly larger than the nationwide provincial average.

What has been Ontario's position? The 1849 Baldwin Act, Ontario's first municipal statute, established principles of "responsible government" and assigned to Upper Canada (today's Ontario) the ultimate legislative authority over municipal governance.[92] It was not until after the turn of the twenty-first century that Ontario began reforming its municipal policy.[93] The Ontario Municipal Act, 2001, which came into effect in 2003, replaced the Dillon's Rule prescribed powers approach with 10 "spheres of jurisdiction" (including highways, transportation, waste management, parking, and public utilities) in which the municipalities had expanded power and flexibility to pass bylaws. The new act also granted municipalities natural person powers, releasing them from the "laundry list" conception of expressly designated municipal authority.[94] But the act reiterated that "[m]unicipalities are created by the Province of Ontario" and imposed on municipalities an onerous series of procedural requirements in handling their finances, highlighting the province's Dillon-like fear of municipal autonomy.[95] The act also went on to codify the traditional rule against municipal bylaw circumvention of provincial or federal legislative powers by stating that municipal bylaws are "without effect to the extent of any conflict with a provincial or federal Act or a regulation made under such an Act."[96] In 2004, Ontario went on to sign a memorandum committing itself to consult with the Association of Municipalities of Ontario before making legislative changes that affected municipalities.

The main development in Ontario's municipal government legislation came several years later with the adoption of The Stronger Toronto for a Stronger Ontario Act, 2006, commonly referred to as the City of Toronto Act, 2006. Following the widely unpopular amalgamation of Toronto in 1998 (an amalgamation of six municipalities with the former Metropolitan Municipality of Toronto to create the City of Toronto), local political actors began pushing for localized power and an increased level of autonomy that matched Toronto's unique position as the country's largest city. In adopting the City of Toronto Act, 2006, the provincial legislation reacted to these pressures by allowing for broader forms of taxation and increased legislative autonomy (subject to continued avenues of appeal to the Ontario Municipal Board and provincial action that is

---

[92] Ironically, this was done in support of the "home rule" principle, in an attempt to shield local government, at the time perceived as equivalent to today's provincial government, from excessive central government control. While the act applied the home rule principle with respect to what today would be considered provincial affairs, it established Dillon's Rule with respect to what today would be included in municipal affairs.

[93] Levi, "Freedom of Canadian Cities," 421.

[94] David Siegel, "Ontario," in Andrew Sancton and Robert A. Young, eds., Foundations of Governance: Municipal Government in Canada's Provinces (University of Toronto Press, 2017), 24.

[95] Levi, "Freedom of Canadian Cities," 432.

[96] Ontario Municipal Act, Section 14(a).

at any time considered "necessary or desirable to the provincial interest").[97] The act's preamble states that the Ontario Assembly "recognizes the importance of providing the City with a legislative framework within which the City can build a strong, vibrant and sustainable city that is capable of thriving in the global economy . . . The Assembly recognizes that it is in the interests of the Province that the City be given these powers." Section 6 of the act further states that the powers of the city "shall be interpreted broadly so as to confer broad authority on the City to enable the City to govern its affairs as it considers appropriate and to enhance the City's ability to respond to municipal issues."

In reality, the effect of the act has been modest. Despite its increased powers of taxation, the only taxes currently levied by the City of Toronto that are unavailable to the rest of the province are its land-transfer tax and billboard tax, together adding approximately 3% to the city's revenue.[98] (The common three primary sources of municipal revenue in Ontario are property taxes, development charges, and user fees.) The act also gave Toronto increased borrowing powers, accompanied by advanced accountability measures. The act also included requirements for Toronto to appoint an auditor general, an integrity commissioner, an ombudsman, and a lobbyist registry, all optional for Ontario's other municipalities.[99]

The consensus regarding the act among policy analysts and local government pundits seems to be that while the act did formally increase Toronto's autonomy, the city council's ongoing hesitation to use its increased powers has significantly undermined the city's empowerment. Furthermore, by the end of 2006, many of the special privileges that had been carved out for Toronto, such as the authority to delegate decision-making power to smaller, community councils, were also afforded to other Ontario's municipalities through ongoing reforms to the province's general municipal legislation.[100] Empirical measures of city autonomy across Canada further suggest that, while there is some variance among provinces in terms of city political status, very limited fiscal autonomy is awarded to any Canadian cities. Toronto's situation in this regard is similar to that of far smaller cities such as Saskatoon (population 250,000, largest city in Saskatchewan) or St. John (population below 100,000, largest city in New Brunswick).[101] Comparative studies of city fiscal autonomy suggest that, with the exception of London (UK), Toronto stands out as the world city most

---

[97] City of Toronto Act, *2006*, SO 2006, c 11, Schedule A. The *Act* came into effect on January 1, 2007.

[98] Harry Kitchen, "Is 'Charter-City Status' a Solution for Financing City Services in Canada—or Is That a Myth?," *University of Calgary School of Public Policy Research Papers* 9, no. 2 (January 2016): 7.

[99] Sancton, "False Panacea," 7.

[100] David Siegel, "Ontario," 25–26; Andrew Sancton, "False Panacea," 9; Harry Kitchen, "Solution for Financing City Services in Canada," 17.

[101] *See* Smith and Spicer, "The Local Autonomy of Canada's Largest Cities."

limited in its taxation powers. This lack of tax flexibility, critics argue, has made Toronto less competitive and fiscally potent than cities such as New York, Paris, and Frankfurt.[102]

Provincial politics also play a role in taming the act's emancipating potential. In 2017, then-Premier of Ontario Kathleen Wynne blocked the introduction of a road tolling plan permitted by the City of Toronto Act that would have helped considerably in financing an essential multibillion-dollar refurbishment of several aging motorways connecting the city with its main suburban areas. The tolling option, initially supported by the premier, would have shifted the bulk of repair and maintenance costs from the city's pocket to the hundreds of thousands of drivers who use the main traffic arteries to commute to and from Toronto on a daily basis. However, facing a pending provincial election in which the suburban Toronto vote was expected to play a large role, the premier vetoed the road tolling option, thereby denying Toronto the opportunity to fund its transit network renovation plan by borrowing against this potential revenue stream.[103] Protests by Toronto mayor John Tory—who called the decision "short sighted" and "the latest in a series of paternalistic responses that undervalue municipal autonomy and the priorities of Toronto"—had no effect.

Public transit has been a perennial bone of contention in Toronto, in particular Toronto's subway system (operated by the Toronto Transit Commission, TTC, owned by the City of Toronto), and the commuter rail system (operated by Metrolinx, a Crown corporation owned by the Province). In 2019, the Ontario provincial government unilaterally introduced and enacted legislation to transfer ownership of four transit expansion projects in Toronto to the Province. Citing the city's supposed inefficiency in launching these projects, the provincial government authorized Metrolinx, rather than the TTC, to oversee the four new projects and prohibited the city from developing other transit projects nearby or similar to them. Among other things, the legislation amended s. 47(1) of the Metrolinx Act, 2006, to provide that the Lieutenant Governor in Council "may, by order, transfer to [Metrolinx], with or without compensation, all or some of the City of Toronto's and its agencies' assets, liabilities, rights and obligations with respect to a project prescribed as a rapid transit project that is the sole responsibility of the Corporation . . ." The same legislation also compels the city and its agencies (including the TTC) to comply with the pertinent provincial directives.[104] The move was accompanied by massive cuts in provincial funding for

---

[102] See, e.g., Enid Slack, "International Comparison of Global City Financing: A Report to the London Finance Commission" (IMFG, 2016); Enid Slack, "How Much Local Fiscal Autonomy Do Cities Have?" (IMFG Perspectives, 19/2017).

[103] Jennifer Keesmaat, "Big Cities Need New Governance," in Bold Ideas: Policy Beyond Canada 150 (Mowat Centre, May 9, 2017).

[104] Getting Ontario Moving Act (Transportation Statute Law Amendment), 2019, SO 2019, c 8; and Robert Mackenzie, "Ontario Aiming to Take Ownership of Toronto Transit Projects,"

transit, healthcare and child care in Ontario cities. In reaction, Mayor Tory went on record stating that "[Toronto's] ability as a city to continue to move forward is in question due to a combination of these very ill-advised budget cutbacks, harsh measures imposed on cities and towns across Ontario without warning, some of them imposed more harshly on Toronto than any of the other cities and towns in the province."[105] In October 2019, the city and province reached a cost-sharing arrangement, which committed city funds to the expansions in exchange for the province's commitment not to take over the city's entire subway system.[106]

Provincial control over the City of Toronto explicitly manifested itself in 2018, when newly elected Ontario Premier Doug Ford (Progressive Conservative Party), a former city councilor and brother of the former Toronto mayor, Rob Ford, introduced legislation to reduce the number of city councilors at Toronto's City Hall from 47 to 25.[107] Arguing that "big government" ought to be slashed, and citing chronic inefficiency in city council and the need to expedite municipal decision-making concerning housing, infrastructure, and transit, Ford suggested the city electoral wards should be aligned with the 25 federal and 25 provincial electoral ridings. To that end, in August 2018 the Ontario government adopted Bill 5, the Better Local Government Act, 2018.[108] When a judge of the Ontario Superior Court of Justice issued a stern ruling that such a change amid a looming municipal elections (October 2018) would violate the

---

Urban Toronto (May 3, 2019); online: http://urbantoronto.ca/news/2019/05/ontario-aiming-take-ownership-toronto-transit-projects.

[105] David Rider, "Toronto Mayor Declares War on Ford Government's 'Ill-Advised Budget Cutbacks,'" *Toronto Star*, May 6, 2019; and Adam A. Donaldson, "Guthrie Continues LUMCO Advocacy in Toronto," *Guelph Politico* (May 7, 2019).

[106] "City, Ford Government Strike Deal on Ontario Line, Province Agrees to Drop TTC Upload," *CBC News*, October 16, 2019. The agreement was adopted by Toronto City Council on October 29, 2019. "Toronto-Ontario Transit Update," City of Toronto, October 29, 2019; online: http://app.toronto.ca/tmmis/viewAgendaItemHistory.do?item=2019.EX9.1.

[107] In 2016, the City of Toronto Council voted to increase the total number of wards from 44 to 47, following a thorough review of demographic trends and population projections to 2030. Section 128(1) of the City of Toronto Act, 2006, gave the city the authority to enact a bylaw to divide or subdivide Toronto into wards or dissolve existing wards. Bylaw no. 464-2017 and no. 247-2017 redivided Toronto from 44 into 47 wards for the 2018 municipal election. The new boundaries were developed through a third-party consultant group and then approved by city council. The review process involved meetings with city councilors, stakeholder groups, school boards, and the public. The consultant group gave voter parity prime importance, but also considered minimum change to wards, population growth (wards intended to be used until 2030, designed to grow into voter parity), the capacity of a councilor to represent the constituents in an area (workload based on number of constituents). The final 47-ward plan deviated from voter parity in order to keep communities of interest together in Sentinel Road, Regent Park, and Church-Wellesley Village. A legal challenge to that decision was dismissed in *Di Ciano v. Toronto (City), [2017] OMBD 1276*. The majority opinion saw no infringement of the "effective representation" constitutional requirement as protection of community growth and interests was considered a valid factor to balance against voter parity at times of boundary redrawing. The dissenting opinion held that boundary drawing should consider voter parity at the time of boundaries are drawn, not with an eye to future elections.

[108] Better Local Government Act, 2018, SO 2018, c 11.

Canadian Charter of Rights and Freedoms' free expression guarantee (s. 2(b) of the Charter),[109] Premier Ford threatened to invoke the charter's override clause, also called the "notwithstanding clause" (section 33). This clause, which had never been used before in Ontario, permits federal and provincial legislation to operate (for up to five years) notwithstanding its apparent violation of certain charter rights.[110] It is worth noting that, of all possible policy areas and the many thousands of contested provincial and municipal decisions made since 1982 (the year the charter was adopted), the first time the Province of Ontario threatened to invoke the notwithstanding clause, it did so as a means of keeping Canada's largest city in line.

Mayor John Tory expressed his outrage, called the proposal "not right and not fair," and suggested a referendum should to be held on the proposed change. Jennifer Keesmaat, former chief city planner and candidate in the October 2018 mayoral elections, went further to suggest that Toronto should establish self-government and secede from the province. The fact remains, however, that under the Canadian Constitution, cities, small or large, are the creations of the provinces. Hence, the Ontario provincial government enjoys broad latitude in shaping the legislative framework governing Toronto, especially during times of majority government, which Ontario has had since June 2018.

As expected, the province appealed the single-judge ruling Ontario Superior Court of Justice. A three-member panel of the Ontario Court of Appeal unanimously stayed the Ontario Superior Court initial ruling on the matter.[111] The provincial government gave an undertaking that it would not invoke the override clause if a stay were granted, which did not affect the decision.[112] The court suggested that the judge "stretch[ed] both the wording and the purpose of s. 2(b) [the free expression guarantee] beyond the limits of that provision."[113] Noting that the charter guaranteed the right to vote and to stand for office only with respect to federal and provincial elections, the court indicated that any disruption to the municipal election did not infringe voters' or candidates' democratic or free expression rights.[114] Though only an interlocutory decision, it signaled that "the judgment under appeal was probably wrongly decided."[115] Following

---

[109] *City of Toronto et al. v. Ontario (Attorney General)*, 2018 ONSC 5151.

[110] Such invocations are rare. Since 1982 there have only been a handful of significant instances in which governments have either invoked or seriously attempted to invoke this clause. Even the change of guards in Ottawa following the 2006 federal election and the ensuing nine years of Conservative government have not changed that trend.

[111] *Toronto (City) v. Ontario (Attorney General)*, 2018 ONCA 761.

[112] *Id.* at para. 8.

[113] *Id.* at para. 12.

[114] *Id.* at paras.13–19.

[115] *Id.* at para. 20.

the decision, Premier Ford expressed his sense of vindication, while the city has continued to litigate the appeal on the merits.[116]

Eventually, a five-member panel of the Ontario Court of Appeal (OCA) released its final ruling on the matter in September 2019.[117] In a 3-2 decision it dismissed the City of Toronto's claims, reaffirming the ultimate constitutional nonexistence of Canadian cities through their complete subjugation to provincial legislation. The majority opinion did not mince words in stating that the City of Toronto's position was unsubstantiated given that the Toronto City Council "is a creature of provincial legislation. Provincial legislation governs everything from its composition to the scope of its jurisdiction."[118] The majority opinion went on to determine that although the city's main argument is framed as a matter of protecting freedom of expression in the context of a municipal election, "in reality the applicants' complaint concerns the timing of the legislature's decision to change the composition of City Council—a change that is undeniably within the legitimate authority of the legislature . . . [A]dditional arguments raised by the City of Toronto and supporting interveners—drawing on unwritten constitutional principles and jurisdictional limits inherent in the division of powers—are similarly erroneous and unsupported by constitutional jurisprudence. In short, the *Act* [to change the structure of the city's highest elected body in the midst of an election] is constitutional, and the appeal must be allowed."[119]

Perhaps most importantly, in its address of Toronto's claim that unwritten constitutional principles may inform the framework established by s. 92(8) of the Constitution Act, 1867, the majority opinion serves as a blatant, "exhibit A"-like illustration of this book's main thesis: "Courts have sometimes used unwritten constitutional principles to fill 'gaps' in the Constitution . . . No such gap exists here . . . this is not the case of constitutional framers having not addressed a social or technical development—like aeronautics or nuclear energy—because they

---

[116] Nick Westoll and David Shum, "Ontario's Appeal Court Sides with Ford Government, Paves Way for 25-Ward Election," *Global News* (September 19, 2018); online: https://globalnews.ca/news/4464728/appeal-court-stay-toronto-city-council/. As of August 2019, the Ontario Court of Appeal had not yet rendered its decision on the merits.

[117] A request for leave to appeal before the Supreme Court of Canada is pending. The application (submitted by the City of Toronto) purports to raise three issues of national and public importance: (i) Does s. 2(b) of the Charter protect expression of electoral participants from substantial mid-election changes? (ii) Can unwritten constitutional principles of democracy or rule of law (including federalism, democracy, protection of minorities, the rule of law, and judicial independence) be used as a basis for striking down the provisions? (iii) Are municipal electors who are given a vote in a democratic election entitled to effective representation? With respect to the third question, the appellants acknowledge that s. 3 of the charter guarantees the right to vote in federal and provincial elections, not municipal, but contend that the court has not determined whether there are limits on the provinces' powers to circumscribe statutory rights to elect municipal representatives once they have been granted.

[118] *Toronto (City) v. Ontario (Attorney General)*, 2019 ONCA 732, para. 1.

[119] *Id.* at paras. 6–8.

simply could not have seen it coming. Municipal institutions, including municipal governing bodies, long pre-dated 1867 . . . [T]he decision was made not to
constitutionalize these institutions, but rather to put them under the jurisdiction
of provincial legislatures."[120] And to finish with a rhetorical exclamation mark,
the court concluded that "[T]here is no open question of constitutional interpretation here. Municipal institutions lack constitutional status."[121] The proper
route to change that, the court stated, is via constitutional amendment, not judicial interpretation.

And so, a constitutional document adopted over 150 years ago, when Toronto's
population was less than 50,000, governs a metropolis home to approximately
20% of Canada's population. What is more, the dramatic urbanization trend
embodied in the rise of the megacity in Canada and elsewhere is not acknowledged as a new development that requires constitutional reframing, but rather
continues to be analyzed through a mid-nineteenth-century constitutional lens,
as if "cities" in the twenty-first century are essentially the same as cities in 1867.

As reflected in the OCA's dissenting opinion, other constitutional jurisprudence has embraced a more "permissive yet restrictive" approach than that char-
acterizing the relationship between Ontario and Toronto. As the SCC stated in
1993, echoing Dillon's Rule, municipalities in Canada may only exercise powers
"expressly conferred by statute, those powers necessarily or fairly implied by the
expressed power in the statute, and those indispensable powers essential and
not merely convenient to the effectuation of the purposes of the corporation."[122]
On this understanding of municipal government, cities were required to go to
the province to seek an amendment of their municipal act whenever a new issue
emerged that required regulation or prohibition.[123]

The influence of Dillon's Rule remained strong in a 1997 case involving
Toronto. *East York (Borough) v. Ontario (Attorney General)* concerned the
amalgamation of several cities around Toronto into a megacity (the City of
Toronto).[124] Those who opposed the legislation challenged it as exceeding the
province's authority under section 92(8) of the Constitution Act, 1867, because it
was allegedly passed without consultation with municipalities and their citizens.
This challenge was unsuccessful at trial and at the Court of Appeal, which held
that municipal institutions lack constitutional status, being mere creatures of the
legislature that exist only if provincial legislation so provides. According to the

---

[120] *Id.* at para. 94.
[121] *Id.* at para. 95.
[122] *R. v. Sharma*, [1993] 1 S.C.R. 650, at para. 26, quoting Stanley M. Makuch, *Canadian Municipal and Planning Law* (Carswell, 1983), 115. *See also R v. Greenbaum*, [1993] 1 S.C.R. 674.
[123] *R v. Greenbaum*, paras. 415–418.
[124] (1997), 34 OR (3d) 789 (Gen Div), aff'd (1997), 36 OR (3d) 733 (CA), leave to appeal to SCC refused [1997] SCCA No 647 [*East York*].

East York decision, municipal institutions have no independent autonomy and may exercise only those powers that are conferred upon them by statute, their powers subject to abolition or repeal by provincial legislation. A request for leave to appeal was dismissed by the SCC without reasons.

Since the 1990s, there has been some movement toward recognizing broader and more flexible city authority in both the legislative and judicial spheres. The 1994 SCC ruling in *Shell Canada Products Ltd. v. Vancouver (City)* exhibited a shift from the old, limited approach to municipal authority.[125] In that case, the Council of the City of Vancouver passed two resolutions that prevented the city from doing business with Shell Canada and declared Vancouver a "Shell-free" zone until Shell Canada stopped conducting business in apartheid South Africa.[126] Justice McLachlin (as she then was), in what has become an authoritative dissent, warned against "confining modern municipalities in the straitjackets of tradition" and asserted that "[i]f municipalities are to be able to respond to the needs and wishes of their citizens, they must be given broad jurisdiction to make local decisions reflecting local values."[127] Here, McLachlin rejected the majority's decision, which held that the resolution was ultra vires as it was not expressly or implicitly authorized by Vancouver's enabling statute and was unrelated to the purposes of the statute, having no identifiable benefit to the citizens of Vancouver.[128] McLachlin's approach has come to play an important role in establishing a more open-minded approach to judicial interpretation of municipal powers. Of course, this approach still bases a municipality's power exclusively on provincial legislation. However, more generous interpretation of this legislation means that cities become able to wield a more robust set of powers. We may view this approach as a judge-made way of responding to the limited constitutional status of municipalities while maintaining provincial legislative supremacy.

By 2000, the SCC had adopted McLachlin's broad and purposive approach to interpreting provincial enabling statutes for municipalities.[129] In *Nanaimo v. Rascal Trucking Ltd*, a trucking company held 15,000 cubic yards of soil on its property. After receiving complaints about noise and dust, the municipality passed a resolution declaring the soil a nuisance and ordering its removal.[130] The SCC noted that the process of determining municipal jurisdiction was an exercise in statutory interpretation and that there was ample authority to support the broad and purposive approach.[131] In 2004, the SCC went on to acknowledge

---

[125] [1994] 1 S.C.R. 231 [*Shell Canada*].
[126] *Id.* at para. 237.
[127] *Id.* at para. 245.
[128] *Id.* at para. 280.
[129] *Nanaimo (City) v. Rascal Trucking Ltd.*, 2000 SCC 13 at paras. 18–31 [2000] 1 S.C.R. 342.
[130] *Id.* at paras. 2–4.
[131] *Id.* at para. 18.

that a "broad and purposive approach to the interpretation of municipal powers" had been embraced by the courts, and that this approach had evolved alongside a trend among the provinces toward drafting more open-ended enabling statutes for municipalities.[132]

Canadian provincial courts of appeal have, by and large, followed suit. In its ruling in *Croplife Canada v. Toronto (City)*, the Ontario Court of Appeal found that it was appropriate to apply the broad and purposive approach, both in interpreting Part II of the already mentioned Ontario Municipal Act, 2001, which sets out general municipal powers and specifically directs courts to apply a broad interpretation under s. 9(1), and also in interpreting Part III, which contains more specific powers and does not explicitly call for a broad interpretation. In this broad and purposive approach to the interpretation of the specific power of municipalities to legislate for the "general health and well-being" of their residents, the court noted that, given the development of jurisprudence since the early 1990s, it would take clear legislative language to return to Dillon's Rule when interpreting the act's specific grants of power.[133] The court also noted that it would be a "retrograde step to apply the former, restrictive approach" to the interpretation of an act designed to "give municipalities in Ontario the tools they need to tackle the challenges of governing in the 21st century."[134]

Another move toward promoting municipal autonomy may be seen in the SCC's 2001 ruling in *Spray-Tech v. Hudson (Ville)*, one of Canada's leading cases on the limits of municipal autonomy. There, the court advocated for the principle of "subsidiarity"—the proposition that "law-making and implementation are often best achieved at a level of government that is not only effective, but also closest to the citizens affected and thus most responsive to their needs."[135] (I shall return to the idea of subsidiarity in Chapter 5.) To that end, the SCC endorsed a collaborative tri-level regime for the regulation of pesticides.[136] Bylaws that regulate areas of shared jurisdiction are valid so long as they do not conflict with federal or provincial legislation. According to the court, the "mere existence of provincial (or federal) legislation in a given field . . . [does not necessarily] oust municipal prerogatives to regulate the subject matter."[137] As the "environment" is not a subject of legislation under the Constitution Act, 1867, the matter is a subject of bi-jurisdictional responsibility.[138] Since the municipal regulations under scrutiny were stricter than both the federal and provincial ones, the SCC

---

[132] *United Taxi Drivers' Fellowship of Southern Alberta v. Calgary (City)*, [2004] 1 S.C.R. 485.
[133] *Croplife Canada v. Toronto (City)* [2005] OJ No. 1896, 10 MPLR (4th) 1, at para. 33.
[134] *Id.* at para. 34.
[135] *114957 Canada Ltée (Spray-Tech, Société d'arrosage) v. Hudson (Ville)*, [2001] 2 S.C.R. 241.
[136] *Id.* at para. 39.
[137] *Id.*
[138] *Id.* at para. 33.

held that, despite the existence of federal and provincial legislation concerning pesticides, the city of Hudson's bylaw regulating the use of pesticides within its territory under the "general-welfare" provision of its enabling statute, the Cities and Towns Act (CTA), was valid. However, in his concurring opinion, Justice LeBel was clear in noting that no real terrain change in municipal government is to be assumed: "A tradition of strong local government has become an important part of the Canadian democratic experience. This level of government usually appears more attuned to the immediate needs and concerns of the citizens. Nevertheless, in the Canadian legal order, as stated on a number of occasions, municipalities remain creatures of provincial legislatures."[139]

Despite these jurisprudential moves toward recognizing enhanced municipal autonomy as an important policy objective, Canadian courts remain cautious to ensure that bylaws do not exceed the proper scope of municipal authority. The courts apply the federalism doctrines of federal paramountcy, "pith and substance," and "interjurisdictional immunity" to ensure that municipalities do not exceed the powers granted to them by their enacting statutes. In order to prevent municipalities from circumventing the limits of their delegated power, courts have often found municipal bylaws ultra vires on the grounds that their pith and substance encroaches on exclusive federal power.[140]

In the recent SCC case of *Rogers Communications Inc. c. Chateauguay*, Rogers, a Canadian communications giant with a major stake in the cable television, wireless, and professional sports markets, obtained federal approval for the siting of an antenna system in the territory of Chateauguay (a suburb of Montreal). The municipality of Chateauguay objected, passing one resolution authorizing the acquisition of the property in question, and then adopting a second resolution that attempted to establish a reserve on the property in question. The municipality argued that its establishment of the reserve was a valid exercise of the powers delegated to it by the province and that it was "protect[ing] the health and well-being of their residents."[141] The SCC held that even a "flexible and generous interpretation of the evidence" revealed that the resolution was intended to prevent Rogers from installing its antenna system on the property in question and thus was in pith and substance about the location of radio-communication infrastructure. Hence, the bylaw represented an interference with the federal government's exclusive jurisdiction over radio communications.[142]

---

[139] *Id.* at para. 49.

[140] For example, in *R. v. Westendorp*, the SCC held that a town's adoption of a bylaw that prohibited solicitation on the town's streets was not an attempt to regulate nuisance but was in pith and substance a prohibition on prostitution and thus an unconstitutional attempt to regulate a matter of federal jurisdiction. *See R. v. Westendorp* [1983] 1 S.C.R. 43, at paras. 20–21.

[141] *Rogers Communications Inc. v. Chateautguay (Ville)*, [2016] 1 S.C.R. 467, para. 75.

[142] *Id.* at para. 44. The SCC advanced a similar approach in 2007, this time relying on the "interjurisdictional immunity" doctrine in determining that the municipality of Vancouver could not regulate the ability of the Vancouver Port Authority (VPA), a federal corporation, to build on its property.

In jurisprudence considering the implications of international treaties in assessing the constitutional validity of municipal bylaws—an increasingly relevant area given the emergence of international standards concerning environmental protection—judicial ambivalence has been the rule. In the *Spray-Tech* ruling discussed earlier, the SCC majority noted Canada's advocacy for the inclusion of the "precautionary" principle (a principle of international environmental law designed to anticipate and avoid environmental damage before it occurs) in "virtually every recently adopted treaty and policy document related to the protection and preservation of the environment."[143] According to the majority, this trend in international law, reflected in Canada's treaty obligations, supported the legitimacy of the impugned bylaw. However, in his concurring opinion, Justice LeBel disagreed, stating that "international sources have little relevance" and that the means to enact the bylaw must be found in Canadian law. In *Croplife Canada v. Toronto*, the Ontario Court of Appeal echoed Lebel, holding that international law sources alone cannot confer power on municipalities and that "if the municipality did not otherwise have the power to enact the by-law, the precautionary principle could not be used as authority for upholding the effectiveness of the by-law."[144]

In summary, Canadian cities, some are among the most diverse in North America and the world, remain constitutionally powerless, and are subject to a pre-megacity constitutional framework adopted in the mid-nineteenth century. Since the 1990s there has been a modest move in both the jurisprudential and the provincial legislative arenas toward granting municipalities more power, all while maintaining provincial constitutional supremacy (and the corresponding federal constitutional silence) with respect to cities.

III. Australia

Arguably even more so than the Canadian case, the "Australian model" of metropolitan governance is widely perceived to be "an extreme form of state government playing a key role."[145] Australia's constitutional order allows for

---

Because the municipality's otherwise valid bylaw infringed on the federal government's power over navigation and shipping, the bylaw did not apply to the VPA. See *Burrardview Neighbourhood Assn. v. Vancouver (City)*, [2007] 2 S.C.R. 86.

[143] *Spray-Tech*, 31–32, *citing* David Freestone and Ellen Hey, "Origins and Development of the Precautionary Principle," *in* David Freestone and Ellen Hey, eds., *The Precautionary Principle and International Law* (Kluwer Law International, 1996), 41.

[144] *Croplife Canada v. Toronto*, para. 71.

[145] Graham Sansom and Jeremy Dawkins, "Australia: Perth and South East Queensland," *in* Enid Slack and Rupak Chattapadyay, eds., *Governance and Finance of Large Metropolitan Areas in Federal Systems* (Oxford University Press, 2013), 10–48, 14.

near-complete state domination of cities and, metropolitan governance more generally. As one expert puts it, Australian states "exercise absolute control over the existence, roles, activities, financial resources and governance structure of local government."[146] Consequently, Australia's large cities—Sydney (metro population 5.2 million; approximately two-thirds of New South Wales's population); Melbourne (metro population 5 million; approximately three-quarters of Victoria's population); and Brisbane (metro population 2.5 million; approximately half of Queensland's population)—are largely at the mercy of state governments, which effectively control a variety of key policy areas including education; health; and policing to planning, land use, infrastructure, and major utilities. While there has been some ambivalence in the High Court jurisprudence concerning the Commonwealth's power to invest in massive urban renewal projects, Australia's major cities remain patently underrepresented under the existing constitutional order.[147]

The near-complete subjugation of cities to state discretion emanates from the Australian Constitution's (1900) establishment of states' residual authority. Unlike sections 91–92 in Canada's Constitution Act 1867, Australia's Constitution does not set out the states' enumerated powers in a list. Instead, it enumerates only the Commonwealth (federal) Parliament's powers, primarily in section 51 with three in section 52. Any legislative area not granted to the Commonwealth in sections 51 or 52 remain with the states.[148] This "residual authority" emanates from section 107 of the constitution.[149] As local government was a subject of colonial legislation prior to confederation and is not one of the

---

[146] Graham Sansom, "The Australian Model of Metropolitan Governance: 'Muddling Through' or Just a 'Muddle'?" (Paper presented at Cities in Federal Theory workshop held at the University of Melbourne, June 20–21, 2019).

[147] There seems to be some uncertainty about the Commonwealth's ability to directly fund local government, as a result of two High Court of Australia decisions: *Pape v Commissioner of Taxation*, [2009] HCA 23; and *Williams v Commonwealth of Australia*, [2012] HCA 23. In its 2013 preliminary report, the Australian Joint Committee on Constitutional Recognition of Local Government identified these two decisions as a significant factor in the need for a new constitutional referendum (paras. 1.71.9, 1.23); online: <https://www.aph.gov.au/Parliamentary_Business/Committees/House_of_Representatives_Committees?url=jsclg/localgovt/preliminaryreport/fullreport.pdf>. In a nutshell, the holding (6:1) of *Williams* was that the making of federal payment under the funding agreement under review was not supported by the executive power of the Commonwealth under s. 61 of the Constitution, and more generally, that the Commonwealth's power to spend "must be found elsewhere in the Constitution or in statutes validly enacted under the Constitution" than in an "implied nationhood power." In other words, the ruling constrains somewhat the federal spending power, which heretofore had been thought to be quite expansive. *See* Nicholas Aroney, "The High Court of Australia: Textual Unitarism vs Structural Federalism," *in* Nicholas Aroney and John Kincaid, eds., *Courts in Federal Countries: Federalists or Unitarists?* (University of Toronto Press, 2017), 63–64.

[148] *See generally* Alan Fenna and Robyn Hollander, "Dilemmas of Federalism and the Dynamics of the Australian Case," *Australian Journal of Public Administration* 72 (2013): 220–227; John Brumby and Brian Galligan, "The Federalism Debate," *Australian Journal of Public Administration* 74 (2015): 82–92.

[149] Commonwealth of Australia Constitution Act (Australia), 1900, s. 107.

powers given to the Commonwealth, the constitutional power to legislate on municipal governance resides with the states. One exception is Australia's capital, Canberra, which is fundamentally different in its legal status from all other Australian cities.[150] It is not part of any state, instead sitting in the federally run Australian Capital Territory, carved out of New South Wales soon after federation. Canberra contains the vast majority of the ACT's population and has no local government, effectively functioning as a city-state.[151]

Australia's states have their own written constitutions, which all recognize local government in some way.[152] However, these state constitutions guarantee little more than the mere existence of local government, subjected to state, rather than to federal, legislative authority.[153] In fact, as Grant and Drew put it, "the constitutional recognition of local government in all instances is contradicted by the ensuing sections of the constitutions."[154] In this way, all state constitutions expressly subject local government power to state legislative authority with little or no qualification while affirming local authority in the abstract.[155] In the words of Grant and Drew, "despite the variability amongst the constitutions, local governments overwhelmingly serve at the pleasure of the state legislatures and consequently are not afforded immunity from them in any absolute sense."[156] As masters of Australian cities, states have enacted city-specific legislation to govern some of the country's large urban centers. The City of Sydney Act 1988, the City of Melbourne Act 2001, and the City of Brisbane Act 2010 are three prime examples. Smaller cities and towns are governed under the states' local government acts. All of the city-specific acts contain provisions for the application of the state's local government act. Generally, they state that the local government

---

[150] This authority is provided by s. 52(i) of the Australian Constitution, which grants exclusive power to the Commonwealth with respect to "the seat of government of the Commonwealth, and all places acquired by the Commonwealth for public purposes."

[151] Graham Sansom, "Canberra, Australia," in Enid Slack and Rupak Chattopadhyay, eds., *Finance and Governance of Capital Cities in Federal Systems* (McGill-Queens University Press, 2009), 16.

[152] These provisions also vary considerably in their level of detail. For example, New South Wales and South Australia both contain only a single, quite general city-enabling section, while Victoria's constitution recognizes local councils over several sections and goes into considerable detail. The relevant provisions in Australian state constitutions are the following: *Constitution Act* (New South Wales), 1902, s. 51; *Constitution Act* (South Australia), 1934, s. 64A; *Constitution Act* (Victoria), 1975, ss. 74A, 74B; *Constitution Act* (Western Australia), 1889, ss. 52–53; *Constitution Act* (Tasmania), 1934, ss. 45A, 45B, 45C; *Constitution of Queensland*, 2001, ss. 70–78.

[153] *See* Cheryl Saunders, "Constitutional Recognition of Local Government in Australia," in Nico Steytler, ed., *The Place and Role of Local Government in Federal Systems* (Konrad-Adenauer-Stiftung, 2005), 47–63. Saunders notes that "only one state, Western Australia, guarantees the elected status of the system of local government, without express reservations to allow parts of the system to be appointed, permanently or temporarily or, as in the case of New South Wales, to provide that local government may be either 'duly elected or duly appointed.'" *Id.* at 55.

[154] Bligh Grant and Joseph Drew, *Local Government in Australia: History, Theory and Public Policy* (Springer, 2017), 184.

[155] *Id.*

[156] *Id.*

act and city-specific act should be read in conjunction, but the latter takes precedence in the event of a conflict.[157] From a fiscal standpoint, the net impact of the specific city acts is at best unclear. A 2013 report by the Australian Parliament's Joint Committee on Constitutional Recognition of Local Government noted that "use of direct funding to local government has increased substantially since the mid-1990s."[158] Yet, on average, local councils in Australia receive approximately 10% of their revenues through state and federal grants.[159] Merely 5.8% of Melbourne's total revenue in 2018–2019 and 2.1% of the City of Sydney's total revenue in 2017–2018 came from such grants.[160]

Due to the limited constitutional authority of local governments, city councils are subject to amalgamation by state governments without their consent. As Cheryl Saunders observes, "state constitutions provide surprisingly patchy protection for local government against arbitrary dismissal."[161] This has been an extremely contentious issue in Australia for several years. According to a former New South Wales Minister for Local Government, in 2011, state-local relations "had deteriorated to a point where it could accurately be described as toxic," largely due to the strain over amalgamation.[162] In 2004, the City of Sydney was amalgamated with South Sydney, despite the objections of the councils. The city later declared that the forced merger had been disruptive and not resulted in significant savings.[163] In 2017, the premier of New South Wales announced that the

---

[157] For example, the *City of Sydney Act 1988* refers to NSW's Local Government Act 1993 as "the Principal Act" and states at section 3, "This Act [with parts excepted] shall be construed with, and as if it formed part of, the Principal Act." Striking a slightly different note, the *City of Brisbane Act 2010* states at section 5, "Generally, the Local Government Act does not apply to the Brisbane City Council or its councillors, employees, agents or contractors. However, particular provisions of the Local Government Act apply, or may apply, to the Brisbane City Council as a local government."

[158] Parliament of the Commonwealth of Australia, Joint Select Committee on Constitutional Recognition of Local Government, *Final Report on the Majority Finding of the Expert Panel on Constitutional Recognition of Local Government: The Case for Financial Recognition, the Likelihood of Success and Lessons from the History of Constitutional Referenda* (Canberra, 2013), para. 2.8; online: <https://www.aph.gov.au/Parliamentary_Business/Committees/House_of_Representatives_Committees?url=jsclg/localgovt/finalreport/fullreport.pdf>.

[159] *See, e.g.,* Australia, Department of Infrastructure and Regional Development, *Local Government National Report 2014–2015* (Canberra, 2017); online: <https://www.regional.gov.au/local/publications/reports/2014_2015/LGN_REPORT_2014-15.pdf> at 4.

[160] Melbourne City Council, *Annual Report 2018–2019*; online: <https://www.melbourne.vic.gov.au/SiteCollectionDocuments/annual-report-2018-19.pdf> at 186, 198; City of Sydney, *City of Sydney Annual Report 2017/18*; online: <https://www.cityofsydney.nsw.gov.au/__data/assets/pdf_file/0004/308344/2017-18-Annual-Financial-Statements-Audited-and-Signed.pdf> at 15–20.

[161] Saunders, "Constitutional Recognition of Local Government in Australia," 55. Saunders notes that only the Queensland and Victoria state constitutions place any constraints on the process by which an elected local authority may be removed, whether by requiring ministerial action (Queensland) or an Act of Parliament (Victoria). *Id.* at 55–56.

[162] Don Page, "New South Wales Local Government reform 2011 to 2014," *in* Brian Dollery and Ian Tiley, eds., *Perspectives on Australian Local Government Reform* (Federation Press, 2015), 117, quoted in Grant and Drew, *Local Government in Australia*, 211.

[163] Anne Davies, "Council Amalgamations: The Good, the Bad and the Ugly," *The Sydney Morning Herald* (June 26, 2015); online: <https://www.smh.com.au/national/nsw/council-amalgamations-the-good-the-bad-and-the-ugly-20150625-ghxz1u.html>.

state was abandoning plans for a further series of council amalgamations. Several of the state's local councils had already been amalgamated, while others were then challenging the decision to amalgamate in court on procedural grounds.[164] The state's process during this consolidation project was widely criticized as unduly opaque and economically unsound.[165]

Meanwhile, at the federal level, there have been three prominent and unsuccessful attempts to amend Australia's Constitution to empower cities. The first, in 1974, would have given the Commonwealth Parliament authority to grant money to local governments as it saw fit. This power would have given local governments both "symbolic" and "financial" recognition.[166] The amendment was rejected in a referendum. This failure had little practical effect, however, as the Commonwealth still managed to fund local governments, first by granting it through the states, and later by granting it directly after Australia's High Court recognized its power to do so under an existing constitutional provision.[167] The second attempt to strengthen the constitutional status of municipalities occurred in 1988. This attempt would have "had no specific practical, functional or financial aspects, being simply symbolic."[168] Again, the amendment failed in a referendum. In 2013, Parliament approved a proposed constitutional amendment aimed at strengthening Commonwealth power to provide funding to cities. As discussed earlier, this attempt was motivated by a pair of High Court decisions that put into some question the flexibility of the federal spending power in Australia.[169] Unlike previous attempts, the government did not put the proposed amendment to a referendum, a condition of its formal adoption, believing that it had no chance of being voted in.[170] Predictably, the academic literature

---

[164] Eamon Waterford, "How Can We Make Local Councils Fit for the Future?," *The Fifth Estate* (June 30, 2018), online: <https://www.thefifthestate.com.au/columns/spinifex/how-can-we-make-local-councils-fit-for-the-future/>.

[165] Graeme Philipson, "Opinion—Amalgamation Issue Just Won't Go Away" (January 8, 2018); online: *Government News* <https://www.governmentnews.com.au/opinion-amalgamation-issue-just-wont-go-away/>.

[166] A.J. Brown, "In Pursuit of the 'Genuine Partnership': Local Government and Federal Constitutional Reform in Australia," *University of New South Wales Law Journal* 31 (2008): 435–466, 441.

[167] *Victoria v. Commonwealth* (1975) 134 CLR 338; *see* Brown, "In Pursuit of the 'Genuine Partnership,'" 443.

[168] Brown, "In Pursuit of the 'Genuine Partnership,'" 445–446. The proposed provision read: "Each State shall provide for the establishment and continuance of a system of local government, with local government bodies elected in accordance with the laws of the State and empowered to administer, and to make by-laws for, their respective areas in accordance with the laws of the State."

[169] *Pape v. Commissioner of Taxation*, [2009] HCA 23; *Williams v. Commonwealth of Australia*, [2012] HCA 23. Another related case, *Williams (No. 2)*, involves restrictions on federal spending absent legislative justification. See *Williams v. Commonwealth of Australia*, [2014] HCA 23.

[170] Grant and Drew, *Local Government in Australia*, 107–113.

is consistently pessimistic on the chances for constitutional empowerment of Australian cities in the foreseeable future.[171]

IV. The European Scene

As we have seen in Chapter 1, contemporary pan-European constitutional discourse is preoccupied with subsidiarity talk and attempts to resolve democracy deficit tensions through jurisprudential and legislative deference to national worldviews, cultural inclinations, and local policy preferences. Yet, while European countries are increasingly vocal in demanding enhanced nullification and opting-out options vis-à-vis the pan-European policies to which they object, they are persistently reluctant even to consider granting anything like these powers to major urban centers within their territorial boundaries.

Europe is home to some of the world's greatest cities. London and Paris—capitals of two major colonial empires—have long been the objects of admiration as "world cities." Rome and Athens—two ancient imperial capitals—draw millions of visitors each year. Meanwhile, Frankfurt and Brussels have become pan-European economic and governance hubs. At the EU level, planners and economists, (but, tellingly, not jurists or public law scholars), refer to the so-called Blue Banana—a megalopolis-like region with a population of 110 million—stretching from London and Manchester in the UK to Milan and Turin in Northern Italy, via parts of France, Belgium, the Netherlands, Germany, and Switzerland. Despite major overhauls in urban governance (e.g., the establishment of the Greater London Authority or the Greater Paris plan), none of these major cities enjoys extended constitutional status or self-governance authority.

The European Charter of Local Self Government provides some basis to believe that European cities may be better off than their counterparts in the United States, Canada, or Australia. The charter was adopted by the Council of Europe in 1985 and came into force in 1988. It protects the basic prerogatives of local government, exercised by directly elected councils, and affirms the capacity of local authorities, within the limits of the law, "to regulate and manage a substantial

---

[171] Brown, "In Pursuit of the 'Genuine Partnership,'" 436. Writing in 2008, Brown predicts that "in the context of a real referendum debate, any proposals similar to those of 1974 or 1988 would almost certainly be destined to fail," as indeed it did in 2013. As recently as June 2019, the Australian Local Government Association, representing 537 councils, adopted a resolution requesting "the Commonwealth Government to initiate a Referendum at the earliest opportunity seeking agreement for recognition of Local Government in the Australian Constitution." The Deputy Prime Minister and leader of the National Party Michael McCormack spoke to the delegates prior to the vote and expressed support for constitutional recognition. However, to date, that resolution has garnered little political traction. See Judy Skatssoon, "Local Councils Vote for a Referendum," *Government News* (June 17, 2019); online: <https://www.governmentnews.com.au/local-councils-vote-for-a-referendum/>.

share of public affairs under their own responsibility and in the interests of the local population." Article 2 denotes that the principle of local self-government must be recognized in domestic legislation and, where practicable, in the constitution. However, in reality, the charter's net effect on enhanced city constitutional power in Europe has been modest at best, as the constitutional status of cities continues to reflect established national constitutional traditions largely unaltered by the charter.[172] What is more, the charter fails to distinguish between small townships and megacities, instead referring broadly to "local government."

Unlike most countries of its population size (85 million) or economic significance, Germany does not feature a real megacity. Due to a confluence of historical contingencies, from the multiple political entities of the pre-Bismarck era to the destruction of World War II and the split of the country and of Berlin from 1945 to 1990, Germany has evolved as a relatively decentralized country. Several German cities, notably Berlin (one of Europe's cultural capitals), Frankfurt (one of Europe and the world's financial centers), and Dusseldorf (at the heart of the Rhine-Ruhr region, one of Europe's heavy industry centers), have evolved into major cities on a continental scale. Berlin, Hamburg, and Bremen enjoy constitutional status as city-states, equal to the status of a canton/province/state—Berlin because it is Germany's capital, the other two because both were independent city-state members of the historic Hanseatic League at the time of German unification in 1871.[173] Yet, this designation is predominantly of administrative significance, and does not entail any enhanced revenue-generation powers or reflect any novel constitutional thinking about the megacity or the urban agenda more generally.[174]

The German Basic Law is silent on the status of cities or large urban agglomerations. At the same time, it protects the regulatory competences of municipalities in local affairs "within the limits prescribed by law" (Art. 28.2). The German Federal Court held that this competence includes local affairs that

---

[172] *See generally* Giovanni Boggero, *Constitutional Principles of Local Self-Government in Europe* (Brill-Nijhoff, 2017); Lando Kirchmair, "International Law and Public Administration: The European Charter of Local Self-Government," *Pro Publico Bono* 3 (2015): 124–135; Chris Himsworth, *The European Charter of Local Self-Government: A Treaty for Local Democracy* (Edinburgh University Press, 2015).

[173] The main privilege the three German city-states have enjoyed vis-à-vis other cities is their systemically better positioning with respect to equalization transfers between the federal government and the Länder (Länderfinanzausgleich). The inclusion of Bremerhaven—essentially an enclave in the state of Lower Saxony—into the city-state of Bremen for the purposes of the German Basic Law was done upon request of the US Navy to allow it access to a main seaport after World War II.

[174] The German Federal Constitutional Court has ruled on a number of occasions, most recently in September 2018, that the constitutional recognition of these three cities as states negates their protection as municipalities under Art. 28(2) Basic Law. In a nutshell, the court is of the opinion that however modest is the practical meaning of these three cities as states, it still exceeds the prerogatives of other German cities. Hence, reliance on protection of municipalities is redundant. *See, e.g.,* 2 BvF 1/15, 2 BvF 2/15: Constitutionality of the 2011 Census Case (judgment of September 19, 2018).

have not been explicitly assigned by law to other levels of government, and may be overridden only in the name of public interest (the definition of which remains vague).[175] However, in practice, the residual power German municipalities enjoy with respect to regulating local affairs not addressed by other laws, has been limited considerably by a large number of federal and Land statutes. The mixed (at best) status of German cities has come to the fore amid the arrival of a very large number of refugees to Germany in 2015 and 2016. A federal quota system distributed the incoming refugees across the country according to tax revenues and population size. Consequently, Germany's large cities received the bulk of incoming migrants, regardless of their existing challenges with respect to density, affordable housing, oversubscribed transit, healthcare, and education facilities, etc. As recent reports suggest, that framework imposed uneven burdens on city-states and large cities.[176] While large German cities, notably Berlin and Hamburg, have shown considerable ability to innovate in order to effectively absorb a large number of newcomers, there remains a huge institutional and constitutional gap between what German cities are expected to do with respect to refugee housing or integration, and their lack of meaningful constitutional standing or even a seat at the policy-making table.[177]

Likewise, there are no provisions in the specific German state constitutions that grant any special treatment to large cities. Munich is only named once in the Bavarian state constitution;[178] neither Cologne nor Dusseldorf is even mentioned in the state constitution of North Rhine-Westphalia; and the Hessian state constitution is silent with respect to Frankfurt, a city that was described in Saskia Sassen's seminal work as a "global city" alongside New York, London, and Tokyo. Moreover, the Rhine-Ruhr metropolitan region—Germany's largest urban agglomeration with 11 million people within the state of North Rhine-Westphalia, maintains multiple administrative coordination bodies but lacks any autonomous constitutional standing or personality.

A similarly non-constitutional entity, the Randstad—a major metropolitan area of over 8 million people in the Southwestern Netherlands, comprising the four largest Dutch cities (Amsterdam, Rotterdam, The Hague, and Utrecht)— is home to over 45% of the Dutch population. While the four cities often

---

[175] BVerfGE 79, 127 (Rastede). For a detailed discussion, *see* Christian Bumke and Andreas Vosskuhle, *German Constitutional Law: Introduction, Cases, Principles* (Oxford University Press, 2019), 418–420.

[176] Bruce Katz, Luise Noring, and Nantke Garrelts, "Cities and Refugees—The German Experience" (Brookings, 2016).

[177] See Bruce Katz and Jessica Brandt, "The Refugee Crisis Is a City Crisis: World Leaders Are Negotiating a Global Compact on Refugees. Urban Leaders Need a Seat at That Table," *City Lab*, October 27, 2017.

[178] Art. 68 states that the Bavarian Constitutional Court shall be formed at the Higher Regional Court in Munich.

engage in inter-municipality cooperation initiatives on matters such as tourism and transportation, the Randstad itself has no independent legal standing, let alone constitutional recognition.[179] The Amsterdam Metropolitan Area (Metropoolregio Amsterdam), a key part of the Randstad region, is an informal voluntary association of 36 municipalities and two provinces (Noord-Holland and Flevoland). Likewise, in the southern Randstad (the urban agglomeration of Western Holland), 23 local authorities cooperate under the Metropolitan region Rotterdam-The Hague. Much like the Randstad region, these associations are voluntary and lack any stature in Dutch public law, constitutional or otherwise, all while approximately three-quarters of the Dutch population live in urban areas, making the Netherlands one of the most urbanized countries in Europe.

Meanwhile in Switzerland, Article 50 of the revised Swiss Constitution (1999) formally signals increased attention to city status as it recognizes the autonomy of communes (in accordance with cantonal law) and warrants that the Confederation "shall take account of the special position of the cities and urban areas as well as the mountain regions" (as Margaret Mead is quoted to have once said, "always remember that you are absolutely unique; just like everyone else"). Article 50 does not establish new competences for cities, nor does it serve as basis for federal or cantonal subsidization of cities. In practice, city status varies across cantons. The canton of Freiburg passed a cantonal act specifically governing placing urban areas under cantonal rule. An intriguing split cantons structure is place in regions where historical faith divisions warrant it (e.g., Basel-Stadt [Basel-City] and Basel Landschaft [Basel-Country]). Geneva is a de facto city-state as the Geneva canton comprises the city and its outskirts. Unlike Geneva, the city of Zürich—Switzerland's most populous city—does not enjoy a de facto city-state status as it is embedded within the considerably broader canton of Zürich. Because political majorities in the canton and the city are allocated differently, electoral rifts commonly arise between the left-leaning city and the conservative bourgeois canton, which often outvotes the city in cantonal as well as national referenda.[180] Attempts to split the canton into two half-cantons to better reflect the city of Zürich's electoral preferences have failed.

---

[179] OECD Territorial Reviews, *The Metropolitan Region of Rotterdam-The Hague, Netherlands* (OECD Publishing, 2016).

[180] The most successful party in the 2019 cantonal parliament elections, for example, was the Swiss People's Party (a right-wing, nationalist-populist party), which took 24.5% of the votes, down from 30% in the 2015 election. That party received considerably more support from rural areas than the city of Zürich, as has traditionally been the case: *see* "Grüne und GLP gewinnen bei Zürcher Wahlen, SVP verliert deutlich—die Schlussresultate in der Übersicht," *Neue Zürcher Zeitung*, March 25, 2019. In the 2015 elections, for example, the party received less than 18% of the votes in the electoral districts within the city of Zürich, it received over 48% in the (rural) municipality of Weiningen. Furthermore, no member of the Zürich city council is from the Swiss People's Party.

In neighboring Austria, the constitution (Bundesverfassung, which has been under reform for nearly 15 years without any final outcome as yet) establishes principles of federalism (especially following a round of constitutional amendments in 1974), albeit of a more unitary variety than in Germany or Switzerland. Article 2 of the Austrian Constitution lists Vienna—capital of Austria and home to a fifth of the country's population—as one of the nine Länder of Austria. Article 108 details the simultaneous competences of Vienna's municipality and Land authorities. Article 5 I B-VG enshrines Vienna as the capital and seat of the supreme federal authorities; Article 25 I B-VG further states that the seat of the national council is in Vienna. As in Berlin, however, these provisions do not assign special powers to Vienna beyond what it has as a Land. Nor is the density factor in any way accounted for. Whereas the Vienna Land population (1.8 million) is spread over 400 square kilometers (155 square miles), the second-most populous Austrian Land—Lower Austria (Niederösterreich)— has a smaller population (1.6 million) than Vienna yet spreads over a territory of nearly 20,000 square kilometers (7,700 square miles), 50 times larger than Vienna. What is more, other than Vienna in its dual status as capital city and as Land, all other Austrian cities with populations larger than 20,000 enjoy similar competences, regardless of their size.

Italy's constitutional order, established in the aftermath of World War II, created a highly decentralized system that emphasized regional autonomy, alongside local autonomy and some residual administrative competences to municipalities. But it was not until 2015 that Italy's major cities were granted enhanced status via Article 114 of the constitution. The amended Article 114 includes "metropolitan cities" among Italy's sub-national entities. An accompanying law (56/2014) assigned that status to 10 cities, which were hitherto part of Italy's 107 provinces (a subregional entity), including Rome (population of 4.5 million), Milan and Naples (each with a population of about 3.2 million).[181] The law created an elected metropolitan mayoral position in each of these cities and granted extended autonomy to the designated cities with respect to matters such as local planning and zoning, provision of local police service, and local transportation. The law did not grant these cities any transformative fiscal autonomy beyond what was needed to assume authority over the devolved governance functions.

---

[181] In 2015, Italy's Constitutional Court confirmed (Judgment No. 50/2015) the constitutionality of the "metropolitan cities" plan despite its top-down nature, in an apparent contravention of Article 133's call for bottom-up, province-led reforms. The court reasoned that plan amounted to a structural reform of local government, whereas Article 133 applies mainly to single provincial boundary modifications. See Giovanni Boggero, "The Establishment of Metropolitan Cities in Italy: An Advance or Setback for Italian Regionalism?," *Perspectives on Federalism* 8 (2016): E-1–22.

What is more, in typical Italian fashion of deference to regionalism, Article 114 also allowed each of Italy's constitutionally recognized regions to grant such status to cities within their respective jurisdiction. Within two years, four additional cities, including Cagliari (population 600,000) and Messina (400,000), were granted similar status by their respective regional governments. And to top off this rather convoluted reform, Prime Minster Matteo Renzi's proposed package of constitutional changes, which would have enhanced the central government's power vis-à-vis the regions while removing the entire "provincial" status from the constitution, was defeated by 59% to 41% in a national referendum held in December 2016. The outcome has been a motley, "half-baked" system of city autonomy that may have nontrivial long-term effects on the autonomy of Italy's large cities, but at its present configuration, reflects a reform halted prior to its completion.

Even in Spain's effervescent quasi-federalist system, where sentiments of regional and territorial identity are deeply rooted in history and reflected in the constitution, big cities do not possess much power. Section 2 of the Spanish Constitution (1978) recognizes the right to autonomy of Spain's "regions and nationalities," and at the same time declares "the indissoluble unity of the Spanish nation." Since 1983, the country has been divided into 17 autonomous communities (comunidades autónomas).[182] Each autonomous community has its own elected Parliament whose members elect a regional government, and is granted a core set of legislative competences.[183] Additional transfers of power from the central government to the autonomous communities are allowed, and has been determined in an ongoing process of bilateral negotiation between the central government and each of the communities, many of which, in particular Catalonia and Andalusia, have accused the central government of dragging its feet in ceding powers to and in clarifying fiscal arrangements with the autonomous communities. There are two further levels of government below the national and regional—provinces and municipalities. Their powers and responsibilities are set out in the Basic Law on Local Government (1985). Additionally, the Local Government Modernization Act (2003) establishes governance

---

[182] These are the following: the Basque Country, Catalonia, Galicia, Andalusia, Asturias, Aragon, Balearic Islands, Canary Islands, Cantabria, Castile and León, Castile-La Mancha, Extremadura, Navarra, La Rioja; and the regions of Madrid, Murcia, and Valencia. In 1995, two Spanish possessions in Northern Africa, Ceuta and Melilla, were added as autonomous cities.

[183] The autonomous communities have control over healthcare and education. Catalonia and the Basque Country have their own police forces. The Basque Country and Navarra also have independent fiscal systems. Catalonia was refused such autonomy in 2012, and so it remains with the national tax redistribution system, which transfers funds to poorer regions from richer ones, like Catalonia. *See* Megan Specia and Rick Gladstone Raphael Minder, "Spain Is a Collection of Glued Regions. Or Maybe Not So Glued," *New York Times*, October 27, 2017.

guidelines for municipalities with populations larger than a predetermined threshold.

The metropolitan area of Madrid (population 6.5 million) is one of the 17 autonomous communities, with a governing body called the Autonomous Community of Madrid (created in 1982 through section 144 of the constitution as a measure of national interest). A special law for Madrid as a capital city— Act on Capital Status and Special Regime of Madrid (2006)—reinforces the existing competences and stipulates some minor decentralization functions from the central government and the Community of Madrid to the city level such as mobility, public safety and security, and infrastructure. The law also regulates the administrative relations between the central government, the Community of Madrid, and the City of Madrid, as well as the city's political and administrative organization. However, as observers of Spanish federalism have noted, since 1980, both the Autonomous Community of Madrid (with respect to Madrid) and the government of Catalonia (with respect to Barcelona) have avoided creating any kind of general government for the two metropolitan areas in order to prevent strong metropolitan councils from becoming rivals to the autonomous communities themselves.[184] Consequently, the self-governance capacity of Madrid and Barcelona is not substantively greater than that of any other Spanish municipality. In other words, in Spain too, neo-secessionist regionalism has been limited to traditional sub-national units.

That the European city, sizable as it may be, is a creature of the state, fully subsumed within broader constitutional entities is also reflected in the tellingly sporadic European Court of Justice (ECJ) jurisprudence on urban standing. In a number of cases determining the validity under EU law of local governments' adopting tax rates lower than national rates, the ECJ deferred to these subnational units' constitutional status and competences within their respective polities, as interpreted and enforced by the national courts. If such local governments have no entrenched status or competences in a given national constitutional order, the ECJ cannot create such status and will therefore not defer.[185]

Let us zoom in on London and Paris, two of Western Europe's largest and most widely recognized cities. Both cities have served as national and world centers of trade, empire, diversity, and governance for centuries. Reflecting fresh thinking in central government policy, both cities underwent major governance overhauls in the last two decades, aimed at sustaining and enhancing their global stature.

---

[184] See, e.g., Francisco Velasco Caballero, "Kingdom of Spain," in Nico Steytler, ed., Local Government and Metropolitan Regions in Federal Systems (McGill-Queen's University Press, 2009), 298–328, 311.

[185] See, e.g., Unión General de Trabajadores de La Rioja (UGTRioja) and Others v. Juntas Generales del Territorio Histórico de Vizcaya and Others, Joined Cases C-428/06 to C-434/06 (September 11, 2008).

A large-scale amalgamation process has taken place in the London region, commencing with the creation of the Greater London Authority in 2000 and continuing while the city hosted the 2012 Olympic Games as well as a host of other world-class summits. Across the channel, the Greater Paris (Le Grand Paris) development plan was launched in 2007, followed by the establishment in 2016 of the Greater Paris Metropolitan Authority and accompanied by a successful bid to host the 2024 Olympic Games. But these grandiose reforms have not generally carried out.

Take London. Its governance structure has undergone several major changes over the past three decades: chief among them is the introduction of a governance system shared between the 33 London boroughs, the mayor, and the Greater London Authority (GLA). This development followed a centrally orchestrated transformation of London from a postindustrial city into a world-class business and banking center, as illustrated by the central government's creation of the London Docklands Development Corporation, which was aimed at cutting red tape and bypassing local authority, ultimately yielding the regeneration of the Isle of Dogs into today's Canary Wharf.

In the 1990s, the central government renewed interest in developing the city. Mega-projects such as the Channel Tunnel Rail Link, the Jubilee Line expansion, the London Eye, and the Millennium Dome and Bridge were centrally funded. Following a referendum held in 1998, the Greater London Authority Act was adopted in 1999, and the GLA was established in 2000. It is made up of an elected mayor of London who acts as a representative for Greater London and its executive, as well as a 25-member London Assembly that acts as the legislative body. Both are elected every four years. The mayor has a strong, executive role while the Assembly has the authority to hold the mayor to account.[186] (The 2000 introduction of directly elected mayoralty allowed for prominent London mayors Ken Livingstone, Boris Johnson, and later Sadiq Khan to gain prominence well beyond the city itself.) Together, they are responsible for the strategic development of Greater London.[187] Since its launch, additional powers have been incrementally conferred upon the mayor of London and the GLA by the Greater London Authority Act 2007, the Police Reform and Social Responsibility Act 2011, the Public Bodies Act 2011, the Localism Act 2011, and the Policing and Crime Act 2017.[188] The entire GLA initiative was part of the Labour government's plan to modernize local government and make it more accessible and responsive to people's concerns. In addition, the government attempted to foster policy cohesion across the London metro area—something that urban planners thought was

---

[186] Parliament. House of Commons (2017), *The Greater London Authority* (05817), 4.
[187] Jack Parker, "Greater London Authority: London Mayor and Assembly," *Insight* (2015): 1.
[188] House of Commons, *The Greater London Authority*, 9, 19.

missing since the disbanding of the Greater London Council in 1986.[189] However, constitutional empowerment of London has never been part of the plan.

Calls for greater autonomy for the city in the wake of the 2016 Brexit referendum were quickly silenced. In the immediate aftermath of the vote, which saw 59.9% of eligible London residents vote to stay in the EU, a public petition emerged calling for the mayor of London, Sadiq Khan, to declare London independent from the UK in order to allow it to continue as a member of the EU.[190] While the petition began as a "frustrated joke, a cry of despair," it rapidly gained public attention with more than 175,000 signatures in the first week.[191] Political leaders quickly weighed in, with Labour Party strategist Spencer Livermore arguing that "[I]ndependence for London within the EU should now be our goal" and favorably comparing the city to Singapore, which seceded from Malaysia.[192] Mayor Khan, on the other hand, did not endorse the underlying idea of secession. However, he went on record demanding more autonomy for the city "to protect London's economy from the uncertainty ahead, to protect the businesses from around the world who trade here and to protect our jobs, wealth and prosperity."[193] In a November 2018 speech at the Center for London, Mayor Khan called for "a new constitutional deal" that would "reset the devolution agenda" and give greater autonomy for London, and said that national governments are "powerless in the face of globalisation and powerless to respond to the needs of local citizens."[194] Despite the UK's deep entanglement in the Brexit saga in recent years, no such constitutional fortification of cities or of London is on the horizon. Moreover, observers agree that the GLA Act left many opportunities for

---

[189] *See* Carolyn Harrison, Richard Munton, and Kevin Collins, "Experimental Discursive Spaces: Policy Processes, Public Participation and the Greater London Authority," *Urban Studies* 41 (2004): 903–917, 905; Karen West et al., "The Greater London Authority: Problems of Strategy Integration," *Policy & Politics* 31 (2003): 479–496, 480.

[190] "Pro-EU Londoners Rebel with 'Lexit' Secession Call," *Agence France Presse*, June 25, 2016. "Londependence," as the movement came to be called, was not an entirely new idea; for example, then-BBC Economics editor Stephanie Flanders wrote an opinion piece outlining the case for an autonomous London in 2013, and Tim Oliver, a Dahrendorf Fellow at LSE IDEAS, argued for a devolved government in January 2016, six months prior to the Brexit vote. *See* Stephanie Flanders, "Should Britain Let Go of London?," *BBC News*, March 26, 2013; online: https://www.bbc.com/news/business-21934564; Tim Oliver, "The UK Needs a Devolved Government for London," *London School of Economics* (blog), January 30, 2016; online: https://blogs.lse.ac.uk/europpblog/2016/01/30/the-uk-needs-a-devolved-government-for-london/.

[191] "Pro-EU Londoners Rebel with 'Lexit' Secession Call,"; Pauline Bock, "'Londependence' May Be a Dream, But More Autonomy for the City Is Not," *The New York Times* (June 28, 2016); online: https://www.nytimes.com/live/eu-referendum/londependence/.

[192] Jack Sommers, "Brexit Vote Sees 'London Independence' Seriously Touted by Labour Lord," *Huffington Post* (June 24, 2016); online: https://www.huffingtonpost.co.uk/entry/eu-referendum-london-independence_uk_576d4c57e4b0d257114993a2?guccounter=1.

[193] Bock, "'Londependence' May Be a Dream."

[194] Dave Hill, "Sadiq Khan: More Autonomy for UK Cities Can Help Combat 'the Politics of Blame and Hatred,'" *On London* (November 7, 2018); online: https://www.onlondon.co.uk/sadiq-khan-more-autonomy-for-uk-cities-can-help-combat-the-politics-of-blame-and-hatred.

the central government to intervene and assert its authority in core urban planning and city governance matters.[195]

Meanwhile, the UK Cities and Local Government Devolution Act 2016 manifests a commitment to "devolve powers and budgets to boost local growth in England," in particular to "devolve far-reaching powers over economic development, transport and social care to large cities which choose to have elected mayors."[196] With the devolution to the cities of powers hitherto exercised by ministers and relating to transport, housing, skills, and healthcare, the government considered it "necessary for the people of the area to have a single point of direct accountability. The Government's view is that for cities, elected mayors for combined authority areas will achieve this and ensure the continuation of strong democracy."[197] In addition to mayoral elections, the act authorizes amalgamation of authorities and the creation of sub-national transportation authorities. Essentially, the act extends the administrative devolution pact with London, to other major urban centers such as Greater Manchester, Liverpool, and Sheffield.

Early in its existence, the GLA was described as "a weak upper tier of local government rather than an embryonic regional authority."[198] While it has taken shape in an era of devolution in UK administrative and constitutional law, the GLA's powers are not comparable to, for example, those of the Scottish Parliament (as delineated by the Scotland Act 1998 or the Scotland Act 2016), the National Assembly for Wales (as defined by the Wales Act of 2006, 2014 and 2017), or Northern Ireland Assembly (as defined by the Northern Ireland Act, 1998). From its creation, there was no political undertone of enhanced self-government in the GLA. Indeed, there are key policy areas in which the GLA has little or no role, including health, education, and social care, among others. Ultimately, the GLA's main role is a strategic one, unifying London's multiple public policy bodies under a shared vision and institutional framework, essentially, relying on the London boroughs to implement its policies.[199] (Tellingly, while the GLA operates out of City Hall—a modern, shell-shaped structure with a glass exterior, designed by internationally renowned architect Norman Foster—the GLA does not actually own the building it is based in, instead holding a 25-year lease.)

Consistent with the GLA's unifying role, the mayor's job is generally to provide leadership across London by "knocking heads together."[200] However, mayoral powers under the GLA vary across policy areas. The mayor effectively has

---

[195] *See, e.g.,* Greg Clark and Tim Moonen, *World Cities and Nation States* (Wiley Blackwell, 2017), 41.

[196] *See* "Cities and Local Government Devolution Act 2016: Explanatory Notes" (2016), para. 1.

[197] *Id.* at para. 2.

[198] Vernon Bogdanor, *Devolution in the United Kingdom* (Oxford University Press, 1999), 275, quoted in Harrison et al., "Experimental Discursive Spaces," 905.

[199] Parker, "Greater London Authority," 3. *See also* West et al., "The Greater London Authority," 485.

[200] House of Commons, *The Greater London Authority*, 8.

full executive authority over functional bodies such as Transport for London, although most of this body's funding comes directly from the Treasury.[201] Matters such as strategic housing funding and (since 2018) the London fire commissioner are directly handled by the GLA, giving the mayor full authority over them.[202] In certain policy areas such as environment, culture, and equal access to healthcare, the mayor has a statutory duty to produce strategy documents that dictate policy direction, but has no power to deliver these strategies. In other policy domains, the mayor only has the power to appoint members to public body boards. The Assembly may, with a two-thirds majority, amend the mayor's annual budget or a mayoral strategy. It also has a general power to hold the mayor and his key advisers to account.[203] Additionally, the secretary of state has the power to guide and limit the GLA's powers.[204]

In short, while the GLA represents a substantial overhaul in the governance of a world city and an extension of mayoral authority in certain policy areas, it remains hard to identify a true shift in power dynamics between the GLA and the central government nearly two decades after the body's adoption. As a strategic administrative body that controls and coordinates other entities and services throughout Greater London, the GLA does not bolster the constitutional status of London as a world city within a unitary system of government. A recent study concluded that, in 2016, "central government is still very much a key player in London."[205] And so, modernization and devolutionist impulses in British government notwithstanding, London has remained entirely subsumed within the British national constitutional order.

Meanwhile, France has manifested a similar duality between government support for grandiose city development and a central grip over the city as a national asset. France has often been thought of as a textbook example of a centralist, "strong state" setting and constitutional order. Paris has long been under control of the French nation-state; it was not until 1977 that a directly elected mayor of the central municipal department of Paris was introduced. And it was not until the late 1990s that the central government began to foster close collaboration among the municipalities comprising the Paris region (Île-de-France)—central Paris alongside seven other municipalities, commonly understood to mean the Paris metropolitan area, and one of the 12 administrative regions in mainland France. A deliberative metropolitan forum was only launched in 2006

---

[201] *Id.* at 7–8.
[202] *Policing and Crime Act 2017* (UK), s. 3.
[203] House of Commons, *The Greater London Authority*, 7.
[204] *London Authority Act 1999* (UK), ss. 30(7)–(9) and ss. 31(7)–(8). Parker, "Greater London Authority," 3.
[205] Clark and Moonen, *World Cities and Nation States*, 41.

and has made strides in facilitating public policy collaboration across the Paris metropolitan area.

Enter the ambitious Greater Paris development project, initiated in 2007 by the central government to promote Paris as a competitive global city. Announced by then-President Nicolas Sarkozy, Greater Paris included massive government investment in infrastructure, transit, planning, and land use, as well as in changes to urban governance structures that would foster further collaboration among the various Paris municipalities.[206] Following an arduous preparation process, the Greater Paris Act gained legislative force in 2010. The initial budgetary focus was on improving the transit system, emphasizing an "urban, social and economic project . . . based on the construction of a new public transportation network."[207] To that end, the act allocated nearly €30 billion for constructing the new Grand Paris Express, with a further €12 billion approved for modernizing existing railways, all in an attempt to overcome the divide between "inside neighborhoods" and "outside neighborhoods" created by the notorious péripherique—a major ring road surrounding the core city.[208] Additionally, the Greater Paris Act created the Society of Greater Paris (SGP) as a public body controlled by three national ministries. The SGP would be responsible for state consultation with municipalities throughout the planning process, in addition to the overall management of the construction and financing for the new railway lines, stations, and installations of the Grand Paris Express.[209]

The Greater Paris Act also introduced territorial development contracts (TDCs), providing legal framework for agreements between state representatives (acting primarily through SGP) and municipalities on issues concerning the development of new housing and public facilities in areas surrounding planned Grand Paris stations.[210] Although they are premised on the notion of voluntary participation on the part of the municipalities, TDCs have been frequently criticized as instruments for the state to reintegrate itself into municipal planning and development.[211] Nonetheless, many municipalities within Paris

---

[206] Henry Samuel, "Nicolas Sarkozy Plans for 'Grand Paris,'" *Telegraph.co.uk* (last modified June 5, 2008); online: https://www.telegraph.co.uk/news/worldnews/europe/france/2080999/Nicolas-Sarkozy-plans-for-Grand-Paris.html.

[207] *2010 Greater Paris Act*, N° 2010–597, June 3, 2010, Journal Officiel de la République Française, n°0128, June 5, 2010 (Art. 1).

[208] Xavier Desjardins, "Greater Paris and Its Lessons for Metropolitan Strategic Planning," *Town Planning Review* 89 (2018): 3–4. The project envisioned the creation of four new metro lines for the Paris metropolitan area, entailing the construction of 200 kilometers (77 miles) of tunnels and 68 new stations, of which two-thirds would be linked to existing metro lines, in the span of 10 to 15 years.

[209] *Id.* at 1.

[210] *See* Caroline Gallez, "Contrats de développement territorialin the Grand Paris project: Towards Negotiated Networked Development?," *Town Planning Review* 85 (2014): 273–286.

[211] Desjardins, "Greater Paris," 6.

have entered into TDCs in order to secure state funding for their projects, to en-sure their voices are heard in the planning process, and to coordinate more effec-tively with other municipalities in negotiations with the state.[212]

A key feature of the project from a governance perspective was the 2016 es-tablishment of the Greater Paris Metropolitan Authority (GPMA), representing an administrative restructuring for the ongoing development of the Paris metro-politan area. Its jurisdiction encompasses 7.5 million people within 12 territorial public entities (one of which is the city of Paris itself), which have been further divided into 131 communes.[213] The GPMA is led by a council of 210 members, 62 of whom represent inner Paris.[214] The GPMA acts primarily as a mechanism to facilitate tax redistribution as well as inter-municipal cooperation for ongoing economic and environmental development.[215]

While the creation of the GPMA represents a shift in the administration of urban planning within Paris, its powers are delimited by strict compliance requirements with the detailed master development plan provided by the Île-de-France region.[216] Essentially, the state has been able to maintain and enhance its grip over planning of Greater Paris via the GPMA. The GPMA's limited political autonomy and largely administrative function have led scholars of urban govern-ance to refer to it as an "empty shell."[217] Some critiques have gone even further, exposing the neoliberal, business-friendly vision of a "global city" that informed the Grand Paris plan from its inception. In her meticulous study of the politics of the Grand Paris plan, my University of Toronto colleague Theresa Enright con-vincingly shows how the Greater Paris project—the most grandiose of its kind in recent memory—is reflective of meta-notions of growth and marketization as hallmarks of an economic capital. The project is also unmistakably French in its conception of the central role that the French state has played in its articulation and implementation.[218] It is hardly surprising, I would add, that its local empow-erment rhetoric notwithstanding, Paris has remained a centrally controlled and

---

[212] Gallez, "Contrats de développement territorial," 280. Where a TDC has not been signed, the SGP is authorized to carry out projects within a 400-mile radius of planned stations after consul-tation with local authorities. *See* "Why Grand Paris," *JLL Grand Paris* (last modified January 2018); online: http://www.grand-paris.jll.fr/en/grand-paris-project/overview/.

[213] Hugo Bessis, "Is the New 'Greater Paris' Authority Too Weak to Get Things Done?," *CityMetric* (last modified March 7, 2016); online: https://www.citymetric.com/politics/new-greater-paris-authority-too-weak-get-things-done-1894.

[214] Desjardins, "Greater Paris," 10.

[215] "Metropolis of Greater Paris," *Métropole Du Grand Paris* (last modified April 15, 2016); on-line: http://www.metropolegrandparis.fr/fr/content/english-version.

[216] Desjardins, "Greater Paris," 12.

[217] *Id.*

[218] Theresa Enright, *The Making of Grand Paris: Metropolitan Urbanism in the Twenty-First Century* (MIT Press, 2016). Importantly, Enright shows that large expenditures for the Grand Paris Express were made not merely or even primarily for the public good but to increase the attractiveness of the region to private investors.

constitutionally dependent entity, especially considering that this world city had its municipal affairs administered by a nationally appointed prefect until 1977. Since assuming office in 2014, outspoken Paris Mayor Anne Hidalgo has been a champion of social progressivism and has taken a few noticeable steps to turn Paris into a more environmentally-friendly city.[219] As discussed in Chapter 4, Hidalgo also introduced a city-based identity card modeled on the IDNYC. Nonetheless, Paris's constitutional non-status remains intact.

A similar picture is evident when we turn our gaze to large urban centers in Central Europe. The Budapest metro region is home to 3 million people— approximately 30% of Hungary's population. In the Czech Republic, over 2.5 million people—approximately 25% of the population—live in the metro Prague region. Belgrade (metro population of 3 million), is home to over 40% of Serbia's population. All of these cities—national megacities when the relative population size measurement discussed earlier is deployed—are constitutionally designated as capitals of their respective countries. Yet none enjoy standing as constitutionally recognized entities. Moreover, some major cities in the region— notably Budapest and Vienna—are considered islands of cosmopolitan liberal policy preferences in otherwise strong right-wing-leaning national electorates. In addition to the centralist impulse to keep large cities under state control, Viktor Orbàn's Fidesz-led government (as of 2018 holding an overwhelming majority of 134 seats in the 199-seat parliament), for example, lacks political incentive to empower opposition-controlled constituencies. (Tellingly, an explicitly anti-Orbàn candidate representing the opposition Democratic Coalition Party won the October 2019 Budapest mayoral elections.)

In most respects, then, large European cities, many of which are the "old world's" most populous urban centers, enjoy even fewer constitutional powers than their counterparts in North America. In fact, American scholars who lament the powerlessness of American cities as reflected in the sanctuary city debate would be interested to know that similar litigation is very sparse in other national settings. While a few major European cities have declared themselves "Solidarity Cities" (in the spirit of the human rights cities networks discussed in previous chapters), these declarations carry more symbolic or aspirational significance than any real legal and constitutional weight. With the exception of Barcelona, where such solidarity city statements have been inseparable from the broader Catalan secessionist impulse, cities that exert pressure against state policies regarding immigration lack any constitutional claim against the state. Examples include Amsterdam, Utrecht, and Tilburg (the Netherlands), Gdansk (Poland), Vienna (Austria), Zürich (Switzerland), and Athens (Greece) through

---

[219] *See* Adam Nossiter, "The Greening of Paris Makes Its Mayor More Than a Few Enemies," *New York Times*, October 5, 2019.

the "solidarity cities" framework within the Eurocities network (a network of more than 130 of Europe's largest cities), as well as the Italian regions of Tuscany [Florence], Emilia-Romagna [Bologna], and Lazio [Rome]. When these cities have taken action, it has been through the provision of services that cater to illegal immigrants, rather than refusing to enforce state immigration policy or challenging the state's central constitutional authority.[220] Moreover, comparative, cross-country reports suggest that, although there has been a strong urban dimension to the refugee crisis since 2015, European cities continue to lack a seat at the table when it comes to funding or policy-making. While large cities are transit hubs and sought-after destinations, the cities themselves remain dependent on central government funding and have little or no influence over the determination of central asylum and refugee policies.[221]

Conclusion

At least two lessons may be drawn from the brief discussion in this chapter. First, in contrast to North America, where litigation is the main channel for debating the constitutional status of urban centers, the megacity discussion in Europe is largely taking place in central government planning and policy-making circles. Relevant constitutional jurisprudence is rare and often inconsequential. This trend may reflect several factors, including the litigious nature of American society; the long legacy of central planning in many European countries; and at least to some extent, the federal structure of the United States, Canada, and Australia as opposed to the unitary nature of many European polities. However, even in federalist European settings such as Germany and Switzerland, litigation concerning city status is rare. Whatever the reason for this clear difference in style may be, in neither setting does the megacity enjoy constitutional standing, instead being largely subsumed within national constitutional structures conceived either prior to the arrival of the megacity (as in North America) or in the post–WWII reconstruction mode of national constitution making.

Second, when it comes to urban agglomeration, the old world of modern constitutionalism has witnessed a great silence. In both North America and Europe, rich and sophisticated constitutional debates have taken place concerning the place of religion in public life; the contours of human dignity; and the place of

---

[220] *See* Harald Bauder and Dayana A. Gonzalez, "Municipal Responses to 'Illegality': Urban Sanctuary across National Contexts," *Social Inclusion* 6 (2018): 124–134.

[221] *See* Bruce Katz and Jessica Brandt, "The Refugee Crisis Is a City Crisis: World Leaders Are Negotiating a Global Compact on Refugees. Urban Leaders Need a Seat at That Table," *City Lab*, October 27, 2017; Ellie Violet Bramley, "Cities Need More Power to Deal with Refugee Crisis: Report," *The Guardian*, April 4, 2016.

national constitutional orders in an increasingly interconnected, globalized world. Discussion about extensive urbanization and its consequences features centrally in political and economic analyses, but is almost entirely absent from the constitutional scene. While the specifics of the constitutional terrain in the United States, Canada, Australia, Germany, the Netherlands, the UK, and France vary greatly, none of these national constitutional orders has paid close attention to the unprecedented urbanization of the last few decades. This large-scale stagnation stands in stark contrast to the constitutional vibrancy concerning urban agglomeration and megacity autonomy in Asia and Latin America. As we shall see in the next chapter, much of the innovation on this front emanates from "new world" constitutional settings not commonly associated with the scholarly and jurisprudential (unofficial) canon of comparative constitutionalism.

3

Constitutional Innovation in Governing the Metropolis

Law, Economics, Politics

As we have seen, the governance of megacities in the constitutional "old world" has been characterized by an ongoing stalemate interspersed with occasional ad hoc action that seldom, if ever, alters the existing constitutional framework. Major North American cities are governed by a largely gridlocked constitutional order adopted between 150 and 240 years ago. Meanwhile in Europe, centrist-national governance traditions have consistently triumphed over city power. Strong emphasis on administrative law, combined with continental European civil law tradition, has rendered urban governance a largely non-constitutional-domain. Even ambitious programs such as "Grand Paris" or the creation of the Greater London Authority did not include any *constitutional* change in the status of those megacities.

In contrast to the stalemate in the constitutional old world, the constitutional "new world" has generated new ideas about constitutional governance of the metropolis. In this chapter, I explore some of the novel approaches that new world central governments have taken to the urbanization groundswell. Specifically, I identify three scenarios exemplifying paths of central government's role in metropolitan emancipation: First, I consider cases—Tokyo, Japan; Seoul, Korea; and China's several special-status cities—in which central governments' constitutional support of megacities reflects astute, long-term planning for regional or national economic growth. Second, I consider instances in which major constitutional reforms are introduced in order to counteract decades of ineffective sub-national dominance over the urban agenda. Drawing on the examples of India and Brazil, I show how deep-seated patterns of intergovernmental power struggles may render such reforms ineffective. I then contrast the rather modest success of such urban empowerment reforms in these two countries with the attempt to usher in a new constitutional era for cities in South Africa as part of the new post-apartheid constitutional order. Third, and finally, I consider cases in which strategic empowerment or disempowerment of megacities has been the product of sheer politics, driven by strategic maneuvering by key stakeholders

City, State. Ran Hirschl, Oxford University Press (2020). © Ran Hirschl.
DOI: 10.1093/oso/9780190922771.001.0001

serving their own immediate political interests, as seen in the constitutional governance of Mexico City, Buenos Aires, Nairobi, Cairo, and Dhaka.

As these three scenarios illustrate, parts of the constitutional new world—Asia, Latin America, and to some extent Africa—have become a living laboratory for novel constitutional thinking on the unprecedented urban agglomeration of the last few decades. In all this experimentation, three factors emerge as the main determinants of constitutional innovation or stalemate in megacity governance: the *necessity* factor—the need for developing world countries to think creatively about urban agglomeration given its astonishing pace in the Global South; the *constitutional* factor—a constitution's amenability to change in favor of the megacity; and finally, the *political* factor—the interplay of political power holders, national and sub-national governments' various interests in enabling or subverting megacity emancipation.

I. Constitutional Empowerment of Megacities as Engines of Economic Growth

In a widely publicized move in 2017, the Saudi government announced plans to build a new megacity—*Neom*—on the Red Sea Coast, as part of its new "Vision 2030" grand plan to move Saudi Arabia away from dependence on oil.[1] The Neom project is backed by more than $500 billion from the Saudi government in collaboration with local and international business consortia. The Saudi government declared Neom to be a supposed "megacity of the future" and a "civilizational leap for humanity." As such, it will operate independently of the "existing governmental framework." Delusional or visionary as this idea may be, it aims to emulate an approach that has been used successfully by several leading countries in Asia: supporting megacity development economically and politically as a means of nationwide modernization, economic transformation, and global branding.[2]

Tokyo provides what is perhaps the earliest example of planned megacity empowerment by a central government as a national project. The Greater Tokyo

---

[1] *See* "NEOM, a $500bn Dream in the Desert: Saudi Arabia Launches a Futuristic Economic Zone," *Economist*, October 26, 2017. Construction of Neom began in 2019 and is expected to be completed within 7–10 years. The new city's airport has already been classified by IATA as an official commercial airport. According to Neom CEO Nadhmi Al-Nasr, "NEOM is a global initiative that will require and expect the whole world to . . . be part of transforming the dream into reality. For that to happen . . . we had to come up with our own law of that zone." Online: https://aawsat.com/english/home/article/1717256/neom-ceo-our-mission-transform-dream-reality-serve-world.

[2] Another illustration of the application of this model may be Doha, capital of Qatar. Backed by massive government support, Doha turned within less than 50 years from a humble city of less than 100,000 inhabitants in the 1970s into a 2.5 million regional hub, hosting world class sporting, political, and economic gatherings.

Area—the largest city in the world—has a population of 38 million. It is comprised of 23 special wards, with the central Tokyo prefecture at its core, which includes some of Tokyo's busiest districts, among them Shinjuku, Shibuya, Ueno, and Shinagawa. The population of the central Tokyo prefecture alone has grown from 3.5 million in 1945, to 11.6 million in 1975, and to 14 million in 2017. Over the years, the southwest expansion of Tokyo has reached Yokohama, itself a city of nearly 4 million people and a major commercial hub, to create an urban sequence that stretches over 5,500 square miles. The public transit figures effectively tell the Tokyo story: the Shinjuku station at the heart of Tokyo's main business district serves 3.6 million people *daily* and is the world's busiest train station with over 1.3 billion passengers per year, followed by Tokyo's Shibuya station with 1.1 billion rides per year. (By comparison, New York's Penn Station and Grand Central each see about 750,000 passengers daily, or about 275 million annually, one-fifth of Shinjuku's usage. Waterloo Station—the busiest train station in London—sees about 300,000 passengers daily, or 110 million annually, about one-twelfth of Shinjuku's usage.) Every visitor to Tokyo can attest to the city's enormous size as well as its cleanliness, efficient transportation system, and low crime rates when compared to large cities in North America.

How did this urban miracle come to pass? Cultural and social factors are, of course, essential. But there is the question of urban governance, too. While Japan is a centralized, unitary nation-state, Chapter VIII of its constitution, which was promulgated in 1946 and came into effect in 1947, entrenches several principles of local self-government. Article 92's "principle of local autonomy" has informed several ordinary statutes, most notably the Local Autonomy Act, which interprets and expands upon this concept. Article 93 further requires local government entities to establish assemblies as their deliberative organs, and that the chief executive officers of all local public entities and the members of their assemblies shall be elected by direct popular vote from within their communities. Furthermore, the Diet (Japan's national parliament) cannot unilaterally change the status of any local government "without the consent of the majority of the voters of the local public entity concerned, obtained in accordance with law" (Article 95). By the time Japan's Constitution came into effect in 1947 and a new framework for local government was established, the seeds of Tokyo's special megacity status had already been planted. Its government's considerable political and fiscal autonomy would eventually turn the Tokyo metropolis into a uniquely powerful entity in Japan's intergovernmental affairs.

State empowerment of Tokyo began during the Meiji era, and continued in the 1930s and 1940s.[3] In 1943, the Tokyo-*fu* (prefecture) and Tokyo-*shi* (city) were

---

[3] Emiko Kakiuchi, "Japan: Tokyo," *in* Ian Shirley and Carol Neill, eds., *Asian and Pacific Cities: Development Patterns* (Routledge, 2013), 98–111.

merged to form the Metropolis of Tokyo (東京都 *Tōkyō-to*)—one of Japan's 47 prefectures—with wartime efficiency being a primary reason for collapsing the dual administrative systems into one.[4] The modern roots of the current 23 special ward system came into effect in 1947 following the enactment of the post–WWII Constitution of Japan (which enshrined local autonomy in Chapter VIII) and the Local Autonomy Law (LAL), which provided a guarantee of local autonomy against national government encroachment.[5] Consequently, the Tokyo Metropolitan Government (TMG) emerged and assumed control over Tokyo's wards. The first election of the governor of Tokyo by popular vote took place during that time; over the years, the elected governor of Tokyo has become one of the most influential political actors in Japan. Additional delineation of the division of powers was laid out in the Decentralization Promotion Law (1995), enacted in anticipation of the greater need for local authority in an aging society.[6] In a further move toward decentralization, the Comprehensive Local Autonomy Law (2000) was adopted, followed by a reform to the National Planning Act (2005), each granting more autonomy to local government in planning and implementation of central government policies.[7]

All these legislative changes constituted Tokyo as a megacity that is both a "prefecture" and a "city," and equipped the new metropolitan entity with significantly more policy authority and fiscal autonomy than other Japanese cities. Key policy areas, ranging from urban planning and zoning, infrastructure, and policing to elementary and secondary education and public health lie with the metropolitan leadership. The fiscal means for such autonomous governance are provided through direct taxation. From the 1950s onward, about 70% of Tokyo's revenue was derived from local taxes, rising to nearly 80% in the 1990s. Today, Tokyo generates approximately 82% of its revenue from local taxation and receives far lower tax reallocation from the central government than any of the world's comparable megacities. Data from 2015 indicates that while Tokyo receives less than 6% of its budget directly from intergovernmental transfers and an additional 12% from shared taxation, London receives 68% of its budget from such intergovernmental transfers.[8] The 2018 budget of the central Tokyo prefecture

---

[4] "History of Tokyo, *Tokyo Metropolitan Government*; online: http://www.metro.tokyo.jp/ENGLISH/ABOUT/HISTORY/history01.htm.

[5] *Id.*

[6] Andrew Stevens and Marie Yoshikawa, "Japanese Mayors—Japanese Local Government and Mayors of Largest Cities," *City Mayors, City Mayor Foundation* (April 2018); online: http://www.citymayors.com/mayors/japanese-mayors.html.

[7] Nobuo Sasaki, "What Type of Decentralization Best Suits Japan?," *Nippon Communications Foundation* (April 22, 2013); online: <https://www.nippon.com/en/in-depth/a01801/>.

[8] *See* Enid Slack, "International Comparison of Global City Financing: A Report to the London Finance Commission" (IMFG, 2016); Enid Slack, "How Much Local Fiscal Autonomy Do Cities Have?" (IMFG Perspectives, 19/2017).

alone was approximately 132 billion USD, more than the national budget of Sweden.[9]

Akin to several other empowered megacities worldwide (see my discussion of Mexico City's constitutional emancipation later in this chapter), Tokyo's special status allowed it to pursue a progressive social agenda. In 2015, to pick one example, Tokyo's Shibuya ward became the first jurisdiction in Japan to issue certificates recognizing same-sex partnerships as "equivalent to marriage," thereby allowing same-sex couples to rent apartments together and granting them hospital visitation rights. City authorities' quest to market Tokyo as a cosmopolitan world city in anticipation of the 2020 Olympic Games in Tokyo has contributed an added impetus (recall the international outcry following Russia's crackdown on gay rights leading to the 2014 Winter Olympics in Sochi). In 2018, the TMG passed a law that prohibits "the Tokyo Metropolitan Government, citizens, and enterprises" from "unduly discriminat[ing] on the basis of gender identity or sexual orientation."[10] Even as the national government remains resistant to legalizing same-sex marriages, 20 municipalities in Japan have followed Tokyo's lead in addressing same-sex preferences and partnerships.[11]

The success of Tokyo's merged prefecture-city status has prompted other major Japanese cities, most notably Osaka, to pursue similar planning and fiscal autonomy. Prime Minister Shinzo Abe and his government supported the Metro Osaka merger plan despite resistance from the Osaka chapter of his own Liberal Democratic Party, which opposed Osaka's controversial mayor, Toru Hashimoto. In 2015, Osaka voters rejected the consolidation plan by a narrow margin, leading to Hashimoto's resignation, although efforts to merge Osaka prefecture and city in a manner similar to the Tokyo arrangement are still ongoing. On several occasions since the early 1990s, the central government has also considered a relocation of the government administration offices from Tokyo in order to ease its urban concentration.[12] Initial ideas of creating a Washington, DC-like capital, alongside a New York-like Tokyo have come and gone, partly due to concerted efforts by the TMG to keep the status quo intact.

All things considered, Japan-Tokyo relations serve as a textbook example of a central government's acknowledgment of the megacity's essential role in national stature, economic development, and possibly even global branding. Fostering

---

[9] Tokyo's 2018 budget stood at 14.4 trillion yen, or approximately 132 billion USD.

[10] *See* "Tokyo: New Law Bars LGBT Discrimination," *Human Rights Watch* (October 5, 2018); online: https://www.hrw.org/news/2018/10/05/tokyo-new-law-bars-lgbt-discrimination; Tokyo Metropolitan Government Ordinance Seeking Realization of the Principle of Respect for Human Rights Outlines in the Olympic Charter, 2018.

[11] *See* Justin McCurry, "Tokyo Dawn: Is the Impenetrable City Finally Opening Up?," *The Guardian*, June 10, 2019.

[12] *See* Vadim Rosmann, *Capital Cities: Varieties and Patterns of Development and Relocation* (Routledge, 2016), 112–113.

Tokyo's world-city stature rather than suppressing it, the Japanese governments of the post–WWII era have created a mutually beneficial arrangement whereby the city gains from the government's empowering, collaborative approach toward fiscal autonomy, while the government has benefited by harnessing the city's size and stature to stimulate national economic development and enhance the nation's competitiveness both regionally and globally.

Another example of a megacity with a special designation from the central government is Seoul (city population 10 million, metro population 26 million). With a history of over 600 years, Seoul is a world-class city and home to approximately half of South Korea's population, as well as the headquarters of virtually all brand-name Korean corporations. The Constitution of South Korea creates five orders of sub-national units. The first tier, directly below the central government, comprises eight provinces, Jeju Island, and eight first-level cities. The eight cities include Busan, Daegu, Daejeon, Gwangju, Ulsan, and Incheon (part of the Seoul metro area) as metropolitan cities; Sejong (see later discussion) as a newly created self-governing city; and Seoul as the only special metropolitan city. According to Article 117 of the Korean Constitution, adopted in 1948 and amended in 1988, "[l]ocal governments shall deal with administrative matters pertaining to the welfare of local residents, manage properties, and may enact provisions relating to local autonomy, within the limit of laws and regulations; the types of local governments shall be determined by law." The accompanying Local Autonomy Act states that the first tier of sub-national government in South Korea comprises a "Special Metropolitan City, a Metropolitan City, a Do (Province) and a Special Autonomous Do." The conjunction of Article 117 and the *Local Autonomy Act* therefore allows Seoul to enjoy a unique constitutional standing.

Scholars often identify Seoul as a business-friendly metropolis, "principally a national platform for the global operations of Korean multinational companies."[13] Its legal and fiscal autonomy, alongside unflagging support from the central government, has allowed Metropolitan Seoul to invest tremendously in public transit and urban planning as well as to launch high-publicity initiatives at the global level, including hosting the 1988 Olympic Games, 2002 FIFA World Cup, and the 2010 G-20 Summit.[14] The central government has nurtured Seoul's national and regional powerhouse status, using the city as South Korea's gateway to globalization and capitalizing on its power to enhance the country's image worldwide.[15]

[13] Greg Clark and Tim Moonen, *World Cities and Nation States* (Wiley Blackwell, 2017), 74.
[14] For a concise survey of Seoul's economic and socio-spatial development, *see* H.M. Kim and S.S. Han, "Seoul," *Cities* 29 (2012): 142–154.
[15] This metropolis/nation link is also evident in Korean popular culture. A recent Korean feature film, *The Mayor* (2017), depicts a bitterly fought mayoral election campaign in which big money, urban affairs, and national politics closely intersect to create an effervescent drama—formally

Less widely discussed, yet equally significant, is the impact of Seoul's status on its ability to tackle social welfare challenges. This ability has proven essential in addressing the rapid population growth the city witnessed in the second half of the twentieth century: Seoul's population rose from 1.5 million in 1955 to over 10 million in 1990. It nearly quadrupled from 1960 (2.5 million) to 1985 (over 9 million) alone. In response, Metropolitan Seoul, in collaboration with the central government, invested considerably in urban development, public transit, and housing, including affordable housing projects. The city's legislative autonomy allowed it to launch a unique residential zoning policy known as Shift, which made it mandatory for developers to include affordable housing as one-fifth of any housing development. By the mid-1990s, the city had added approximately 200,000 new units for low-income residents. Currently, there are over 270,000 public housing units in Seoul, with the metropolitan government vowing to build over 60,000 additional units by 2022. In comparison, New York City strives to have 200,000 such units by 2024.

Seoul's prime status in South Korea's governance system has made the mayor of Seoul one of the most significant political figures in the country. The mayoralty transformed in 1995 from a centrally appointed office to an elected one. Today, the position is commonly perceived as a springboard to influential positions in national politics, as close as it gets to a realization of Benjamin Barber's *If Mayors Ruled the World*, discussed in Chapter 1.[16] Goh Kun, mayor of Seoul from 1988 to 1990 and from 1998 to 2002, served as prime minister of Korea for two stints immediately thereafter (1997–1998, 2003–2004). Lee Myung-bak served as Seoul mayor from 2002 to 2006 and then moved on to serve as president of Korea from 2008 to 2013.[17]

Of course, the ramifications of Seoul's political and economic centrality are not all positive. The city's position has raised concerns about the concentration of Korea's business corporation headquarters in Seoul, and the potential that this concentration creates for overly cozy business-government relations, regulatory loopholes, and large-scale corruption. These concerns draw fuel from the repeated convictions of South Korea's leaders for accepting bribes from the country's family-owned conglomerates, or chaebol, which control vast swaths

fictional but inspired by real events. Some readers may also recall that the Korean pop (K-pop) hit *Gangnam Style*—the first YouTube video to reach one billion views, currently with over three billion views—is inspired by the popular perception of Gangnam, Seoul's main business district. Its music video was shot in Gangnam and depicts some of the district's iconic buildings.

[16] Benjamin Barber, *If Mayors Ruled the World* (Yale University Press, 2013).
[17] In 2018, a Seoul district court sentenced Lee for 15 years in prison on charges of bribery, embezzlement, and abuse of power, and ordered him to pay a 13 billion won ($11.5 million) fine. The court ruled that Lee had accepted bribes from some of South Korea's largest companies in return for favorable decisions and government policies.

of the economy. Seoul's economic primacy has also led to persistent brain drain from Korea's other large cities, notably Busan and Daegu, both in the country's southeast.

To further illustrate the centrality of Seoul to Korean statehood, as well as the unflagging constitutional support that the city receives (en route setting the stage for the discussion later in the chapter of the political origins of megacity constitutional status), let us consider the politics behind the proposal to build a new administrative capital for Korea. As a presidential candidate for the New Millennium Democratic Party, Roh Moo-hyun pledged to relocate the adminis-trative function of Seoul, capital of Korea for 600 years, to a newly constructed city, Sejong. Sejong carries symbolic, national unification weight, named after Sejong the Great, the fifteenth-century king of Korea who is credited with cre-ating the first native phonetic alphabet system for the Korean language.[18] Ostensibly, the move was intended to take some of the pressure off Seoul. The change would also transfer some government functions approximately 70 miles to the south of the country, that is, farther away from the border with North Korea (Seoul is located merely 25 miles away from the border). It was also meant to break up the geographical concentration of the Korean economy. At the time, Seoul was the home base for more than a half of all manufacturing companies, 95 out of the 100 largest Korean corporations, and two-thirds of the country's best universities.[19]

However, observers of Korean politics point out that there might have been a less noble, more political motive behind Roh's idea to erect Sejong as a new capital. The proposed location of Sejong was politically significant, sitting be-tween North and South Chungcheong provinces.[20] Chungcheong is the country's "swing region," which often proves key in deciding presidential elec-tion campaigns between candidates from Gyeongsang in the southeast and Jeolla in the southwest. The less populous Chungcheong has never produced a pres-ident, but it can determine which province does. Accordingly, candidates face significant pressure to appeal to Chungcheong's voters. Enter Roh's 2002 capital relocation proposal, which predictably was extremely popular in Chungcheong, also enjoying considerable support elsewhere. Roh deployed populist rhetoric in advocating the relocation, "painting it as crucial to his broader program of dismantling the political and socio-economic 'establishment,'" and portrayed his critics as "reactionary conservative elements with vested real-estate interests in Seoul, who were only thwarting his efforts to consummate the process of

---

[18] *See* Rossmann, *Capital Cities*, 116.
[19] *Id.*
[20] *See* Chie Sang-Hun, "City's Evolution Offers Lessons in Korean Politics," *New York Times*, March 3, 2010.

democratization."[21] In December 2002, Roh was elected president. Soon thereafter, the National Assembly passed the government-sponsored bill (which came into effect in January 2004) for the construction of a new administrative capital. A constitutional war ensued.

Petitioners representing the main opposition to the plan—chiefly the Grand National Party headed by Park Geun-hye; and the Seoul mayor, Lee Myung-bak (at the time, a personal political rival of Roh)—filed a constitutional challenge, arguing that the relocation plan amounted to constitutional amendment, and as such could only be done through a national referendum as warranted by the required constitutional amendment procedure. In October 2004, only a few months after the Korean Constitutional Court had criticized Roh for violating election law during the 2004 campaign,[22] the court released what is considered one of its most politically significant decisions to date.[23] In an 8-1 decision, the court held that, although the constitutional text does not entrench the status of Seoul as the capital of Korea, the fact that Seoul had served as capital for six centuries made its status a customary constitutional convention. "Matters not explicitly stated in the text of the constitution may . . . be recognized as part of an unwritten or customary constitution. Especially, matters that were self-evident and presupposed at the time of drafting the constitution may be left out of the text." Because a customary constitutional norm establishes that Seoul is the country's capital, even though it is not in the written constitution, this status cannot be changed without a national referendum, required for all constitutional amendments under Article 130 of Korea's Constitution.

The Seoul city government, which campaigned against relocating the capital, was thrilled. "I express my respect for the historic decision," then-Mayor Lee Myung-bak said. "The victory is not only for the Seoulites but for all citizens of our country."[24] Prior to the ruling, he raged against the plan, saying he would stop it "even if I have to mobilize the military."[25] But in 2007, Lee Myung-bak then launched his bid for the national presidency. Farewell Seoul interests, hello Chungcheong interests. To appeal to the Chungcheong voters, Lee pledged his support for the capital relocation. He later went on record to admit that his change of heart on the matter was designed to win votes. This miraculous change

---

[21] Chaihark Hahm and Kim Sung Ho, "Constitutionalism on Trial in South Korea," *Journal of Democracy* 16 (2005): 28–42, 38.

[22] *The Presidential-Impeachment Case*, Case No. 2004 HeonNa 1 (Judgment of May 14, 2004).

[23] *Relocation of the Nation's Capital Case I* [16-2(b) KCCR 1, 2004 Hun-Ma 554 et al., Oct. 21, 2004].

[24] Ser Myo-ja, "Top Court Halts Capital Move," *Joong Ang Daily*, October 22, 2004.

[25] Chie Sang-Hun, "City's Evolution."

of mind seemed to have worked well. In 2008, Lee was elected president of Korea, a five-year position that he held until 2013.[26]

Following the Constitutional Court's 2004 ruling, President Roh's political stature was damaged. In early 2005, however, he pulled together a revised plan, somewhat reduced in its scope, to relocate most but not all of the government institutions to the planned Sejong. A new constitutional challenge was launched in response to the revised plan. In November 2005, the court released its decision: this time it approved (7-2) the planned change on the ground that the revised plan was not aimed at changing the status of Seoul as capital, meaning that it was not a constitutional change and did not require a national referendum.[27] The majority of judges stated "We do not find that the agencies located in the [newly planned city] perform central political and administrative functions that amount to control over national policies." Reflecting retrospectively on the court's earlier ruling on the matter, three of the majority justices writing concurrently noted that they did not "recognize the customary constitution that Seoul is the capital," and wrote that they "do not believe that it is necessary to amend the written constitution to change the customary constitution," thereby distinguishing their view of the law from the court's earlier ruling on the matter. The dissenting opinion adhered to the original one and stressed that the revised plan would transfer approximately three-quarters of South Korea's government agencies to the new city, effectively dividing the nation's capital. Whatever the legal significance of the decision, very little has changed on the ground. As of 2018, more than a decade after the constitutional crisis concerning the capital relocation, Sejong's population stands at less than 300,000. While a few government offices have been relocated to the city, Seoul remains the major hub of government operation as well as the uncontested business and economic capital of South Korea.

A different variant of the long-term, enabling approach toward megacity governance is apparent in China's notion of centrally administrated municipalities (CAMs): Shanghai, Beijing, Tianjin, and Chongqing. The "mega" in each of these four cities is profound. The metro population of Chongqing is over 30 million. Meanwhile, Beijing's population is estimated at 25 million, and neighboring Tianjin's population is estimated at 16 million. These two municipalities, along with Shijiazhuang and Xiong'an, compose the core of the Jingjinji urban cluster whose population has surpassed 110 million. Shanghai's metro population is estimated at 34 million. When neighboring cities such as Kunshan, Wuxi,

---

[26] In 2018, five years after the conclusion of his presidency, Lee Myung-bak was convicted in a slew of corruption charges. Earlier that year, his successor Park Geun-hye had been removed from office, convicted on similar charges, and ultimately sentenced to 24 years in prison.

[27] *Relocation of the Nation's Capital Case II* [17(b) KCCR 481, 2005 Hun-Ma 579, 763 (consolidated), Nov. 24, 2005].

Haining, Hangzhou, Nanjing, and Hefei are taken into account, the population of the Yangtse River Delta urban region exceeds 150 million.

Commencing in 1927, 11 major Chinese cities, including Beijing, Shanghai, and Tianjin, were established as municipalities, essentially designating these cities as the highest-ranked regional urban centers. Following the establishment of the People's Republic of China (PRC) in 1949, a number of cities were granted a similar status, bringing the number of central municipalities to 14. In 1954, 11 of these municipalities were reassigned a status of sub-provincial cities, effectively becoming capitals of their provinces. Conceived as centers of regional economic development, the remaining three cities—Beijing, Shanghai, and Tianjin—were granted CAM status. While Tianjin temporarily reverted back to sub-provincial city status between 1958 and 1967 before it was restored as a CAM, Beijing and Shanghai have maintained their CAM status over the past 65 years. In 1997, the southwest city of Chongqing, formerly part of the province of Sichuan, was also granted that status, alongside a significantly enlarged territory under its jurisdiction (the largest of all four CAMs). This was done in order to promote a "go west" policy as well as to allow it to serve as a main gateway to the Three-Gorges Dam project—the world's largest power station.[28]

Article 30 of China's 1982 constitution establishes the notion of CAMs ("The country is divided into provinces, autonomous regions and municipalities directly under the Central Government"); assigns to CAMs a constitutional status equivalent to that of provinces; and stipulates that these province-level megacities are held directly accountable for and controlled by the central government.[29] China's unique spatial governance structure comprises four CAMs, 22 provinces (official Chinese reports include Taiwan in that category for a total of 23), and five autonomous regions, all in what is formally a unitary state but practically has evolved as an intricate quasi-federal system. Article 89(4) of the constitution further warrants that one of the tasks of the PRC State Council is "to exercise unified leadership over the work of local organs of State administration at various levels throughout the country, and to formulate the detailed division

---

[28] Tse-Kang Leng, "Centrally Administrated Municipalities: Locomotives of National Development," in Jae Ho Chung and Tao-chiu Lam eds., *China's Local Administration: Traditions and Changes in the Sub-National Hierarchy* (Routledge, 2009), 40. Since its CAM designation, the Chongqing municipal authority has invested enormous resources in new transit infrastructure, parks, cultural facilities, and other public amenities.

[29] A similar notion is expressed in the constitution of Vietnam, where a constitutional division was established in 1992 and further reinforced in 2013 between provinces and "cities directly under the central authority" or "centrally run cities," referring to Hanoi and Ho Chi Minh City. Such constitutional designation entrusts these two Vietnamese megacity authorities with considerably wider policy-making tools than those available to other cities. *See also* the constitution of Kazakhstan (with respect to Almaty and Astana [as of 2019, renamed Nur-Sultan]); the constitution of Guatemala (Guatemala City); the constitution of Kyrgyzstan (Bishkek and Osh); and the constitution of Zimbabwe (Bulawayo and Harare).

of functions and powers between the Central Government and the organs of State administration of provinces, autonomous regions and municipalities directly under the Central Government." In addition, from the mid-1980s onward, 15 large cities were assigned a "sub-provincial cities" status. These include rapidly growing megacities such as Guangzhou, the capital of Guangdong Province (metro population 25 million); Shenzhen (metro population 23 million; also within the Guangdong Province); and Chengdu, capital of Sichuan Province (metro population 18 million).

Additionally, the Ministry of Housing and Urban-Rural Development introduced in 2010 a National Urban System Plan that included the designation of major cities as National Central Cities (NCCs), tagged as centers of regional modernization and economic development. The original designation included five such cities: Beijing, Shanghai, Tianjin, Guangzhou, and Chongqing. In the decade since the adoption of the plan, four additional cities have been designated as NCCs: Chengdu, Wuhan, Zhengzhou, and Xi'an.

In a complementary move, China's hukou (household registration) system—introduced in the 1950s to monitor the population, control internal migration, and prevent the emergence of slums in urban centers—was reformed several times. The hukuo system remains highly controversial as it dis-incentivizes population movement to large urban centers by restricting and qualifying essential legal protections and locality-based social services newcomers are entitled to.[30] Since it is estimated that nearly 300 million people moved to China's cities since the early 1980s, the limitations have had severe effects on social and economic inequality in contemporary China. To mitigate these effects, a major overhaul in 2014 allowed over 100 million internal migrant workers to register in the cities where they live, thereby enabling them and their families to access essential social services, including education and healthcare benefits.[31] For the most part, the hukou system remains tiered depending on the size of the migrant workers' destination city: the larger the destination city is, the stricter the criteria for residence registration and entitlement to social services. In that way, the authorities aim to control population movement and direct internal migration to mid-size cities rather than to already crowded metropolises, en route preventing the emergence of vast shantytowns at the outskirts of megacities. Experts agree that while further reforms to the hukou system are urgently required, the gradual ease of

---

[30] The literature on the hukou system's pitfalls is voluminous. For a recent account, see Alexsia T. Chan and Kevin J. O'Brien, "Phantom Services: Deflecting Migrant Workers in China," *The China Journal* 81 (2019): 103–122.

[31] *See* Bettina Gransow, "International Migration in China—Opportunity of Trap?," *Focus Migration Policy Brief* 19 (December 2012).

legal restrictions on internal migration since the 1980s has contributed to the relative success of China's centrally planned approach to urbanization.[32]

While clearly not uncontroversial, China has won appreciation from international think tanks and consulting firms for its approach to megacity constitutional empowerment, combined with multilevel (national, regional, and local government) coordination on the urban development front, all within a centrist framework of megacity contribution to national economic development. In its recent *Global Cities Report*, for example, AT Kearney, one of the world's foremost consulting firms, includes a section entitled "Learning from the East—Insights from China's Urban Success." The report praises China's holistic approach to cities, its empowerment of municipalities, and its tremendous public investment in infrastructure and the skilled workforce in an attempt to making Chinese cities more attractive to residents and to international business alike.[33]

Shanghai—arguably the crowning economic development jewel in China's CAM model—has become one of Asia's major financial centers, alongside Tokyo, Hong Kong, and Singapore. Its rapid metamorphosis from a gray factory city into a regional and global megacity has been analyzed extensively.[34] Observers agree that turning Shanghai into a world city would not have been possible had it not become a Chinese "state project" in the 1990s. "By the mid-1990s," write Greg Clark and Tim Moonen in their comparative account of nation-state/world city relations, "the central government and city government had begun to combine effectively to make Shanghai the productive engine of the Yangtze River Delta region . . . Central government . . . unloaded some of the financial burden on Shanghai municipality and also transferred more powers for it to generate its own revenue. District level and municipal government in Shanghai acquired a range of administrative powers, such as planning, financial management, infrastructure system maintenance and foreign trade."[35] Shanghai's designation as a centrally administered city has come to fruition and paid off big time.

[32] Kam Wing Chan, "Achieving Comprehensive *Hukou* Reform in China," *Paulson Policy Memorandum*, December 2014; Kam Wing Chan, *Urbanization with Chinese Characteristics: The Hukou System and Migration* (Routledge, 2018); Liqiu Zhao, Shouying Liu, and Wei Zhang, "New Trends in Internal Migration in China: Profiles of the New-Generation Migrants," *China & World Economy* 26 (2018): 18–41.

[33] Erik R. Peterson et al., *Global Cities Report* (ATKearney, 2018); online: https://www.atkearney.com/global-cities/2018.

[34] *See, e.g.,* Xiangming Chen, ed., *Shanghai Rising: State Power and Local Transformation in a Global Megacity* (Minnesota University Press, 2009).

[35] Clark and Moonen, *World Cities and Nation States*, 181. *See also* Chaolin Gu et al., "Spatial Planning for Urban Agglomeration in the Yangtze River Delta," *in* Jiang Xu and Anthony G.O. Yeh, eds., *Governance and Planning of Mega-City Regions* (Routledge, 2011), 236–266.

Another illustrative case is Shenzhen—one of the most rapidly developing cities in China.[36] It is assigned a "sub-provincial city" status alongside 14 other main cities, a status that grants it considerable planning and development powers. In 1980, it was designated as one of China's Special Economic Zones, associated with flexible, economic growth-oriented policies. Over the last half century it has emerged from a modest market town with a population of 30,000 into a bustling metropolis with 23 million inhabitants, a major financial and IT center (home to Huawei's headquarters), and the third largest seaport in the world (after Shanghai and Singapore). While in the 1990s, Shenzhen was a massive factory of cheap goods, it has morphed into a "world city" featuring high-skill industries and a growing proportion of white-collar professionals. The city's relative autonomy, backed by the provincial and central government's support, has allowed its authorities to launch extensive urban development and public transportation projects, as well an eco-friendly taxi industry. The construction market is booming; in 2016, more skyscrapers were built in Shenzhen alone than in the entire United States combined. Yet due to massive emigration into the city—it is estimated that 90% of the Shenzhen's residents were born elsewhere—housing prices are skyrocketing. With several high-volume border crossing points and a 15-minute high-speed train ride to neighboring Hong Kong, the possibility of the rise of a de facto, if not a de jure, metropolis of 50 million people at the Pearl River delta seems more likely than ever. Whatever one may think of the pros and cons of such extraordinarily rapid urban development, it is indisputable that Shenzhen's emergence as one of China's and Asia's megacities draws upon the provincial and central governments' unflagging political, economic, and legal support.

To be sure, virtually none of the various special-status urban center designations were driven by a participatory democracy or individual freedom outlook. Nor do these designations reflect a central government acknowledgment of regional or urban self-determination aspirations or enhanced representation impulses. The two elevated megacity designations—CAMs and sub-provincial cities—were assigned by the central government of a single-party polity with a highly dubious human rights record. These designations have been driven by a mix of economic development considerations; administrative governance factors (efficient governance of a 1.4 billion-person polity is a challenging task); and various strategic calculi by pertinent political stakeholders at central, provincial, and urban levels. Moreover, one could credibly question

---

[36] See generally Mary Ann O'Donnell, Winnie Wong, and Jonathan Bach, eds., *Learning from Shenzhen: China's Post-Mao Experiment from Special Zone to Model City* (University of Chicago Press, 2017).

whether Shanghai's economic ascent in the last three decades does not simply reflect the government's embrace, at least to some extent, of Western economic ideals and financial market-friendly policies that the PRC originally opposed. Nonetheless, the concept of a megacity status that matches the status of a province is worthy of consideration by policy makers and public law thinkers, even when it serves only to promote efficacious governance or macroeconomic development goals. We are, after all, facing a twenty-first-century world in which cities with populations over 50 or 100 million are no longer wild science fiction projections.

A case in point is Hong Kong, a bustling metropolis, one of Asia's main business centers, boasting the highest number of visitors per year (nearly 28 million) of all the world's cities. It sports the largest concentration of high-rises in the world, and the highest population density in any high-income country, with parts of the city (e.g., Kowloon) sporting density of over 50,000 people per square kilometer (129,500 per square mile). Overseen since 1997 by an authoritarian regime in Mainland China known for its disrespect for freedom of political speech and its deep antipathy for any opposition to its rule, the city's governance structure nonetheless reflects a unique approach to megacity management. Until the 1991 handover agreement between the UK and China, Hong Kong was a British Dependent Territory. On July 1, 1997, it became a Special Administrative Region (SAR) of the Peoples' Republic of China, governed according to a unique "one country, two systems" motto.

According to the Hong Kong Basic Law, China has exclusive jurisdiction over foreign affairs and defense while Hong Kong authorities are in control of all other matters. That means the government of Hong Kong controls essential policy portfolios such as immigration, media, education, transportation, and housing. As Hong Kong is a major economic hub for international corporations, taxation is a key policy area. The Basic Law (Art. 108) warrants that the taxation system in Hong Kong remains independent of, and different from, the taxation system in Mainland China. In addition, Art. 106 grants Hong Kong independent public finance whereby no tax revenue is handed over to the central government in China. Consequently, the tax paid by Hong Kong residents is used exclusively for the SAR's purposes. The common law legal tradition applies to Hong Kong, and so interpretation of tax rules and adjudication on tax-related matters are handled exclusively by local tribunals. What is more, using the name "Hong Kong, China," the SAR is free to enter economic relations with other countries and participate in international organizations, notably the World Trade Organization.

However, as scholars of Hong Kong constitutional law repeatedly note, the apparently clear distinction of competences between Mainland China and Hong Kong authorities is subject to several limitations, most importantly the ultimate power vested in the Standing Committee of the National People's Congress to interpret the Basic Law, and to invalidate Hong Kong's laws.[37] Observers note that this ability is a potentially powerful constitutional governance tool as, ultimately, the meaning of the Basic Law is not in Hong Kong's hands. To date, China has interpreted the Basic Law on five occasions, most recently in 2016; three of these were upon Hong Kong's request.[38] In 2016, China, through the Standing Committee of the National People's Congress, preempted a Hong Kong court ruling by disallowing two elected pro-"Hong Kong Independence" legislative councilors from serving on the grounds that they had failed to take the oath as stipulated in Article 104 of the Basic Law, thereby refusing to pledge allegiance "to the Hong Kong SAR of the People's Republic of China."[39] The Standing Committee also has the power to declare a "state of emergency" in Hong Kong.

Readers may recall the imprisonment of the leaders of the massive protests that took place in Hong Kong in 2014, known collectively as the "umbrella revolution." The protests began after the Standing Committee issued a decision regarding proposed reforms to the Hong Kong electoral system, perceived at the time as effectively establishing the Chinese Communist Party authority to pre-screen the candidates for the chief executive of Hong Kong. Likewise, an attempt in 2019 to adopt an extradition bill that would allow suspects to be extradited from Hong Kong to Mainland China triggered massive protests in Hong Kong, escalating to near chaos at times. The protestors' initial concern was that such legislation would erode the "one country, two systems" principle, and would allow a de facto subjection of Hong Kong residents to Chinese law. Ultimately, the proposed bill was repealed but the protests marched on for months, triggering aggressive police response, but not deployment of Chinese forces. Local council elections held in late 2019 saw a landslide victory for the pro-democracy movement. While the Coronavirus outbreak pushed the crowds off the streets, there is no end in sight to the underlying SAR versus Mainland China tension.

At the same time, China seems fully aware of Hong Kong's strategic significance to its aspirations of becoming a global economic powerhouse. Hong Kong's long-standing market economy tradition, international stock exchange culture, and British legal system provide assurances to global investors. Experts

---

[37] See, e.g., Cora Chan, "Subnational Constitutionalism: Hong Kong," in David S. Law, ed., Constitutionalism in Context (Cambridge University Press, forthcoming in 2020); Albert H.Y. Chen, "The Autonomy of Hong Kong under 'One Country, Two Systems,'" in Tai-lok Lui, Stephen W.K. Chiu, and Roy Yep, eds., Routledge Handbook of Contemporary Hong Kong (Routledge, 2019), 33–51; Danny Gittings, Introduction to the Hong Kong Basic Law, 2nd ed. (Hong Kong University Press, 2016); Johannes Chan and C.L. Lim, eds., Law of the Hong Kong Constitution (Thomson Reuters, 2015); Yash Ghai, Hong Kong's New Constitutional Order: The Resumption of Chinese Sovereignty and the Basic Law, 2nd ed. (Hong Kong University Press, 1999).

[38] Chen, "The Autonomy of Hong Kong under 'One Country, Two Systems,' " 40–41.

[39] See Chief Executive of the HKSAR v. President of the Legislative Council, FAMV 7/2017 (Court of Final Appeal, Aug. 25, 2017). The two legislative councilors were disqualified. Subsequently, four other legislative councilors were disqualified on similar grounds. See Chen, id. at 47.

of comparative urban politics have suggested that, in terms of policy making on the ground, Hong Kong received "careful and timely support from the Chinese central government through most of the two decades since the handover of power."[40] In the meantime, massive, centrally-planned infrastructure projects support the status of Hong Kong as one of the pillars of the Pearl River Delta region, alongside attempts to strengthen its connection to Mainland China. A fast train line connects Hong Kong with Shenzhen and Guangzhou, constructed in 2018, further blurring the Hong Kong/China boundary and facilitating the emergence of a major urban region at the Pearl River delta. A 34-mile (55 km) bridge connecting Hong Kong, Macau, and the mainland city of Zhuhai in a plan to merge 11 southern cities into a single economic powerhouse. The six-lane structure, which also includes a section of undersea tunnel to allow shipping to the Pearl River delta, links 70 million people across a region boasting a combined annual GDP of over $1.5 trillion—higher than the gross GDP of Australia or Mexico. The $20 billion project, which took a decade to complete, aims to create a megalopolis dubbed the "Greater Bay Area."[41] In short, Hong Kong also exemplifies the uniquely Chinese conceptualization of megacities as catalysts and focal points of large-scale economic development. This approach draws on a mix of constitutional devolution and municipal autonomy alongside central monitoring and massive investment in infrastructure.

II. Constitutional Quest for Influence over the Urban Agenda

In a second scenario of innovation in megacity constitutional governance outside Europe and North America, major constitutional amendment or overhaul, often associated with a new political agenda, aims to advance a bold urban agenda. Rather than looking to cities as hubs of national economic growth, as in the examples discussed earlier, the concern here is to ameliorate conditions in largely disenfranchised, impoverished, and severely underfunded megacities by strengthening local government. Some of these attempts are more successful than others, mostly as they encounter active resistance by decentralized, sub-national units eager to retain control of cities. Two prime examples are India and Brazil. Both countries—large federal jurisdictions that contain some of the world's biggest cities and most notorious urban slums—launched major

---

[40] Clark and Moonen, *World Cities and Nation States*, 153. *See also* "Why Hong Kong Remains Vital to China's Economy," *The Economist*, October 1, 2014.
[41] Natasha Khan, "China's New 34-Mile Bridge Links Up 70 Million People in Planned Megalopolis," *Wall Street Journal*, October 22, 2018.

constitutional reforms aimed at empowering cities. In these two cases, the long-standing reality of sub-national control over cities, along with the politics of intergovernmental affairs, has brought about mixed results.

India is set to be a main site of urbanization in the coming years. Recent reports project a dramatic growth in India's urban population in the next three decades, with perhaps as many as 400 million additional people residing in cities by 2050. Even today, India is home to some of the world's most massive megacities, notably New Delhi and Mumbai, each with an estimated population ranging between 25 and 30 million inhabitants. Other megacities include Kolkata (state of West Bengal), Bangalore (Karnataka), Chennai (Tamil Nadu), and Hyderabad (until 2014 in Andhra Pradesh; in 2014, the new state of Telangana was created, and Hyderabad was made its official capital). Each has a core city population of more than 10 million and metro area estimates of between 15 and 25 million. Some of these megacities have succeeded in attracting large-scale private sector investment. Bangalore, for example, has become India's IT and biotechnology capital. At the same time, India's megacities are home to some of the world's poorest neighborhoods, home to some of the most vulnerable and marginalized urban residents. In Mumbai's Dharavi slum, 700,000 people live within little more than two square kilometers (roughly 0.77 square mile); 52.5% of Mumbai's population occupy 9% of the city's land, living in neighborhoods deemed illegal by the state and lacking almost any infrastructure or services. The housing shortage is dire; estimates indicate that 65% of Mumbai households live in single-room units.[42] A confluence of legal, political, and economic factors prevent affordable housing supply or regulated improvement of slum dwellings. India's federal system has traditionally left most urban governance responsibilities to state governments, with little attention paid to addressing urban agglomeration at the national level. In 1993, a pair of constitutional amendments were adopted that aimed to address local government. The 73rd Amendment deals primarily with governance of rural settlements and townships, while the 74th Amendment addresses cities. The latter defines a metropolitan area as "an area having a population of one million or more comprised of one or more districts and consisting of two or more Municipalities or Panchayats or other contiguous areas." Article 243W(a) of the constitution allows state legislatures to "endow the Municipalities with such powers and authority as may be necessary to enable them to function as institutions of self-government . . ." Such law "may contain provisions for the devolution of powers and responsibilities upon Municipalities at the appropriate level." (Note that Article 243W does not require states to

---

[42] See Marie-Hélène Zérah, "'Transforming Mumbai' or the Challenges of Forging a Collective Actor," in Dominique Lorrain, ed., Governing Megacities in Emerging Countries (Ashgate, 2014), 97–152.

devolve power to cities, but instead suggests that state legislatures *may* do so if they are so inclined, and also that state legislatures preserve discretion over the scope and nature of devolved powers.) The 12th Schedule attached to the 74th Amendment lists 18 concrete policy areas, including urban planning and urban poverty alleviation, wherein state legislature may devolve power to city authorities. In addition, Article 243ZE provides for the establishment of metropolitan planning committees for each designated metropolitan area. On paper, then, the 74th Amendment represents a serious exercise in constitutional empowerment of cities and local government more generally.

In practice, however, the actual impact of this constitutional change on urban self-government has been varied at best, with most observers assessing its real effect as minimal. Because of the traditional strength of the states in Indian politics, and the significance of state governors' support for national parties and their leaders, the 74th Amendment left the actual designation of "metropolitan areas" in the hands of state governors, provided the designations meet the criteria in the amendment as well as "such other factors as they deem fit." Essentially, state governors are free to determine their own criteria for classifying urban centers within their respective states. Due to the liberal discretion that state governors possess, "classification of cities in India tends to be driven more by political factors than a cohesive framework."[43] States have generally been reluctant to abdicate responsibilities and provide unconditional funds to local governments. Governors tend to withhold metropolitan status from cities, as such designation would result in reduced state control over these urban centers alongside greater state financial obligations toward the newly designated municipalities.[44] Consequently, state governments maintain legislative, administrative, and financial control over cities. State-controlled agencies continue to dominate key city-related policy areas, ranging from transportation and housing to land use and low-income neighborhood improvement. Studies further suggest that the establishment of metropolitan planning committees (as per Article 243ZE) suffers from too many structural and political barriers, making the process protracted and sporadic.[45] Moreover, comparative accounts show that, as a result of India's state-deferential approach to urban governance, urban governments are responsible for only 3% of the total public expenditure, compared to 20% to 35% in China, reflecting Indian urban authorities' lack of fiscal autonomy and resources.[46] Aggregate studies on cities across India suggest that Indian cities generate on average less

[43] Michael Castle Miller, "The Urban Situation," *Indonesian Journal of International and Comparative Law* 4 (2014): 1047–1066, 1061.
[44] *Id.*
[45] *See* K. C. Sivaramakrishnan, "Revisiting the 74th Constitutional Amendment for Better Metropolitan Governance," *Economic and Political Weekly* 48, no. 13 (March 30, 2013).
[46] Clark and Moonen, *World Cities and Nation States*, 103.

than 40% of their budgets, while the remainder, over 60%, comes from higher levels of government.[47] Inevitably, urban authorities resort to private sector investment, which often comes with business-friendly strings attached. Other studies have gone as far as suggesting that, in some instances, the states' unwillingness to devolve power has left local governments totally unable to operate, existing only in form and lacking any substantive content.[48]

Constitutional jurisprudence concerning the scope and nature of the 74th Amendment is scant. In the few cases where the Supreme Court of India was called upon to rule on these matters, it adopted a deferential line, siding with the general understanding of the 74th Amendment as granting state governments the authority to determine whether and to what extent to devolve powers to local government. In a 2006 ruling concerning a challenge to a State of Maharashtra legislation that allowed the state to intervene in municipal planning (one of the policy heads enumerated in the 12th Schedule discussed earlier), the Supreme Court held that "Article 243W contains merely an enabling provision, and it does not mean that the State is obligated to provide for such a statute."[49] The adoption of the 74th Amendment, the court held, does not change the exclusive state authority with respect to local government empowerment. Other rulings similar in nature issued by the Supreme Court and by several State High Courts, confirmed that local governments may not exercise independent powers beyond those granted to it by state legislation, and, importantly, that the 74th Amendment does not grant municipalities a right to levy taxes on their own.[50]

Granted, India's constitutional deference to states on urban development matters may produce relative success stories of urban governance, but only when state authorities are so inclined. The ascendance of Bangalore (metro population of over 12 million), in the southwestern state of Karnataka, arguably India's most notable urban renewal success story, has been consistently cultivated by state authorities through massive public investment in infrastructure (e.g., the Bangalore-Mysore corridor expressway, connecting Bangalore with its closest major city; the International IT Park, a research facility dedicated to supporting tech firms; the Kempegowda International Airport, serving nearly 35 million passengers annually; and top international carriers such as Emirates, Lufthansa, Air France, British Airways, and Singapore Airlines). Additionally, the Karnataka state government adopted industrial policies that encouraged and

---

[47] See "Annual Survey of India's City-Systems 2017 (ASICS)," *Janaagraha Centre for Citizenship and Democracy*; online: http://janaagraha.org/asics/report/ASICS-report-2017-fin.pdf.
[48] See George Mathew and Rakesh Hooja, "Republic of India," *in* Nico Steytler, ed., *Local Government and Metropolitan Regions in Federal Systems* (McGill-Queen's University Press, 2009), 166–198.
[49] *Shanti G. Patel v. State of Maharashtra*, Special Leave Petition (civil) 63/2006 (January 31, 2006).
[50] See, e.g., *Sakshi Gopal Agarwal v. State of Madhya Pradesh*, 2003 (4) MPHT 1 (Madhya Pradesh High Court, August 29, 2003).

incentivized technology companies to establish themselves in Bangalore. Within years, high-tech giants such as Texas Instruments, IBM, and Tata did so, leading to popular reference to Bangalore as the "Indian Silicon Valley." (All told, even today, Bangalore continues to feature large pockets of extreme poverty, with hundreds of slums, home to roughly a quarter of the city's population.)[51]

Prime Minister Narendra Modi's national government has prioritized national planning in the area of megacity development and has thrown its support behind Mumbai's modernization and infrastructure renewal efforts through various joint-venture and fund-matching schemes. Yet, under the current constitutional framework, it is the government of the State of Maharashtra—until 2014 a traditional bastion of the Congress Party—that calls the shots on Mumbai governance. The state, not the national government, has full control over the appointment of the municipal commissioner of Mumbai, the city's chief executive officer (as the mayor is a largely ceremonial position).[52] Furthermore, while metro Mumbai's population constitutes approximately a quarter of Maharashtra's overall population, due to India's electoral system, the Greater Mumbai region has only 6 of the State of Maharashtra's 48 MPs in a national parliament of 543 elected MPs. It is further estimated that, even though more than 40% of Maharashtra's population lives in urban centers, merely 25% of the Lok Sabha ("House of the People"— the lower house of India bicameral parliament) are from urban areas. This, in turn, creates further disincentive for the Maharashtra government to adopt pro-Mumbai policies at the expense of other statewide stakeholders. The result is that the State of Maharashtra, rather than the central government of Mumbai itself, has control over the governance and fiscal autonomy of Mumbai—one of the world's largest and densest megacities.

A similar institutional and political incentive structure produces underrepresentation of large urban centers elsewhere in India. Chennai's current population of 10 million has grown exponentially in recent years and now constitutes about 15% of Tamil Nadu's population. But Chennai is represented by merely 3 of Tamil Nadu's 39 MPs in the national parliament. Ahmedabad (population 8.5 million) accounts for approximately one-eighth of the state of Gujarat's population (70 million) but has merely 2 of the state's 26 seats (one-thirteenth). The list of underrepresented urban areas goes on and on. What is more, according to Articles 81 and 82 of the Indian Constitution (as amended by the

---

[51] According to a recent study, "the number of slums in Bangalore has grown from 159 in 1971 to over 2000 slums (notified and non-notified) in 2015. Those living in slums accounted for just over 10% of the city's population in 1971 and an estimated 25 to 35% in 2015." *See* "Survey-Based Socio-economic Data from Slums in Bangalore, India," *Scientific Data* (January 2018); online: https://www.nature.com/articles/sdata2017200.pdf.

[52] From 2014 to 2019, the governor of Maharashtra was Chennamaneni Vidyasagar Rao of the ruling BJP Party. As of September 2019, the governor is Bhagat Singh Koshyani, also of the BJP.

87th Amendment, 2003), apportionment of Lok Sabha seats within and among states is based on the 2001 census and is frozen until 2026 (de facto until after the national census in 2031), the year the country's population is expected to stabilize. By 2031, the population figures drawn upon to allot parliamentary seats to each state will be six decades old. While the 87th Amendment did allow for redistricting within states based on the 2001 population figures, state authorities are reluctant to do that for fear of political reprisal, all while the total number of seats assigned to each state may not be altered. Consequently, the massive urbanization trend in India over the last few decades is not reflected in either intra- or inter-state electoral seat allocation.

In short, while constitutionalization has certainly enhanced the status of local governments in India's multi-tiered federation, a confluence of constitutional and political factors, notably the political significance of states and their governors and the consequent constitutional deference to their interests, continue to hinder the successful implementation of urban empowerment in India. Consequently, in a country where some of the world's biggest cities are situated, and where one-fifth of global urban growth in the coming decades is projected to take place, there is little room within the constitutional federalism framework for the central government to engage directly with local government. Unlike in Japan, South Korea, or China, "in India, fear of the large city and the aggregation of municipal power are still regarded as potential threat to provincial leadership."[53] The adoption of the 74th Amendment has not accomplished much in altering this situation, as it left the urban agenda largely in the hands of subnational governments. The main exception is Delhi, India's largest city, which is granted a sui generis National Capital Territory (NCT) status.[54] Delhi is jointly administered by the Government of India and the Government of NCT Delhi through an elected Legislative Assembly and Council of Ministers headed by an appointed lieutenant governor (currently Anil Baijal, former home secretary of India). This joint governance structure has been a source of strain at times when the central government attempts to override policies adopted by the Delhi governing bodies.[55]

---

[53] K.C. Sivaramakrishnan, *Governance of Megacities: Fractured Thinking, Fragmented Setup* (Oxford University Press, 2015), 225.

[54] The 69th Amendment (1991) of the Constitution grants the National Capital of Delhi special status with its own democratically elected government and legislative assembly.

[55] Drawing on principles of representative democracy and state autonomy, the Supreme Court of India ruled in July 2018 that the NCT Council of Ministers for Delhi has the executive power to take action in all the fields in which the Delhi legislative assembly can pass laws (as per Article 239AA(3) of the Constitution, including the State list [barring land, police, and law and order] and the Concurrent List of the Seventh Schedule). The court further held that decisions of the NCT Council of Ministers are binding upon the lieutenant general, and that in case of disagreement, the LG cannot bring governance to a standstill. *See* Civil Appeal No. 2357/2017, *Government of NCT Delhi v. Union of India* (decision released July 4th, 2018); online (full judgment): https://sci.gov.in/supremecourt/2016/29357/29357_2016_Judgement_04-Jul-2018.pdf.

The federally driven constitutionalization of the urban development agenda in Brazil has been more active and more successful, although it too is tamed by vast socioeconomic inequalities and by the vagaries of national and intergovernmental politics in a large federal country. Brazil's urban expansion in the twentieth century is well documented; whereas in 1900, 10% of the country's population was urban, in 2000, the number was closer to 80%. One of the consequences of such rapid, nearly uncontrolled urbanization was the emergence of large urban *favelas*—informal settlements of mostly poor and disadvantaged populations. In the early 1980s, the harsh realities of Rio de Janeiro's slums became synonymous with "third world" (to use the terminology of that time) shantytowns; and, more generally, political disenfranchisement of the poor, urban neglect, and state incapacity in the developing world. Today, many of the economic and political challenges facing Brazil's megacities remain—notably in São Paulo (metro population 22 million) and Rio de Janeiro (metro population 14 million). Nonetheless, Brazil's 1985 transition to democracy and the ensuring aggressive campaign for a "right to the city" represent a positive counterpart to India's Amendments 73 and 74.

In 1986, a national constituent assembly was established, tasked with writing a new constitution in a socially progressive spirit, "daring and innovative without parallel in the constitutional history of Brazil and a rare occurrence even in comparative law."[56] Extensive popular input was sought via public hearings and public submissions of proposed provisions and amendments. Following a charged debate, the new federal constitution was adopted in 1988. It included Article 182, warranting that "urban development policy, carried out by the municipal public authority, according to the general guidelines fixed by law, is intended to order the full development of the social functions of cities and to guarantee the well-being of their inhabitants." In other words, an embryonic "right to the city" was born, the first of its kind in world constitutions. This constitutional provision alone has had significant effects on urban planning and zoning processes in Brazil.

According to Article 182.1, each city with at least 20,000 inhabitants—over 85% of Brazil's population live in cities that meet this criterion—must have a master plan approved by the city council as their basic tool for urban development and expansion policy.[57] Article 183 further states that "an individual who possesses as his own an urban area of up to two hundred and fifty square meters,

---

[56] J.G.L Coelho and A.C.N. Oliveira, *A nova Constituição—avaliação do texto e perfil dos constituintes* [The New Constitution: Evaluation of the Text and Profile of the Assembly Constituents] (Revan, 1989), 20.

[57] In 2015, the Federal Supreme Court ruled that municipalities may adopt specific, not hitherto discussed planning and zoning regulations, as long as those are compatible with the broader scope of an approved master plan.

for five years without interruption or opposition, using it as his or as his family's residence, shall acquire title over it, provided he does not own another property." In other words, "adverse possession" principles, aimed at preventing forced evacuations of long-term dwellers by land developers, were constitutionally recognized. Perhaps even more importantly, the inclusion of these two provisions in the new constitution signaled a transition to a new era wherein elements of urban governance and reform are federally protected against encroachment by sub-national governments, local authorities, or private sector actors.

The federal entry into the urban governance scene was complemented by the adoption of the City Statute in 2001 as well as the establishment of the Ministry of Cities and the National Cities Council in 2003. The City Statute—the first of its kind in Latin America—regulates the implementation of Articles 182 and 183, and explicitly acknowledges the right to a sustainable city in Brazil's large urban centers.[58] It prioritizes the collective good and "social function" of urban life and urban land (essentially meaning placing emphasis on due attention to improving the living conditions of Brazil's urban poor and to the notion that urban land should not sit vacantly when it can serve a useful public purpose). The City Statute further defines guidelines that must be observed by federal, state, and local governments to ensure a democratic civil society voice in city management. Created by President Luiz Inácio Lula da Silva upon his election in 2002, the federal Ministry of Cities (shut down by newly elected uber-conservative President Jair Bolsonaro in 2019) was aimed at further expanding the federal stake in urban affairs while offering solutions to unsuitable housing and infrastructure in Brazil's ever-expanding cities; its portfolio included responsibility for urban development policy and sectoral policies for housing, sanitation, and urban transportation. (It is estimated that in the 15 years of its existence prior to its recent termination, the Ministry of Cities was able to offer new housing solutions to 4 million families; however, the actual quality and reliability of these new solutions is contested.)[59] In 2004, Brazil became the first developing country to join the Cities Alliance—a significant international network for urban development, supported by the UN-Habitat, the World Bank, and the World Association of Major Metropolises.

As well-intended as these constitutional and legal initiatives might have been, the political reality in Brazil at both the federal and the intergovernmental levels

---

[58] *See* Edesio Fernandes, "The City Statute and the Legal-Urban Order"; and Jose Roberto Bassul, "City Statute: Building a Law," both *in The City Statute of Brazil: A Commentary* (Cities Alliance, National Secretariat for Urban Programmes & Brazil Ministry of Cities, 2010), 55–70, 71–91.

[59] Gregory Scruggs, "Ministry of Cities RIP: The Sad Story of Brazil's Great Urban Experiment," *The Guardian*, July 18, 2019. Scruggs suggests that whereas "[H]istorically, the federal government had left favela upgrading to state and city governments . . . during the ministry's flush years, Brasília got involved, too: it put 33.5bn reais into more than 3,500 favelas nationwide."

is such that the actual, on-the-ground effects of these reforms have been largely dependent on political alignment between federal, state, and megacity leaders. When such alignment exists, federal and state support for megacity projects is likely; conversely, when there is a change of power, there is a tendency to discontinue funding for urban development projects.[60] As noted earlier, one of the first actions of newly elected President Bolsonaro (on January 1, 2019, his first day in office) was to abolish the Ministry of Cities created by the Lula administration. In its early days, the Ministry of Cities, headed by Olívio Dutra—founding member of the Workers' Party and former Mayor of Porto Alegre—allowed urban reformers to present their progressive ideas to the Ministry.[61] The Ministry's redistributive policies and massive investment in alleviating living conditions in Brazil's poor urban neighborhoods did not mesh well with Bolsonaro's expressly conservative agenda. Refolded into the Ministry of Regional Development, the cities portfolio has been entrusted again to tight central government control with little representation for bottom-up voices or ideas.

From 2001 to 2005, and again from 2013 to 2017, the city of São Paulo, the largest metropolitan concentration in South America, was headed by a mayor from the Workers' Party (PT), the party that had led the federal government from 2002 to 2016. The strong ties between these mayors and the ruling party are clear. From 2001 to 2005, the Mayor was Marta Suplicy; and from 2013 to 2017, the mayor was Fernando Haddad, both of the PT. Suplicy went on to serve as senator as well as federal minister of tourism (2007–2008), and minister of culture (2012–2014), all under the PT government. Haddad was the minister of education in the PT-led federal government from 2005 to 2012, before his four-year term as mayor of São Paulo. He then returned to play a key role with the PT at the federal level. In 2018, the Workers' Party selected him as the vice-presidential candidate for the October 2018 elections and later elevated him to presidential candidate once the imprisoned Lula was banned from running. During those alignment years, federal funding for city development was generous. In 2013, in response to the Movimento Passe Livre demonstrations that advocated for free public transit in the city, the federal Ministry of Cities agreed to spend approximately $18 billion improving urban transport. However, with the impeachment of President Dilma Rousseff of the PT in 2016, that funding came to a halt.

Furthermore, the constitutional reform aimed at city empowerment has not done much to improve megacity representation at the federal level. Brazil's parliament is bicameral: the Senate (upper house) comprises 81 seats, with three senators from each of the 26 states as well as from the federal district. The result is that, akin to the US Senate, densely populated states (where Brazil's

[60] Clark and Moonen, *World Cities and Nation States*, 126.
[61] Scruggs, "Ministry of Cities RIP."

megacities are located) are chronically underrepresented. The State of São Paulo, for example, has approximately 45 million people, while the State of Roraima has approximately half a million inhabitants. Consequently, each senator from São Paulo represents approximately 15 million inhabitants, while each Roraima senator represents only about 170,000 inhabitants. The House of Representatives (lower house) is based on proportional representation. Here, too, megacities are patently underrepresented. Because the 1988 constitution requires that each state be represented in the lower house by a minimum of eight deputies and a maximum of 70, São Paulo—which in a truly proportional system would have between 60 and 90 times as many representatives as small states like Roraima, Acre, and Amapá—only has 8.75 times as many.[62] Put differently, a São Paulo voter's vote is worth about one-tenth of a voter in any of these three states.

In summary, in this second scenario of constitutional response to urbanization, central government's attempt to involve themselves in the urban development sphere in order to address often dire governance needs. However, results have been modest, owing to preexisting constitutional impediments alongside engrained patterns of politically motivated cooperation or resistance by subnational governments.

An important contrast within this group of constitutional responses to the challenge of the city is the post-apartheid Constitution of South Africa, enacted in 1996. As part of its distinct democratizing break away with the country's political and constitutional past, the new South African constitution was aimed at empowering local government while curbing provincial power. To that end, Article 40(1) holds that "government is constituted as national, provincial, and local spheres of government which are distinctive, interdependent and interrelated." Chapter 7 (sections 151–164) of the constitution further marks a fundamental shift away from the pre-1996 order.[63] It builds upon and operationalizes Article 40(1) as it endows municipalities with the ability to legislate and administer regulations in a number of areas (e.g., municipal planning, health services, public transport, trade), and, most importantly, the ability to raise funds in these areas, subject to some oversight by provincial and national governments. As the Constitutional Court (Justice Johann Kriegler) noted shortly after the new constitution came into effect: "The constitutional status of a local government is thus materially different to what it was when Parliament was supreme, when not only the powers but the very existence of local government depended entirely on superior legislatures. The institution of elected local government could then have

---

[62] *See* Gilberto Marcos et al., "The Supreme Federal Court of Brazil: Protecting Democracy and Centralized Power," *in* Nicholas Aroney and John Kincaid, eds., *Courts in Federal Countries: Federalist or Unitarist?* (University of Toronto Press, 2017), 103–134, 114.

[63] Robert Cameron, "The Upliftment of South African Local Government?" *Local Government Studies* 27 (2001): 97–118, 102.

been terminated at any time and its functions entrusted to administrators appointed by the central or provincial governments. That is no longer the position. Local governments have a place in the constitutional order, have to be established by the competent authority, and are entitled to certain powers, including the power to make by-laws and impose rates."[64]

Chapter 7 of the Constitution sets out three categories of municipalities, of which a "category A municipality" refers to major urban centers, currently governing the metropolitan areas of Johannesburg (metro population 10 million), Cape Town (4.5 million), and Durban (3.5 million), as well as the smaller urban areas of Bloemfontein and East London. The creation of such unified metropolitan governments, and by extension integrated urban space, was a direct response to the apartheid policy of excluding certain neighborhoods (notably Soweto in Johannesburg) from city boundaries and administration, thereby depriving these neighborhoods from representation, services or subsidies. Chapter 7 further provides that a municipality has the "right to govern, on its own initiative."[65] Section 156 of the Constitution provides three avenues for municipalities to exercise their power: executive authority, the right to administer, and the authority to make and administer bylaws. In addition, Section 156(5) enables municipalities to exercise any power incidental to the effective performance of their functions.[66] Municipalities' significant revenue raising functions are further entrenched in Section 229 of the Constitution, which confers the ability to impose rates on property and surcharges on fees for services as well as other taxes if authorized by national legislation. The Constitutional Court has referred to the municipal revenue raising power as an "original power," clarifying the fact that the imposition of rates and surcharges does not require enabling federal legislation.[67] Consequently, a decade after the adoption of the new constitution, South African municipalities were estimated to have raised more than three-quarters of their operating revenue through their own taxation functions.[68] Additionally, municipal governments are further entitled to an equitable share of the revenue

---

[64] *Fedsure Life Assurance Ltd & Others v. Greater Johannesburg Transitional Metropolitan Council & Others* 1999 (1) SA 374 (CC), 1998 (12) BCLR 1458 (CC), at para. 38.

[65] Section 151(3).

[66] What is meant by 'incidental' was elaborated by the Constitutional Court in *In re: DVB Behuising (Pty) Limited v. North West Provincial Government and Another* 2001 (1) SA 500 (CC), 2000 (4) BCLR 347 (CC). While this case dealt with provincial incidental powers, the Constitutional Court held that powers usually falling within the domain of the national government were intra vires the provincial government as they were "inextricably linked to the other provisions of the Proclamation." The same standard would very likely apply to municipal incidental powers.

[67] *City of Cape Town v. Robertson* 2005 (2) SA 323 (CC), 2005 (3) BCLR 199 (CC), at para. 56.

[68] National Treasury, *Local Government Budgets and Expenditure Review 2001/02–2007/08* (2006), Figure 2.5.

raised nationally to enable it to provide basic services and perform the functions allocated to them.[69]

The general consensus among observers of municipal affairs in South Africa is that the constitutional recognition of local government has been effective in allowing cities to provide improved services to their residents. This seems to hold true even when a major city (e.g., Cape Town) is governed by an opposition party (the Democratic Alliance).[70] This is not to say that the relations between major South African cities and the other orders of governments do not occasionally sour. However, unlike in India or Brazil, the constitutional order and the constitutional jurisprudence stemming from it successfully shield cities from the exclusive grip of federal or provincial governments. That shield has been reaffirmed in several landmark rulings of the South African Constitutional Court pertaining to intergovernmental disputes under the 1996 constitution.[71] In its ruling in *City of Johannesburg Metropolitan Municipality v. Gauteng Development Tribunal* (2010), to pick one example, the Constitutional Court ruled that cities have exclusive authority over municipal planning, including zoning and land use management, and that national or provincial powers may not be used in ways that usurp or subvert municipal planning powers. In another important ruling (*Maccsand v. City of Cape Town*) two years later, the Constitutional Court ruled that while intergovernmental cooperation is to be favored, a national competence may be limited by the exercise of a municipal competence.[72] Specifically, the court held that the granting of mineral mining rights by the national government cannot not circumvent municipal zoning decisions.

In other words, in contrast to the attempt at constitutional emancipation of cities in India where no real alteration of the political and constitutional power structure occurred, or to Brazil where bitter political divide has loomed

---

[69] A municipality's claim to an equitable share of national revenue was found to be justiciable in *Uthukela District Municipality & Others v. President of the Republic of South Africa & Others* 2002 (5) BCLR 479.

[70] *See, e.g.*, Robert Cameron, "Vertical Decentralisation and Urban Service Delivery in South Africa: Does Politics Matter?." *Development Policy Review* 32 (2014): 81–100.

[71] Johannesburg, for example, was involved in major litigation against the Gauteng Development Tribunal, a provincial body that has equivalent and parallel authority to the municipality to regulate land use. In a judgment that was affirmed by the Constitutional Court, the Supreme Court of Appeal declared two chapters of the *Development Facilitation Act 67 of 1995* unconstitutional as they encroached on the authority of municipalities to engage in 'municipal planning' as set out in Part B of Schedule 4. *See City of Johannesburg v Gauteng Development Tribunal* (335/08) [2009] ZASCA 106); confirmed by the Constitutional Court in *City of Johannesburg Metropolitan Municipality v Gauteng Development Tribunal and Others*, 2010 (6) SA 182 (CC). More recently, the city launched a legal challenge against the chairman of the National Building Review Board. In this case, the Constitutional Court confirmed the ruling of the High Court of South Africa, Gauteng Division that S. 9 of the *National Building Regulations and Building Standards Act*, which empowered the board to exercise appellate review powers over municipal decisions, was unconstitutional. *See City of Johannesburg Metropolitan Municipality v. Chairman of the National Building Review Board* 2018 (5) SA 1 (CC).

[72] *Maccsand (Pty) Ltd v. City of Cape Town and Others* 2012 (4) SA 181 (CC).

large over the city empowerment issue, the constitutionalization of city status in South Africa reflected a genuine breaking with the past. While large South African cities are still marred with daunting challenges, the constitutionally entrenched three-tier governance system allows urban centers a meaningful voice in addressing these issues.

III. Blatant Politics and the Constitutional (Dis)Empowerment of Megacities

Until 2014, the Constitution of Russia designated the country's two most populated cities, Moscow (population of approximately 13 million) and St. Petersburg (5.5 million) as cities of federal significance—a status that seems obvious given these cities' rich histories and huge political, economic, and cultural significance.[73] This constitutional designation allows Moscow and St. Petersburg to have their own governors, parliaments, constitutions (provided their provisions do not contradict the Federal Constitution), constitutional courts, and the authority to legislate in a host of policy areas. All other cities in Russia lack this status and must therefore bargain for power-sharing terms with their respective superior regional governments.

When the Russian Federation annexed the Republic of Crimea in March 2014 following a political crisis in Ukraine, the Crimean city of Sevastopol (population of approximately 400,000; the 12th largest city in Ukraine, and equivalent in population to the 50th largest city in Russia) became the third constitutionally designated city of federal significance. As of March 21, 2014, Article 65 of the Russian Constitution officially lists three cities—Moscow, St. Petersburg, and Sevastopol—as cities of federal significance. In other words, when political interests so warrant, cities may be awarded (or stripped of) constitutional status overnight.[74] Ukraine's response was quick. In 2016, the Ukrainian constitution was amended to designate Kyiv and Sevastopol as having special status and self-government powers, resembling those of oblasts and districts.[75]

---

[73] Constitution of Russian Federation 1993 (revised 2014), Art. 65.

[74] Political interests of various sorts may also apply in stripping cities of their special status, as indicated by the politics behind the establishment of Brasilia as the capital of Brazil (Rio de Janeiro was the capital until 1961); the establishment of Abuja as the capital of Nigeria (replaced Lagos as the capital in 1991); Astana ("our capital" in Kazakh) as the capital of Kazakhstan (Almati was the capital until 1998; Astana's name itself was changed on March 20, 2019, to Nur-Sultan in honor of Kazakhstan's long-serving president Nursultan Nazarbayev who stepped down on that day after nearly three decades in office); or Naypyidaw as the capital of Burma/Myanmar (replaced Yangon (Rangoon) as capital in 2006). See, e.g., Edward Schatz, "What Capital Cities Say about State and Nation Building," *Nationalism and Ethnic Politics* 9 (2003): 111–140.

[75] Constitution of Ukraine, 1996 (revised 2016), Art. 118, Art. 133, Art. 140.

Istanbul (metro population 15 million) is Turkey's main city, a bridge between the Near East and Europe, and a major economic and transportation hub for the entire region. Whereas the city's population accounts for 18% of Turkey's population, the city generates 37% of Turkey's GDP. Control of the city therefore carries significant political benefits, concrete and symbolic. For 25 years, from 1994 to 2019, the city's mayors represented the ruling AKP Party or its predecessor, the FP (the Virtue Party, Fazilet Partisi), beginning with the mayoral term of Recep Tayyip Erdoğan, now Turkey's strongman-president.[76] Then, in 2019, AKP candidate and former Prime Minister Mr. Binali Yıldırım lost the mayoral election by a slim margin to the main opposition party (CHP) candidate, Mr. Ekrem İmamoğlu. It was hardly surprising, after a quarter century of AKP control over the city, when President Erdoğan launched an appeal to the Supreme Election Council, the judicial composition of which his government administration affects.[77] Alleging "some electoral officials were not civil servants and some result papers had not been signed," Erdoğan sought annulment of the Istanbul mayoral election results.[78] The board granted Erdoğan his wish, declared the Istanbul election results void, and set a new election date for June 2019. Article 79 of the Turkish Constitution states that "[N]o appeal shall be made to any authority against the decisions of the Supreme Election Council." And so, election results were annulled and a new round was ordered. The majority of Istanbul's voters, however, refused to bow; in a defiant response to Erdoğan's warnings to his supporters that losing Istanbul would mean losing Turkey, they re-elected İmamoğlu as mayor. In his acceptance speech, İmamoğlu acknowledged the challenge of managing Istanbul's massive refugee population and the city's close to $5 billion debt amid political prosecution from the center, saying "[T]here will be trials, there will be litigation ... I know I won't sail in calm seas. But I'm here to face everything positively."[79] Good luck.

---

[76] The four Istanbul mayors during that period were Recep Tayyip Erdoğan (1994 to 1998); Ali Müfit Gürtuna (1998 to 2004); Kadir Topbaş (2004 to 2017); and Mevlüt Uysal (2017 to 2019).

[77] The Supreme Electoral Board, established in 1950, is a constitutional institution that is tasked with securing electoral integrity country-wide. Its decisions are binding and final without being subject to any judicial review. As Bertil Emrah Oder notes, "the government has extended the tenure of Supreme Electoral Board members to one year (till 2020 and 2023 respectively) before the municipal elections. This reinforces the perceptions of a political bias in the Board. Ignoring the principle of stability, the Constitutional Court has declared this strategic and hasty intervention into the institutional design of electoral monitoring as constitutional since the terms of members are not defined in the Constitution (E. 2019/14, K. 2019/16, 14 March 2019)." See Bertil Emrah Oder, "A Do-Over for Istanbul: Gripping Electoral Law and Democratic Resilience," Ferfassungsblog: On Matters Constitutional (May 27, 2019); online: https://verfassungsblog.de/a-do-over-for-istanbul-gripping-electoral-law-and-democratic-resilience/.

[78] "Turkey Election Re-Run Angers Victorious Opposition," BBC (May 7, 2019); online: https://www.bbc.com/news/world-europe-48177740.

[79] See Laura Pitel, "Istanbul's New Mayor Warns Erdogan against Curbing His Powers," Financial Times, June 28, 2019.

These examples bring us to the third scenario, in which political power holders drive constitutional empowerment (or disempowerment) of megacities as a matter of sheer political calculus and desire for concrete gain. When a strong political incentive presents itself—real or symbolic—to constitutionally empower a megacity, empowerment becomes likely, particularly in settings where the constitutional framework is legally amenable to change. And vice versa: in settings where megacities have lost constitutional power, this disempowerment has often worked in favor of major power holders' political interests. While such self-interested political maneuvering is often associated with "small town" politics, it commonly manifests itself in central governments' attitudes toward megacity emancipation.

Let us consider a few examples of politically-driven constitutional change in the status of some of the world's largest cities, namely Buenos Aires, Mexico City, Nairobi, Cairo, and Dhaka. Taken together, these diverse examples illustrate the significance of political interests in explaining shifts in national governments' willingness to bolster the constitutional status of cities.

Argentina is a federal democracy with a presidential system of government and a bicameral legislature. The federation consists of 23 provinces and Buenos Aires as an autonomous city (*Ciudad Autónoma*) within the federation.[80] Buenos Aires gained its special constitutional status as an autonomous city as part of the 1994 constitutional overhaul in Argentina.[81] Article 129 of the Argentine Constitution warrants that Buenos Aires shall have an autonomous system of government akin to that of the 23 provinces. Prior to this reform, Buenos Aires had been a federal district for 125 years. The 1994 reform rescinded the president of Argentina's prerogative to directly appoint the city's mayor, as had been the case since 1880, and allowed Buenos Aires to have its own legislative assembly. This empowering transformation in Buenos Aires's constitutional status, following over a century of stalemate, provides a textbook example of how the changing interests of political power holders may transform the constitutional status of megacities.

According to the Constitution of Argentina (Articles 121–123), provincial governments are important political and administrative entities. They adopt

---

[80] Martín Ardanaz, Marcelo Leiras, and Mariano Tommasi, "The Politics of Federalism in Argentina and Its Implications for Governance and Accountability," *World Development* 53 (2014): 26–45.
[81] The full version of Article 129 of the Argentine Constitution (1994) reads: "The City of Buenos Aires shall have an autonomous system of government, with its own legislative and jurisdictional powers, and a head of government who shall be elected directly by the people of the City. A law shall guarantee the interests of the National Government while the City of Buenos Aires is the capital of the Nation. Within the framework established in this article, the National Congress shall convene the inhabitants of the City of Buenos Aires so that, through the representatives that they elect for this purpose, they enact the organizational statute of the City's institutions."

their own constitutions and elect their own governors, legislatures, and provincial institutions without intervention by the federal government. They enjoy
authority over vital areas of public policy (e.g., education, health), and are also
in charge of executing national public policies such as social welfare programs.
These provincial prerogatives are complemented by the constitution's residual
power clause, according to which provinces reserve all powers not delegated to
the federal government. Gaining a constitutional status akin to that of a province was therefore a major institutional augmentation of Buenos Aires's political
stature within the Argentine federation.

From 1868 until 1993, there had been no change in the status of Buenos Aires
despite its metropolitan area being home to more than a third of Argentina's
population and accounting for over 60% of Argentina's GDP. How, then, did the
enhancement of the city's status come about? The city of Buenos Aires's constitutional empowerment was agreed upon as part of the 1993 Pact of Olivos between Carlos Menem of the neo-Peronist Justicialist Party (PJ) and president of
Argentina (1989–1999); and Raúl Alfonsín, the former president (1983–1989)
and leader of the opposition Radical Civic Union (UCR) Party.[82] The last years
of Alfonsín's term saw one of Argentina's major economic crises of the last half
century. Consequently, Menem won the 1989 elections by a landslide. His economic "convertibility plan" was endorsed by most voters, leading to his PJ's
success in the 1991 and 1993 midterm elections. Prior to the 1994 reform, the
presidential term of office was fixed at six years with no re-election option (reflecting the post-military junta era sentiment in Argentine politics). As the end
of his six-year term drew near, Menem sought a constitutional amendment that
would allow him to run for another term. In order to lift the constitutionally
entrenched six-year term limit through a constitutional amendment, Menem required a supermajority of two-thirds of both houses of the Argentine Congress—
an unlikely possibility given the composition of the upper house at that time.
A constitutional pact with the opposition UCR Party became Menem's best bet.
Secret meetings between Menem and Raúl Alfonsín ensued, resulting in a new
constitutional deal. Menem's main benefit was the UCR's agreement to support
a constitutional amendment that would allow for his re-election for a second,
four-year term. In return, the opposition gained enhanced representation in the
Senate and in judicial appointment processes. Even more importantly, however,
the capital city of Buenos Aires—a major anti-Peronist district—would become
an autonomous region apart from the province of Buenos Aires. It would have its
own political representation and elected mayor, effectively ensuring UCR control of the newly created autonomous region.

---

[82] The memorandum of understanding was signed in the official presidential residence, the Quinta
de Olivos, hence *Pact of Olivos*.

The new constitutional deal was approved by Congress in December 1993 and later by a constituent assembly, paving the way for Menem's re-election in the 1995 presidential election and en route for the constitutional empowerment of one of Latin America's major urban centers as an autonomous constitutional entity within the Argentine federation. Following the adoption of the Pact of Olivos, the Menem-led administration did everything in its power to delay the delegation of new powers to Buenos Aires.[83] Ultimately, however, it had to comply with Transitory Clause 15 of the 1994 national constitution, which required the election of the newly empowered Buenos Aires chief of government and constituent assembly.[84] In July 1996, the elections were finally held and saw the UCR Party candidate (Fernando de la Rúa) election as chief of government, and a landslide win in the constituent assembly elections for a coalition of parties that favored maximum autonomy to the city. The constitutional transformation in the status of Buenos Aires was completed with the proclamation of its new constitution in September 1996. As we shall see in Chapter 5, that empowerment later provided the institutional capacity for Buenos Aires to advance major environmental protection policy initiatives.

A more recent illustration of megacity constitutional empowerment driven by domestic politics is the transformation of Mexico City from a federal district to a full-fledged state. The city's estimated population in 2018 was 22 million, and it has been listed among the 10 most populous cities in the world for the last 40 years. Under the 1917 constitution, the capital city was set up as a creature of the national government. Until the recent change in its constitutional status, the city's official name was the Federal District (Distrito Federal), or as almost everyone called it, the "D. F."

The idea to return Mexico City to its residents by turning it into an independent state with constitutional status similar to that of all other sub-national governments of the Mexican confederation was raised occasionally throughout the twentieth century, but never gained real traction until the mid-1980s. Calls for local autonomy in Mexico City began to gain momentum following a devastating earthquake in 1985 and citywide disappointment over slow and unorganized federal and state relief efforts.[85] In 1987, the federal government responded to growing demands by granting the city a locally elected governing body with a narrow scope of legislative authority. A subsequent reform in 1996 gave the

---

[83] For a detailed discussion of the political context for, and aftermath of the change in the status of Buenos Aires, see Miguel de Luca et al., "Buenos Aires: The Evolution of Local Governance," in David J. Myers and Henry A. Dietz, eds., Capital City Politics in Latin America: Democratization and Empowerment (Lynne Rienner, 2002), 65–94.

[84] Id. at 86–88.

[85] Diego Rabasa, "Mexico City Is 'Crowdsourcing' a New Constitution. But Will It Change Anything?," The Guardian, June 2, 2016.

citizens of Mexico City the ability to elect their own executive head of government, a mayoral position that had previously been filled by presidential appointment.[86] In 2000, Andrés Manuel López Obrador (president of Mexico as of 2018) was elected mayor of Mexico City (the official title is Head of Government of the Federal District). During his term in office, López Obrador of the center-left party of the Democratic Revolution (Partido de la Revolución Democrática, PRD) gained national and international recognition as an activist, a visionary mayor (he was a runner-up in the 2004 international mayor of the year contest), and a keen advocate for city emancipation as a necessary tool to enhance democratic representation and to effectively fight poverty. The federal government was less impressed with Obrador's quest to emancipate Mexico City. Not only did the federal government seek to retain its budgetary control over the city as a federal district, but its right-wing populist leader, Vicente Fox of the National Action Party (Partido Acción Nacional, PAN), also viewed Obrador as a political threat to his administration, the mayor having skillfully built on his municipal leadership to become a prominent political figure on the national stage. Consequently, Obrador's call to free Mexico City of the federal grip failed to take off at the federal level.

López Obrador left the Mexico City mayoralty in late 2005 in order to run as the PRD candidate for the 2006 presidential elections. He lost that election by a slim margin of less than 250,000 votes to Felipe Calderón of the PAN. The ideological and political animosity continued between the PAN-led federal government under Calderón and the PRD-led Mexico City leadership of Mayor Marcelo Ebrard. In 2007, amid these tensions, Mayor Ebrard introduced legislation that decriminalized abortion in the district. Later, in 2009, he introduced another piece of progressive legislation that established gay marriage in the district. In a symbolic act of autonomy in 2007, Mexico City's municipal government supported a move by local activist groups to adopt a "Mexico City Charter for the Right to the City."[87] The Charter's drafting process included mass public consultations held at the city's central plaza (the Zócalo), a symbolic locus of Mexican statehood. Mayor Ebrard continuously emphasized the strategic value of the drafting process, so that "the city we dream can become reality." The drafting process concluded in 2009, yielding one of the most socially radical bills of rights ever drafted, in bold opposition to the national government's

---

[86] Viridiana Rios, "Mexico City Will Become a State," *Wilson Center: Mexico Institute* (last modified June 3, 2016); online: https://www.wilsoncenter.org/article/mexico-city-will-become-state.

[87] For a comprehensive review of the drafting process as well as the vision behind the Mexico City Charter for the Right to the City, and the Charter's provisions, *see* http://www.hic-gs.org/content/ Mexico_Charter_R2C_2010.pdf [July 2010]. For an academic account of the drafting process, *see* Ana María Sánchez Rodríguez, "The Right to the City in Mexico City," *in* Barbara Oomen, Martha F. Davis, and Michele Grigolo, eds., *Global Urban Justice: The Rise of Human Rights Cities* (Cambridge University Press, 2016), 220–236.

conservative, business-friendly worldview. In an attempt to create some international buzz around the city's quest for emancipation, the completed draft of the Mexico City Charter for the Right to the City, officially adopted in 2010, was presented at the Fifth World Urban Forum organized by the UN-Habitat in Rio de Janeiro. The mayor of Mexico City was present. Mexico's federal government did not join the celebration.

A breakthrough came following the 2012 presidential elections, won by Enrique Peña Nieto of the centrist-statist PRI (Partido Revolucionario Institucional)—the dominant political party in Mexico throughout much of the twentieth century. In December 2012, President Enrique Peña Nieto struck a deal with the PRI's two main rival political parties, PAN and PRD, to endorse the so-called Pacto por México (pact for Mexico). This pact involved a comprehensive series of energy, education, fiscal, and telecommunication reforms aimed at giving a major boost to Mexico's stagnant and crisis-laden economy, and at overcoming the gridlock in Mexican politics since the Ernesto Zedillo presidency (1994–2000).[88] The mayor of Mexico City, Miguel Ángel Mancera of the PRD, was among the prominent politicians with whom Peña Nieto bargained. In exchange for the mayor's support for the pact, and the PRD's support for it more generally, Peña Nieto agreed to back amendments to the Mexican Constitution that would turn Mexico City into the 32nd "federal entity"—basically on par with a state. And so, approximately a century after the Mexican Revolution and the adoption of the 1917 constitution, a national political pact that required Mexico City's support allowed the city to release itself from the federal state grip and its government to control a considerably larger part of its budget. As celebratory signs all over the city declared, "Adiós DF, Hola CDMX" (goodbye federal district [DF], welcome Mexico City, [*Ciudad de Mexico*, CDMX]).[89]

Mexico City's promised new status required two constitutional changes: an amendment to the national constitution assigning full state status to Mexico City and the adoption of a state constitution. To address the first requirement, Article 44 (originally designating Mexico City as a federal district) and Article 122 (defining the parameters of governance applicable to the federal district) of the national constitution were amended in 2016.[90] This officially allowed for a change in the status of Mexico City from a federal district to a state named Mexico City. The amended Article 122 states that Mexico City is an autonomous

[88] For an astute political analysis of the pact and its aims, *see* Andres Sada, "Explainer: What Is the Pacto por México?," *Americas Society/Council of the Americas* (March 11, 2013).

[89] *See* Gregory Scruggs, "The People Power behind Mexico City's New Constitution," *City Lab* (last modified February 3, 2017); online: https://www.citylab.com/equity/2017/02/the-people-power-behind-mexico-citys-new-constitution/515637/.

[90] On the history and process of amending the Mexican Constitution, *see* Mauro A. Rivera León, "Understanding Constitutional Amendments in Mexico: Perpetuum Mobile Constitution," *Mexican Law Review* 9 (2016): 3–27.

entity within the Mexican federation, with respect to "everything related to its domestic regime, and its political and administrative organization."[91] It further stipulates that "the government of Mexico City is responsible for its local powers, as established in the Mexico City Constitution," and defines the prerogatives of the newly established state's governing institutions in a way similarly to other Mexican states. Importantly, the amended Article 122 states that "Mexico City will adopt for its domestic regime a republican, representative, democratic, and laic form of governance. Mexico City public power shall be divided for its exercise into the legislative, executive, and judiciary. Two or more of these powers shall not be vested in a single person or corporation, nor the Legislative shall be vested in a single individual. Mexico City Constitution, according to its jurisdiction, shall establish norms and guarantees for the enjoyment and protection of human rights as provided by article 1 of this Constitution."[92]

President Peña Nieto announced the approval of these enabling amendments by saying, "[a] long-awaited wish has become a reality: Mexico City has been recognized as a state with genuine autonomy . . . [T]he amendment marks the culmination of a debate that began with the discussion of the Constitution of 1824 and has been present for nearly two centuries. During this period, new states have been incorporated until today, when Mexico City was finally acknowledged as a federal state."[93]

With the amended provisions of the national constitution in place, the stage was set for the adoption of a new state constitution for Mexico City. Mere days after the constitutional reform gained assent at the federal level, a unique, first-of-its-kind exercise of megacity constitution writing began. There were three major steps. First, a committee of legal experts, academics, and activists selected by Mayor Mancera produced a draft state constitution. The draft was then published widely in print and online, and extensive citizen response was sought in an open "crowdsourcing" exercise. Finally, a 100-member constitutional assembly comprising 60 members elected by city residents and 40 drawn from Congress (14), Senate (14), or appointed by the mayor (6) and the country's president (6) considered the popular input and negotiated the document's final version. Reflecting Mexico City's progressive spirit, the composition of the assembly was heavily criticized by left-leaning groups for the excessive inclusion of presidential appointees, and more generally for the overrepresentation of federal and party interests. Criticism notwithstanding, the constitution-making process

---

[91] The original text reads: "La Ciudad de México es una entidad federativa que goza de autonomía en todo lo concerniente a su régimen interior y a su organización política y administrativa."

[92] I am grateful to Luis Sanchez Soto for the translation of the original Spanish text into English.

[93] President Enrique Peña Nieto, "Mexico City's Political Reform is a triumph of dialogue, democracy and its inhabitants" (Official press release, January 29, 2016); online: https://www.gob.mx/presidencia/prensa/31782.

marched on. In its year-long deliberations, commenced in September 2016, the assembly held 21 plenary sessions, considered 544 suggestions by assembly members and 978 proposals by citizens, with an estimated direct participation of over 10,000 people.[94] The outcome, symbolically dubbed the "CDMX Carta Magna," officially came into effect in September 2018, despite not having been put to an approval referendum as initially recommended.

The elaborate constitution-making process produced a socially progressive and all-inclusive document that boosts the city's autonomy within Mexico's federal system and gives the mayor more power, all while devolving some decision-making to neighborhood-level elected councils. The document also includes provisions protecting LGBTQ+ rights, cultural diversity, education, green spaces, as well as a general "right to the city" along the lines discussed earlier in the book, with the hope of protecting vulnerable and marginalized populations from the forces of real estate speculation, police brutality, economic exclusion, and gentrification.[95] Alongside criticism of the drafting process as well as of the constitution falling short of committing to extensive social housing and collective property schemes, observers have noted that the process brought about unprecedented citizen engagement; city-based collective identity; and identification with core values of democracy, transparency, and self-government.

In summary, where there is a will, there is a way. For nearly a century, Mexico's federal government had no incentive to empower Mexico City. Similarly to the constitutional empowerment of Buenos Aires, however, a long stalemate in megacity status ended when a deal that included the emancipation of Mexico City appeared beneficial to Mexico's main political actors. In return for the city's support for a national political pact, the federal government agreed to change the city's constitutional status from a federal district to an autonomous state. A process of amending the national constitution and of writing a constitution for Mexico City was launched, and it implemented practices of democratic participation and representation in constitution making that is seldom seen at the international, national, or municipal level. Ultimately, one of the most progressive constitutions ever drafted emerged, following one of the most open and inclusive constitution-making processes ever conducted. Noble and idealistic as it all sounds, this enhancement to Mexico City's self-government power only became possible once a political constellation conducive to the change presented itself.

---

[94] Alejandra Reyes, "The Evolution of Local Government in Mexico City: Pursuing Autonomy in a Growing Region," *IMFG Perspectives* 25/2019, 12.

[95] For a comprehensive elaboration of the constitution-making process and the content of the new Mexico City Constitution, *see* "Political Constitution of Mexico City: Background and Fundamental Advances," *CDMX, Unit for Political Reform of Mexico City*; online at: Constitucion_CDMX_antecedentes_En.pdf.

In an interesting postscript, López Obrador became Mexico's president in 2018. Soon after taking office, the former mayor of Mexico City and champion of city autonomy initiated a six-year plan to move as many as 31 government agencies out of Mexico City, intending to decentralize government and spread civil service job opportunities across the country. In a 400-page plan published upon his election, López Obrador suggests that the country's "exacerbated centralism"—with "practically the entire federal government" and many major businesses concentrated in Mexico City—has led to overpopulation in the capital while smaller cities remain underdeveloped.[96]

In contrast with these city-empowering changes, political interests, either of a devolutionary, power-diffusing brand or of a blatant democracy-taming type, may drive revisions to megacity status in the opposite direction to what we see in Mexico City. One of the telling examples of taming city power in the name of devolution and democratic reforms is provided by the Constitution of Kenya (2010) and its impact on Nairobi—the largest city in Eastern Africa and one of the major metropolitan centers in the entire continent. Nairobi has a core city population of 4.4 million, and a metro area population of 9.5 million. Since Kenya acquired its independence in 1963, Nairobi has served as the country's capital, seat of national government, and center of economic and political power. Until 2010, it was governed as one of eight administrative territorial subdivisions of the national government, reflecting Kenya's centrally controlled quasi-federalism inherited in 1963 and maintained until the 2010 constitutional reform. Stark ethnically- and politically-driven regional disparities in development, infrastructure, services, and overall socioeconomic status existed between the relatively well-off Nairobi and the adjacent Central Province, and the left-behind North Eastern Province or the northwest of the Rift Valley Province. These regional gaps were sustained during the first four decades of Kenya's independence through an intricate patron-client system fostered during the presidencies of Jomo Kenyatta (1964–1978) and Daniel arap Moi (1978–2002).

In the early 2000s, political support for the traditional patronage system was undermined following shifting constellations of power at the center, accompanied by increasing opposition from Kenya's historically marginalized regions and ethnic groups. The hope for real change with the coming to power of the National Rainbow Coalition (led by Mwai Kibaki, member of the Kikuyu community, president of Kenya until 2013) quickly faded. The 2007 presidential elections shaped up as a showdown between statist-centrist elites and devolutionist challengers, highlighting Kenya's blatant ethno-regional inequalities. Political turmoil, at times violent, ensued both before and after the December

---

[96] See Simon Schatzberg, "'There's No Other Option': The Radical Plan to Move Mexico's Government," *The Guardian*, October 2, 2018.

2007 elections, as the Kibaki government either failed to effectively address the hot-button issue, or proactively sabotaged any serious attempt at decentralization (as the chief opposition, the Orange Democratic Coalition, led by presidential hopeful and devolution proponent Raila Amolo Odinga, claimed).[97] Following a close election, Kibaki was declared the winner. In early 2008, political protests against the Kibaki government (associated with Kikuyu) turned vicious. A humanitarian crisis developed. As anti-Kikuyu sentiments grew, the push for devolution through constitutional reform regained strength as a potential remedy to Kenya's stark inter-ethnic and inter-regional inequalities. Promoted by intense international mediation efforts, and ultimately accepted by most political factions, devolution eventually became the centerpiece of the new constitution, adopted in 2010, following a long and arduous drafting process.

The 2010 constitution abandoned the eight-province structure and adopted instead a new 47-county system. County boundaries correspond almost identically to those of the former districts comprising the eight provinces. However, in stark contrast with the eight-province structure, the new order grants the counties a significant degree of autonomy, as well as their own elected governors, in an attempt to reduce local government's traditional subjection to the clientelistic and ethnicity-based political economy. Article 10 of the new constitution identifies "sharing and devolution of power" as one of "the national values and principles of governance in this Article [that] bind all State organs, State officers, public officers." Article 174 lists the objects of devolution as including promotion of democratic and accountable exercise of power; recognition of diversity; provision of self-governance powers to the people; to "recognise the right of communities to manage their own affairs and to further their development," and "to facilitate the decentralisation of State organs, their functions and services, from the capital of Kenya." Importantly, Article 203 stipulates that in every fiscal year "the equitable share of the revenue raised nationally that is allocated to county governments shall be not less than fifteen per cent of all revenue collected by the national government." Article 204 further establishes an equalization fund (0.5% of annual national revenue) "to provide basic services including water, roads, health facilities and electricity to marginalised areas to the extent necessary to bring the quality of those services in those areas to the level generally enjoyed by the rest of the nation, so far as possible." Observers have described

---

[97] Observers of Kenyan constitutional politics suggest that Kibaki and his allies opposed decentralization both as a means to retain the centralized presidential system which they controlled, and also because they feared the effect of devolution on their Kikuyu coethnics living in areas where they would be outnumbered by other ethnic groups should devolution take place. I thank Karol Czuba for sharing his doctoral dissertation, "Microfoundations of State-Making: Extension of State Power in the Drylands of Ethiopia, Kenya, and Uganda" (2019), in which he makes that point (p. 85). *See also* Eric Kramon and Daniel N. Posner, "Kenya's New Constitution," *Journal of Democracy* 22 (2011): 89–103.

this constitutionally-enshrined devolution matrix as a critical turning point in the country's constitutional history and a "game changer in Kenya's politics of development."[98]

At the same time, Article 184 of the 2010 constitution gives the national government the power to define local government. The Urban Areas and Cities Act, 2011, translates Article 184 into guidelines for public life. It classifies urban areas and cities, lays out the structure of governance in these areas, and outlines responsibilities such as planning and delivery of services.[99] Importantly, it sets out a threshold of 500,000 residents for city designation, conferred by the president upon a Senate resolution.

The 2010 constitution recognizes Nairobi as one of the country's 47 counties—the Nairobi City-County, the smallest, yet most populous, of the counties. The devolution that attended this change of status is said to have strengthened, and indeed, given birth to, Nairobi's self-governing powers. The two elected governors of Nairobi County since devolution, Evans Kidero (2013–2017) and Mike Sonko (2017–present), have been powerful individuals who have openly challenged the once-dominant national government, despite both being affiliated with President Uhuru Kenyatta's political party (Kidero with the National Alliance, and Sonko with the ruling Jubilee Alliance umbrella party into which the National Alliance merged in 2016). Elected by Nairobians, they are also more representative of the city's diverse population than previous administrators and, to secure re-election, must attempt to accommodate their constituents' demands. Quite notably in a city long perceived as dominated by Kikuyu interests—but inhabited mostly by other ethnic groups, the largest of them the Luo—neither Kidero nor Sonko belongs to the Kikuyu ethnic group.

However, enhanced autonomy does not ensure effective governance. Because of Nairobi's designation as a county, statute dictates that it is to "be governed and managed in the same manner as a county government," meaning that the city does not have a city board or council. Meanwhile, the county assembly's sizable 123-member council—85 elected members alongside 38 nominated members—renders effective governance difficult. Nairobi's most significant woes in the new constitutional order are economic. Prior to devolution, as the seat of the national government and the preeminent economic center, Nairobi (alongside the neighboring highland counties) received the bulk of economic resources. This is no

---

[98] Karuti Kanyinga, "Devolution and the New Politics of Development in Kenya," *African Studies Review* 59 (2016): 155–167, 163; Ellen M. Bassett, "Urban Governance in a Devolved Kenya," in Carlos Nunes Silva, ed., *Governing Urban Africa* (Palgrave Macmillan, 2016), 73–98; Jeffrey Steeves, "Devolution in Kenya: Derailed Or On Track?," *Commonwealth & Comparative Politics* 53 (2015): 457–474. For a recent assessment of the devolution process, *see* James Thuo Gathii and Harrison Mbori Otieno, "Assessing Kenya's Cooperative Model of Devolution: A Situation-Specific Analysis," *Federal Law Review* 46 (2018): 595–613.
[99] Bassett, "Urban Governance in a Devolved Kenya," 84.

longer the case, with these resources having been redirected to other counties, most notably to Northern Kenya, once almost entirely neglected by the government. Nairobi's county government budget is the largest in the country, but the per-capita budget of Turkana—with approximately one-quarter of the capital's population—is considerably higher.[100] As well, the newly created Nairobi County assumed the debts of the city government.[101] Additionally, the county has to address challenges of extreme poverty, including failing or nonexistent infrastructure in some of the most impoverished and densest neighborhoods in the world, notably the Kibera slum, considered the largest urban slum in Africa. Public transit development plans and corresponding eviction orders clash with constitutionally guaranteed rights to housing, to land ownership and to fair hearings. Consequently, the Nairobi County government has struggled to provide the services that it is constitutionally mandated to deliver to the city's inhabitants.

Nairobi's continuing economic and political importance and the relative wealth of its population have moderated the impact of the redistribution of resources to some extent, but the capital, along with the neighboring Kikuyu highland counties, definitely have not benefited from devolution as much as most of the rest of Kenya.[102] In short, constitutional devolution reform aimed at strengthening the autonomy of local government vis-à-vis the central government has resulted in fortification of Kenya's historically disenfranchised hinterlands at the expense of the city of Nairobi. With the weakening of Nairobi's status as the locus of national government, there appears to have been a parallel weakening, or at least overlooking, of its status as Kenya's and East Africa's major urban center. That process has taken a considerable toll on the provision of municipal services in Nairobi. Ultimately, in early 2020 the national government

---

[100] Nairobi County has more than 4 million residents and a county budget (2017–2018 fiscal year) of 33 billion Kenyan shillings, or approximately 9,500 shillings per person per annum. That figure is lower if one takes into account informal estimates of the city's population at over 4.5 million. Turkana County, in the country's northwest corner, has 900,000 inhabitants (a quarter of Nairobi's population), and a county budget (2017–2018) of 11 billion Kenyan shillings (one-third of Nairobi's), or approximately 12,200 shillings per person per annum. The Elgeyo-Marakwet County (in the former Rift Valley Province), to pick another example, has 400,000 residents and a county budget (2017–2018) of 5 billion Kenyan shillings, or approximately 12,500 shillings per person per annum, approximately 30% higher than in Nairobi.

[101] Garth Myers, "A World-Class City-Region? Envisioning the Nairobi of 2030," *American Behavioral Scientist* 59 (2015): 328–346.

[102] Observers further suggest that the difficulties that Governors Kidero and Sonko have faced during their terms in office (Kidero failed to secure a second term as the county governor) could be attributed in part to their relative lack of resources. Internal Nairobi City County politics has been marred with bitter rivalries. Polycarp Igathe, elected deputy governor of Nairobi City County in 2017, to pick merely one example, resigned four months into his term citing lack of trust by Sonko as plans for decongesting and cleaning up parts of Nairobi were being contemplated. In December 2019, Sonko was arrested for a few days on corruption charges during his tenure as governor.

took over the capital city from the Nairobi County, and announced it would manage the city directly as a national government affair.[103]

In contrast with the democracy-enhancing decentralization attempt in Kenya and its effect on the status of Nairobi, the planned relocation of Egypt's capital and Dhaka's bifurcation saga provide telling illustrations of a democracy-taming impulse that drives deflation of megacity power. With a metro population of approximately 19 million people, Cairo is the largest city in the Middle East and a close second in Africa (after Lagos). It is home to about one-fifth of Egypt's population, and has served as symbolic center of Egyptian statehood for generations. Tahrir Square, a major public square in downtown Cairo, has been the location and focus of massive political demonstrations, most notably the massive popular protests that led to the January 2012 Egyptian revolution and the ousting of President Hosni Mubarak.

That uprising led to the rise to power of the hitherto banned Muslim Brotherhood and to the June 2012 election—what observers consider the first free elections in Egypt—of Mohamed Morsi (of the Freedom and Justice Party founded by the Muslim Brotherhood) as president. That radical change shifted control over the Egyptian state for the first time in Egypt's modern history away from the military-backed statist political establishment. As well, it strengthened the place of Islamic Shari'a in Egypt's constitutional and political order.[104] To that end, a new constitution was adopted in December 2012. As is well known, a counterrevolution, essentially a military coup d'état led by field marshal Abdel Fattah el-Sisi, and backed by the statist establishment, took place in June 2013. El-Sisi became president, Morsi was put in jail, and a new constitution restoring the pre-2012 order was adopted. Throughout these dramatic events, portrayed by observers as part of the so-called Arab spring, virtually all foreign media coverage centrally featured Cairo and Tahrir Square as a symbolic battle ground (much like Tiananmen Square in Beijing or the Zócalo in Mexico City) between the establishment and the people.

And then, out of the blue, and following nearly 1,000 years of Cairo serving as the capital of Egypt, the el-Sisi government announced its plan to relocate the

---

[103] To that end, President Uhuru Kenyatta created a new unit—the Nairobi Metropolitan Services (NMS)—to handle the takeover of some functions of Nairobi county. In March 2020, Major General Abdallah Mohammed Badi, a Kenya Airforce officer, has taken over the NMS, effectively handling the administration of Nairobi county on behalf of the national government.

[104] On the day of his election, Morsi wasted no time in announcing publicly in a speech in Tahrir Square (where else) that he would reform Egypt's Constitution to better reflect principles of Shari'a. The constitution introduced in December 2012 by President Morsi not only reproduced Article 2 (stating that principles of Islamic Shari'a are "the" source of legislation), but also introduced Article 219, which uses technical terms from the Islamic legal tradition to define what is actually meant by "the principles of the Islamic Shari'a" as stated in Article 2. That constitution also guaranteed (Article 4) that al-Ahzar would be consulted on matters of Islamic law; Article 11 stated that the state is to "protect ethics and morality and public order"; and Article 44 prohibited the defamation of prophets and religious messengers, such that it may be interpreted as prohibiting blasphemy.

locus of the government to a newly built administrative capital, about 30 miles (45 kilometers) away from Cairo. The official reason? Cairo's dilapidated infrastructure, overly crowded streets, chronic traffic jams, and overall image as an old, worn-out megacity with little appeal for international corporations. By contrast, the new, yet-to-be-named capital is to include an airport, a massive green space twice the size of New York's Central Park, an opera house, 20 Chinese-built skyscrapers (including the tallest skyscraper in Africa at 345 meters), 32 ministerial office blocs, and a diplomatic quarter with space for more than a hundred embassies.[105] In a message of tolerance amid Islamic extremism, the new capital also hosts Egypt's largest church (the brand new Cathedral of Nativity of the Coptic Church), located right beside one of the region's largest mosques. The development is touted by its creators as "the entrance to a new city, a new lifestyle, a new community, and a new worldwide center of attraction."[106]

And who is orchestrating and supervising the construction of this promised urban paradise? The Administrative Capital for Urban Development (ACUD)— a joint venture between the Egyptian Army (51%) and a government land development agency (49%) is in charge of the actual construction of the city, while the army is supervising the construction companies involved in the project. The costs of constructing this new capital are estimated to be in the tens of billions (a 2015 estimate suggested $40 billion), financed by the Ministry of Defence and a projected sale of soon-to-be vacated government buildings in Cairo.[107]

What could have possibly pushed the el-Sisi government to launch this mega project at the time it did? The failing-Cairo justification provided by government officials may well reflect an important part of the story. However, Cairo's urban problems had been brewing for decades prior to the capital relocation decision. The city's overpopulation, crowded streets, and dated infrastructure did not start in 2014, nor did these problems significantly worsen at that time. The army's deep involvement in the project, as well as the project's timing, immediately after the military's loss of power in the 2011–2013 period, suggest that there may be another factor at play: the army's quest to shield the government from large-scale civic protest in prominent public spaces; and to prevent repetition of the widely televised Tahrir Square-centered popular uprising that overthrew President Mubarak, another high-ranked military officer who became president.[108] "In the

---

[105] See Heba Saleh, "Egypt's President Sets Sights on Megacity to Rival Cairo," *Financial Times*, December 17, 2017.

[106] Ruth Michaelson, "'Cairo Has Started to Become Ugly': Why Egypt Is Building a New Capital City," *The Guardian*, May 8, 2018.

[107] Just to jump-start this megaproject, the government, through the Ministry of Defence, borrowed $12 billion from the International Monetary Fund. *See* Michaelson, *id.*

[108] It is widely believed that an extreme version of a similar "fear of the big city" impulse was a main driving force behind the Myanmar/Burma military rulers' 2005 decision to relocate that country's capital from the port city of Yangon (Rangoon)—the country's major city (7 million) and political nerve center—to the newly built Naypyidaw ("royal city" in Burmese), located some 200 miles

new capital," said former Brigadier General Khaled el-Husseiny Soliman, the international coordination manager of the aforementioned ACUD, "the army will be in command and control center and will manage and control the whole city via the center."[109] In another interview, he went on to suggest that "[T]he new capital will be a much more orderly city, where people and vehicles will be under constant surveillance . . . [I]t's a unique city, a modern city; it means cameras everywhere."[110] Enough said.

Article 222 of Egypt's 2014 Constitution states that "Cairo is the capital of the Arab Republic of Egypt." It also states that the House of Representatives and the Supreme Constitutional Court are to be headquartered in Cairo, although both are allowed to hold their sessions elsewhere in Egypt in "exceptional circumstances" or "in cases of emergency." Article 226 sets out the constitutional amendment rules. In essence, changes to the relevant constitutional articles must be approved by a two-thirds majority of the House of Representatives and gain majority support in a public referendum. Considering that el-Sisi was re-elected as president in March 2018 winning more than 97% of votes, none of these conditions must seem overly daunting from the government's point of view.

Let us also consider the Dhaka bifurcation saga—another telling illustration of an antidemocratic impulse that may stand behind change in megacity status. The Dhaka metro region in Bangladesh has approximately 19 million people and is one of the world's densest megacities, with approximately 45,000 people per square kilometer (116,550 per square mile). Its population is projected to reach over 50 million people before the end of the twenty-first century. Inequalities abound—approximately 40% of the city's population lives on 5% of the land, with density in Dhaka's slums estimated at seven times higher than in the rest of the city. The city is also at high risk of flooding due to a combination of unfavorable weather conditions, severe climate change impact, and a chronically dysfunctional sewage system. The bitter political war between the two major parties in Bangladesh—the socialist-secularist Awami League and the Bangladesh Nationalist Party (BNP)—has turned the governance of Dhaka into a key battlefield for national politics.

inland. See Daniel Gomà, "Naypyidaw vs. Yangon: The Reasons Behind the Junta's Decision to Move the Burmese Capital," in Lowell Dittmer, ed., Burma Or Myanmar? The Struggle for National Identity (World Scientific Publishing, 2010), 185–204; Alan Sipress, "As Scrutiny Grows, Burma Moves Its Capital," Washington Post, December 28, 2005; David Logan, "Myanmar's Phantom Capital: Why Did Myanmar's Generals Build a New Capital in the Middle of Nowhere?," The Globalist, September 28, 2013.

[109] Cited in Rachel Elbaum, "Egypt Builds a New Capital City to Replace Cairo," NBC News, August 10, 2018.
[110] Cited in Jane Arraf, "Egypt Builds a New Capital City," NPR News, August 1, 2018.

With a population of 160 million, Bangladesh is the eighth most populous country in the world. The country gained its independence in 1972 following a vicious independence war fought against Pakistan (prior to gaining its independence, Bangladesh was named East Pakistan). With the exception of a military regime (1982–1990) and a national caretaking government from 2006 to 2008, either the Awami League or the BNP have led Bangladesh government since independence. Prior to the military coup of 1982, Bangladesh was governed by Mujibur Rahman (founding father of Bangladesh and founder of the Awami League) from 1972 to 1975, and later by Ziaur Rahman (founder of the BNP) from 1975 to 1981. Upon the end of the military regime in 1990, the BNP was in national power from 1991 to 1996 and from 2001 to 2006, led by Khaleda Zia (widow of Ziaur Rahman). The Awami League, led by the forceful Sheikh Hasina Wazed, daughter of Mujibur Rahman, has been in power from 1996 to 2001, from 2009 to 2014, and from 2014 to the present. In February 2018, Khaleda Zia, now leader of the opposition BNP, was convicted for corruption and sentenced to a lengthy prison time, allowing Prime Minister Sheikh Hasina Wazed and the Awami League to weaken their main political nemesis. Consequently, in the most recent national elections held in December 2018, Awami League garnered 288 seats of the country's 300-seat parliament. In short, for a near half century, Bangladesh politics has been completely overshadowed by a vicious duel between two dynasties, each following a modern-day version of an "I am the state" approach.

Back to megacity governance. In an unprecedented move in the region, the Awami League-led government announced in 2011 that the Dhaka City Corporation (DCC)—Dhaka's governing body—would be split into the Dhaka North City Corporation (DNCC, 36 wards) and the Dhaka South City Corporation (DSCC, 56 wards). Citing the inefficiency and incompetency of the DCC, the government promoted the division as a move toward modernization and as necessary to improve service provision in a megacity in need of major reforms.[111] What the government did not say—but every observer of Bangladeshi politics knew—is that taking control of the DCC and ousting the mayor of Dhaka, Sadeque Hossain Khoka (2002 to 2011), a leading politician in the BNP, was the real motivation behind the move. Once it emerged victorious in the national election in late 2008, the Awami League government made a concerted effort to prevent the Dhaka mayoral elections from taking place, advancing a host of administrative reasons not to hold the elections. Eventually, the government introduced the bifurcation plan on November 23, 2011. It was hastily approved by the Awami League-controlled parliament five days later

---

[111] See "Splitting Dhaka: Model or Mistake," *Future Challenges* (February 27, 2012); online: https://futurechallenges.org/local/searchlight/splitting-dhaka-model-or-mistake/).

(reports in local media suggest the parliamentary debate on the Dhaka split bill lasted nine minutes), and the split of one of the world's largest megacities came into force on December 1, 2011. Upon approval of the abolition of the DCC and the split of Dhaka into DNCC and DSCC, the government moved on to appoint administrators to lead the new entities, while the mayor and councilors (of the BNP) were pushed out of office.

For the first four years of their existence, both the DNCC and the DSCC were staffed by nominated Awami League supporters. (The BNP boycotted the 2014 national elections and has not been officially represented in parliament since). In the first elections for the DNCC and DSCC held in 2015, Annisul Huq—a successful entrepreneur and TV host endorsed by Awami League—won the DNCC leadership, while Sayeed Khokon of the Awami League and son of Dhaka's first mayor, Mohammad Hanif (1994–2002), assumed the leadership of the DSCC. Annisul Huq died in 2017, leaving the DNCC vacant until the 2019 election of Atiqul Islam, another businessman backed by the Awami League. A year later, Khokon was replaced as mayor of South Dhaka by Sheikh Fazle Noor Taposh—an Awami League member of parliament.

The real utility of the sudden split has been questioned repeatedly by scholars and observers.[112] As expected, the BNP has vehemently condemned it. A one-day citywide shutdown was declared to protest the split. Because the Constitution of Bangladesh designates Dhaka as the country's capital, there were calls for a referendum on the city split. Ousted Mayor Khoka attempted to challenge the constitutionality of the bifurcation before the Bangladesh High Court, as did other BNP supporters prior to the elections for the two newly created entities. The High Court rejected all petitions, citing orderly passing of the Local Government (City Corporation) Amendment Act of 2011, under which DCC was bifurcated into two city corporations. And so the Awami League-led government's objective of splitting Dhaka for partisan purposes was fulfilled. The BNP Mayor of Dhaka was forced to depart, and the ruling party was able to bring Dhaka—Bangladesh's most significant political setting, now transformed into Dhaka North and Dhaka South—under its control. Meanwhile, the actual management of Dhaka—the official reason for the divide—is getting worse. Several years after the bifurcation plan took place, the Economist Intelligence Unit declared Dhaka the fourth-least livable city as of 2017, one spot below Port Moresby (Papua New Guinea) and just ahead of Tripoli (Libya), Lagos (Nigeria), and war-torn Damascus (Syria). But despite such appalling results, the split was a success from the perspective of the government, who viewed it simply as a means of accomplishing the political conquest of Dhaka.

---

[112] *See* Patricia Barta and Syed Zain Al-Mahmood, "Dhaka's Partition Seen Making Matters Worse," *Wall Street Journal*, October 14, 2013.

Conclusion

In stark contrast to most other areas of constitutional law, much of the innovative constitutional thinking concerning megacity governance emanates from the new world of constitutionalism, in particular from Asia, Latin America, and parts of Africa. While most leading political theory and social science accounts of cities and urbanization have been written by scholars from and of the Global North, when it comes to actual constitutional innovation in those areas, it is the world beyond Europe and North America that has taken the lead. Such fresh thinking may be a part of national constitutional transformation (e.g., Brazil, South Africa) or driven by various central planning factors, intergovernmental considerations, blatant politics, or by a combination of these factors.

What explains the fact that constitutional innovation in this area is more likely to emanate from the new world? One obvious factor is necessity. As indicated in earlier chapters, much of the extensive urbanization of the last few decades has taken place outside North America and Europe. As we have seen, approximately 88% of the 3.2 billion increase in the world's urban population growth between 1960 and 2018 has taken place in Asia, Africa, and Latin America, compared to only 12% in Europe and North America. This trend is bound to intensify in the coming decades. While this may seem unintuitive for comparative constitutionalists who are newcomers to the world of megacities, it is hardly surprising that serious thought has been devoted to the urbanization challenge in regions and polities that are bound to carry the brunt of it. In such settings, pressure to address the megacity challenge may come from various sources: central governments concerned with their polity's future, megacity leaders operating under mounting pressures to deliver reasonable quality public goods to already oversubscribed and ever-more populous urban centers, or civil society groups and international NGOs determined to improve living conditions and opportunities in some of the world's poorest metropolises.

Two other plausible factors are constitutional flexibility and political incentives. Unlike in the old world of constitutionalism, where constitutional structures and traditions are essentially carved in stone, the constitutional scene outside of Europe, North America, and Australia may be more susceptible to change, either due to its relative newness (as say in Brazil or South Africa), recent overhauls (as in Kenya), or the constitutional order's unfiltered reflection of political control (as in China). In such settings, it may be easier for pertinent stakeholders to willingly and effectively engage in constitutional change concerning major challenges such as extensive urbanization, environmental protection, or socioeconomic inequality. When seen through that prism, it is unsurprising that novel, at times even revolutionary, thinking with respect to massive urban agglomeration and the "right to the city" emanates from Asia, Latin America, and Africa.

And, as often is the case, the political context and incentive structure within which constitutional change takes place explains much of its timing, scope, and content. As we have seen, none of the various constitutional megacity transformations discussed here may be explained without close attention to the surrounding political environment and the changing incentives of power holders, which often serve as driving forces. This political dimension is obvious in the cases of Buenos Aires, Mexico City, Cairo, and Dhaka, but extends to explain various aspects of megacity emancipation or restraint in virtually all settings explored in this chapter. Armed with these insights, we may reflect back upon the discussion in the previous chapter examining constitutional stalemate in megacity governance in the constitutional old world. In that part of the constitutional universe, urban agglomeration is extensive but does not pose an existential threat to the power holders; pertinent constitutional frameworks are difficult to change; and, above all, political incentives to empower megacities rarely present themselves. Without some confluence of these factors in favor of city emancipation, such a radical constitutional change is unlikely to take place.

4

Attempts at City Self-Empowerment

The stark gap between city centrality and the virtual constitutional silence on urban power pushes ambitious cities and city leaders to advance notions such as international city networks, human rights cities, and environmentally friendly cities, or to adopt "right to the city" charters. In this chapter, I address such attempts by constitutionally voiceless cities and mayors to advance their agendas and causes by looking beyond the statist constitutional order, either through the advancement of "urban citizenship" schemes—often in the form of residency-based certificates or identification cards that allow their holders to access essential city services, or, more frequently, through international networking and collaboration based on notions such as "the right to the city," "sustainable cities," "solidarity cities," and "human rights cities." For the most part, such initiatives have a socially progressive undercurrent to them, addressing policy areas such as air quality and energy efficient construction, affordable housing and alleviation of poverty, enhanced community representation, or accommodating policies toward refugees and asylum seekers. Such intercity pooling and cooperation may prove particularly effective in policy areas *not directly addressed or hermetically foreclosed by statist constitutional law* (notably, environmental protection). It may also positively affect the daily lives of undocumented migrants who must rely on services provided by the city in lieu of state-provided ones.

These transnational city networks do not amount to anything close to Murray Bookchin's radical ideas (discussed in Chapter 1) about a transnational confederation of cities as an anti-statist, revolutionary force that would strive to dethrone and triumph over the state. Nonetheless, they doubtlessly represent a step in the direction of Benjamin Barber's call to convene a global parliament of mayors that would foster intercity learning and facilitate effective problem solving in policy areas that cities, rather than states, may be better situated to address.[1] What is more, due to the inherently statist outlook of constitutional orders and the predominant lack of city standing, such international city networking initiatives may raise awareness of the urban agenda at the national or international levels.

---

[1] Benjamin R. Barber, *If Mayors Ruled the World: Dysfunctional Nations, Rising Cities* (Yale University Press, 2013). For a radical view of municipal confederalism as an alternative to the state, *see* Murray Bookchin, *Urbanization without Cities: The Rise and Decline of Citizenship* (Black Rose Books, 1992).

City, State. Ran Hirschl, Oxford University Press (2020). © Ran Hirschl.
DOI: 10.1093/oso/9780190922771.001.0001

At the same time, the actual *constitutional* bite of such international inter-city consortia is limited in a state-dominated constitutional universe. With few exceptions, these proposals live *beside* the formal constitutional or international law frameworks that govern national jurisdictions, rather than existing as a part within these frameworks. As such, these networks are unlikely to help urban centers to effectively pursue policies that are *consistently at odds* with the ends of their national governments, or with the order of authority established by the constitutional frameworks within which they operate. For similar reasons, urban citizenship initiatives may positively affect the daily lives of undocumented immigrants living in the metropolis, but they remain rather toothless when it comes to constitutional institutions, litigation, and jurisprudence. Furthermore, while they challenge the largely uncontested "seeing like state" underpinnings of contemporary political membership regimes, they seem to offer little response to the nonexistence of cities qua order of government in constitutions, and in constitutional thought more generally.

I. International City Networks

Environmental protection is not only an area of increasing significance but also of extensive city activism.[2] Cities enjoy two key strategic advantages here. First, as environmental protection is a relatively new regulatory area that has only gained public awareness over the last few decades, most national constitutional orders remain silent on the matter, thereby allowing cities to carve out a regulatory niche for themselves with respect to environmental protection. Second, policy areas that often fall within ordinary municipal regulatory jurisdiction (e.g., water supply, waste management and recycling, intra-city traffic control, noise levels, parks and recreation, neighborhood zoning, and construction permits) have significant environmental protection potential. The conjunction of these strategic advantages has allowed cities to take the lead in implementing environmentally friendly policies, from creating bus and bicycle lanes to developing green spaces and insisting on energy efficient buildings. Some cities (e.g., Copenhagen) have implemented radical measures (e.g., banning diesel engines, incinerating garbage to generate heat and electricity) aimed at making them completely carbon-neutral within the foreseeable future.[3] More often than not, such measures are

---

[2] *See, e.g.*, Katrina Wyman and Danielle Spiegel-Feld, "The Urban Environmental Renaissance," Public Law Research Paper No. 19-08, NYU School of Law, 2019, *California Law Review* (forthcoming); Jolene Lin, *Governing Climate Change: Global Cities and Transnational Lawmaking* (Cambridge University Press, 2018); and Sara Hughes, Eric Chu, and Susan Mason, eds., *Climate Change in Cities: Innovations in Multilevel Governance* (Springer, 2018).

[3] *See, e.g.*, Derek Robertson, "Inside Copenhagen's Race to Be the First Carbon-Neutral City," *The Guardian*, October 11, 2019.

not met with enthusiasm by central governments, particularly when city politics and national politics are controlled by opposing political parties.

Certain aspects of environmental protection have become major areas of international intercity collaboration. Prime examples are the C40 Climate Leadership Group, ICLEI—Local Governments for Sustainability, the World Mayors Council on Climate Change, Climate Alliance and Energy-Cities. The C40 network was created and led by cities since 2005 and aims to connect more than 90 of the world's largest urban centers, representing over 600 million people and one-quarter of the global GDP.[4] Its focus is on "tackling climate change and driving urban action that reduces greenhouse gas emissions and climate risks, while increasing the health, wellbeing and economic opportunities of urban citizens." Importantly, each member city is required to have a plan of its contribution toward the goal of constraining global temperature rise to no more than 1.5 degrees Celsius above preindustrial levels. ICLEI, which includes over 1,500 cities from 124 countries, was founded in 1990 by the UN. It focuses on environmental and sustainability action plans to lower emissions, increase the use of recyclable resources, make cities resilient to climate change by strengthening vulnerable neighborhoods, and on building inclusive and safe communities. The World Mayors Council on Climate Change was founded in 2005 following the implementation of the Kyoto protocol to serve as "an alliance of committed local government leaders concerned about climate change." To that end, it promotes the Global Cities Covenant on Climate, which supports action plans for emission reduction, and encourages cities to report on greenhouse gas reduction to a carbon cities climate registry.

Climate Alliance and Energy-Cities—both founded in 1999—bring together thousands of municipalities in Europe to fight climate change. The Energy-Cities network strives to influence EU policies on energy, environmental protection, and urban policy by publishing position papers to lobby the EU and the European Energy Union and by initiating energy reduction pilot projects. Cities Alliance is composed of some of the major local government networks discussed here (e.g., C40, ICLEI, Metropolis, UCLG), 12 national governments (e.g., Brazil, South Africa, the United States, UK, Germany, France), private foundations (e.g., the Ford Foundation), NGOs (e.g., Habitat for Humanity), universities (e.g., NYU), and multilateral organizations (e.g., UN-Habitat, the World Bank, and the UNCDF—the UN Capital Development Fund). Each member municipality in the Climate Alliance must pass a resolution committing itself to cutting CO2 emissions by 10% every five years. The network also fosters partnerships with Indigenous peoples in the Amazonian region as a means of

[4] *See* https://www.c40.org/cities; Jolene Lin, *Governing Climate Change*, ch. 5, "Transnational Urban Climate Governance via Networks: The Case of C40."

guarding its massive rainforest. Every alliance member has also made a pledge to abstain from using tropical woods from unsustainable sources and to use Forest Stewardship Council-certified timber in public procurement. Additionally, the alliance pushes for better funding for climate policy in the EU and internationally, houses working groups on climate change, and conducts projects such as the creation of a Germany-wide database of cycling traffic and a campaign to raise awareness among cities about the environmental impact of their financial investments.

International city networks for environmental governance were also very visible at the UN Climate Change Conference in Bonn, Germany (November 2017), held to mark the second anniversary of the Paris Climate Agreement. In light of the Trump administration's decision to withdraw from that agreement, the call by American urban leaders, notably Michael Bloomberg (former mayor of New York City) to have a seat at the table was significant. Presenting a universalist outlook, California Governor Jerry Brown noted that "the fires are burning in California [and] [t]hey'll be burning in France, burning all around the world" if countries fail to reduce emissions.[5] A few weeks later (December 2017), over 50 mayors from around the world (including mayors of Mexico City, Paris, Vancouver, and Chicago) gathered at the North American Climate Summit in Chicago and signed the Chicago Climate Charter, a pioneering international charter on climate change that seeks to allow cities to commit to the Paris Climate Agreement. It engages with the agreement directly and commits its signatory parties to achieve, in their respective cities, "a percent reduction in greenhouse gas emissions equal to or greater than our nations' Nationally Determined Contributions to the Paris Agreement."[6] At the C40 World Mayors Summit in Copenhagen (October 2019), mayors of more than 90 of the world's biggest cities gathered together to voice support for a "Global Green New Deal"; at that occasion, Los Angeles Mayor Eric Garcetti, who rallied US mayors to commit to the Paris Climate Agreement after Trump announced in 2017 his intention to withdraw the country, said he would ask the UN secretary general, António Guterres, to give American cities a new role in UN climate talks.[7]

"City resilience" has been a major theme of international city networking initiatives. CityNet, which was founded in 1987 and brings together 135 municipality members, aims to facilitate connections between cities and other actors in order to "establish sustainable and resilient cities in the Asia Pacific Region." Its activities are supported by the UNDP, UN-Habitat, and UNESCAP. In 2013,

[5] "Jerry Brown to Trump: 'Get Out of the Way,'" *ABC News*, December 12, 2017.
[6] For a full version of the charter and list of its signatory parties, *see* "North American Climate Summit"; online: https://northamericanclimatesummit.splashthat.com/.
[7] Richard Orange, "US Mayors Seek to Bypass Trump with Direct Role at UN Climate Talks," *The Guardian*, October 10, 2019.

the Rockefeller Foundation similarly created the 100 Resilient Cities network "to help cities worldwide build resilience to the growing social, economic, and physical challenges of the 21st century." To that end, the network has committed itself to hiring a chief resilience officer and creating a city resilience strategy for each member city; to building an urban resilience marketplace with a network of industry leaders, private and nonprofit; to "train[ing] municipal leaders to be resilience champions"; and to influencing global leaders and policy makers toward funding and building resilient cities. The network draws on external research, internal monitoring, and reporting from cities to monitor progress. Among its members are many of the world's megacities, including Buenos Aires, Los Angeles, London, Seoul, Rio de Janeiro, Lagos, Jakarta, and New York.

Another important policy area addressed by international city and mayor networks is human rights and social inclusion. For example, Climate Alliance advocates before international organizations, funds local and national government projects addressing rapid urbanization in the Global South, and holds major conferences on the problems of development and poverty eradication in cities. One of Cities Alliance's major programs is the Cities without Slums Action Plan, which Nelson Mandela launched in 1999. It sets to significantly improve the lives of over 100 million slum dwellers worldwide by 2020. The plan was endorsed by 150 heads of state at the UN Millennium Summit in 2000. In 2004, UNESCO founded the International Coalition of Inclusive and Sustainable Cities (ICCAR) to "promote and reinforce anti-discrimination policies in cities, fight racism, discrimination, xenophobia and exclusion." Each of the network's regional coalitions (e.g., Africa, Europe, Asia and the Pacific, Latin America and the Caribbean, United States, and Canada) has a 10-point action plan. The points vary among regions, but cover areas such as housing, equal opportunity employment, immigrant integration, tolerance education, and reducing disparities in sentencing of minority groups. The Integrating Cities network was founded in 2010 in London to "provide equal opportunity for all residents, to integrate migrants, and to embrace the diversity of their populations that is a reality in cities across Europe." It includes 33 European cities and has recently added Toronto as its first non-European member. Signatories to the Integrating Cities Charter agree to actively communicate their commitment to equal opportunity, ensure equal access and non-discrimination, and facilitate engagement from migrant communities. Meanwhile, a dense web of smaller scale intercity policy coordination has formed through organizations such as Eurocities, which brings together the local governments of over 130 of Europe's largest cities and 40 partner cities, collectively governing 130 million citizens across 35 countries. Eurocities addresses urban challenges in Europe, most notably concerning multiculturalism, immigration, and the refugee and asylum crisis European cities have been facing over the last few years.

Other major city networks aim to go beyond policy-specific projects to pro-mote a common voice for cities worldwide. The World Organization of United Cities and Local Governments (UCLG), founded in 2004, brings together many preexisting local and regional government associations with an aim "to represent and defend the interests of local government on the world stage." To advance that cause, the UCLG has a strategic partnership with the EU, as well as a cooperation agreement with the UN-Habitat, and lobbies for a formal advisory role for local governments within the UN. This network of networks has over 240,000 city and town members around the world, as well as over 175 regional government asso-ciations. The UCLG Committee on Social Inclusion, Participatory Democracy and Human Rights, founded in 2005, articulates and advances a common voice for the global municipal movement in these areas. It aspires to engage in advo-cacy and city-to-city learning projects concerning spatial justice, participation in urban life, social cohesion, anti-discrimination, and promotion of historical memory. Metropolis, the World Association of the Major Metropolises—now the metropolitan section of the UCLG—was established in 1985 and has a cur-rent membership of 137 of the world's largest metropolitan areas. It engages in sustainability knowledge sharing and represents metropolitan governments be-fore international organizations such as the UN, the World Health Organization, and the World Bank.

Some of these local government networks have been influential in global gov-ernance. ICLEI was instrumental in pushing the UN's Agenda 21 action plan for environmental protection at the 1992 Rio de Janeiro Earth Summit.[8] UCLG signed an agreement of cooperation with UN-Habitat and formed a strategic partnership with the EU.[9] Mayors for Peace has jointly presented with the UN Parliamentarians for Nuclear Non-Proliferation at the UN General Assembly.[10] Local government networks were also crucial in shaping the New Urban Agenda, the Habitat II summit, and the Paris Agreement on climate change.[11] Furthermore, city networks have been recognized at global climate negoti-ations since 2010 with the implementation of the United Nations Framework Convention on Climate Change Conference of Parties.[12]

---

[8] Michele Acuto, "City Leadership in Global Governance," *Global Governance* 19 (2013): 481–498.

[9] United Cities and Local Government, "Advocacy and Partnerships" (2018); online: UCLG https://www.uclg.org/en/action/international-agenda.

[10] Chadwick F. Alger, "Expanding Governmental Diversity in Global Governance: Parliamentarians of States and Local Governments," *Global Governance* 16 (2010): 59–79.

[11] Alaina J. Harkness et al., "Leading Beyond Limits: Mayoral Powers in the Age of New Localism" (Brookings Institute, Centennial Scholar Initiative, 2017); online: https://www.brookings.edu/re-search/leading-beyond-limits-mayoral-powers-in-the-age-of-new-localism/.

[12] Sharon Dawes and Mohammed A. Gharawi, "Transnational Public Sector Knowledge Networks: A Comparative Study of Contextual Distances," *Government Information Quarterly* 35 (2018): 184–194.

This web of international city and mayor networks is ever-expanding. As a recent report by the Brookings Institute observes: "[M]ayors are flexing their muscle on the global stage, generating coordinated action on issues like climate change where many national governments are falling behind, and pushing for more formal recognition in an international system that remains organized around the nation state."[13] Consequently, international city networks involve some of the world's most visionary thinking about challenges facing cities in general, and megacities in particular. Virtually all relevant UN agencies, many of the world's major cities, as well as some of the world's most prominent representatives of the urban voice on environmental protection, resource and energy conservation, sustainability, resilience, human rights, social inclusion, and eradication of poverty, have come together to advance a progressive agenda on these and other related matters. Scholarly accounts confirm that such networks facilitate knowledge exchange, allow municipalities to effectively aggregate their voices, engage in international governance, better represent people's needs, and act faster than nation-states on certain international issues.[14]

But while these intercity initiatives have managed a renewal of cities' status on the international stage, they have had little or no effect on the constitutional sphere. To a large extent, these networks fly under public law's radar.[15] Virtually none of the international city networks enjoys full legal personality in either constitutional or international law. Local government networks are unable to bring claims to the International Court of Justice or other pertinent international tribunals for breaches of international obligations. Accountability, compliance, and enforcement mechanisms deployed by such networks are not fully developed, and often lack external authority. Moreover, many national constitutions grant the national government exclusive power over foreign affairs. This means municipalities, small or large, have very limited legal authority to enter into agreements with intergovernmental organizations. What is more,

---

[13] Harkness et al., "Leading Beyond Limits." Other scholarly accounts too suggest that mayors are turning to city networks because their resources are decreasing while their roles are becoming increasingly complex and require technical knowledge. *See, e.g.,* Ileana Porras, "The City and International Law: In Pursuit of Sustainable Development," *Fordham Urban Law Journal* 36 (2009): 537–601.

[14] *See, e.g.,* Michele Betsill and Harriet Bulkeley, "Looking Back and Thinking Ahead: A Decade of Cities and Climate Change Research," *Local Environment* 12 (2007): 447–456; Devani G. Adams, "Why We Cannot Wait: Transnational Networks as a Viable Solution to Climate Change Policy," *Santa Clara Journal of International Law* 13 (2015): 307–331; Hari M. Osofsky and Janet Koven Levit, "The Scale of Networks: Local Climate Change Coalitions," *Chicago Journal of International Law* 8 (2008): 409–436; Helmut Philipp Aust, "Shining Cities on the Hill? The Global City, Climate Change and International Law," *European Journal of International Law* 26 (2015): 255–278; Joana Setzer, "Testing the Boundaries of Subnational Diplomacy: The International Climate Action of Local and Regional Governments," *Transnational Environmental Law* 4 (2015): 319–337.

[15] For an early assessment of the legal status of such networks, *see* András Sajó, "Transnational Networks and Constitutionalism," *Acta Juridica Hungarica* 47 (2006): 209–225.

sub-national governments in constitutional orders where municipalities derive their power from the state (e.g., United States, Canada) are able to severely limit cities' international activities.[16] While it is not uncommon for these networks to intervene in constitutional litigation via amicus briefs or as interveners, their activities—whether at the political, educational, or advisory level—are seldom carried out through constitutional litigation channels, and rarely affect constitutional change.

II. The "Right to the City" in Practice

Another significant development in this realm is the use of the "right to the city" concept to support the so-called human rights cities movement. But notwithstanding its frequent invocation by sociologists, philosophers, and urban activists, the exact meaning of the "right to the city" from a formal legal standpoint remains nebulous at best. As we saw in Chapter 1, this bold and potentially revolutionary concept, introduced by Henri Lefebvre, has never been fully concretized or operationalized, neither by Lefebvre himself nor by later thinkers. What is more, the supposed content of the right has shifted over time. Initially put forward as a radical response to advanced capitalism through redistribution and collective ownership of urban spaces and assets, the right to the city came to encompass claims for accommodation and recognition of diversity, identity, and difference within urban spaces. Today, one would be hard-pressed to name more than a handful of instances in which the right to the city has been incorporated into constitutional law, having concrete and justiciable, not merely symbolic meaning. This is not to say that this right is not a useful legal concept (after all, the right to strike and workers' rights more generally did not become widely accepted legal rights until many years after the initial introduction of ideas about exploitation and power imbalances in the workplace that led to their eventual legalization). Nonetheless, there can be no question that the right to the city is conceptually fuzzy, or that central governments are, by and large, uninterested in concretizing the right or incorporating it into constitutional or public law.

---

[16] For instance, between 2013 and 2015, a movement to oppose environmental protection under the UN Agenda 21 agreement and to protect private property rights led state representatives in Arizona, Georgia, Mississippi, Texas, New Hampshire, and Alabama to introduce legislation to ban municipalities from entering into agreements with intergovernmental organizations participating in Agenda 21. The bills passed in Alabama, New Hampshire, and Texas. *See* Elwood Earl Sanders Jr, "Is It Constitutional for an American Municipality to Join ICLEI?," *Appalachian Journal of Law* 13 (2014): 127–146; John Celock, "New Hampshire Lawmakers Kill Agenda 21 Ban," *Huffington Post* (February 6, 2013); online: https://www.huffingtonpost.com/2013/02/06/new-hampshire-agenda-21_n_2633364.html?guccounter=1.

In 2000, the European Charter for Safeguarding of Human Rights in the City included the first attempt to legally formalize the right to the city. Article I ("Right to the City") states: (1) "[T]he city is a collective space belonging to all who live in it. These have the right to conditions which allow their own political, social and ecological development but at the same time accepting a commitment to solidarity"; and (2) "The municipal authorities encourage, by all available means, respect for the dignity of all and quality of life of the inhabitants." The charter resulted from preparatory work initiated in Barcelona in 1998 during the "Cities for Human Rights" Conference, which was organized to commemorate the 50th Anniversary of the Universal Declaration of Human Rights. Hundreds of mayors and political representatives participated in the event and united their voices to call for a stronger political acknowledgment of cities' importance in safeguarding human rights in a highly urbanized world. The 41 participating European cities adopted the "Barcelona Engagement," a roadmap for drafting a political document aimed at fostering the respect, protection, and fulfillment of human rights at a local level. During the next two years, a dialogue about the charter ensued between various European cities, civil society representatives, and human rights experts. The draft was discussed and finally adopted in Saint-Denis (Paris) in 2000. Since then, a European conference is held every two years to share the progress made by signatory cities (more than 400 today) toward implementing the charter.

A World Charter on the Right to the City followed suit in 2005. It was the culmination of various civil society initiatives, mostly in Latin America, and inspired in part by the City Statute, which was adopted in Brazil in 2001 (discussed in some detail in Chapter 3). Here, too, the emphasis on formalizing the right to the city is on inclusiveness. Article I (1) of the World Charter states: "All persons have the Right to the City free of discrimination based on gender, age, health status, income, nationality, ethnicity, migratory condition, or political, religious or sexual orientation, and to preserve cultural memory and identity in conformity with the principles and norms established in this Charter." Article I (2) further stipulates:

> The Right to the City is defined as the equitable usufruct of cities within the principles of sustainability, democracy, equity, and social justice. It is the collective right of the inhabitants of cities, in particular of the vulnerable and marginalized groups, that confers upon them legitimacy of action and organization, based on their uses and customs, with the objective to achieve full exercise of the right to free self-determination and an adequate standard of living. The Right to the City is interdependent of all internationally recognized and integrally conceived human rights, and therefore includes all the civil, political,

economic, social, cultural and environmental rights which are already regulated in the international human rights treaties.

A similar mix of broad aspirations, emphasis on human rights and inclusion,
and lack of concrete legal stature characterizes the Global Platform for the Right
to the City, a civil society initiative established during the International Meeting
of the Right to the City, held in São Paulo in November 2014. According to the
initiative, the right to the city entails the "right of all inhabitants, present and
future, permanent and temporary, to use occupy and produce just, inclusive
and sustainable cities, defined as a common good essential to full and decent
life." Conceived in this way, the right to the city emphasizes substantive equality
notions that are similar to or possibly surpass those encompassed by economic
and social rights (e.g., the rights to housing, healthcare, education, welfare, food,
and water), and declares the applicability of such notions to every city dweller regardless of her formal status vis-à-vis the state.

A handful of individual cities, notably Montréal (2006), Mexico City (2010),
and Gwangju (2012), adopted charters committing themselves to a right to the
city platform. In all these instances, the emphasis is on social justice and inclusion. The Montréal Charter of Rights and Responsibilities (MCRR), for example,
commits the city to work with its inhabitants to build a framework for citizen's
rights and reciprocal responsibilities. It promotes values such as sustained
struggle against poverty and discrimination, respect for justice and equity, and
commits to transparent management of municipal affairs based on citizen involvement and to building trust in democratic organizations. As the first of its
kind on a city level, the Montréal Charter has received much international attention, including recognition at the 2006 UN-Habitat World Forum III for its
focus on inclusion, urban policies, and local democracy. In 2012, the Montréal
Charter was revised through public consultation in accordance with a provision
of the charter that provides for periodic evaluation to make improvements. In
this revision, new city commitments were added, further expanding the city's
commitment to values of democracy, environmental protection, and sustainable
development.

Its groundbreaking vision notwithstanding, the concrete legal stature of the
MCRR remains limited, being a mere municipal bylaw. The MCRR is binding
on all Ville de Montréal elected officials, managers and employees, including
those working for boroughs or para-municipal or city-controlled corporations.
The commitments therein are also binding on any person or organization per-
forming duties on behalf of the city. However, section 86.1 of the *Charter of Ville
de Montréal* provides that the MCRR "may not serve as the basis for a judicial or
jurisdictional remedy nor . . . be cited in judicial or jurisdictional proceedings."
Consequently, the only available recourse to ensure compliance with the MCRR

is with the Ombudsman de Montréal. While the MCRR allows the ombudsman to intervene and investigate decisions that were voted by City Council, the Executive Committee, or a Borough Council, the external *constitutional* capacity of the MCRR rights or of the Montréal Ombudsman to enforce resolutions are narrow at best.

Instead of adopting comprehensive human rights charters of their own, some cities have opted to commit themselves to specific international human rights treaties. The concreteness of such an approach carries certain advantages in terms of accountability and enforcement capacity. In 1998, San Francisco became the first city in the world to commit itself to the Convention on the Elimination of All Forms of Discrimination Against Women (CEDAW)—widely considered the main international human rights treaty focusing on women's rights—through the adoption of a local CEDAW Ordinance. The ordinance requires the City and County of San Francisco to take action in the form of preventive measures to ensure that its resources, policies, and actions do not intentionally or unintentionally discriminate against women and girls from any community. The San Francisco's Department on the Status of Women has since supported many municipal legislation initiatives aimed at advancing the status of women in the city. Over the years, other major American cities, including Los Angeles; Washington, DC; Pittsburgh; and New Orleans followed suit. Campaigns to adopt similar ordinances are underway in Boston and New York City. A declaration of a city's commitment to CEDAW has important political significance, particularly as the United States remains one of only seven countries worldwide that have not ratified CEDAW.[17] Daring as such city ordinances may be, the federal government remains the unchallenged entity representing the entire country in all matters concerning human rights international treaties.

In other instances, city ordinances may signal a looming national shift. While same-sex marriage is not recognized in Japan's constitutional law (e.g., Article 24 of the Japanese Constitution) or civil code (Articles 731 to 737 of the Civil Code), several major Japanese cities have been advancing a progressive agenda on the rights of LGBTQ persons and same-sex couples. In 2015, the district of Shibuya, in central Tokyo, began issuing "proof of partnership" certificates to same-sex couples that facilitated joint home rental agreements or hospital visits of ailing same-sex spouses. Other districts in Tokyo and major cities (e.g., Osaka) followed suit. Likewise, in preparation for the 2020 Tokyo Olympic Games, and possibly as a response to the anti-LGBTQ legislation passed in Russia prior to the Winter Olympics in 2014 (Sochi), the Tokyo Metropolitan Government passed a law that prohibits "the Tokyo Metropolitan Government, citizens, and

---

[17] The list includes Iran, Somalia, South Sudan, and Sudan.

enterprises" from "unduly discriminat[ing] on the basis of gender identity or sexual orientation." The new law also commits the government of Tokyo to "conduct measures needed to make sure human rights values are rooted in all corners of the city and diversity is respected in the city."[18] Yuriko Koike, governor of Tokyo since 2016 and the first woman to ever hold that senior position, pledged when elected that the Olympics "will be a touchstone for the creation of a new Tokyo." She also mentioned that one of her goals as governor would be to create a diverse city "where everyone . . . can actively participate in society and lead fulfilling lives." Given Tokyo's major stature within Japan, it may well be that a more inclusive agenda toward LGBTQ rights soon finds its way to Japan's constitutional domain.

In recent years, the advancement of the right to the city at the municipal level has been closely entangled with cities' efforts to establish themselves as "human rights cities."[19] The trend has been conceptualized as reflecting the proliferation of human rights discourse and human rights regimes beyond the state.[20] Human rights city initiatives may be driven by principled motives such as city leaders' genuine commitment to human rights, their frustration with the city's constitutional non-status, reflecting ideological gaps between progressive cities and conservative governments. It may be driven by cities' or mayors' interest in fostering their reputation, nationally or internationally, as inclusive and socially progressive polities. It may also simply reflect a question of scale: cities are perhaps better suited to enforce human rights commitments than the very large and often detached state apparatus. Some scholars of human rights cities have suggested that, at least in the United States, the trend may have some concrete legal bite; interpretation of federal intervention in state affairs as "appropriate" may ensure that human rights protection does not fall below federal standards, thereby shielding cities from preemptive rights-curtailing legislation by states.[21] Either way, the hope driving the human rights cities trend is that cities can and will "deliver where nation states have failed,"[22] ideally leading

[18] See "Tokyo: New Law Bars LGBT Discrimination," Human Rights Watch (October 5, 2018); online: https://www.hrw.org/news/2018/10/05/tokyo-new-law-bars-lgbt-discrimination.

[19] On the scope, potential, and challenges of the "human rights cities" trend, see Barbara Oomen, Martha F. Davis, and Michele Grigolo, eds., Global Urban Justice: The Rise of Human Rights Cities (Cambridge University Press, 2016); Barbara Oomen, "Human Rights Cities: The Politics of Bringing Human Rights Home to the Local Level," in Jeff Handmaker and Karin Arts, eds., Mobilising International Law for 'Global Justice' (Cambridge University Press, 2018), 208–232. Among the cities experimenting with human rights legislation that seminal collection discusses are Barcelona, Mexico City, Montréal, Utrecht, and San Francisco.

[20] See, e.g., Oomen, "Human Rights Cities."

[21] See, e.g., Martha Davis, "The Upside of the Downside: Local Human Rights and the Federalism Clauses," St. Louis University Law Journal 62 (2018): 921–938.

[22] Barbara Oomen, "Introduction: The Promise and Challenges of Human Rights Cities," in Oomen, Davis, Grigolo, Global Urban Justice, 2.

to "a new urban utopia: a place where human rights strive to guide urban life."[23]

Prominent examples of such human rights city initiatives are Barcelona's City of Rights program and New York City's Commission on Human Rights. The former is aimed at "including the human-rights-based approach in public policies, and at designing and implementing policies on human rights based on thematic priorities, such as developing the right to the city and citizen rights, the fight against hate speech and discrimination and work for full citizenship."[24] The latter, "is charged with the enforcement of the Human Rights Law, Title 8 of the Administrative Code of the City of New York, and with educating the public and encouraging positive community relations."[25]

The adoption of the Gwangju Human Rights Charter in 2012, and the subsequent establishment in Gwangju of the World Human Rights Cities Forum in 2014 represent an important case in point of a human rights city initiative outside North America and Europe. The city of Gwangju has acquired a somewhat legendary status in the fight for democratization in South Korea. The Gwangju Uprising of May 1980, in particular, has become a milestone in Korean citizens' pro-democracy stance. Driven by the popular Gwangju Democratization Movement, the uprising cost the lives of hundreds of people, killed by government forces. Over the years, the Gwangju Uprising has had a profound impact on South Korean politics and history. In 1995, following immense popular pressure, the senior politicians and army generals responsible for the massacre in Gwangju, including former Presidents Chun Doo-hwan and Roh Tae-woo, were indicted and sentenced to life in prison. Ultimately, the convicts were pardoned and a national reconciliation campaign was launched. May 18th was declared a national memorial day, a law acknowledging bereaved families was enacted, and the cemetery where many of the victims are buried was declared a national cemetery.

In this spirit, the human rights administration of Gwangju, the first city-level administration of its kind in Korea, was established in 2010. The preamble of the Gwangju Human Rights Charter further references the city's human rights legacy and states that the charter is established "with a view to realizing the Universal Declaration of Human Rights and promoting democracy and justice." In 2014, the city hosted almost 500 city delegates from around the world at the World Human Rights Cities Forum to explore the establishment of a "Global Alliance of Human Rights Cities for All." The first principle of the Gwangju Guiding

[23] Michelle Grigolo, *The Human Rights City: New York, San Francisco, Barcelona* (Routledge, 2019).
[24] https://ajuntament.barcelona.cat/dretsidiversitat/en/barcelona-city-rights.
[25] "Inside the NYC Commission on Human Rights," https://www1.nyc.gov/site/cchr/about/inside-cchr.page.

Principles for a Human Rights City adopted in that forum declares: "The Human Rights City respects all human rights recognized by the existing relevant international human rights norms and standards such as the Universal Declaration of Human Rights and national constitutions. The Human Rights City works towards the recognition and implementation of the right to the city in line with the principles of social justice, equity, solidarity, democracy and sustainability."

As with the international declarations concerning the right to the city discussed earlier, such broad commitments signal the adopting city's genuine commitment to international human rights standards as well as to an inclusive, socially progressive public policy agenda. The symbolic, educational, and public awareness effects of such commitments are considerable and ought not to be taken lightly—certainly not in a nationalist-populist age where an exclusionary "us vs. them" rhetoric is prevalent. Such city charters may also have some self-determination effects in signaling the community's commitment to a shared set of values. Nevertheless, akin to other types of self-generated emancipatory moves by cities, the real legal effect of such human rights city charters is unclear at best, as in most instances they lack formal status in claims made vis-à-vis states or central governments, and they cannot replace or operate in lieu of polity-wide constitutional guarantees of pertinent rights and entitlements. The compliance and enforcement mechanisms created by such charters are limited. Even avid proponents of the human rights cities idea note that very few of the charters adopted to date create effective legal remedies that allow individuals or groups claiming human rights violations to seek any meaningful legal relief.[26] What is more, with a few exceptions where political incentives so warrant (I discuss these exceptions in detail in Chapter 3), national governments cannot be bound by such policy initiatives. Unlike constitutional rights commitments at the national level, it is unclear what actual "duties" city rights create. In other words, human rights cities may promise various rights protections, but the actual duty to realize such rights is often well beyond cities' legal ambit. No support or resources are provided by the state, which remains the primary, and often the only, relevant agent and duty bearer of human rights commitments vis-à-vis the international arena.[27]

While such initiatives have generally not encountered enthusiasm on the part of national governments, international city networks have made some symbolic (though seldom legally binding) strides at the international arena. In 2017, to pick one example, more than 150 city leaders from around the world released

---

[26] See, e.g., Cynthia Soohoo, "Human Rights Cities: Challenges and Possibilities," in Oomen, Davis, Grigolo, Global Urban Justice, 257–275.

[27] See Johanna Kalb, "The State of the City and the Future of Human Rights: A Review of Global Urban Justice," Columbia Human Rights Law Review 75 (2017): 75–97, 88.

the Mechelen Declaration, demanding representation at the drafting process of the UN's Global Compact on Migration and Global Compact on Refugees. The two global compacts were eventually adopted in Marrakesh in 2018, prompting the same network of mayors and city leaders to sign a second declaration calling for the full and formal recognition of the role of local authorities in the implementation, follow-up, and review of both compacts. In response, the UN High Commissioner on Refugees enthusiastically embraced the city leaders' declaration in a speech highlighting the necessity of working with city leaders to solve the global refugee crisis.[28]

A European variant of the human rights city notion has been formed over the last few years under the auspices of the *Eurocities* framework discussed earlier, in the context of the refugee influx to Europe. In response to restrictive policies adopted by their respective national governments and to strong anti-immigrant rhetoric by nationalist-populist parties, progressive leaders in cities from Athens to Barcelona to Amsterdam, have declared their cities "solidarity cities" committed to humane, accommodating treatment of newcomers. Public statements by Barcelona's mayor, Ada Colau, represent the spirit of the solidarity cities network: "[W]here are our European values of solidarity, humanity and dignity when it comes to the refugee crisis? The response at the national and EU level is clearly not enough, but cities have stepped up. We, the cities, are acting, and we are joining Solidarity Cities to work for an urgent and humane response to the situation."[29] At the height of the refugee crisis, Colau led a delegation of European mayors for direct talks with EU migration and regional policy authorities. She went on to denounce "Spain's immoral management regarding the refugee crisis," which she described as "deeply shaming." "Cities are part of the solution . . . we have expertise and are willing to help . . . regrettably, local governments are not taken into account." In a typical statist fashion, the EU's Migration Commissioner Dimitris Avramopoulos assured the solidarity cities delegation that he "took note" of Colau's demands, but emphasized that EU support to local authorities is always carried out "through the Member States."[30] Enough said.

[28] Chrystie Flournoy Swiney and Sheila Foster, "Cities Are Rising in Influence and Power on the Global Stage," *City Lab* (April 15, 2019).

[29] Eurocities, "Solidarity Cities—Cities Delivering on Refugee Reception and Integration" (October 17, 2016); online: http://www.eurocities.eu/eurocities/documents/Solidarity-Cities-cities-delivering-on-refugee-reception-and-integration-WSPO-AETKWL; the "Solidarity Cities" network was launched in October 2016 during a EUROCITIES meeting in Athens.

[30] Reported in *Catalan News* (April 5, 2016); online: http://www.catalannews.com/politics/item/barcelona-s-mayor-reports-to-the-ec-spain-s-immoral-management-of-the-refugee-crisis.

III. Urban Citizenship

Possibly the most consequential development in urban self-empowerment along the lines of the right to the city is in the concept of "urban citizenship," an abstract idea given effect through city issuance of identification cards or residence certificates that allow their holders access to local public services. Much has been written about the history, forms, and meanings of citizenship as a political and legal concept, commonly conceived as delineating the relationship between sovereign states and their residents.[31] While local citizenship was common for centuries, the rise of the modern nation-state brought political membership, with all the commitments, rights, and duties that come with it, under state control. An intricate state apparatus evolved, handling matters such as population registry, passport issuance, immigration control, and naturalization tests, all founded on membership in the national body politic as the ultimate basis of belonging.[32] In that Westphalian matrix, the local, domicile- or community-based nature of membership largely eroded. Today, however, as several scholars have noted, the increasingly complex reality of multilevel policy making, service provision, and law enforcement in the modern state creates a de facto patchwork of different membership-related statutes operating simultaneously.[33] From a normative angle, political theorists such as Avner de-Shalit and Rainer Bauböck have advanced an intriguing notion of urban citizenship (or "city-zenship"), envisioned as an alternative or as a complement to extant models of state-based membership.[34] While such ideas remain theoretical, in practice, several American cities have introduced municipal identification card systems that provide cardholders, including undocumented migrants, with formal identification, as well as access to essential services such as public schooling, libraries, and public health facilities.

A prominent example is the New York City municipal identification card program (IDNYC), which was launched in 2015. Mayor Bill de Blasio introduced

---

[31] Ayelet Shachar et al., eds., *The Oxford Handbook of Citizenship* (Oxford University Press, 2017); Derek Heater, *A Brief History of Citizenship* (NYU Press, 2004); Rogers M. Smith, *Civic Ideals: Conflicting Visions of Citizenship in US History* (Yale University Press, 1999).

[32] *See, e.g.*, John C. Torpey, *The Invention of the Passport: Surveillance, Citizenship and the State* (Cambridge University Press, 2009); Rogers Brubaker, *Citizenship and Nationhood in France and Germany* (Harvard University Press, 1998).

[33] *See, e.g.*, Willem Mass, "Multilevel Citizenship," *in* Ayelet Shachar et al., eds., *Oxford Handbook of Citizenship* (Oxford University Press, 2017), 644–668; Linda Bosniak, "Status Non-citizens," *id.* at 314–336; Linda Bosniak, *The Citizen and the Alien: Dilemmas of Contemporary Membership* (Princeton University Press, 2007).

[34] *See, e.g.*, Avner de-Shalit, *Cities and Immigration: Political and Moral Dilemmas in the New Era of Migration* (Oxford University Press, 2018); Rainer Bauböck, "Reinventing Urban Citizenship," *Citizenship Studies* 7 (2003): 137–158. *See also* Murray Bookchin, *The Rise of Urbanization and the Decline of Citizenship* (Sierra Club Books, 1987).

its aim in these words: "For too long, hundreds of thousands of New Yorkers struggled to get affordable, accepted, U.S.-issued proof of identification. As a result, they could not enter their child's school during school hours, open a bank account, or present identification when needed to law enforcement. In a City that is strengthened by its diversity and celebrated for its inclusiveness, too many New Yorkers were living in the shadows. With IDNYC, my team and I set out to right that wrong and to help all our people lead lives full of respect and recognition."[35] To this end, the IDNYC serves as a valid form of identification for entering schools and city buildings, as well as for interactions with the New York City Police Department. The card also offers free memberships to city-run cultural institutions, may be used as a library card, provides discounts at pharmacies and at supermarkets, and allows access to banks and other benefits.

Most importantly, this form of municipal ID is free and available to all residents of New York who are 14 years of age or older and who can provide documentation of identity (including a foreign passport, consular identification card, or driver's license) and New York residency, regardless of their formal immigration status.[36] As a city-controlled manifestation of membership that is available without federal documentation, the card offers a partial answer to the fractured nature of citizenship in America and elsewhere. As Linda Bosniak points out, America's hybrid federalist structure grants the federal government control over membership in the national community through its power over admission or removal of immigrants and conferral or denial of citizenship, while the regulation of migrants' daily lives, be they documented or undocumented, is largely in the hands of sub-national or local authorities.[37] The IDNYC, by formally recognizing local membership, brings the power of admission (for certain limited purposes) more in line with the practical reality of governance. Similar municipal ID programs have been introduced to various degrees of success in other American cities, including San Francisco (SF City ID Card), Philadelphia (PHL City ID), and Chicago (Chicago CityKey).[38]

Some observers see the introduction of such municipal ID programs as a potentially terrain-changing legal development in asserting city powers, and in creating a new form of citizenship for their residents.[39] Indeed, there is little doubt that the launch of municipal identification cards in several major American cities

---

[35] Tamara C. Daley et al., "IDNYC: A Tool of Empowerment: A Mixed-Methods Evaluation of the New York Municipal ID Program" (Westat, 2016); online: https://www1.nyc.gov/assets/idnyc/downloads/pdf/idnyc_report_full.pdf.

[36] *See* Kendra Sena, "Municipal IDs: Local Governments and the Power to Create Identity Documents" (Albany Law School, Government Law Center, 2018); online: https://www.albanylaw.edu/centers/government-law-center/Immigration/explainers/Documents/2018-08-08%20Municipal%20ID%20Explainer%20AS%20POSTED.pdf.

[37] Bosniak, *The Citizen and the Alien*.

[38] New Haven's Elm Card, launched in 2007, was the first of its kind in this context.

[39] *See, e.g.*, Kenneth Stahl, *Local Citizenship in a Global Age: How Cities Are Changing What It Means to Be a Citizen* (Cambridge University Press, forthcoming 2020); Amy C. Torres, "'I Am

positively affects the daily lives of undocumented immigrants in those cities. It also signals a novel concretization of the right to the city, at least in the American context. However, these programs have no effect on the *constitutional* standing of cities and their residents. Although municipal ID card legislation does typically contain language explicitly extending card benefits regardless of immigration status, none of the municipal ID laws overrides the operation or enforcement of federal immigration law itself. There is nothing in any existing municipal ID legislation that attempts to regulate immigration, or that interferes with the execution of national immigration policy. Nor is there anything with real constitutional significance in such legislation that alters the status or authority of the issuing cities. In other words, municipal IDs do not create new legal entitlements for undocumented immigrants or other cardholders; they simply "facilitate access to municipal and other services for which cardholders are already eligible."[40]

Several major European cities, (e.g., Madrid, Paris), have also been experimenting with municipal ID cards. The Paris variant, *Carte Citoyenne-Citoyen*, modeled on the IDNYC, was introduced by Mayor Anne Hidalgo in the wake of the terror attacks of 2015 as a gesture of accommodation and inclusion amid national anger targeted at immigrants. However, the gesture remains largely symbolic as the competences of French municipalities are limited (even compared to their American counterparts), and the uptake of the Carte Citoyenne-Citoyen in the outer ring of metropolitan Paris, where most alienated immigrant communities live, remains modest at best.[41] Meanwhile, in Germany, several cities (e.g., Munich, Hamburg) have been pondering various urban citizenship initiatives in the wake of the refugee crisis that brought more than a million refugees to that country. However meaningful these moves may be as gestures of compassion and hospitality, their legal, let alone constitutional impact, is limited, as German municipalities are obliged to act as reporting agents for national authorities. National law requires all residents to register at their local registration offices (*Einwohnermeldeamt*), which assess their legal status and report foreigners to the municipal foreign office (*Ausländeramt*), which in turn reports visa and status violations to federal authorities. Additionally, national law requires landlords to provide information about their tenants; as of 2015, registration with one's municipality requires a landlord-approved form

Undocumented and a New Yorker': Affirmative City Citizenship and New York City's IDNYC Program," *Fordham Law Review* 86 (2017): 335–366.

[40] Sena, "Municipal IDs," 3.
[41] Phil Wood, "Urban Citizenship—Making Places Where Even the Undocumented Can Belong, Background Paper" (Intercultural Cities, November 2018), 9; *see also* online: https://www.paris.fr/cartecitoyenne.

stating who exactly is living in the unit.[42] In short, the legal or constitutional room for the realization of urban citizenship in Germany is very slim.

Another variant of limited legal urban citizenship is found in the Netherlands, where both EU and non-EU foreign subjects registered as city residents may vote in municipal elections (non-EU citizens must have lived in the Netherlands uninterrupted for at least five years). Non-EU residents of Amsterdam may also vote in the District Council (*Bestuurscommissie*) elections provided they have been registered in the city for more than three years.[43] However, these local political participation rights depend upon successful registration in one's municipality, an act requiring a valid passport, residence permit, a certified copy of one's birth certificate, and other formal documentation that effectively precludes residents without formal status from participating.

Municipal identity cards, in theory and in practice, are certainly not an inconsequential development. At the very least, they plant the seeds for building distinct urban identity, separate from the national equivalent. However, in the vast majority of instances, they affect neither the cardholders' nor the issuing cities' constitutional status or standing. In fact, the entire notion of a distinct "urban citizenship," either as an alternative to national citizenship or even as complementary to it, runs up against the very conceptualization of modern statehood and the statist outlook of its constitutional order. Moreover, bold as the notion of urban citizenship is, it seems to be concerned with the supposed lack of citizenship rights of the city's individual dwellers—the vast majority of whom are already equal members of the sovereign national entity within which their home city is located, and as such enjoy the entire gamut of constitutional protections to which any other member of the polity is entitled. Urban citizenship does not address what seems to be a major cause of city underrepresentation: *the nonexistence of cities qua order of government* in constitutions, constitutional jurisprudence, and constitutional thought more generally.

What is more, advancing urban citizenship through municipal identity cards is effectively confined to a handful of progressive cities in North America and Europe, from New York and San Francisco to Amsterdam and Paris. Nevertheless, as we saw earlier, the vast majority of urban growth and agglomeration has taken place in the Global South. Self-proclaimed city power in the form of municipal identity cards, even in its currently sporadic and limited form, happens largely outside the big urbanization scene in India, China, Brazil, the Philippines, Indonesia, and Nigeria. As mentioned earlier in this book, the

---

[42] Harald Bauder and Dayana A. Gonzalez, "Municipal Responses to 'Illegality': Urban Sanctuary across National Contexts," *Social Inclusion* 6 (2018): 124–134, 129.

[43] *See* https://www.iamexpat.nl/expat-info/official-issues/elections-netherlands-voting-rights-expats.

challenges facing Kinshasa, for example, are enormous—its population has increased from 400,000 to 13 million in the space of only half a century, a 32-fold increase in a city where the annual GDP per capita ranges between $200 and $500. As discussed in Chapter 5, Dhaka contains 20 million residents living with a city-wide density of 46,000 people/km^2 (119,140/mile^2). Consider how much greater is the population density in Dhaka than it is in other cities: it is 5 times that of New York City, 7 times San Francisco, 12 times Paris, 16 times Toronto, and nearly 30 times Melbourne. It is hard to see how the challenges of Kinshasa, Dhaka, Mumbai, Lagos, and other huge cities of the Global South are resolved by thought-provoking yet abstract accounts of urban citizenship that project a New York, Paris, or San Francisco political and demographic reality on fundamentally dissimilar urban settings in the Global South.

Conclusion

Even as influential cities emerge, the state and its accompanying statist constitutional vision are reluctant to give away governance power. What cities need is a more robust constitutional standing. Lacking such power, city leaders are pushed to align their policies with broader state interests and/or with big business and private sector resources, often adopting these domains' visions of the public good en route. Whereas transnational organs and economic corporations hold considerable leeway vis-à-vis the statist constitutional order, cities do not. Lacking any meaningful "exit," "flight," or "forum shopping" capacity, aspiring cities increasingly turn to limited acts of autonomy and defiance (notably in the realm of undocumented migration and accommodation of difference), or, more commonly, to international city networking, predominantly in areas such as environmental protection, sustainability, and human rights, drawing on attractive yet abstract notions such as the "right to the city." These developments, embryonic as they are, may have significant symbolic, educational, and at times practical significance. However, more often than not, such moves are not pursued in sync with central governments, and occur within a rigid, city-restricting constitutional framework. National constitutional orders' reluctance to acknowledge, let alone promote city power, does not seem to weaken even amid the ever-thickening nexus of intercity policy collaborations and quasi-legal commitments. Consequently, the net potential of such initiatives and collaborations to bring about real *constitutional* (i.e., not merely aspirational, reputational, or educative) change in megacity status appears limited as long as it is not accompanied by a change in the constitutional status of cities as rights granting and rights guaranteeing actors. Granted, every constitutional revolution must begin somewhere. Progressive city attempts at self-emancipation, and more specifically transnational city networks, may be seen as an initial step toward the formation of a distinct urban identity and perhaps also the realization of a parliament of cities notion, often associated with Barber's *If Mayors Ruled the World*. However, these networks currently lack the most basic prerogative of parliaments, namely the ability to self-govern and help shape the general law of the land.

5

Rethinking City Constitutional Status

This chapter develops several possible justifications for the constitutional empowerment of cities. Fortunately, this task does not begin as a *tabula rasa*.
Several key arguments, both normative and practical, have already been put
forward in support of the emancipation of urban centers and their residents on
the basis of what we might term general constitutional principles. These include
arguments that rely on principles of anti-discrimination and calls for fair and
equal inclusion of historically disenfranchised groups; such arguments are particularly relevant to city life given the diverse demographic composition and
challenging socioeconomic reality of many large urban centers. Although detailed comparative data on urban diversity are hard to come by, the data that do
exist point in a clear direction: metropolitan areas are distinctly more diverse
than micropolitan or rural areas. Indeed, the defining characteristic of metropolis demographics and everyday urban life is super-diversity, where various
dimensions of diversity—racial, religious, ethnic, linguistic, political, sexual,
and socioeconomic—constantly intersect with each other.[1] More often than not,
urban poverty is closely correlated with race or ethnicity. This trend holds true in
many contexts: in large American cities, where African American communities
live in inner city poverty; in African cities (e.g., Nairobi) where slum dwellers
often belong to minority ethnic groups; and in European urban centers such as
Paris or Brussels, where Muslim immigrants from Northern Africa are concentrated in poverty-ridden neighborhoods a short drive away from the upscale
Champs-Élysées or Grand Place/Grote Markt.

Other familiar arguments for city autonomy invoke a different element of the
constitutional canon: economic and social rights. Here we often witness calls for
core minimum guarantees to address the challenge of poverty or homelessness in
cities. Within this group of rights, the right to housing is particularly relevant to
urban life. In the high-income world, government-regulated affordable housing
is often in short supply. In many low-income countries, it is either rare or nonexistent. Residents of informal settlements and slum neighborhoods live in harsh
conditions, and can face threats of eviction with no available alternatives—often
to make way for joint business-government "development" projects.

---

[1] *See* Steven Vertovec, "Super-Diversity and Its Implications," *Ethnic and Racial Studies* 30
(2007): 1024–1054.

City, State. Ran Hirschl, Oxford University Press (2020). © Ran Hirschl.
DOI: 10.1093/oso/9780190922771.001.0001

Another argument for city empowerment is connected to addressing the increasing pressures of migration. The vast majority of newcomers, whether invited or not, settle in big cities and become integral parts of urban life. Issues of immigrant settlement and integration therefore tend to bear more directly on cities than on the countryside.

These and related arguments are powerful and may, if heeded, lead to significant improvement in the living conditions of countless city dwellers. Their strength lies in the fact that, as general constitutional principles, they may apply to *any* social setting, urban or not. Equal opportunity, anti-discrimination, economic, social, and immigrant rights are frequently invoked in debates over the politics of the urban domain, but none of these concepts was developed specifically in response to the urban context. The fact that debates involving these rights often take place in large city settings has much to do with the demographic and socioeconomic realities in these settings, not with the independent normative, qualitative, or analytical value of the rights themselves.

As we have seen in Chapter 1, when it comes to city-centered arguments per se—arguments that respond directly to the urban condition itself, based on the notion that the city is a distinct political entity and a social domain—available ideas tend to be rather abstract and typically lack legal specificity and constitutional substance. Action-guiding theories, whether deontological or consequential, as well as the aspirational aims of social movements that stem from urban realities, may have moral leverage but limited constitutional sway. In this category of arguments, already explored in detail in Chapter 1, two bold ideas stand out: Henri Lefebvre's intriguing yet fuzzy notion of a "right to the city"; and pragmatic calls à la Benjamin Barber for mayors "to rule the world."

Taken together, however, extant arguments for enhanced city power do not seem to acknowledge or appreciate the full scope of urban centers' *constitutional* powerlessness. Specifically, existing threads of argument suffer, in my view, from the following flaws: (i) they are too often spatially blind and non-city specific; (ii) they are highly abstract (e.g., the right to the city), with little or no constitutional dimension or operationalization; and (iii) they overlook crucial aspects of urban agglomeration, in particular in the Global South, ranging from extreme density and limited economic leverage of cities to systemic political underrepresentation and a structural constitutional bias in favor of a state-centered perception of legal spatiality and the constitutional and institutional order it upholds.

As we have seen throughout this book, the scale, intensity, and magnitude of urban agglomeration worldwide is unprecedented. Any attempt to find fresh answers to the real, complicated, and as yet unresolved challenges that the surge of the megacity poses to contemporary constitutional thought requires us to venture beyond existing arguments. My goal here is to enrich the discussion concerning the constitutional empowerment of cities by exploring several lines of thought that have been addressed sparsely at best by comparative constitutional law and theory.

First, I highlight the systemic political *underrepresentation* of urban voters in countries ranging from the United States, Canada, and Australia to Brazil and India. In these countries, constitutionally entrenched electoral malapportionment of large cities, dilution of urban votes within larger units, and anti-urban biases of single member first-past-the-post electoral systems combine to create a de facto "one person, half a vote" reality for urban dwellers. Drawing on the rich literature on electoral system design, I propose that mixed urban-rural electoral districts within an overarching proportional representation system may begin to remedy this systemic underrepresentation of urban voters.

Second, constitutional empowerment of cities is necessary to reduce their structural dependence on the deep pockets of big business. With their ever-expanding populations, large cities face increasing demands for services. Yet they lack meaningful constitutional standing or sufficient taxation authority to satisfy those demands. Consequently, the cities are prone to becoming beholden to market forces and the deep pockets of corporations.

Third, I argue that, as a growing majority of the world's population resides in cities, it will be impossible to meaningfully address either rising economic inequality or climate change without the direct involvement of city government. At the very least, tackling these problems, among the most burning public policy challenges of our time, will require us to assign additional powers to those at the front lines of policy delivery. The constitutional empowerment of cities, and their consequent fiscal independence from business and central government, is likely to allow cities greater capacities to pursue an affordable housing and environmental protection agenda, and to do so more freely, creatively, and aggressively.

Fourth, I introduce the density factor into the discussion about city and city-dweller empowerment. Extreme density is defined as a very high population-to-space ratio on a large scale without viable exit options. As I explain, such conditions, commonly found in megacities in the developing world, call into question the practical utility of constitutionally-entrenched economic and social rights: in particular the right to housing and the right to health. While formal recognition of these rights in national constitutions is at its all-time peak, their actual realization is severely limited by acute urban density. I further suggest that involuntary extreme density may justify granting enhanced political and constitutional voice to more vulnerable residents of megacities in the Global South—the new frontier of extensive urbanization worldwide.

Fifth, I propose an adaptation of the concept of equalization—commonly deployed for redistributive and standardization purposes among sub-national units—to also apply to the ever-intensifying urban agglomeration trend. The comparative data are resounding: in the current age of the city, socioeconomic gaps *within* metropolitan regions, and consequently, intra-metropolis transfers, are just as relevant, if not more relevant, to a fiscal equalization conversation as is the traditional sub-national unit-based matrix of inter-jurisdictional redistribution. Inter-regional equalization schemes that overlook the tremendous intra-metropolis gaps find support in the statist outlook and national methodology embedded in contemporary constitutional thought. These schemes embrace and perpetuate the overly simplistic "city = haves" perception, allowing the real urbanite "haves," whether in Toronto, Paris, or Mumbai, to hide behind regional and sub-national unit average- and median-income figures that dilute stark intra-metropolis inequalities.

Finally, I suggest that extensive urbanization and the rise of very large cities require us to re-examine certain assumptions regarding democratic theory and effective representation based on established principles of stakeholding and subsidiarity. At the very least, I argue, our current "age of the city" calls for a rethinking of orthodox federalism theory and practice, according to which province- and state-sized entities are the default constituent unit of the federation, while cities—ubiquitous and vital to every social, economic, and political aspect of contemporary life—are virtually nonexistent in the discourse. By corollary, I suggest that notions of subsidiarity—commonly deployed in transnational constitutional discourse—have theoretical purchase, and could be productively invoked in discussions concerning enhancement of urban centers' constitutional power.

I. One (Urban) Person, Half a Vote

The commitment to the "one person, one vote" principle is central to constitutional democracy. The intersection of demographic concentration in many urban areas with constitutionally protected malapportionment leads certain electoral systems to systematically underrepresent cities and their residents. As we have seen in earlier chapters, constitutionally entrenched limitations on equal representation of urban voters affect large cities as diverse as Toronto, Mumbai, and São Paulo. For example, due to a Supreme Court of Canada ruling that allows electoral district size to deviate up to 25% from the provincial average, some rural ridings in Ontario have a little over 60,000 voters, while some urban ridings in Toronto have nearly double that number of voters. Furthermore, because the constitution of Brazil requires that each state be represented in the lower house by a minimum of 8 deputies and a maximum of 70, São Paulo, which in a truly proportional system would have between 60 and 90 times as many representatives as small states like Roraima, Acre, and Amapá, only has 8.75 times as many.[2] Put differently, a São Paulo citizen's vote is worth about one-tenth of a vote in any of these three states. And while metro Mumbai's population constitutes approximately a quarter of Maharashtra's overall population, due to India's electoral system, the Greater Mumbai region comprises only 6 of the State of Maharashtra's 48 MPs in a national parliament of 543 elected MPs. According to the current constitutional framework governing the matter, the next reallocation of seats will take place in 2031 (based on the 2026 decennial census). By that time, the parliamentary allotments will be based on population figures six decades old.[3] Such infrequent allocation stretches the effects of malapportionment in an inherently anti-urban way. As city population growth has increased at a much higher rate than in rural areas, impeded reapportionment leads to further underrepresentation of cities.

In other settings (e.g., Zürich, Chicago) the political voice of city inhabitants is reduced and practically subsumed by larger sub-national units. More often than not, this effect helps to dilute the potential influence of progressive urban voices. In the United States, politically motivated redistricting and gerrymandering—controlled by state legislators—has effectively reduced the power of urban areas by slicing them up or redrawing districts such that the rural parts of each district overwhelm urban areas.[4] Some observers go as far as suggesting that partisan gerrymandering is the primary reason that major cities have not enjoyed much political clout within the states that contain them.[5] Attempts to challenge the present practice of districting on constitutional grounds before the US Supreme Court have failed. In its 2018 ruling in *Gill v. Whitford*, dealing with blatant partisan gerrymandering in Wisconsin, the court remanded the case to

---

[2] *See* Gilberto Marcos et al., "The Supreme Federal Court of Brazil: Protecting Democracy and Centralized Power," *in* Nicholas Aroney and John Kincaid, eds., *Courts in Federal Countries: Federalist or Unitarist?* (University of Toronto Press, 2017), 103–134, 114.

[3] Milan Vanishav and Jamie Hinston, "India's Emerging Crisis of Representation," *Carnegie Endowment for International Peace* (March 14, 2019); online: https://carnegieendowment.org/2019/03/14/india-s-emerging-crisis-of-representation-pub-78588.

[4] Examples are many. Texas, to pick one, features an obvious set of such heavily gerrymandered congressional districts designed to overwhelm progressive city neighborhoods in Austin, Houston, and San Antonio. TX 10 (elected a Republican) stretches from the conservative suburbs of Houston, through a large rural area, and right into the heart of Austin; TX 17 (elected a Republican) includes a large rural area in East Texas (and the cities of College Station and Waco), and then into the northern suburbs of Austin; TX 21 (elected a Republican) includes parts of downtown San Antonio and downtown Austin, as well as a large rural area in the Hill Country to the west; TX 25 (elected a Republican) stretches from the conservative suburbs of Fort Worth, through a huge rural area, and right into downtown Austin. A counter attempt to create a majority-minority district through blatant gerrymandering is TX 35, which includes the historically Black East Austin as well as the East Side of San Antonio (includes some wealthy areas) and a highway connecting them.

[5] *See, e.g.,* Brentin Mock, "Where Gerrymandering Is Containing City Power," *City Lab,* January 10, 2017. Among the chief illustrations Mock discusses is Wisconsin's Legislative Assembly District 22, once a Democrat seat on the coast of Lake Michigan in 2008, "gets swallowed in 2012 by Districts 23 and 24, and then somehow ends up far west of Milwaukee," now a Republican seat, a switch resulting directly from the gerrymander.

lower courts, citing the plaintiff's difficulty in establishing harm.[6] Consequently, in the State Assembly elections held in November 2018, 54% of the popular vote, largely concentrated in urban areas, supported Democratic candidates, but the Republicans wound up maintaining their 63-seat majority. In its recent landmark ruling in *Rucho v. Common Cause* (2019), the court held (5-4 along traditional conservative-liberal ideological lines) that partisan redistricting is a political question, not reviewable by federal courts, and therefore ought to be addressed by Congress or by state legislatures, not by the judiciary.[7] Taken together, these trends have proven to systematically weaken the political representation of cities and their residents and negatively impact predominantly urban policy issues such as transit, density, and affordable housing.

Furthermore, comparative data on single member first-past-the-post electoral systems (such as those in place in the United States, Canada, and India) demonstrate that city underrepresentation is further exacerbated by the aggregate wide margin (typically left-leaning) candidate wins in urban electoral districts compared to more moderate margin (here, right-leaning) candidate wins in rural districts.[8] Because educated, socially progressive voters often pack into cities, they essentially dilute their own voting impact through excessive concentration.[9] In his book, *Why Cities Lose?*, political scientist Jonathan Rodden argues that, while support for the left has historically been clustered in cities among the industrial working class, today, left-wing parties comprise coalitions of diverse urban interest groups, from racial minorities to cosmopolitan urban elites and the creative class. These parties win big in urban districts but struggle to capture the suburban and rural seats necessary for legislative majorities. While "left party candidates run up extremely wide margins of victory in their core urban bastions," right-wing candidates win in crucial suburban and rural constituencies, often with smaller margins.[10] Consequently, as Rodden shows, "Republicans win seat shares well in excess of their share of the vote."[11] Partisan bias in US legislative elections therefore does not result solely from intentional partisan and racial gerrymandering, but also emerges from patterns of human geography or "unintentional gerrymandering."[12] The result is a strong relationship between

---

[6] *Gill v. Whitford*, 138 S. Ct. 1916; 585 U.S. ___ (2018).

[7] *Rucho v. Common Cause*, No. 18-422, 588 U.S. ___ (2019).

[8] *See, e.g.,* Jonathan Rodden, "The Geographic Distribution of Political Preferences," *Annual Review of Political Science* 13 (2010): 321–340; Jonathan Rodden, *Why Cities Lose: The Deep Roots of the Urban-Rural Divide* (Basic Books, 2019).

[9] For a discussion of what the trend may mean in traditionally Republican states in the United States, *see* Derek Thompson, "American Migration Patterns Should Terrify the GOP," *The Atlantic* (September 17, 2019).

[10] Rodden, *Why Cities Lose*, 6.

[11] *Id.* at 5.

[12] *See* Jowei Chen and Jonathan Rodden, "Unintentional Gerrymandering: Political Geography and Electoral Bias in Legislatures," *Quarterly Journal of Political Science* 8 (2013): 239–269. The authors show that in many states, Democrats are inefficiently concentrated in large cities and smaller

the geographic concentration of Democratic voters and systemic electoral bias favoring Republicans. A consistently similar trend may be identified in other multi-district, single-member, first-past-the-post-electoral systems, such as in Canada, Australia, and the UK.[13] Computational models further suggest that in territory-based electoral systems, hypothetical "rural parties" enjoy better representation than "urban parties" as in most instances there is asymmetry in the spatial distribution of voters: urban party voters tend to congregate together in a tight area, while rural party voters occupy much larger territory, surrounding urban centers on all sides.[14]

The aggregated differential effect of muted voice and lack of ability to advance policy choices concerning a range of issues affecting cities is dramatic. Although scholars and activists have called out the problem, cities often encounter difficulties in addressing these discrepancies as a result of constitutional datedness, hard-to-change electoral systems, and other unfavorable institutional and political conditions. Oftentimes, cities lack proportional voice in the bodies that make crucial decisions concerning many of the very policy issues that affect them. (As we have seen, in the United States, state governments control the electoral redistricting or gerrymandering enterprise). And because gerrymandering of state electoral districts often results in electoral districts that are misaligned with municipal boundaries, urban representation in state legislatures is often weakened.[15] The divergence here from equal voice and stakeholding ideals is obvious.

What can be done to overcome this deficiency? Innovative ideas such as joint or mixed urban-rural electoral districts have the potential to alleviate city underrepresentation, and the widening urban-rural divide more generally. Initial arguments about the advantages of such districts, and how they function, have already been put forth. For example, in their quest for an optimally inclusive electoral and party system, Frances Rosenbluth and Ian Shapiro advocate for larger electoral districts that encompass both rural and urban areas, and include more diverse populations to enhance the competitiveness of congressional elections.[16]

---

industrial agglomerations such that they can expect to win fewer than 50% of the seats when they win 50% of the votes.

[13] In the UK, Rodden reveals, the Conservative Party and the Labour Party have received nearly similar cumulative number of votes from 1950 to 2017; yet during that time period, the Conservatives have been in power nearly two-thirds of the time. Likewise, in Australia, the Australian Labor Party and its right-wing competitors have split the popular vote since 1950, yet the right has been in power for 68% of the time.

[14] Allan Borodin et al., "Big City vs. the Great Outdoors: Voter Distribution and How It Affects Gerrymandering," *Proceedings of the Twenty-Seventh International Joint Conference on Artificial Intelligence (IJCAI-18)* [2018]: 98–104.

[15] *See, e.g.,* Kenneth A. Stahl, "Preemption, Federalism and Local Democracy," *Fordham Urban Law Journal* 44 (2017): 133–179.

[16] Frances McCall Rosenbluth and Ian Shapiro, *Responsible Parties: Saving Democracy from Itself* (Yale University Press, 2018), 24.

They further note that "[P]olitical parties are best able to formulate good public policy when their members of Parliament (MPs) come from districts that are more similar to one another, since only then will the MPs be willing to delegate decision-making authority to party leaders to formulate and implement policy. And only internally diverse districts will produce parties that have the interests of the whole country in mind."[17] Proposing reforms for the British electoral system, they further argue that "the most effective institutional adjustment would be to establish larger, more diverse electoral districts that include urban, suburban, and rural voters in roughly the same proportion as in the country as a whole." Such districts, they suggest "would return MPs to office who see the whole picture."[18]

Another intriguing idea in this context is an electoral system termed "rural-urban proportional representation" (RUP). In a RUP system, advanced by a think tank named Fair Vote Canada, proportional representation exists across the map, but this representation is structured differently in urban areas than in rural areas.[19] Urban ridings have multiple seats per riding, with the number of seats proportionate to the riding's population. Rural ridings have only one member per riding. Because these rural, single-member ridings do not provide proportional representation, rural voters are additionally represented by "top-up" seats, allocated proportionally to "top up" the representation of rural, non-plurality voters.[20] Thus, RUP aims to respond directly to the political implications of urban agglomeration, distinguishing between the needs of cities and those of rural areas and attempting to accommodate the diversity of political perspectives in dense urban areas. And it does so without compromising the representation of rural voters.

"Top up" or "adjustment seats" are common in Northern European electoral systems as a means for addressing spatial underrepresentation, whether urban or rural. Sweden employs a two-tier proportional representation system where 310 of the total 349 parliament members are selected first through permanent seats (designated to each of the country's 29 constituencies based on population size), and second through 39 "adjustment seats" (where a party's comparative figure was largest following the permanent seats). Denmark is divided into three

---

[17] *Id.* at 64.
[18] *Id.* at 239.
[19] "Rural-Urban Proportional," *Fair Vote Canada*; online: https://www.fairvote.ca/rural-urban-proportional/. The RUP system is partly based on the electoral system that Alberta and Manitoba used provincially early in the twentieth century. There, cities had proportional representation in multi-member ridings with a single transferable voting system, while rural ridings were single member. A deficiency with the old Alberta-Manitoba approach was that it left rural voters out of proportional representation. RUP fixes this problem by adding rural top-up seats.
[20] *Id. See also* "What Is Rural-Urban Proportional?," *CBC* (November 5, 2018); online: https://www.youtube.com/watch?v=8bAECs8NUBI.

electoral provinces, each of which is divided into 10 multi-member districts, which are further subdivided into a total of 92 nomination districts. The 175 seats nationwide (4 additional seats are reserved to Faroe Islands and Greenland) represent 135 constituency seats, and 40 compensatory seats distributed proportionally among the three electoral districts. Iceland's parliament is composed of 63 seats, 54 of which are allocated across the country's six constituencies based on the proportion of votes in each, with 9 "adjustment seats" distributed based on national aggregation of the vote.

Another way to address the chronic underrepresentation of cities is to draw on principles of so-called non-territorial federalism. Unlike classical federalism, in which representation is territory-based, in non-territorial federalism, certain communities and interests that are geographically spread across a given polity may be granted fixed quota-based representation or autonomy over community-defining issues. Non-territorial federalism is usually thought of as a response to multiethnic, multi-religious. and multilinguistic tensions, offering secure representation to different constituent groups in major decision-making bodies. While far from an ideal solution, in part due to its tendency to ossify and rigidify the lines of distinction defining the represented groups (ignoring the messier reality of intersecting and overlapping identities), non-territorial federalism holds the advantage of adding new dimensions of representation within deeply diverse societies. The Lebanese parliament is comprised according to a set of quotas for various Christian, Muslim, and Druze communities, accompanied by an agreed-upon split of the country's main executive power holders among Maronite Christians, Sunni Muslims, and Shia Muslims. In New Zealand, to pick another example, the Maori have a reserved quota in the 120-member national parliament. Belgium features a mix of territorial and non-territorial representation, with Flemish-, Walloon-, and German-speaking communities given autonomy over core language and education policies. It does not require a major leap of imagination to realize that the same logic could be applied to address certain city-specific interests that get lost due to today's systemic patterns of urban underrepresentation in national and sub-national legislatures.

II. Ceding the City to Big Business?

In the first two decades of the twenty-first century, city leaders, and particularly elected mayors, have assumed greater importance as political actors both operating and gaining prominence beyond the local level.[21] However, cities—the

---

[21] A few "household names" that come to mind here are Michael Bloomberg (former mayor of New York), Ken Livingstone and Boris Johnson (former mayors of London), Sadiq Khan and Anne Hidalgo (present mayors of London and Paris, respectively). For a useful discussion of the still scant

entities these mayors are in charge of—are often constitutionally voiceless, locked within rigid constitutional orders, and lacking any real exit options. The power to engage in "forum shopping," and thus wield the threat of capital flight, as any private corporate actor might do, is not available to the city, arguably the most significant sub-state public corporation. Consequently, many cities have opted for a common yet contested path of action: collaboration with the private sector in areas or projects of joint interest. Such collaborations, whether small or large scale, often follow a similar pattern. Private sector entities help fund or co-sponsor urban development projects in areas such as education, healthcare, architecture, culture, or sports and leisure. In return, cities successfully push for concessions and business-friendly policies in areas such as taxation, zoning, or building permits.

One significant effect of cities' deficient constitutional status is their limited ability to tax and generate revenue. The systemic underfunding and chronic austerity of cities, alongside the ever-growing demands of infrastructure and social services, leave them badly in need of financial support. Often, private financiers offer to fill this void for a political price, placing city government in an inherently uneasy relationship with big business. As cities grow more and more dependent on large corporations, they become more prone to promote decisions, policies, and regulations that favor corporate over public interests.

A vibrant scholarly thread within critical urban geography points to this structural dependency of cash-starved cities, often short shifted by national and provincial governments, on investments by the private sector for urban development. Combined with hegemonic neoliberal worldviews, cities may become beholden to the interests of big business and advanced capitalism.[22] With very few exceptions, this important critique has not yet penetrated the field of constitutional law.[23]

In an important opinion piece published in 2018, Richard Schragger points out that in the late twentieth and early twenty-first centuries, the dogma overwhelmingly argued that cities would forever be limited by the mobility of capital. Hence, "cities have no choice but to adopt pro-market policies and pursue alliances with powerful business interests in the pursuit of growth."[24] In return for investments and joint ventures, cities may adopt business-friendly policies as an attempt to attract big business and prevent capital departure, or to ensure

literature on mayors as political actors, see Richard Stren and Abigail Friendly, "Big City Mayors: Still Avatars of Local Politics?," Cities 84 (2019): 172–177.

[22] See, e.g., Neil Brenner and Nikolas Theodore, eds., Spaces of Neoliberalism: Urban Restructuring in North America and Western Europe (Blackwell, 2002).
[23] For an important exception, see Richard Schragger, City Power (Oxford University Press, 2016).
[24] Richard Schragger, "Cities on a Hill?," Boston Review, February 14, 2018.

that private sector money continues to co-fund projects. Corporations can cred-ibly threaten to engage in "forum shopping," forcing cities to cater to business interests by softening regulations, lowering rent for office spaces, and encour-aging corporate initiatives. City-business partnerships thus become a necessary mode of urban governance.[25] By contrast, if cities secured enhanced constitu-tional standing vis-à-vis other levels of government and gained direct taxation powers, their structural dependency on big business would diminish, in turn bolstering cities' bargaining capacity vis-à-vis the corporate world, and subse-quently increase the likelihood that cities adopt policies that cater to all their constituencies and residents, across the spectrum of wealth and income.

Let us consider in some detail a few aspects of the city-business alliance. The connection between cities and capital is well established in sociological and eco-nomic thought. The seminal works of Max Weber on the role of urban autonomy in Europe's rise, or Paul Krugman's influential thinking on urban agglomeration and economies of scale are merely a few examples. The idea that cities, oftentimes within the same polity, may compete with each other for investment, capital, and highly skilled people has become voguish in late twentieth and early twenty-first century theorizing about urban governance. The need for certain cities to "rein-vent" themselves in this period as a result of deindustrialization and globaliza-tion lent credence to the theory of intercity competition. Such competition may take several concrete forms, many of which are of the business-friendly type. While innovation scholars such as Richard Florida hail urban clustering of talent and creativity as essential for city competitiveness, neo-Marxist critics such as David Harvey point to the importance of urban concentration in shrinking the time and space needed to gather human capacities. Cities also provide a multi-plier of riches for property owners and businesses. It is within cities that rent, for example, generates extra surplus from non-material goods such as trendy neighborhoods, reduced travel time, etc. At the very least, the huge volume of daily human traffic concentrated in megacity centers creates a paradise for advertisers. And as many megacity centers are often marketed as glitzy and fash-ionable, big business strives to associate itself with that supposed trendiness and symbolic power, by establishing headquarter offices in the city's core business districts or sponsoring landmark buildings within (e.g., skyscrapers, sports facil-ities, and museums). In short, big cities and big business seems to be entangled in a long-standing love affair.

In a recent article, Saskia Sassen, author of the seminal *The Global City*, points to a new stage in this ongoing relationship: the organized capital takeover of

---

[25] Advocates of such partnership emphasize their potential to serve as fertile ground for the provi-sion of services in a more nimble fashion. See e.g., Kriston Capps, "How Local Governments Came to Embrace Business Partnerships," *City Lab*, November 10, 2017.

megacities through major corporate acquisitions of property at the heart of cities.[26] Sassen cites 2016 estimates of approximately $220 trillion as the global value of these urban-centered real estate assets. It is reasonable to estimate that the value is even higher today. Such accumulation of assets, she suggests, marks the repositioning of the city as a valuable commodity, particularly because the value of the acquisition "increasingly resides in ownership or control of the building itself, rather than how the building is used . . . [M]any of these buildings function rather as a way of storing capital."[27] The majority of corporate acquisitions of that nature take place in the world's top 100 cities as measured by their GDP, but the pattern quickly expands to other cities as well.[28] Sassen further notes the low utility function of these corporate acquisitions: many of the buildings are underused.[29] Thus holding the property itself, rather than its actual use, is increasingly becoming the main purpose of such possessions. In this regard, corporate control of prime city property stands in stark contrast with the ever-escalating price of modest housing, and the shrinking capacity of the working and middle classes to find residences in core city areas. This pattern of acquisitions is supported by a strict legal regulatory nexus that allows for foreclosures and evictions, often hitting low-income households. In short, Sassen argues, city buildings, and by extension the city's space, are increasingly taken and controlled by corporate ownership.

Although there is limited systematic comparative data on real estate ownership and use, single-market studies support Sassen's claim of increased corporate concentration of ownership. A 2016 study found that just 20 landlords hold more than 150,000 of New York City's approximately 2.2 million rental units, yielding a total income of over $2 billion per year for their owners.[30] Another study suggests that as of 2017, the Canary Wharf Group, co-owned by the government of Qatar, is London's largest landowner, with over 21 million sq. ft. of property, more than the landholdings of the City of London itself (17.5 million sq. ft.) or Transport London (15 million sq. ft.).[31] Corporate entities such as Aviva and BNP Paribas own more property space than the Crown Estate, the UK government, or the City of London.[32] Evidence of similar trends in cities in the developing world is scattered, but the direction is consistent: more corporate development in prime city property. Ho Chi Minh City, to pick one example, has seen more than a third

---

[26] Saskia Sassen, "The City: A Collective Good?," *Brown Journal of World Affairs* 23 (2017): 119–126. *See also* Saskia Sassen, "Who Owns Our Cities—and Why This Urban Takeover Should Concern Us All," *The Guardian*, November 24, 2015.

[27] Sassen, "The City: A Collective Good?," at 121.

[28] *Id.* at 123.

[29] *Id.* at 122.

[30] Will Parker, "Rentopoly: Who Owns New York?," *The Real Deal*, July 1, 2016.

[31] Emanuele Midolo, "Who Owns London?," *Property Week*, March 16, 2017.

[32] *Id.*

of its historic buildings demolished in the last two decades, clearing space for fancy commercial and shopping projects located in dozens of new high-rises, including the Landmark 81—one of the world's newest supertalls.[33] Shoppers entering a generic exemplar of the new malls "are greeted by a blast of air-con and a glitzy showroom featuring a bright yellow Lamborghini Huracán supercar and three different models of Bentley."[34] In Luanda, another large city projected to have well over 10 million people within the next few years, "inequality is stark: wealth has been hoarded by the elite and the rights of ordinary citizens are trampled on. Many are forcibly evicted to create new developments where they can't afford to live."[35] In short, big money is taking over megacities, near and far.

When cities attempt to hold the corporations that flourish in their midst to account for soaring housing prices, shortage of public housing, and increasing homelessness, the all-too familiar threat of capital flight rears its head. In 2019, the Seattle City Council unanimously passed a $275 per employee tax on Seattle businesses to fund affordable housing and prevent homelessness. Amazon pushed back by ending construction of a downtown tower, suggesting it would sublease instead. Fearful of alienating the city's flagship corporate employer, city officials backtracked. A month after the tax proposition's passing, the city council repealed it. Similarly, in San Francisco, capital flight threats have emerged in response to repeated attempts by the city to adopt anti-homelessness tax measures targeting top-earning corporations. The most notable of these attempts has been the so-called Proposition C, approved in 2018 by 61% of the city voters, failing to clear the two-thirds threshold required under California law.[36] Litigation is ongoing on whether the two-thirds threshold rule applies to Proposition C.[37] While several San Francisco-based corporations supported the proposal, notable others opposed it, reportedly including Twitter, Zynga, and Square.[38] The capital flight argument was advanced even by socially progressive politicians, who warned that adopting Prop C would run the risk of deterring local job creation

[33] Nick van Mead, "'Redefine the Skyline': How Ho Chi Minh City Is Erasing Its Heritage," *The Guardian*, January 21, 2019.

[34] *Id.*

[35] Sean Smith, "After the Oil Boom: Luanda Faces Stark Inequality," *The Guardian*, January 22, 2019.

[36] Under California's 1978 Proposition 3, local (municipal) governments in California have limited ability to increase property tax rates and are required to have new taxes approved by a two-thirds majority of the popular vote.

[37] In July 2019, the San Francisco Superior Court found that "a two-thirds majority is required to pass a special tax initiative placed on the ballot by government officials," but a simple majority is sufficient for proposals from voters.

[38] *See* Kate Conger, "San Francisco Approves Business Tax to Fund Homeless Services," *New York Times* (November 7, 2018); online: https://www.nytimes.com/2018/11/07/technology/san-francisco-business-tax-homeless.html.

by tech giants, or even cause them to move away altogether, taking the middle-class and service jobs with them.[39]

The extensive urban form of corporate welfare is another troubling aspect of the cozy relationship between big cities and big business. Even as influential cities emerge, the state and the accompanying statist constitutional vision are reluctant to give away governance power. City leaders are between a rock and a hard place. They must either align their interests with broader state interests and/or with big business and private sector resources. As cities cannot forum shop or "relocate," they are drawn to other ways to try to improve their lot—for example, by competing for mobile resources, such as talent, wealth, or the headquarters of major industries or corporations. In the widely documented Amazon search for a location for its second headquarters (dubbed "HQ2"), a bidding war emerged among 238 cities in the United States, Mexico. and Canada, a tally later reduced to 20 finalists, each of which offered significant tax breaks, infrastructure incentives, and other benefits to lure the company. Several contenders, among them some of America's largest metro regions (e.g., Los Angeles, Chicago, Atlanta, Philadelphia) offered incentive packages estimated at several billions of dollars each.[40] While politicians understandably saw this as a valuable opportunity for their cities to create or strengthen their branding as high-tech hubs, economists and other policy-makers sounded a more cautious note, raising concerns about the use of public money in serving the interests of one of the world's richest and largest companies by market value.[41] Ultimately, Amazon selected two rather predictable destinations: Chrystal City in Arlington, Virginia—at the outskirts of Washington, DC, where US government agencies are located; and Queens, New York City—adjacent to America's and the world's largest business center. In NYC, the approval process was finalized only after the city gave up its local veto on the planning process, agreeing that control over the process will be held by the state. While attempting to convince Amazon that housing for its potential employees would be affordable, the city offered no suggestions as to how Amazon (valued at approximately 700 billion dollars) could contribute to the city's affordable housing shortage.[42] Likewise, there was no accounting in the city bid for the recreational or educational opportunities funded through the public purse, while Amazon itself, it was revealed in 2019, paid a "[w]hopping $0 in Federal

---

[39] Reported in Michael J. Coren, "San Francisco's Big Business Tax to Fight Homelessness Is a Warning for Tech," *Quartz* (November 9, 2018); online: https://qz.com/1455577/san-franciscos-big-business-tax-to-fight-homelessness-is-a-warning-for-tech/.

[40] Leanna Garfield, "Cities Are Throwing Hundreds of Millions at Amazon to Land HQ2—Here's How They Stack Up," *Business Insider*, April 4, 2018.

[41] *See, generally*, Nathan Jensen and Edmund Malesky, *Incentives to Pander: How Politicians Use Corporate Welfare for Political Gain* (Cambridge University Press, 2018).

[42] *See* Priya S. Gupta, "The Fleeting, Unhappy Affair of Amazon HQ2 and New York City," *Transnational Legal Theory* 10 (2019): 97–122, 109.

Taxes on $11.2 billion profits" for the 2017 and 2018 tax years.[43] In response to mounting public criticism of the financial promises made to Amazon, valued conservatively at $3 billion in tax breaks, subsidies and infrastructure incentives, Amazon announced in early 2019 that it would cancel the planned Long Island City location. New York State Governor Andrew Cuomo and other officials have approached Amazon and Jeff Bezos (including via an open letter in the *New York Times*), announcing their continued commitment to hosting one of the two new headquarters and pleading for the company to reinstate the plan. (In late 2019 it was announced that Amazon has signed a new lease for 335,000 square feet space in the Hudson Yards neighborhood on Manhattan's West Side, without any apparent "sweeteners" or financial incentives funded by the public purse).[44]

The Amazon spectacle is only the tip of the iceberg. As I have explained, cities' structurally limited revenue generation capacity, and their fiscal dependency on national and sub-national governments, creates a state of chronic underfunding, which has in turn pushed American cities into the arms of big business. Fierce competition ensues among cities within the United States that strive to lure corporations to establish their headquarters or major production and distribution hubs in their midst. A few years ago, the so-called Border War between the Kansas and Missouri parts of Kansas City spent huge amount of taxpayer money to lure companies to move across state lines within the same metro area.[45] In many respects, this bidding process is a race to the bottom, as cities are caught in a cruel contest to outdo each other in providing incentives to big business, often paying out of public coffers. Some accounts suggests that local government in America spend as much as $90 billion a year in tax breaks and other financial incentives to lure corporate headquarters and factories.[46] Other, more modest estimates assess the amount in the vicinity of $25 billion to $50 billion per annum.[47] A 2018 deal to bring Taiwanese tech firm Foxconn, to mention but one example, to Wisconsin involved an estimated $3–5 billion in tax incentives. A study assesses the "tax breaks per new job creation ratio" in this transaction at anywhere from $350,000 to about $1.5 million in tax subsidies per newly created

---

[43] *Id.*, 15, *citing* Laura Stampler, "Amazon Will Pay a Whopping $0 in Federal Taxes on 11.2 Billion Profits," *Fortune Magazine*, February 15, 2019), as well as data provided in *The New Republic, The Guardian*, and in a report by *The Institute on Taxation and Economic Policy.*

[44] *See* Keiko Morris, "Amazon Leases New Manhattan Office Space, Less Than a Year After HQ2 Pullout," *Wall Street Journal*, December 6, 2019).

[45] *See* Derek Thompson, "Amazon's HQ Spectacle Isn't Just Shameful—It Should Be Illegal," *The Atlantic*, November 12, 2018.

[46] *Id.*; Louise Story, "As Companies Seek Tax Deals, Governments Pay High Price," *New York Times*, December 1, 2012.

[47] *See, e.g.,* Timothy Bartik, "Who Benefits from Economic Development Incentives? How Incentive Effects on Local Incomes and the Income Distribution Vary with Different Assumptions about Incentive Policy and the Local Economy" (W.E. Upjohn Institute Technical Report No. 18-034, 2018).

job, depending on the actual number of new jobs the deal will eventually help generate.[48] The watchdog group Good Jobs First further reports that among the main beneficiaries of similar tax abatement pledges by cities are some of the world's most profitable firms, including Facebook, Google, and Amazon.[49]

In the majority of cases, city support for big business takes the form of massive tax breaks, expedited land allocation, planning and construction processes, favorable budget allocation for public works (e.g., improved transit to/from company sites), and other such perks from the public purse. In return, the arrival of a business giant to a given city is said to create new, high-quality jobs and to indirectly boost the city's reputation and competitiveness. However, some studies and journalistic investigations question this assumption. A 2018 study titled "Unfulfilled Promises" suggests that, while Amazon fulfillment centers help generate gains in warehousing- and storage-related jobs, they do not generate broad-based employment growth in the cities that host them.[50] In other words, the massive financial incentives that cities and counties are eager to offer Amazon and other corporate entities of like caliber do not generate reciprocal value in actual net job creation. Additional investigations have found that American cities with relatively high inequality levels are more likely to offer companies tax abatements in order to attract their business than cities with relatively egalitarian income distribution.[51] Another recent study suggests that even though there is a substantial variation across states and cities in the use of business incentives, there is little correlation between the level of incentives a company receives and the economic growth in the localities that provide the incentives.[52] For instance, Nathan Jensen's comprehensive study of the impact of firm-specific location incentives in the United States on actual employment opportunities found that such incentives "have no discernible impact on firm expansion, measured by job creation."[53] These incentives, Jensen further argues, are often redundant, as the majority of firms would have made the same decision to relocate, expand, or stay put even without incentives. Likewise, Richard Florida, one of the most influential authors on urban and region competitiveness, found "virtually no

[48] Dominic Rushe, "'It's a Huge Subsidy': The $4.8bn Gamble to Lure Foxconn to America," *The Guardian*, July 2, 2018.

[49] *Id.*

[50] Janelle Jones and Ben Zipperer, "Unfulfilled Promises," *Economic Policy Institute*, February 1, 2018.

[51] *See* Mike Maciag, "Big Business Tax Breaks May Worsen Income Inequality," *Governing*, May 23, 2018. The study reports that in the fiscal year 2016 alone, New York City lost revenue in the amount of $3.5 billion for various tax abatement reasons. Chicago lost $600 million for similar reasons.

[52] Bartik, "Who Benefits from Economic Development Incentives?"

[53] Nathan Jensen, "Job Creation and Firm-Specific Location Incentives," *Journal of Public Policy* 37 (2017): 85–112; *see, generally*, Nathan Jensen and Edmund Malesky, *Incentives to Pander: How Politicians Use Corporate Welfare for Political Gain.*

association between business incentives and any measure of economic performance, including wages, incomes, and unemployment."[54]

Perhaps the most grotesque episode of city corporate welfare dynamics in the
United States involved Chicago's parking meters. In 2008, the city, under Mayor
Richard Daley, struck a deal with Morgan Stanley to lease all of Chicago's parking
meters for 75 years (2008 to 2083) for approximately $1.15 billion, in order fill
acute budget holes without raising property taxes.[55] Recent audits on parking
meters revenue in Chicago suggest that the investors, effectively owned by the
government of Abu Dhabi, will have recouped their investment by 2021, with
a full 62 years of parking revenue in one of America's largest cities still to come.
And it becomes even more incongruous. According to the lease agreement, the
City of Chicago must reimburse investors for every parking space that became
temporarily unavailable for whatever reason, including for public works. In
2017 alone, the city paid investors over $21 million under that category alone.
Attempts by Mayor Rahm Emanuel's administration to renegotiate the terms of
the lease deal or to have it declared illegal on ground that public space cannot
be sold were dismissed by the courts. Therefore, an Abu Dhabi-controlled con-
sortium of investors will continue to pocket the entire amount of public parking
fees in Chicago for the next half century. One is left to scratch one's head in
asking how financially clueless and desperate the city must have been back in
2008 when it agreed to this deal from hell. For the purpose of our discussion, it is
safe to conclude that no city with meaningful legal or constitutional control over
revenue generation would even imagine a deal like the Chicago parking meter
lease. However, without such control, cities struggling to meet the needs of their
populations while operating under a near-permanent state of austerity may find
that selling public assets to private entities becomes one of the very few available
options.

In other parts of the world, cities are faced with similar challenges. While
EU law restricts the incentives that member states can offer to companies,
corporations still enjoy considerable protections under EU law. For example,
large cities accuse Airbnb and other online holiday rental platforms of raising
neighborhood housing costs by taking countless rental units out of the long-
term housing rental supply that is available to locals. However, due to EU liberal imperatives concerning digital commerce, city authorities remain limited
in the ability to regulate the short-term rental market. The phenomenon has
reached new heights in tourist destinations such as Paris, Berlin, Amsterdam,

[54] Richard Florida, "Handing Out Tax Breaks to Businesses Is Worse Than Useless," *City Lab*,
March 7, 2017.
[55] Fran Spielman, "Parking Meter Deal Keeps Getting Worse for City as Meter Revenues Rise,"
Chicago Sun Times, April 15, 2018; Chris Lentino, "Chicago to Pay $20 Million to Parking Meter
Company in 2018," *Illinois Policy*, November 2, 2017.

and Barcelona, where Airbnb and its counterparts have countless listed units (in Paris alone, Airbnb has about 65,000 listed homes). As major European cities sought to limit that trend and push housing prices down, Airbnb turned to EU law. In 2019, the Advocate General of the European Court of Justice endorsed that claim and issued an opinion that, under EU law, Airbnb is considered a digital information provider, not a traditional real estate agent, and as such can continue to "colonize" the market for short-term rentals at the expense of the needs and interests of long-term residents.[56] Cities, home to these commercial transactions, have little or no say in the matter.[57] Given the vulnerable constitutional status of cities in low- and middle-income countries in other parts of the world, we are left to speculate as to potential enormity of the sellout by cities of public assets, not to mention the aggressive advancement of business interests in urban centers.

Other types of urban transformations come to mind involving the ethically questionable proximity of these business interests and city governance: (i) "charter cities" that involve leasing of massive chunks of land to consortia of private developers who build and run autonomous cities or gated communities, supposedly free of state bureaucracy and corruption;[58] (ii) new city projects throughout the world that, like Saudi Arabia's Neom, follow a pattern of "corporatization" whereby entire neighborhoods (even cities) are built jointly by governments and the private sector and then run by CEOs and sales companies as complete business enterprises in subversion of democratic governance processes;[59] (iii) so-called smart cities, where technological advancements developed by giant corporations are deployed to run and monitor key aspects of everyday city life, thereby entrusting invaluable data to the hands of tech giants; and (iv)

[56] *See* Case C-390/18, Opinion of ECJ Advocate General (delivered on April 30, 2019); online: http://curia.europa.eu/juris/document/document.jsf?docid=213504&text=&doclang=EN&pageIndex=0&cid=1668049).

[57] Daniel Boffey, "Airbnb Should Be Seen as a Digital Service Provider, ECJ Advised," *The Guardian*, April 30, 2019; Jon Henley, "Ten Cities Ask EU for Help to Fight Airbnb Expansion," *The Guardian*, June 20, 2019. However, in 2020, in a case involving two apartment owners in Paris who were fined by the city for having rented out their spaces through Airbnb without authorization, the ECJ Advocate General issued a qualifying opinion according to which EU law's so-called "Services Directive" (2006) permits national and local authorities to restrict the freedom to provide services (e.g., through an authorization process) as long as such restrictions may be justified by "overriding reasons relating to the public interest," in this case "combating a housing shortage and seeking to ensure the availability of sufficient and affordable (long-term) housing (in particular in large cities), as well as the protection of the urban environment." *See* Opinion of Advocate General Bobek, Joined Cases C-724/18 and C-727/18 *Cali Apartments SCI (C-724/18) HX (C-727/18 v Procureur général près la cour d'appel de Paris, Ville de Paris* (delivered on April 2, 2020).

[58] *See* Rahul Sagar, "Are Charter Cities Legitimate?," *Journal of Political Philosophy* 24 (2016): 509–529.

[59] *See, e.g.*, Sarah Moser, "New Cities: Old Wine in New Bottles?," *Dialogues in Human Geography* 5 (2014): 31–35. Moser estimates that there are 150 such new city projects throughout the Global South, in various stages of planning, construction, or actual inhabitation.

forced evictions of poor neighborhoods—increasingly common in major cities in less economically developed countries—so that prime urban property may be developed, often without adequate compensation or corresponding invest-ment in alternative public housing solutions. Much has been written about the gentrification of hitherto rundown urban areas, involving demographic changes reflective of broad "market forces," the laws of supply and demand, and so on. However, with forced evictions, city and state authorities are proactively collabo-rating with big business to promote such actions.

The upshot of these studies is as obvious from a constitutional design stand-point as it is unsettling from a normative one: due to their lack of robust con-stitutional status, cities often lack suitable independent budgets or sufficient revenue-generating mechanisms. Faced with rising demands for services, structural dependency on funding from higher levels of government, and con-sequently with chronic budget shortfalls, cities turn to big business as their fi-nancial lifeline. The result is privatization of public assets and excessively business-friendly policies.

It is hard to see how this dynamic could change unless lawmakers tackle its root cause: cities' lack of autonomous constitutional standing, taxation authority, and other legally warranted means of revenue generation. Such enhanced city power would substantively change the balance vis-à-vis national or sub-national governments—dominators of cities for the last two centuries.

III. Public Housing, Environmental Protection

As cities become home to an ever-growing majority of the world's population, the need to engage cities in addressing major challenges such as climate change and economic inequality becomes ever more pressing. With 55% of the world popu-lation currently living in cities, rising to over 70% within the next few decades, it is hard to envision any kind of effective response to these challenges without the direct involvement of city government. This provides further justification to em-power cities constitutionally. Doing so is likely, not only to reduce cities' struc-tural dependence on corporate actors (and the strings that come with it), but also to allow cities to adopt more aggressive policies regarding social integration, affordable housing, and environmental protection, clearly distancing themselves from business interests that are agnostic at best (and oftentimes proactively op-posed) to progressive action on these and other closely related matters.

Much has been written about the rising costs of housing in major urban centers, in part due to business control of prime real estate in the city core, "pricing out" the working middle classes and pushing them into suburbia, while confining the lower classes in often decayed urban neighborhoods. At a time when more constitutions than ever before (45% as all national constitutions as of 2019) guarantee the right to housing, housing remains the least affordable human right of all.[60] The global financial crisis of 2007–2010 exacerbated matters considerably, bringing austerity measures down on already cash-strapped municipalities.[61] A comprehensive 2015 study by the UN suggests that "the social housing waiting lists in the United Kingdom are at 1.8 million, 1.7 million in France . . . the United States is experiencing a shortage of 5.3 million social housing units. The waiting period for social housing in the Russian Federation is 20 years."[62] Meanwhile, in many Global South metropolises struggling to cope with population growth, huge shantytowns have emerged at the city outskirts, while poor inner-city neighborhoods have been removed en masse in the name of hastily designed "development" projects that are often closely aligned with business interests.[63]

City governments hoping to combat these trends have commonly looked to public housing projects (sometimes referred to as affordable housing, social housing, or subsidized housing)—decent housing solutions owned and managed by the city and made available to city residents for a subsidized or protected rent, based on a set of socioeconomic, mixed-use, and diversity criteria. Other programs combine public housing with regulatory measures such as rent or price control or privately owned units to ensure availability of affordable housing. More often than not, the demand far exceeds the supply. Arguably, cities with enhanced constitutional autonomy and levying power would be in a position to increase economic self-sufficiency and to reduce city dependence on external funding, thereby allowing for more resources to go to public housing programs.

While a comprehensive study of the effect of city constitutional power on public housing is of course beyond the scope of this book, the anecdotal evidence is clear. The city-state of Singapore—the closest example currently on offer of a self-governing metropolis with state-like features—is not only one of the most successful social experiments in managing social and cultural diversity, but is also the world leader in providing affordable housing solutions to its residents. Within a span of less than two decades, from the time Singapore acquired full sovereignty in the mid-1960s to the mid-1980s, the percentage of residents in public housing rose from 20% to over 70%. Recent reports estimate the current

---

[60] "Social Housing in the UNECE Region: Models, Trends, and Challenges" (United Nations Economic Commission for Europe, 2015); online: www.unece.org/fileadmin/DAM/hlm/documents/Publications/Social_Housing_in_UNECE_region.pdf.

[61] *See* Matthew Desmond, *Evicted: Poverty and Profit in the American City* (Broadway Books, 2017); Susanne Soederberg, "Evictions: A Global Capitalist Phenomenon," *Development and Change* 49 (2018): 286–301.

[62] "Social Housing in the UNECE Region."

[63] For a typical illustration of such dynamic, see the political and legal saga surrounding the eviction of residents of the Kibera informal settlement in southwest Nairobi.

percentage of public housing residents at 82% (or roughly 4 million) of Singapore's permanent population, down from a peak of 87% a few years ago.[64] Similarly, as discussed in Chapter 3, Seoul's legislative autonomy allowed it to launch a unique residential zoning policy that made it mandatory for developers to include affordable housing as one-fifth of any housing development. By the mid-1990s, the city had added approximately 200,000 new units for low-income residents. As of 2018, there are more than 271,000 public housing units in Seoul.[65] (In comparison, New York City strives to have 200,000 such units by 2024; a 2018 citywide survey found that NYC's housing authority requires no less than $32 billion over five years just to meet capital repairs needs in its public housing units.)[66] In late 2018, Seoul's metropolitan government announced 5000 new public rental units would be added each year, and vowed to provide more than 60,000 new public housing units for sale by 2022.[67] Meanwhile in Hong Kong—formally, if not always practically, one of the most autonomous metropoles in the world, approximately one-third of the population resides in public housing, and an additional 15% resides in public sale and subsidized home ownership units.[68] To be sure, Hong Kong remains one of the most economically unequal cities in the world. Unsubsidized home ownership is virtually beyond reach for most middle-class families and is seen as one of the reasons for the 2019 political upheaval in Hong Kong.[69] However, the fact remains that without any government regulation of Hong Kong's high-demand/low supply housing market, Hong Kong residency would be confined only to the super rich.

While social housing rates are considerably lower elsewhere, urban constitutional autonomy consistently makes a difference. Social housing rates in Hamburg (8.5%) and Berlin (6%)—both city Länder—are more than double the national average in Germany (3%). In January 2020, Berlin passed legislation

---

[64] HDB Annual Report 2018/19: Key Statistics; HDB (2019); online: https://www20.hdb.gov.sg/fi10/fi10221p.nsf/hdb/2019/ebooks.html. *See, generally,* Kyunghwan Kim and Phang Sock Yong, *Singapore's Housing Policies 1960–2013* (KDI School and World Bank Institute, 2013); Beng Huat Chua, "Navigating between Limits: The Future of Public Housing in Singapore," *Housing Studies* 29 (2014): 520–533.

[65] Kim Se-jeong, "Seoul's Evolving Public Housing Policy," *Korea Times* (March 21, 2018); online: http://www.koreatimes.co.kr/www/nation/2018/11/281_245940.html.

[66] Sally Goldenberg, "At $31.8 B, NYCHA's Unmet Capital Needs Dwarf Government Allocations," *Politico,* July 2, 2018; online: https://www.politico.com/states/new-york/city-hall/story/2018/07/01/at-318b-nychas-unmet-capital-needs-dwarf-government-allocations-495925.

[67] Claire Lee, "Seoul City to Provide 5,000 Public Housing per Year," *Korea Herald* (September 26, 2018); online: http://www.koreaherald.com/view.php?ud=20180926000167.

[68] Kwok Yu Lau and Alan Murie, "Residualisation and Resilience: Public Housing in Hong Kong," *Housing Studies* 32 (2017): 271–295.

[69] In October 2019, the Hong Kong government introduced a new plan to expand and renew public housing. Governor Carrie Lam declared that "every Hong Kong citizen and his family will . . . [should] be able to have their own home in Hong Kong, a city in which we all have a share." According to the new plan, unused land in the northern territories will be made available, with first-time buyers to receive financial support.

that places a freeze on rental prices for more than 1.5 million Berlin apartments for a period of five years, thereby taming rising costs that were driving out lower- and middle-income earners.[70] In Brussels, which enjoys special constitutional status as a bilingual capital city region—social housing is at the highest percentage (12%) among Belgium's large cities (e.g., 8.3% in Antwerp). The City of Johannesburg, drawing on its expansive constitutionally assigned land use and planning powers (see detailed discussion in Chapter 3), has adopted legislation requiring that all future residential private development projects with 20 units or more include 30% affordable homes, regardless of the project's location. The stated goal of the policy is to address the substantial inequality and segregation that persist in South Africa's largest metropoles.[71] In September 2019, Johannesburg won the Sustainable City and Human Settlements Award from the UN for its partnership with local developers to build South Hills (nearly 6,000 housing units) in the south of the city. The UN recognized the city's "outstanding demonstration in promoting sustainable cities and human settlements, as well as the implementation of sustainable development goals." The project features a mix of fully subsidized homes, subsidized rental units, and open-market units, with over 90% of the units within local legislation's definition of affordable housing. None of these new inclusionary policies would have been possible without the constitutional entrenchment of city powers in the post-apartheid Constitution of South Africa.

Conversely, megacities that face ever-growing demand for social housing but lack meaningful constitutional, planning, or taxation powers, are practically held hostage by state authorities' overarching mandate, pushing city authorities to the hands of big business's deep pockets. (Recall the City of Chicago parking meters lease fiasco described earlier.) As discussed in Chapter 2, Australian cities are constitutionally subjected to Australian states. Sydney, to pick one example, is at the near-complete constitutional mercy of the government of New South Wales. Even though the city has set the target for public housing within its jurisdiction at 7.5%, its capacity to deliver on this commitment is severely constrained by the refusal of the New South Wales government to allow for the necessary zoning adjustments or to increase the proportion of affordable housing in new construction on the large portions of state-owned land within the city. A recent study of public housing in Sydney thus concludes that "if local government is to create a sizable affordable housing sector, it is vital that the State and Federal Government

---

[70] *See* Melissa Eddy, "Berlin Freezes Rents for 5 Years in a Bid to Slow Gentrification," *New York Times*, January 31, 2020.
[71] *See* Justice Malala, "Why Are South African Cities Still So Segregated 25 Years after Apartheid?," *The Guardian*, October 21, 2019.

play a major role. Local governments, however powerful and well-resourced, do not have the capacity to do it by themselves."[72]

In 2018, well aware of the need for more power to tackle the acute affordable housing shortage in megacities, the cities of Amsterdam, Barcelona, London, Montreal, Montevideo, New York, and Paris presented to the UN a Municipalist Declaration of Local Governments for the Right to Housing and the Rights to the City.[73] The declaration calls for more city powers to regulate the real estate market (that would require a shift in city powers as well as the ability to limit, in the name of a worthy cause, constitutionally entrenched property right clauses); more funds to expand and improve public housing stocks (independent taxation powers would certainly help here); and additional tools (constitutional powers, anyone?) to co-produce public-private community driven alternative housing.[74] However, as explained in Chapter 4, regardless of their symbolic, political, or practical significance in raising awareness to the public housing cause, such international city networks, and indeed all of their signatory parties, lack constitutional standing in their respective countries. Moreover, in some instances, supranational constitutional norms may in fact limit the power of cities, pitted as they are against protected property rights, freedom of contract, and of commerce—for example, major European cities' attempts to constrain online platforms that affect the urban housing market such as Airbnb and its counterparts.[75]

Along with rising economic inequality, climate change is one of the most menacing challenges of our time. In this area, large cities are at the forefront. They are major energy consumers, air polluters, and waste producers; recent reports suggest cities are responsible for consuming two-thirds of the world's energy and produce over 70% of global carbon emissions.[76] The World Bank estimates that by 2030, the waste produced globally will reach 7 million tons per day.[77] The waste problem is acute in emerging cities; a 2013 article in *Nature* suggests that "[L]andfills such as Laogang in Shanghai, China; Sudokwon in Seoul; the now-full Jardim Gramacho in Rio de Janeiro, Brazil; and Bordo Poniente in Mexico

---

[72] Alan Morris and Benjamin Hanckel, *Local Government and Housing in the 21st Century: The City of Sydney's Approach to the Supply of Affordable Housing* (University of South Australia, UTS, 2017), 13.

[73] https://citiesforhousing.org/.

[74] *Id.*

[75] *See, e.g.*, "UnFairbnb: How Online Rental Platforms Use the EU to Defeat Cities' Affordable Housing Measures" (Corporate Europe Observatory, May 2018); Daniel Boffey, "Airbnb Should Be Seen as a Digital Service Provider, ECJ Advised," *The Guardian*, April 30, 2019; Jon Henley, "Ten Cities Ask EU for Help to Fight Airbnb Expansion," *The Guardian*, June 20, 2019.

[76] *See* "Why Cities? Ending Climate Change Begins in the City," *C40*; online: https://www.c40.org/ending-climate-change-begins-in-the-city.

[77] Silpa Kaza et al., *What a Waste 2.0: A Global Snapshot of Solid Waste Management to 2050* (World Bank Group, 2018), 24.

City vie for the title of the world's largest."[78] New York, Mexico City, Tokyo, Los Angeles, Mumbai, Istanbul, Jakarta, and Cairo—all huge metropolises—are considered the world's biggest urban wasters.[79] (That Tokyo—twice as large as New York or Mexico City—is not the world-leading trash-producing megacity reflects behavioral patterns and cultural norms, but also Tokyo's legal status, leading to its enhanced regulatory powers in this critical yet often overlooked policy area.) At the same time, as cities grow larger and larger, their residents become immediate victims of extreme heat waves, poor air quality, and rising sea levels. The consequences are harsh and immediate. Megacities such as Jakarta, Dhaka, and Lagos face imminent flooding risk, with severe sanitation hazards affecting their water supply, sewage, and waste management systems. In 2019 alone, environmental emergencies were declared in Mexico City, Lahore, Mumbai, and Delhi, where air quality has fallen to an all-time low, far below minimum acceptable standards, putting tens of millions at immediate health risk. Much as in the realm of public housing, the constitutional empowerment of large cities, bringing extended policy-making authority and taxation powers, is likely to give metropolitan centers an enhanced capacity to address climate change effectively.

As we have seen in Chapter 4, international city networks have been very active in the area of climate change. However, as already mentioned, such networks lack formal constitutional standing, do not affect participating cities' constitutional status in their respective countries, and appear to have only marginally (at best) affected national governments' exclusive status as signatory parties to binding international treaties on climate change. The constitutional empowerment of cities could support policy-making independence of city authorities (en route lowering their reliance on private sector support), thereby allowing cities to effectively bypass national government complacency in combating climate change.

Buenos Aires provides one of the clearest illustrations of the effect constitutional empowerment can have on city power to tackle climate change. As explained in Chapter 3, a changing political constellation in Argentina allowed the City of Buenos Aires to gain a constitutional status similar in practice to that of a province. (According to Article 129 of the Argentine Constitution, "[T]he City of Buenos Aires shall have an autonomous system of government with power of legislation and jurisdiction, and the head of its government shall be directly elected by the people of the City"). The newly-acquired constitutional

---

[78] Daniel Hoornweg, Perinaz Bhada-Tata, and Chris Kennedy, "Environment: Waste Production Must Peak This Century, *Nature*, October 30, 2013.

[79] Christopher A. Kennedy et al., "Energy and Material Flows of Megacities," *Proceedings of the National Academy of Sciences of the United States of America* (PNAS) 112 (2015): 5985–5990, 5986; online: https://www.pnas.org/content/pnas/112/19/5985.full.pdf.

status considerably enhanced the city's autonomous policy-making authority. Aided by bottom-up pressure from city residents and the political will of its leaders, Buenos Aires has turned into one of the most active cities in the world in the fight against climate change, establishing a new Environmental Protection Agency of the Autonomous City of Buenos Aires in conjunction with other government levels.[80] To pick one example, in an international award winning move, Buenos Aires converted the four center lanes of the 20-lane Avenida 9 de Julio—the widest avenue in the world—into bus lanes, dramatically reducing $CO2$ emissions.[81] It also introduced an intricate system of bicycle lanes alongside vast pedestrian-only areas, planted tens of thousands of trees throughout the city, invested in urban drainage, established an environmental protection agency, granted status to many unofficial litter pickers ("cartoneros"), and has put an effort into cleaning up the Rio Matanza-Riachuelo, along which the land was deemed non-livable within 35 meters of its banks in 2008 by Argentina's Supreme Court.[82] The city's Climate Change Adaptation and Mitigation Act (adopted September 2011) warrants an update to the city's environmental action plan every five years.

In summary, a constitutional framework conducive to city action can go a long way in allowing megacities to govern more justly and effectively. To be sure, there is no single solution to economic inequality or global climate change, but cities have the potential ability, and oftentimes the political will, to lead in both fights. Enhanced constitutional standing, accompanied by greater taxation and legislation capacity, is likely to aid cities that wish to do so, to take considerable measures toward the realization of the right to housing and to environmental protection.

IV. The Density Factor

Density seldom features in democratic theory discussions about cities, let alone in the almost nonexistent constitutional theory discussions about urban agglomeration. Nonetheless, density is a key defining feature of cities. Throughout their history, from antiquity to modern times, cities' main defining attribute is

---

[80] For a detailed review, see Charles Newbery, "Environment: Buenos Aires Green Campaign Looks to Youth Environmental; Priorities Include River Clean-Up," Financial Times, April 4, 2017; Francesca Perry, "Everyone Praises Green Copenhagen. But What if Your City has 20m People?," The Guardian, April 2, 2015; "Buenos Aires: Latin America's rising star," CPD Net; online: https://www.cdp.net/en/cities/cities-scores/a-list-stories#464f18360a31a99b8003db4c668244c0.

[81] This project won the 2014 Sustainable Transport Award.

[82] M 1569 XL Beatriz Silvia Mendoza and Others v. National State of Argentina in Regards to Damages (Damages stemming from the environmental contamination of the Matanza-Riachuelo River) [Supreme Court of Argentina; July 8, 2008].

their greater density relative to their surroundings. The essence of contemporary urban life lies in the close proximity of a very large number of people living in a complex nexus of buildings and streets, providing and consuming countless goods and services, all generating frequent and diverse human interactions, from the earthly to the abstract.

In many fast-growing megacities, the density factor has significance on a far more concrete and immediate level. As we have seen, the vast majority of urban expansion over the last six decades took place in the Global South. Furthermore, urbanization in Asia, Africa, and Latin America is projected to account for a whopping 96.2% of the urban population growth worldwide from 2018 to 2050. In Africa alone, urban population increased from 53 million in 1960 to 548 million in 2018—more than a 10-fold increase within half a century, and is projected to further increase to 1.34 billion by 2050. Meanwhile, in Asia, the urban population grew from 360 million in 1960 to approximately 2.26 billion today, and is projected to further increase to 3.47 billion by 2050. Demographic projections for the next three decades further suggest that more than one-third of the growth of the world's urban population between 2018 and 2050 will occur in India (where more than 400 million additional urban dwellers are projected), China (more than 250 million), and Nigeria (190 million).[83]

Massive urban swelling also entails changing density parameters, and by extension serious sanitation and public health concerns. In some instances, the current figures are staggering. Consider this: density in Jakarta—considered one of the worst megacities in the world in terms of traffic jams and air pollution—is 15,000 people/km^2 (38,850/mile^2)—nearly three times denser than London. However, when put in the context of density in other megacities in the Global South, Jakarta does not even come close to the "top." Estimates of the average population density in Manila vary from 20,000 people/km^2 (51,800/mile^2) to over 70,000 people/km^2 (181,300/mile^2)—depending on whether the reference point is the City of Manila (population 1.8 million) or Metro Manila (population 25 million)—but an often cited figure is 43,000 people/km^2 (111,370/mile^2). Dhaka—considered the densest city in the world—sports roughly similar figures (approximately 46,000 people/km^2 [119,140/mile^2]).[84] For comparison purposes (see Figure 5.1), in Hong Kong, one of the densest major urban areas in the high-income world, that figure stands at approximately 6,800 people/km^2 (17,600/mile^2).

---

[83] See World Urbanization Prospects: The 2018 Revision (Population Division of the UN Department of Economic and Social Affairs [UN DESA], 2019).

[84] A 2014 study estimates that more than 60% of the total population in Bangladesh lives in slums. A 2016 study by the UN-Habitat puts that figure at 55%. From 1997 to 2014, over a period of 17 years, the country saw an increase of 66% in the number of slums. See, generally, S.M. Atia Naznin and Shawkat Alam, "Judicial Remedies for Forced Slum Evictions in Bangladesh: An Analysis of the Structural Injunction," Asian Journal of Law and Society 5 (2018): 1–31.

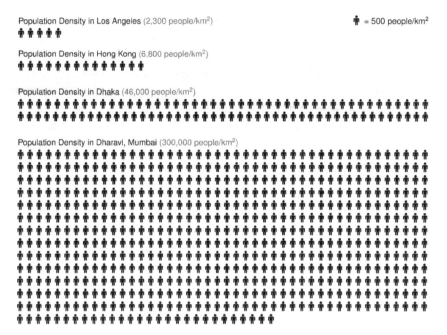

Figure 5.1 Comparative Urban Density

In other major cities in high-income countries, the figures are considerably lower (e.g., Paris 3,800 [9,850]; Berlin 3,100 [8,000]; Toronto 2,800 [7,250]; Nagoya 2,500 [6,475]; Los Angeles 2,300 [6,000]; Melbourne 1,600 [4,150]). If the entire world population (7.6 billion) lived in similar density conditions as Dhaka or Manila, it would fit within the area of Oklahoma or the combined space of the Czech Republic, Austria, and Slovenia with no one living anywhere else in the world.[85]

More unsettling still, density in some poor neighborhoods in developing world megacities is far higher than the overall figures for Dhaka or Manila. Rocinha, a Rio de Janeiro favela, has population density of 50,000 people/km² (129,500/mile²). The Karachi Central neighborhood (Karachi), Kibera (Nairobi; Africa's biggest urban slum), and the Tondo neighborhood (Manila) all have density of 70,000 people/km² (181,300/mile²). In Mabatini and Mlango Kubwa (both in Nairobi), it is 80,000 people/km² (207,200/mile²) and 90,000 people/

---

[85] The current population of these three small European countries is 21 million. Squeezing the entire world population into these three countries would mean that the space that is currently occupied by *each* resident of the Czech Republic, Austria, and Slovenia would be occupied by approximately 355 people.

km^2 (233,000/mile^2), respectively. And in Lalbagh Thana, Chowk Bazar Kotwali Thana (all in Dhaka), Mathare North (Nairobi), and Zaveri Bazaar (Mumbai), the density exceeds 100,000 people/km^2 (259,000/mile^2). By comparison, the densest area in Hong Kong is Kowloon with approximately 50,000 people/km^2 (129,500/mile^2). The general density in Mumbai—one of the densest cities in the world—is 27,000 people/km^2 (70,000/mile^2). As shown in Figure 5.1, in Dharavi—a slum neighborhood in Mumbai—700,000 people live within little more than 2 square kilometers (0.77 square mile), with a population density of nearly 300,000 people/km^2 (777,000/mile^2). That's the equivalent of the entire world population, 7.6 billion, squeezed into Vermont or into the German state of Hesse.[86]

Serious sanitation concerns and failing infrastructure pose major existential challenges even in less-extreme megacity settings. Dhaka's sewage system is chronically dysfunctional.[87] Lagos and Kinshasa struggle with waste management and consequent contamination of water sources. One-third of Manila's population lives in improvised shelters, often with constant fear of intense flooding due to frequent typhoons, poor trash disposal management, and clogged drains and waterways.[88] Parts of Jakarta (city population over 10 million; metropolitan population 30 million) are sinking at a rate of 25 cm per year, and face imminent flooding.[89] This is one of the main reasons for the Indonesian government's revival of attempts to relocate the nation's capital to a different site.[90] Quite apart from the flooding risk—40% of the city sits below sea level—the city is considered one of the world's worst for traffic congestion and air quality. The Sentiong River, which streams through Kemayoran in Central Jakarta, is so polluted that it is known by locals as *kali item* or the black river.[91] In

---

[86] This reflects a much broader housing crisis in Mumbai; it is estimated that 65% of Mumbai households live in single-room units. *See* Marie-Hélène Zérah, "'Transforming Mumbai' or the Challenges of Forging a Collective Actor," *in* Dominique Lorrain, ed., *Governing Megacities in Emerging Countries* (Ashgate, 2014), 97–152.

[87] Poppy McPherson, "The Dysfunctional Megacity: Why Dhaka Is Bursting at the Sewers," *The Guardian*, March 21, 2018.

[88] Gönna Ketels, "Relocating to Escape Flooding in Manila—a Blessing or a Curse?" *DW Deutsche Welle* (July 23, 2019); online: https://p.dw.com/p/3MJrp.

[89] Michael Kimmelman, "Jakarta Is Sinking So Fast, It Could End Up Underwater," *New York Times*, December 21, 2017; Philip Sherwell, "$40bn to Save Jakarta: The Story of the Great Garuda," *The Guardian*, November 22, 2016.

[90] In August 2019, President Joko Widodo announced that due to various considerations, notably inequality, the overburden on Jakarta, and environmental risks, the national capital would be relocated. The new capital will be built in East Kalimantan, Borneo (density of less than 30 people per square kilometer [78 per square mile], compared to Jakarta's 15,000 per square kilometer [38,850 per square mile]). *See* Linda Poon, "Why Indonesia Wants to Move Its Capital Out of Jakarta," *City Lab*, May 6, 2019; Kate Lynos, "Why Is Indonesia Moving Its Capital City?," *The Guardian*, August 27, 2019.

[91] Kate Lamb, "Cover-Up: Jakarta Hides Foul River with Giant Net before Asian Games," *The Guardian*, July 26, 2018.

preparation for the 2018 Asia Games held in the city, the authorities had to conceal the black river underneath a huge black plastic cover to respond to health hazards and aesthetic challenges. Even São Paulo—Brazil's largest city—suffers from recurrent citywide water outages and frequent daily or weekly water supply rationing.[92] In these and other megacities, density is associated with extreme inequality in living conditions.

With such extreme overpopulation, infrastructure, and inequality challenges, it is hardly surprising that the relative contribution of megacities to global GDP is projected to decrease in the coming decades from approximately 15% to approximately 10%. With such long-term trends, the image of the economically successful "global city" of the 1990s is bound to be challenged, and perhaps even replaced, by the "megacity," struggling amidst ever-increasing demand for infrastructure, utilities, and services, and frequently forced to cut deals with the corporate world and adopt business-friendly policies to help make up for its chronic scarcity of public revenue. As all of these data suggest, extreme density is a particularly common feature of developing world megacities. Over half of Delhi's population (25 million in total), to pick one example, occupies less than 10% of the city's land. The other half, or less, occupies more than 90% of the city's land. In Dhaka, approximately 40% of the city's population lives on 5% of the land, with an intra-city density variance of 1:13 (a space occupied by a single person in a spacious neighborhood is occupied by 13 persons in densely populated ones). The Philippines's National Capital Region (Manila and vicinity, often referred to as Metro Manila, which includes 16 municipalities) has an overall density of 21,000 people/km^2 (54,500/mile^2), more than 60 times the national average of 340 people/km^2 (880/mile^2). Manila City, with density of 43,000 people/km^2 (111,500/mile^2) is approximately 126 times denser than the country's average.

This in turn poses a major challenge to the realization of economic and social rights (ESR), commonly understood as one of the main constitutional responses to poverty and to growing socioeconomic inequalities more broadly. ESRs have increasingly been formally constitutionalized in recent years, either as aspirational aims or as justiciable rights. A large number of national constitutions alongside several international treaties and covenants commit governments, at least formally, to the realization of minimum standards of social welfare. Specifically, over 70% of national constitutions protect the right to health, and over 45% of national constitutions protect the right to housing.[93] Almost all

[92] Claire Rigby, "São Paulo—Anatomy of a Failing Megacity: Residents Struggle as Water Taps Run Dry," *The Guardian*, February 25, 2015.

[93] *See* Evan Rosevear, Ran Hirschl, and Courtney Jung, "Justiciable and Aspirational Social Rights in National Constitutions," *in* Katherine Young, ed., *The Future of Economic and Social Rights* (Cambridge University Press, 2019), 37–65; Courtney Jung, Ran Hirschl, and Evan Rosevear, "Economic and Social Rights in National Constitutions," *American Journal of Comparative Law* 62 (2015): 1043–1094.

national constitutions also include a generic protection of "the right to life" or "human dignity," either in lieu of, or in addition to, a set of concrete ESRs. And yet, the actual effect of such formal protection of ESRs depends to a large extent on political will, state capacity, and on-the-ground conditions that determine the feasibility of delivering core minimum living conditions to all. Provision of ESRs is especially difficult in the enormous urban centers of the Global South.[94] This difficulty is likely to further increase given extensive urbanization trends, acute infrastructural deficiencies, and limited city power, rendering the formal protection of ESRs ineffective. In particular, overwhelming population numbers congregated in dense urban areas challenge the feasibility of suitable housing solutions to all, instead giving way to the informal economy, severe housing, health and safety hazards, and often times to quick-fix forced evictions.

While extreme density poses a major challenge to the realization of ESRs, certainly in low- and lower-middle income megacities in the Global South, it has been largely absent from discussions surrounding city empowerment. The implications of extreme density conditions on issues such as sanitation, housing, transportation, education, and healthcare are obvious. But surprisingly, very little has been written on the constitutional implications of the stark density gaps that many cities contain. To the extent that constitutional theory addresses density, it confines its concern to guaranteed "core minimum" arguments made in the context of ESRs.[95] The focus of this rights discourse is on the eradication of poverty through the provision of basic needs. However, under conditions of extreme variance in density, the core minimum approach tells only part of the story. It lacks attention to the distinctive spatial, on-the-ground conditions that make the fulfillment of the core minimum structurally unattainable. When it comes to matters where density is crucially important (e.g., sanitation, health, housing, education), it is implausible to ignore the glaring inequalities that attach to residing on "this or that" side of the density tracks.

Akin to other circumstances of structural disadvantage, those people who are adversely affected by conditions beyond their control deserve to have their interests protected. This may require the creation of remedial mechanisms, which may range, depending on the given country, from institutional measures such as special councils, ombudspersons, public advocates charged with investigative powers to affirmative action programs and to "density impact" assessments (e.g., modeled along the lines of environmental impact assessments of new plans and policies). It is also possible to envision novel political representation procedures

---

[94] See, e.g., Dan Brinks and Varun Gauri, "The Law's Majestic Equality? The Distributive Impact of Judicializing Social and Economic Rights," *Perspectives on Politics* 12 (2014): 375–393.

[95] See Jeff King, *Judging Social Rights* (Cambridge University Press, 2012); see also Katharine G. Young, *The Future of Economic and Social Rights* (Cambridge University Press, 2019).

designed to ensure that the voices of those most affected by density-based hardship are taken into account in those decisions that may shape their basic life conditions. The list could go on.

I suggest that, under certain circumstances, *extreme* and *involuntary* density (think of the slum dwellers in major developing world cities as distinct from the primarily voluntary density in Manhattan) should be taken into account in pertinent law and policy making and, where relevant, reflected in allotment of political voice. The relevant density conditions could be characterized by and measured through a large-scale (i.e., neighborhoods, quarters, cities) people-per-space (PPS) ratio with no available means of exit.

It is no secret that property and representation have a long, often exclusionary, track record. Ideas about land, spatial proximity, and political voice are common in the history of political thought, and need not be replicated here. Locke spoke about cultivation as a criterion for ownership of vacant land. And for centuries, land ownership was the basis for power, wealth, and political voice. Kant spoke about a rifle firing range as a distance yardstick for human interaction. In the post-revolution administrative division of France, there are regions, departments, and communes. The departmental seat of government (*préfecture* or *chef-lieu de département*) was determined according to the time taken to travel on horseback from anywhere in the department, with an aim for the prefecture to be accessible on horseback from any town in the department within a day's ride. Similar spatial intuitions were present in the United States, from Jefferson's equal lots plan for the Rectilinear Survey (1784) to the "160 acres per person" principle established by the *Homestead Act* (1862). Friedrich Engels famously depicted the dense maze of poor worker neighborhoods in mid-nineteenth-century Manchester, hidden from the view of the upper classes and featuring dilapidated and unfitting dwellings, poor sanitation, piles of waste, narrow unlit alleys, and little or no public spaces. Meanwhile, communal ownership of land by members of an agrarian collective has been one of the hallmarks of early socialist thought, from the Soviet Kolkhoz to the Israeli Kibbutz. And in modern labor law, statutory minimal space per worker is a common criterion for workplace safety licensing. In short, density-related arguments have been put forth in various legal, political, and spatial contexts. However, in the context of constitutional rights and their realization, the density factor has been left largely unexplored.

In democratic electoral law, "one person, one vote" is the foundational, widely established axiom. In principle, each qualified individual who is a member of a given democratic polity, regardless of her assets, social strata, gender, race or ethnicity, is entitled to participate in the political process. Here, individual persons are the primary, formally equal "units" or "atoms" from which the democratic voting universe is made, according to which measure voting rights are allotted, ballots are cast, and electoral outcomes are calculated. Spatial conditions do not play a role in determining individual-voter entitlement.

By contrast, in condominium regulations, space is the basic principle in calculating operation fees. Here, the main units are the condominium apartments, regardless of the number of people living in each. Units within a given condominium are either charged an equal fee per unit by the condominium operator, or are charged differentially based on their size, measured in square meters, square feet, etc. At times, other spatial factors (e.g., balconies, exposure, floor level, proximity to stairwell or elevator) are accounted for. However, relative density per unit does not features into condominium fee structure. In property tax law too, tax rates are calculated on the basis of space (e.g., square meters per taxable unit), and sometimes also based on the taxable space's designated function (living, industrial, entertainment, etc.) or estimated market value. The density factor, here relating to how many people live or share a given taxable unit, does not play a role in calculating property tax.

Consider two perfectly identical living units in the same building. Both have similar space, say 800 square feet and all other pertinent variables are equal. In unit A there is 1 resident. In unit B, there are 10 residents. If we apply the democratic principle of "one person, one vote," unit B has 10 votes whereas unit A has 1. For the purposes of condominium fee regulations, both units pay a similar amount as their overall size is identical. But must we always consider population and space in isolation from one another for governance purposes? I suggest that under certain circumstances, a density factor measured on the basis of the PPS ratio may have some purchase, in particular when dealing with issues or policy areas particularly affected by density such as sanitation, transportation, or public safety. The default rule would remain one person, one vote. However, those living in situations of extreme density could have enhanced input into the decision-making process for matters closely related to the deleterious impact of such density on the fulfillment of their basic rights and protections as equal members of a given city or state.

Consider the illustration of four hypothetical scenarios shown in Figure 5.2.

In Scenario A, two groups of people live on an equal-size space. The PPS factor is obviously higher for the larger of the two groups (5,000 people). However, applying the higher PPS value here is not going to make a difference compared to the "one person, one vote" principle because members of that group comfortably outnumber the people in the other group regardless of the PPS value. A similar outnumbering occurs in Scenario B; here, when a simple "one person, one vote" principle is applied, the larger group enjoys greater electoral voice, regardless of the fact that its PPS value is higher (more people/smaller space). So far so good. But what about Scenario C? Here each of the two groups has an equal number of people as the other group (let us say, 1,000 people in each group).

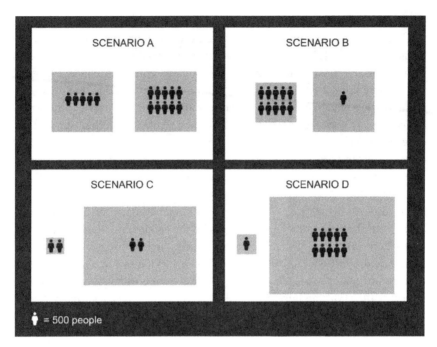

Figure 5.2 People-per-Space (PPS) Ratio

When a "one person, one vote" principle is applied, the two groups have equal weight. However, one group lives within a considerably smaller space than the other group. Hence its PPS value is far higher than that of the other group. At least where PPS values are involuntarily very high, applying the PPS factor in policy decisions where density is a key factor would grant those living under extreme density with enhanced political voice and policy input. In Scenario D, the larger group of people holds the clear electoral advantage under the one person, one vote rule. However, since the area occupied by the 5,000-people group (here 20cm^2) is 20 times the size of the area occupied by the 500-people group (1cm^2), the PPS value for the 500-people group is two times higher (10% of the people over 5% of space) than that of the 5,000-people group. If we take the PPS ratio into account in apportioning voting power, assuming there are urgent, severe density-related problems plaguing this area, each member of the 500-person group would be assigned a greater political voice with respect to matters where density is an essential factor, provided living under density conditions is largely unchosen and without viable "exit" options.

Without delving into well-known paradoxes embedded in the notion of majority rule (e.g., the Condorcet paradox), the idea here would not be to replace the "one person, one vote" principle with another, "density first." As we have seen earlier in this chapter, even a more consistent application of the "one person, one vote" principle would considerably enhance the constitutionally discounted political voice of people living in megacities such as Toronto, Mumbai, or São Paulo who are underrepresented compared to voters in non-urban areas. However, where there are extreme density gaps *within* a single metropolitan area (e.g., intra-city gaps or gaps between the inner city and the suburbs), the PPS ratio may be accounted for via some sort of collective representation mechanism of plural or weighted voting arrangement (e.g., ensuring representation in any binding decision-making process or giving extra electoral weight to those most vulnerable or adversely affected, as discussed earlier). This would allow people living under involuntary extreme density to have added power in key policy decisions related directly to the extreme density conditions they live in. Such an approach aligns with theoretical attempts to reconcile the apparent incompatibilities between democracy and justice so that "power in any decision-making process should be proportional to individual stakes."[96] Inevitably, some majorities that decide some policy issues "are composed of individuals with relatively low stakes imposing their wills on minorities with greater stakes."[97] The legitimacy of such non-contextual decision-making processes is questionable inasmuch as it fails to reflect the distinctive interests of those who have the greatest and most acute stake in and are most directly affected by the density challenge. Implementation of weighted voice or related institutional innovations in decisions related to public services such as public transit, sanitation, healthcare, education, and housing—all are especially density sensitive—may alleviate the consequences of extreme urban density in ways that current practices—forced evictions, willful avoidance of public investment, or reliance on invisible market forces—have not.

Voting systems experts would need to develop the details of this new conceptualization of democratic representation within cities. Properly implemented, this new approach would offer residents of extreme-density neighborhoods such as Nairobi's slums, Mumbai's squatters, or Rio de Janeiro's favelas, considerably better political representation than they currently have. It would help address the very different experiences and life opportunities in extremely high- versus relatively low-density areas without directly altering the income disparities, property ownership, and accumulation of wealth principles so dear to the heart of the capitalist logic. In other words, the development and application of a density-sensitive matrix for political voice is timely and relevant, not only in the context of megacities, but also for poor, extreme-density neighborhoods within large urban centers.

---

[96] Harry Brighouse and Marc Fleurbaey, "Democracy and Proportionality," *Journal of Political Philosophy* 18 (2010): 137–155, 138. For further discussion of plural/weighted voting, *see also* Trevor Latimer, "Plural Voting and Political Equality: A Thought Experiment in Democratic Theory," *European Journal of Political Theory* 17 (2018): 65–86.

[97] Brighouse and Fleubaey, *id.* at 143.

V. Intra-Metropolis Equalization?

Most megacities and large metropolitan areas have larger populations than entire countries, let alone sub-national units. What is more, these cities face similar or greater fiscal inequalities than we see among traditional sub-national
units (e.g., states, provinces, regions, etc.). As the extensive urbanization of
the last half century is merely a prelude to the projected urban agglomeration
over the next few decades, the traditional constitutional conceptualization of
fiscal equalization among national subunits needs to be updated to encompass
intra-metropolis inequalities. A recognition of the megacity as a constitutional
entity, I suggest, would support the application of established constitutional
concepts such as equalization to address stark intra-metropolis inequalities.
Constitutional recognition could help to realize the notion, discussed earlier in the chapter, that due to their relative proximity, spatial and conceptual,
to their residents, cities may be more effective problem solvers than central
governments. Intra-metropolis equalization would help alleviate the ever-
increasing socioeconomic gaps within urban centers, inter alia through the
transfer of resources from wealthy parts of the metropolis to needy ones so as to
promote parity of public services across the megacity. A failure to do so, I argue,
reflects the fixation of constitutions on the pre-megacity vision of spatial statism
and the accompanying methodological nationalism upon which constitutional
orders and contemporary fiscal equalization concepts are still largely based. The
equalization status quo strongly indicates the datedness of tired spatial constitutional governance notions, conceived as part of nation-building efforts in
multifocal, largely non-urbanized settings such as the late eighteenth-century
United States, or mid-nineteenth-century Canada, Brazil, or Germany. Let us
unpack this argument.

   Conventional narratives pit the urban elites against the rural have-nots.
However, stark differences exist between large cities within the same country.
New York City and Detroit are obvious examples, the first associated with the
glossy side of global capitalism whereas the latter is often portrayed as a casualty of that very force. What is more, recent studies highlight the growing inequality hidden in every neighborhood of the city. Even in Europe and North
America, let alone in most parts of the Global South where tremendous socioeconomic and infrastructural inequities exist among neighborhoods, a center-
periphery divide is evident *within* large city centers.[98] Within the United States,

---

[98] For a recent account of such intra-city differences, *see* Colin McFarlane, Jonathan Silver, and
Yaffa Truelove, "Cities within Cities: Intra-Urban Comparison of Infrastructure in Mumbai, Delhi
and Cape Town," *Urban Geography* 38 (2017): 1393–1417.

intra-city inequality has been on a constant rise over the last four decades. Data suggest that since the 1970s, the United States has experienced a steady increase in income inequality alongside a substantial increase in residential segregation by income.[99] Comprehensive studies of income distribution in hundreds of OECD cities point to stark differences in both income levels and inequality within metropolitan areas, even for those within the same country. Strikingly, in most OECD countries, *income inequality in metropolitan areas is higher than the national average.* Within metropolitan areas, larger ones tend to feature higher levels of household disposable income but also higher income inequality.[100] Similar studies focusing on the United States find that "the country's big cities tend to have higher income inequality than the country as a whole." In the early 2010s, a high-income household (measured as the 95th percentile) located in the 50 biggest American cities earned about 11 times as much as a low-income household (measured as the 20th percentile), while the equivalent national ratio was 9 to 1.[101] By the end of the decade, these disparities were even more exacerbated. A recent study of economic inequality patterns in America's urban centers shows conclusively that large metro areas tend to be the most economically unequal.[102] The rising salaries of highly skilled professionals (e.g., lawyers, bankers, engineers, high-tech innovators) have tended to congregate in large cities—with the not unpredictable increase in prime urban real-estate assets being owned by the "haves" in their wake. In other areas, wages are stagnant if not, in fact, in retreat. As a result, the country's six largest metro areas— New York, Los Angeles, Houston, Dallas, San Francisco, and Washington, DC—have become the country's most economically unequal cities. This in turn suggests that in today's increasingly stratified societies, "something we often

[99] *See* Alessandra Fogli and Veronica Guerrieri, "The End of the American Dream? Inequality and Segregation in US Cities," Working Paper 26143 (National Bureau of Economic Research, 2019); Douglass Massey, Jonathan Rothwell, and Thurston Domina, "The Changing Bases of Segregation in the United States," *The Annals of the American Academy of Political and Social Science* 626 (2009): 74–90.

[100] *See* Justine Boulant, Monica Brezzi, and Paolo Veneri, "Income Levels and Inequality in Metropolitan Areas: A Comparative Approach in OECD Countries," *OECD Regional Development Working Papers*, 2016/06 (OECD Publishing, 2016); online: http://dx.doi.org/10.1787/5jlwj02zz4mr-en.

[101] Annie Lowrey, "Study Finds Greater Income Inequality in Nation's Thriving Cities," *New York Times*, February 20, 2014; online: https://www.nytimes.com/2014/02/20/business/economy/study-finds-greater-income-inequality-in-nations-thriving-cities.html?ref=todayspaper, with reference to the Brookings Report, *All Cities Are Not Created Unequal* (February 20, 2014).

[102] Jaison Abel and Richard Deitz, "Why Are Some Places So Much More Unequal Than Others?," *Economic Policy Review* (Federal Reserve Bank of New York, forthcoming); online: https://www.newyorkfed.org/medialibrary/media/research/epr/2019/epr_2019_wage-inequality_abel-deitz.pdf.

think of as undesirable (economic inequality) has been a signal of something positive in big cities (a strong economy)."[103]

Detailed studies of intra-city inequality in some of the world's largest cities reveal an even more unsettling reality. One recent study suggests that in New York, perhaps the world's glitziest metropolis, the top 1% earns approximately 40 times the average income of the bottom 99% of families. The county of New York (Manhattan) is the second-most unequal county in the United States, with the top 1% earning 113 times the average income of the bottom 99% families (the national average for such ratio is 26 to 1).[104] According to a 2017 report by the New York City Independent Budget Office, 0.1% of the New York's earners account for 24% of total income per annum reported in the city. While 1% of the filers made over 40% of the total income citywide, the bottom half taken together accounted for 5.6% of that total (down from 7.4% a decade earlier, suggesting that the income gaps are not only huge but continue to expand).[105] Yet another recent study points to the spatial dimension of inequality: "Stark disparities can be found in neighborhoods that are within minutes of each other: the median household income for a tract near Central Park exceeds $200,000, while an East Harlem neighborhood just a few blocks away is under $16,000."[106]

Meanwhile, in London and Paris—Europe's foremost "global cities"—intra-city inequality is significant and ever-growing. London has a disproportionately large percentage of the UK's poorest and richest households: 15% of London residents are in the top decile and 14% in the bottom decile of UK income distribution. No other region has a more disproportionate share of the top and bottom deciles. Furthermore, the income of the top 10% of London residents amounted to 29% of citywide total income, which is more than the bottom half of households put together. The average household income in the top decile is roughly 8 times higher than that of the bottom 10%, while the nationwide average of that ratio is 4.9.[107]

Paris, with its surrounding region of Ile-de-France, is one of the most unequal in France. While the region of 12 million people boasts 31% of France's total

[103] Emily Badger and Kevin Quealy, "Watch 4 Decades of Inequality Drive American Cities Apart," *New York Times*, December 2, 2019.

[104] Estelle Sommeiller and Mark Price, "The New Gilded Age: Income Inequality in the United States by State, Metropolitan Area and County," *Economic Policy Institute*, July 19, 2018. *See also* S. Roberts, "Gap Between Manhattan's Rich and Poor Is Greatest in U.S., Census Finds," *New York Times*, September 17, 2014.

[105] Nathan Tempey, "NYC's Top 0.1 Percent Makes Four Times The Income of the Bottom Half of Earners," *Gothamist* (April 20, 2017); online: http://gothamist.com/2017/04/20/income_disparity_nyc.php.

[106] Linda Poon, "Mapping the Stark Rich-Poor Divide in Major U.S. Cities," *City Lab*, December 13, 2016.

[107] Adam Tinson, Carla Ayrton, Karen Barker, Theo Barry Born, and Otis Long, London's Poverty Profile (Trust for London, 2017), 41.

GDP, a full 15% of its residents survive on less than €990 per month, and half of these residents live with less than €750 per month.[108] A recent account suggests that while Paris's Ile-de-France region has a slightly lower proportion of poor people compared to the national figures, "its poverty intensity—the indicator for how much further down the poverty line the poorest are—is higher than in any of the other poorest regions of France."[109] In the Seine-Saint-Denis section of Paris (population 1.7 million, in the north and northeast parts of the metropolitan area) the poverty percentage is 27%, the average income is two-thirds of the region's median income, and 22 of its 36 wards are among the poorest 50 wards in Paris.[110]

My hometown Toronto "has the dubious distinction of being the child poverty capital of Canada; one-in-four children in Toronto lives below the poverty line."[111] Studies of broader demographic trends suggest that the middle-income area of the city shrank dramatically (from well over 50% to less than 30% today), while the high-income area increased slightly and low-income area increased substantially: from 19% of the city's neighborhoods in 1970 to 53% in 2005.[112] During that period, extremely low-income neighborhoods grew from 1% to 9%. And whereas in the 1970s, most low-income neighborhoods were in the inner city (i.e., faced dire challenges but had relatively good access to public transit and services), in the early twenty-first century, low-income households are concentrated in the northeastern and northwestern parts of the city, with relatively poor access to transit and services.[113] Fittingly, almost half of Toronto census tracts (48%) are low income, with residents bringing in between 37% and 60% of the average Greater Toronto Area income.[114] Meanwhile, in Toronto's wealthiest areas, incomes have more than doubled since 1980 from $163,000 to $420,000 in today's dollars.[115] According to the 2016 census, in Forest Hill, one of Toronto's richest neighborhoods, the average annual income per capita before taxes

---

[108] See "Alarm over Steep Rise in Poverty in Paris Region," *The Local* (April 11, 2016); online: https://www.thelocal.fr/20160411/alarm-over-steep-rise-in-poverty-in-paris-region, referring to a study by Caritas France.

[109] See "Inégalité: Where Are the Richest and Poorest Parts of France?," *The Local* (February 22, 2019); online: https://www.thelocal.fr/20190222/members-qa-what-are-the-richest-and-poorest-areas-of-france.

[110] *Id.*

[111] Jennifer Keesmaat, "Big Cities Need New Governance," *Bold Ideas: Policy Beyond Canada 150* (Mowat Centre, May 9, 2017).

[112] David Hulchanski, *The Three Cities within Toronto: Income Polarization among Toronto's Neighbourhoods, 1970–2005* (Cities Centre, University of Toronto, 2010).

[113] *Id.*

[114] Statistics Canada, *Census Profile Series* (2016).

[115] Michaela Dinca-Panaitescu, David Hulchanski, Michelynn Laflèche, Laura McDonough, Richard Maaranen, and Stephanie Procyk, *The Opportunity Equation in the Greater Toronto Area: An Update on Neighbourhood Income Inequality and Polarization* (United Way Toronto and York Region, November 2017).

exceeds $240,000 (nearly five times higher than the citywide average); while merely a few subway stations away, residents of Regent Park, one of Toronto's poorest neighborhoods, earn an average annual income per capita before taxes of 26,000, about half of the citywide average and about 10% of the equivalent figure in Forest Hill.[116]

The City of Chicago, to pick another, familiar example, is a very different place for those living on the "Magnificent Mile" (North Michigan Avenue) and for those living in the crime- and poverty-stricken Riverdale or Englewood neighborhoods. The city is struggling to cope with gang violence and shooting incidents. In 2017 alone, the city had approximately 2,800 shooting incidents and 3,500 shooting victims, of whom 650 were murder victims; that shocking number actually represents a decline from over 750 murder victims in 2016. In one weekend in August 2018, 63 people were shot in the city. Whereas African Americans comprise approximately one-third of Chicago's population, they account for approximately 80% of the firearm murder victims in the city in 2015, 2016, and 2017. The vast majority of these murders took place in Chicago's south and west sides, heavily populated by Hispanics and African Americans. In 2017, Donald Trump threatened to send federal forces to the city (governed by Mayor Rahm Emanuel of the Democratic Party) if the city authorities fail to cut violence and crime rate. At the same time, courts have repeatedly struck down City of Chicago restrictions on carrying firearms within city jurisdiction.

Brussels, to pick another example, is often portrayed as the powerful nerve center of the European Union, and the target of much "Euro-skeptic" talk throughout the continent. Yet behind the shiny surface lurks another Brussels: a city heaving with poverty, where almost one in three live on the breadline, and where more than half of those who work in the city and use its services do not live or pay their taxes there. Two of Brussels's communes (boroughs)—Molenbeek and Schaerbeek—are among the poorest and most-densely populated areas in Belgium, and are considered nests of Islamic radicalization. These inner-city boroughs have grown dramatically in their populations due to incoming migration without any corresponding change in the institutional framework that governs the city's legislative authority, resource allocation, or service provision capacity. Similar pockets exist in other major European urban centers, from the Sevran suburb in northeast Paris (data suggest that near 40% of Sevran's population lives below the poverty line), to the Marxloh neighborhood in Duisburg (its low-income immigrant composition has grown from mere 18% in the 1975 to 55% at present). The latter, at the heart of the German Rhine-Ruhr region—Germany's largest urban agglomeration—is dubbed a "no-go" zone by German

---

[116] See Laurie Monsbraaten, "Toronto Region Becoming More Divided Along Income Lines," *Toronto Star*, November 1, 2017.

media; reports from 2016 and 2017 suggested that even police were hesitant in entering the Marxloh neighborhood at that time. Similar socioeconomic divides within megacities exist elsewhere. These and other examples underscore the fact that the conventional image of megacities as glitzy, cohesive entities reflects a partial, and often inaccurate, view of the negligible or nonexistent constitutional stature of huge urban centers.

Obviously, the new megacity of the Global South—as in Karachi, Dhaka, or Lagos—is a very different creature than the global city à la New York, London or Paris, some of the usual suspect examples in the "global cities" literature. Whereas the common global city image depicts a supposedly opulent business, media, and entertainment center, the vast majority of megacity inhabitants in these and many other ever-expanding urban agglomerations in the Global South are poor laborers and their families or those displaced from rural areas who have moved to the city within the last decade or two who struggle to find shelter and are met with rapidly rising housing prices even in lower-income neighborhoods, failing or nonexistent infrastructure, an inadequate public transit system along-side chronically jammed roads, oversubscribed and rundown schools, and overburdened healthcare facilities often charged with serving vast, economically disadvantaged and marginalized populations. State capacity in many densely populated Global South metropolitan areas is low. Consequently, crime rates are high, informal economy practices abound, and "street smarts" reign. In certain neighborhoods, even running water, functional garbage disposal, and sewage systems are considered luxuries. In such urban settings, residents of better-off, middle-class neighborhoods must also learn to cope with weak law enforce-ment capacity alongside high levels of noise, traffic congestion, air pollution, and ethnic tensions typical to large urban centers. Even in medium-development countries, major urban centers feature considerable variance in infrastructure, public services, and living conditions. While Shanghai and Shenzhen may be tomorrow's global cities, Chongqing (in Southwest China), to pick an example of a less well-known new megacity, has an estimated population of 30 million. While its infrastructure is considerably more suitable than that of Kinshasa or Manila, it too lacks any Paris- or New York-style supposed glamor.

Economic disparities within Global South megacities are even more striking than the inequality gaps in major North American or European cities. A recent report suggests, for example, that taken as a whole, Mumbai's population has an estimated wealth of $950 billion, which makes the city the 12th richest in the world in terms of total wealth, ranking ahead of major urban centers like Paris and Toronto. Much of this prosperity is due to the combination of a large billion-aire population and the presence of India's oldest and most prominent stock ex-change. At the same time, "more than half of the city's population lives in slums, or areas of extreme poverty that often lack access to clean water, electricity, and public transportation. With an estimated 6.5 million people residing in these conditions, Mumbai has the largest slum population of any city in the world."[117] The effect of such stark economic inequalities on health, living conditions, educational choices, or career opportunities is dramatic. To pick an obvious example, even the most rudimentary and supposedly universal responses to the Coronavirus threat—hand washing and so-called "social distancing"— are not readily available to residents of shantytowns that often lack basic sanitation facilities.[118] As one resident of the Paraisópolis neighborhood in São Paulo put it: "How are we going to take care of each other and ourselves if we live crammed in one little house? How are we going to wash our hands if we don't have running water all the time?"[119]

The long-term indicators speak for themselves. According to a 2016 study, life expectancy in the Jardim Paulista neighborhood in central São Paulo's is 79.4 years. Contrast this with the Cidade Tirandentes area at the east edge of the metropolis, where life expectancy is 57.3 years, or the Anhanguera neighborhood in the northeast edge of the city where it is 56.4 years, or the Jardim Ângela neighborhood on the southwestern periphery of the city, where life expectancy is 55.6 years. In other words, only 15 kilometers (less than 10 miles) away, individuals live on average almost 24 fewer years than residents of a different neighborhood.[120]

What does the theory of fiscal equalization have to offer in this context? In its common guise, it draws on solidarity, redistributive, and standardization rationales, all aimed at mitigating the gaps, on a national scale, between the revenue/expenditure ratios of "have" and "have-not" regions or sub-national units. This theory suggests that principles of responsible government entail a duty to ensure roughly equal provision of public services throughout a given polity's territory. As some regions or subunits within the polity are in better economic shape than others (e.g., due to predetermined geographical and environmental conditions, availability of natural resources, demographic characteristics, and/ or availability of employment opportunities, all of which may help entice or

---

[117] Aria Bendix, "Drone Photos of Mumbai Reveal the Places Where Extreme Poverty Meets Extreme Wealth," *Business Insider* (October 3, 2018); online: https://www.businessinsider.de/ aerial-drone-photos-mumbai-extreme-wealth-slums-2018-9?r=US&IR=T.

[118] *See, e.g.,* Catherine Davison, "Under Corona Virus Lockdown, Delhi Slum Residents Struggle to Get Water," *Deutsche Welle* (April 9, 2020); online: https://www.dw.com/en/under-coronavirus-lockdown-delhi-slum-residents-struggle-to-get-water/a-53073487

[119] *See,* Andres Schipani and Bryan Harris, "Brazil's Gangs do What Bolsonaro Won't: Enforce a Lockdown," *OZY* (March 29, 2020); online: https://www.ozy.com/around-the-world/brazils-gangs-do-what-bolsonaro-wont-enforce-a-lockdown/294080/. See also Caio Barretto Briso and Tom Phillips, "Brazil Gangs Impose Strict Curfews to Slow Coronavirus Spread," *The Guardian* (March 25, 2020); online: www.theguardian.com/world/2020/mar/25/brazil-rio-gangs-coronavirus.

[120] Nick Van Mead and Niko Kommenda, "Living on the Edge: São Paulo's Inequality Mapped," *The Guardian,* November 27, 2017.

deter economically stronger population), fiscal transfers among subunits are warranted inasmuch as they help equalize or standardize the provision of basic services across the polity.

While applied indirectly in the United States, fiscal equalization is commonly implemented elsewhere. Equalization transfers from central to sub-national governments are "a pervasive feature of virtually all nations with multiple levels of government, including federations (Australia, Belgium, Canada, Germany, Spain), multi-sphere governments (South Africa), and unitary-type states (Japan, the Scandinavian countries)."[121] They are also commonly used in multi-member supranational entities such as the European Union. "In some cases, equalization is a stand-alone program based on an explicit formula (Australia, Canada), while in other cases it may be implicit and embedded in other grant programs or revenue-sharing arrangements (Germany, USA). In all cases, the transfers redistribute from better off to less well-off jurisdictions."[122] The significance of equalization is highlighted "not only by the extent of its use and the fact that it often comprises a substantial share of central government spending, but also from the fact that the requirement for equalization may be found in the relevant national constitution (Canada, Germany, South Africa)."[123]

Let us consider Germany—a prime example of a constitutional equalization system. Article 104b of Germany's Basic Law provides that the Federation may "grant the Länder financial assistance for particularly important investments by the Länder and municipalities (associations of municipalities) which are necessary to: (1) Avert a disturbance of the overall economic equilibrium; (2) Equalize differing economic capacities within the federal territory; or (3) Promote economic growth." The Basic Law also provides that the Federation and the Länder shall "have an equal claim against current revenues to cover their necessary expenditures" and that the coordination of financial requirements shall be pursued "in such a way as to establish a fair balance, avoid excessive burdens on taxpayers, and ensure uniformity of living standards throughout the federal territory."[124] The Basic Law also provides for an intricate system of horizontal distribution of tax revenue, financial equalization among Länder, and supplementary federal grants elaborated in Article 107 and the Federal Fiscal Equalization Act, and redistributed on the basis of Länder fiscal capacity.[125] Länder with below-average

[121] Robin Boadway, "The Theory and Practice of Equalization," *CESifo Economic Studies* 50 (2004): 211–254, 211. *See also* Peter Mieszkowski and Richard Musgrave, "Federalism, Grants, and Fiscal Equalization," *National Tax Journal* 52 (1999): 239–260.

[122] Boadway, "The Theory and Practice of Equalization," at 3.

[123] *Id.*

[124] German Basic Law, Article 106 para (3).

[125] Federal Ministry of Finance, "Financial Relations Between the Federation and the Lander on the Basis of Constitutional Financial Provisions," *Report* (updated 2018: 41); online: https://www.bundesfinanzministerium.de/Content/EN/Standardartikel/Press_Room/Publications/Brochures/2019-03-12-financial-realations-federation-2018-pdf.pdf?__blob=publicationFile&v=3.

revenues will receive grants that cover between 60% and 95% of the gap between the Länder's revenue and the average revenue of all Länder. Simply put, whether a given Land will receive or will make equalization payments depends on whether its "financial capacity index"—the sum of its revenue—is "below or above the 'equalization index' "—the average financial capacity of the Länder."[126] The actual equalization effect on "have-not" Länder has been very significant. In 2014, to pick one example, the formerly East German Länder had lower financial capacity than all but one of the formerly West German Länder. Even the most well-off formerly East German Länder, Brandenburg, was 9.7% lower in its financial capacity than the national pre-equalization average. By contrast, 8 of the 10 formerly West German Länder had financial capacities that were at least 95% of the national equalization index. Of these 10, 4 Länder had financial capacities that exceeded the equalization cut-point index. As the data for 2014 indicates, after equalization, the wealthiest Land, Bavaria (interestingly, from 1950 to 1989 a constant recipient of equalization transfers), had a financial capacity of 106% of the equalization index, down from 117% prior to equalization. On the other hand, Bremen went from a financial capacity of 72% of the equalization index to 91.4%. (While this constitutionally established inter-Land transfer has had a considerable effect, inequality within the city of Frankfurt in the State of Hesse has grown to be the highest in Germany, and, by some accounts, in the whole of Europe.)[127]

The significance of inter-regional equalization transfers is also supported by the active resistance to them from sub-national units on the paying end. Examples abound, from northern Italian provinces to Bavaria (Germany) or Alberta (Canada). Meanwhile, massive secessionist protests have occurred in oil-rich provinces of Venezuela (Zulia), Bolivia (Pando, Santa Cruz, Tarija) and Nigeria (the Niger-Delta region).[128] In these and other similarly situated settings, economically prosperous or resource rich sub-national units demand renegotiation of their respective countries' fiscal federalism constitutional pacts in an attempt to reduce their contribution shares. They would not initiate such politically risky struggles if the costs of equalization were insignificant. Although the existence of such protests by no means shows that inter-regional fiscal transfers succeed in reducing inequality, they do suggest that wealthy regions often feel the brunt of such transfers.

The actual forms and effects of nationwide equalization transfers vary from one polity to another. A comprehensive comparative exploration of such equalization schemes falls beyond the scope of this chapter. But since I have already

---

[126] *Id.* at 42.

[127] "Income Inequality Ranking of the World's Major Cities," *Euromonitor International* (October 31, 2017); online: https://blog.euromonitor.com/income-inequality-ranking-worlds-major-cities/.

[128] Nigeria has 36 states. Approximately 35% of the entire Nigeria's GDP is produced in eight delta states; 80% of oil produced in Nigeria is produced in three states (Akwa Ibom, Delta, Rivers).

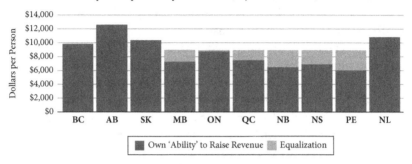

Fiscal Capacity and Equalization, by Province (FY 2018–19)
Displays each province's own fiscal capacity, the equalization payment
required to bring it up to an 'average' level, and the 'adjustment payment'
to fix the pool of equalization paid. In 2018/19, adjustments totalled $1.76b.

Figure 5.3 Fiscal Capacity and Equalization by Province

Figure redrawn from Trevor Tombe, "Unpacking Canada's Equalization Payments for 2018–19"
(University of Calgary: School of Public Policy); https://www.policyschool.ca/unpacking-canadas-
equalization-payments-2018-19/.

described the stark intra-metropolis socioeconomic divisions in Toronto area,
home to roughly a fifth of Canada's population, it would be valuable to compare
that large, non-equalized setting with the pan-Canadian, national subunit-based
equalization matrix. Canada's fiscal federalism is entrenched in the Constitution,
which provides that "Parliament and the government of Canada are committed
to the principle of making equalization payments to ensure that provincial
governments have sufficient revenues to provide *reasonably comparable levels
of public services at reasonably comparable levels of taxation*."[129] A province's per
capita equalization payment is intended to "level up" provinces whose fiscal capacities do not match the national average.[130] A complementary Fiscal Capacity
Cap mechanism ensures that those provinces receiving equalization payments
are not financially better situated than provinces not receiving equalization
payments. The cap is necessary because not all of a province's actual revenue capacity is included in the calculation of its fiscal capacity.

The chart above (Figure 5.3) provides a snapshot of the amount of support
Canadian provinces received through equalization payments per capita in
2018–2019. Alberta's own ability to raise revenue more than doubles that of New

[129] Section 36(2) of the Constitution Act, 1982, emphasis added.
[130] Jean-Francois Nadeau, "2014–2015 Federal Transfers to Provinces and Territories," *Office of the
Parliamentary Budget Officer* (2014: p ii); online: http://www.pbodpb.gc.ca/web/default/files/files/
files/TransferPayments_EN.pdf.

Brunswick or Prince Edward Island, but the gaps are mitigated by equalization transfers.

The basic structure of equalization payments in Canada is grounded in the federal government's calculation of each province's "fiscal capacity": the potential annual revenue per capita from resource extraction[131] and four tax bases: sales/consumption, personal income, property, and business income.[132] If any province's fiscal capacity is calculated to fall short of the national average for that year, the federal government will offer equalization payments to top it up. A second major component of equalization payments in Canada is adjustment payments. Equalization payments are distributed each year as a fixed share of Canada's GDP. If the amount required to equalize the "have-not" provinces exceeds this fixed share, the payments to each province are reduced on a per capita basis. If the amount required to equalize the provinces is less than the fixed share, the surplus is distributed to the provinces again on a per capita basis.

The Canadian system of national province-based equalization does not differentiate between provinces with small populations (e.g., Prince Edward Island, population 150,000) and provinces with very large populations (e.g., Ontario, population over 14 million, nearly 100 times larger than PEI). Consequently, intra-provincial, and by extension intra-metropolis socioeconomic gaps, are infinitely more likely to occur in Ontario and are left unaccounted for by this matrix. It is up to provincial governments themselves, exclusive constitutional hegemons of Canadian cities, to address such pervasive inequalities as they see fit.

What makes equalization transfers from Alberta (one of Canada's richest provinces) to New Brunswick or PEI (two of Canada's less well-off provinces) justifiable in principle, but renders similar transfers between Forest Hill (one of Toronto's richest neighborhoods) and Regent Park (one of the city's poorest neighborhoods) a non-starter? The answer is in the exclusive conceptualization of the national, not the metropolitan, as the relevant demos, collective, or solidarity basis. When thinking through such an exclusively statist prism (embedded in methodological nationalism), the normative obligation to support our less well-off compatriots in other parts of the country appears intuitive, while our fellow urbanites living a few blocks or subway stops away seem irrelevant. Existing attempts to challenge the hegemonic national solidarity basis have often come from Kantians or universalists who claim humanity, not the nation, to be a suitable basis for redistributive justice. Alternatively, ideas about a

---

[131] Provincial revenues from natural resource extraction is calculated as actual revenue per capita. Only 50% of this amount is counted within the formula in order to preserve the incentive to develop a province's resources.

[132] Calculated as the amount that would be available to each province if it were to adopt tax rates equivalent to the national averages.

non-territorial basis for federalism within a given polity have been invoked in discussions about constitutional design for multiethnic or multi-linguistic societies. Here, guaranteed quota-like representation by ethnicity, religion, race, or linguistic community is deployed.[133] However, very little attention has been paid in this context to the possibility of a spatial proximity, metropolis-oriented basis for redistributive policies as complementary to the national and international redistributive matrixes. That moral tilt is translated into legal and practical guidelines for fiscal equalization based on sub-national unit fiscal imbalances, but not on *intra-metropolis inequalities,* even in instances where actual population size or scope of socioeconomic inequalities arguably make the metropolitan framework an equally if not even more relevant framework for inter-jurisdictional transfers as the prevalent national or supranational framework.

Once we supplement the idea of the nation-state as the basic collective solidarity unit with a notion of the metropolis as another important and relevant constitutional entity that similarly warrants equalization of services and standards, a transfer of resources among city wards may become a constitutionally viable option. To be sure, the concrete legal and practical details must be well thought-out. But the basic building blocks of such a novel megacity-centered redistributive matrix are already in place: city ward and electoral riding grids exist and are ordinarily used for national, sub-national or municipal electoral processes, as is reliable data on intra-metropolis socioeconomic gaps, tax revenue gaps, differences in schooling, housing, or healthcare options (such intra-metropolis gaps, as we saw earlier, far exceed national differences in many cases). Recognition of the megacity as an entity with constitutional standing would open up the possibility of implementing such a novel intra-metropolis equalization scheme. It would help change the conventional conceptualization of the megacity as a unified locus of the "haves," a club to which the vast majority of residents in global cities clearly do not belong. It would help prevent the rich and ultra-rich urbanites from ignoring stark intra-metropolis inequalities in favor of region- or sub-national unit-based statistical figures. It would also help expose and alleviate the stark and ever-increasing socioeconomic gaps within the metropolis, as both the scope of inequalities and the size of populations affected by intra-metropolis gaps exceed nationwide gaps that are addressed constitutionally. (Recall: Mumbai's accumulated wealth makes it the 12th richest city in the world, all while 6.5 million of its residents live in slums—a contrast that is not captured

---

[133] Discussion about indigenous justice in Canada and elsewhere have also generated calls for self-determination and self-government of First Nation communities, conceptualized as partly autonomous, "third order" of government alongside the federal government and the provinces. See the final report of Canada's Royal Commission on Aboriginal People (1996). For a recent discussion, see *First Nations Governance Project: Phase I* (First Nations Financial Management Board and the Institute on Governance, 2018).

by India's state-based fiscal equalization formulae. Likewise, in Toronto, average income per capita in rich neighborhoods is nearly 10 times the citywide average and 20 times the equivalent figures in the city's poor neighborhoods). Perhaps most importantly, an ameliorated equalization matrix that takes the megacity seriously would help shake up the rather stagnant constitutional thought of spatial governance, which fixates on state- or province-based federalism, regions, or electoral districts while failing to address the urban agglomeration that the world is now seeing on a massive, unprecedented scale.

The equalization point raises a broader concern: in the current "age of the city," what is the suitable constituent "unit" in the theory and practice of federalism and other multilayer spatial governance structures? As we have seen in Chapter 1, historically, the confederation idea brought together multi-tribe, multi-nation, and multi-city entities, but contemporary studies and practices of federalism have almost exclusively taken the state and its equivalents (provinces, Länder, cantons, regions, emirates, etc.) as the fundamental unit of analysis. In this dominant discourse, cities, home to the majority of mankind, ubiquitous and crucial to every aspect of twenty-first-century society, culture, economics, and politics, are virtually absent, aptly described as "the forgotten stepchildren of both federal politics and scholarship."[134]

VI. Cities, Stakeholding, and Subsidiarity

This critique of the lack of intra-city equalization formulae in world constitutions leads us to one of the most glaring shortcomings in contemporary constitutional thought, namely, the near-complete omission of cities from discussions about subsidiarity, stakeholding, and democratic self-governance. What are we to make of this conspicuous gap in the legal and scholarly discourse?

The basic premise here, and the subject of a handful of writings drawing surprisingly scant attention, is the intuitive notion at the heart of localism, self-government, and subsidiarity arguments: in any given system, the closer power is to the people, the more democratic and truly representative the system is. Subsidiarity principles warrant that, to the extent possible, every level of authority should perform only those tasks that cannot be performed at a more local level. Because many areas of urban governance significantly affect city dwellers' lives, local governance should not be filtered through, let alone exclusively determined by, national politics. City politics is closer to the people than national politics, both in terms of scale and sheer numbers and in the nature of the issues

---

[134] Loren King, "Cities, Subsidiarity, and Federalism," *in* James Fleming and Jacob Levy, eds., *Federalism and Subsidiarity: NOMOS LV* (New York University Press, 2014), 295.

it addresses. Therefore, enhancing the status of city politics and bolstering city power would be in line with ideals of place-based governance and local democratic interpretations of participation and representation. Ultimately, this line of thought suggests that the question of city power is not one of efficiency (an elaboration of that line will come later), but is about democratic self-governance.[135]

Another influential argument for enhanced city power is grounded in an idea widely referred to as "stakeholding theory" or the "all affected interests" principle.[136] As Mark Warren notes, the principle that "all those affected by a collective decision should be included in the decision is long-standing, dating at least back to the Justinian Code (V,59,5,2).[137] Specifically, "what touches all must be approved by all" (*Quod omnes tangit debet ab omnibus approbari*). Essentially, the point here is that those affected by public policy decisions should be represented in the decision-making bodies, or alternatively, compensated for their lack of representation.

In contemporary variants of the argument, a more refined claim is advanced: power in a democracy should be distributed in proportion to the people's stake in the decision under consideration. The more people's interests are affected by a public policy decision, the more they should be involved in making it, either directly or through elected representatives.

As normatively appealing as the stakeholding principle is, its consistent implementation seems impractical. As Robert Goodin notes, in an interconnected world, where spheres, domains, and boundaries are hard to delineate or define, most decisions could affect any number of people, effectively requiring that "virtually everyone everywhere [gets] a vote on virtually everything decided anywhere."[138] However, even if an ideal application of the stakeholding principle is impractical, it remains an intuitively just directive with considerable purchase in support of megacity constitutional standing. As we have seen, the mismatch between the city's ever-expanding service provision responsibility and its lack of power and autonomy reveals a critical democracy deficit.

Cities and city dwellers often make disproportionally high contributions to national well-being while carrying massive burdens and responsibilities in areas such as social integration, policing and crime prevention, housing and sanitation infrastructure, and a host of service provision duties in other areas. What is more, in many urban centers, a huge number of daily commuters work in the

---

[135] *See* Schragger, *City Power*.

[136] While there have been numerous interpretations of stakeholding, as well as the all-affected or all-subjected principles, an influential articulation is found in Robert E. Goodin, "Enfranchising All Affected Interests, and Its Alternatives," *Philosophy & Public Affairs* 35 (2007): 40–68.

[137] Mark E. Warren, "The All Affected Interests Principle in Democratic Theory and Practice" (Working Paper, Institute for Advanced Study, Vienna, June 1, 2017).

[138] Goodin, "Enfranchising All Affected Interests, and Its Alternatives," 68.

city, but pay their taxes in the suburbs where they live. To put it bluntly, cities provide services, collect the garbage, and clean the streets daily for millions of people who are not "paying customers." The result is too often a growing gap between publicly funded schooling, healthcare, or infrastructure in medium- to high-income suburbs that are typically well above equivalent services in most core urban settings. City dwellers are thus doubly disadvantaged: they help subsidize services that are open to all users, whether or not they reside in the city or pay taxes to its coffers, and they also lack independent voice in determining whether their city ought to have any revenue generating powers vis-à-vis the various communities that rely upon its infrastructure.

Closely related ideals such as subsidiarity—commonly invoked in discussions about the place of national identity in supranational quasi-constitutional orders—may plausibly be deployed in the megacity context. Subsidiarity refers to the norm favoring the preservation or allocation of power to local authorities rather than central ones. This simple idea, with its many variants, is widely acknowledged as an important guiding principle in the ordering of state and society.[139] As with federalism, discussions about subsidiarity have made only scant reference to city constitutional empowerment, despite the principle's seemingly obvious application in that context. It is possible to think of subsidiarity in combination with the rethinking of the "unit" in federalism, or to rank them in priority order in relation to their potential applicability to cities. Yishai Blank—one of the pioneering thinkers in this area—argues that subsidiarity is a better model than federalism on which to integrate local governments into the dynamic of global, multilevel governance.[140] Federalism, as we just saw, has a favorable predisposition toward the "state" as a sovereign territorial sphere, while subsidiarity does not privilege any particular level of government.

Let us explore the subsidiarity angle in some depth. Originating in the early seventeenth-century political thought of Johannes Althusius, the notion of subsidiarity was initially motivated by the desire to shield the religious autonomy of local authorities from interference by more central authorities, and to secure "a coherent political order while accommodating diverse religious views."[141] On Althusius's view, small-scale human associations like families, cities, and realms possess not only a historical, but also a normative, priority in political

---

[139] N.W. Barber and Richard Ekins, "Situating Subsidiarity," *American Journal of Jurisprudence* 61 (2016): 5–12, 5. *See also* Andreas Føllesdal, "Survey Article: Subsidiarity," *Journal of Political Philosophy* 6 (1998): 190–218, 190; Andreas Føllesdal, "The Principle of Subsidiarity as a Constitutional Principle in International Law," *Global Constitutionalism* 2 (2013): 37–62, 37–38; Andreas Føllesdal, "Competing Conceptions of Subsidiarity," *in* James Fleming and Jacob Levy, eds., *Federalism and Subsidiarity: Nomos LV* (New York University Press, 2014), 214–230, 214.

[140] Yishai Blank, "Federalism, Subsidiarity, and the Role of Local Governments in an Age of Global Multilevel Governance," *Fordham Urban Law Journal* 37 (2010): 509–558.

[141] Føllesdal, "Survey Article: Subsidiarity," 201.

arrangements.[142] Sovereignty is taken to reside with the constituent units rather than the federal entity. The basis of the central authority's political legitimacy is thought to be a joint delegation by the constituent units.[143]

According to another religiously infused conceptualization of subsidiarity commonly referred to as the Catholic variant (based on various writings on Catholic social thought, formalized by an 1891 ordinance by Pope Leo XIII), subsidiarity serves to mediate the tension between "supranational harmonization and unity, on the one hand, and local pluralism and difference, on the other."[144] On this view, subsidiarity is based on respect for the dignity of the human individual, which is taken to be "ontologically and logically prior to the state or other social groupings."[145] The Catholic variant translates this basis of individualism into the imperative to protect the position of private (religious) groups from the encroaching arm of the regulatory state.

Contemporary political theorists justify subsidiarity on the grounds of republicanism (Philip Pettit), non-domination (Hoi Kong), or liberal contractualism (e.g., Kant, Rawls, Scanlon, Barry, Habermas). This underlying set of values suggests that the theoretical defense of subsidiarity begins with the premise that a legitimate social order must be justifiable in principle to all affected individuals.[146] Modern subsidiarity's preference for sub-unit authority is grounded in two twin notions: (1) that individuals have interests in procedural control over social institutions, and (2) that it is desirable to protect individuals' legitimate expectations with regard to institutional change.[147] Consequently, this conception of subsidiarity contends that central authorities should seek to facilitate the democratic and informed decision-making of subunits, which cannot in principle refer only to sub-national states.[148]

The most powerful argument for subsidiarity as it applies to urban agglomeration and city power is the principle of decentralization. As Wallace Oates has written, "public policy and its implementation should be assigned to the lowest level of government with the capacity to achieve the objectives."[149] The theoretical underpinning here is twofold: efficiency-based (essentially, the idea that local government is best situated to do the job), and democratic governance (decision-making power should be allocated to a democratic unit that can

---

[142] Nicholas Aroney, "The Federal Condition: Towards a Normative Theory," *American Journal of Jurisprudence* 61 (2016): 13–31, 23–24.

[143] Føllesdal, "Survey Article: Subsidiarity," 201.

[144] Paulo Carozza, "Subsidiarity as a Structural Principle of International Human Rights Law," *American Journal of International Law* 97 (2003): 38–79, 40.

[145] *Id.*

[146] Føllesdal, "Survey Article: Subsidiarity," 210.

[147] Føllesdal, "Survey Article: Subsidiarity," 210–213.

[148] Føllesdal, "Subsidiarity and the Global Order," 212–213.

[149] Wallace Oates, "An Essay on Fiscal Federalism," *Journal of Economic Literature* 37 (1999):1120–1149, at 1122 n. 6.

successfully legislate in a way that is accountable and located as close as possible to those affected).

A similar sentiment is expressed in an array of constitutional contexts, from the opening provisions of the Treaty on European Union to the European Court of Human Right's invocation of the "margin of appreciation" doctrine, and from the German Basic Law to the Supreme Court of Canada's occasional reference to subsidiarity in its federalism jurisprudence. According to Article 1 of the Treaty on the European Union, decisions should be "taken as openly as possible and *as closely as possible to the citizen*" (emphasis added). Article 5(3) further warrants that "[U]nder the principle of subsidiarity, in areas which do not fall within its exclusive competence, the Union shall act only if and in so far as the objectives of the proposed action cannot be sufficiently achieved by the Member States, either at central level or at regional and local level, but can rather, by reason of the scale or effects of the proposed action, be better achieved at Union level." The principle of subsidiarity is commonly deployed in international and transnational human rights regimes, most notably the margin of appreciation jurisprudence of the European Court of Human Rights, discussed in some detail in Chapter 1.[150] Article 72 of the German Basic Law provides a formula for the exercise of federal jurisdiction that is inspired by the principle of subsidiarity. Article 72(2) sets out the conditions for the instances that necessitate federal legislation. In so doing, it appears to incorporate a criterion of "necessity" for the justification of central intervention.[151]

While the concept of subsidiarity is not entrenched in the Canadian constitutional order and so its status as an operative principle in Canadian federalism remains unclear, the Supreme Court of Canada refers to it occasionally, notably in cases involving urban governance.[152] In its decision in *Spraytech* (2001)— discussed at some length in Chapter 2—the Supreme Court of Canada defined the principle of subsidiarity as "the proposition that law-making and implementation are often best achieved at a level of government that is not only effective, but also closest to the citizens affected and thus most responsive to their needs, to local distinctiveness, and to population diversity."[153] This definition of

---

[150] *See, e.g.*, Samantha Besson, "Subsidiarity in International Human Rights Law—What Is Subsidiary about Human Rights?," *American Journal of Jurisprudence* 61 (2016): 69–107, 78; Gerald Neuman, "Subsidiarity," *in* Dinah Shelton, ed., *The Oxford Handbook of International Human Rights Law* (Oxford University Press, 2013), 360–378, 369; Yuval Shany, "Toward a General Margin of Appreciation Doctrine in International Law?," *European Journal of International Law* 16 (2005): 907–940, 912; Carozza, "Subsidiarity as a Structural Principle of International Human Rights Law," 40–41.

[151] *See* Jürgen Bröhmer, "Subsidiarity and the German Constitution," *in* Michelle Evans and Augustus Zimmermann, eds., *Global Perspectives on Subsidiarity* (Springer, 2014), 129–156, at 144.

[152] *See* Eugénie Brouillet and Bruce Ryder, "Key Doctrines in Canadian Legal Federalism," *in* Peter Oliver, Patrick Macklem, and Nathalie Des Rosiers, eds., *The Oxford Handbook of the Canadian Constitution* (Oxford University Press, 2017), 415–432, 425.

[153] *114957 Canada Ltée (Spraytech, Société d'arrosage) v. Hudson (Town)*, 2001 SCC 40, at para. 3.

subsidiarity effectively incorporates the rationales of effectiveness, geographical proximity and democratic accountability, flexibility and responsiveness, and diversity.[154]

As we have seen earlier in this chapter and throughout this book, urban agglomeration has reached new heights, and is projected to continue to rise. Consequently, cities face unprecedented pressures to provide suitable services, including housing, sanitation, transportation, healthcare, and education to their ever-growing populations. Perhaps even more importantly, cities stand at the front line of major public policy challenges ranging from managing multiculturalism, diversity, and social integration to handling widening socioeconomic gaps, crime prevention, poverty, and homelessness. The sheer scope and nature of these challenges warrant substantial representation in the policy-making venues that deal with them. What is more, as large cities frequently stand at the receiving end of large-scale domestic and cross-border migration, they are highly affected by policy decisions made at higher levels of government relating to mobility and international relations, with little or no standing at the pertinent decision-making fora. If we are to take ideals of subsidiarity and stakeholding seriously, it is therefore unclear, as Daniel Weinstock notes, why "both theoretical discussions about, and the practice of, real-world federal arrangements [should stop] at the level of Provinces, länder, U.S. state and the like . . ." and continue to exclude cities.[155]

The diversity of urban polities adds yet another justification to admit cities, in particular large cities where plurality of ideas and shifting, issue-based majorities, are inherent, into stakeholding- and subsidiarity-based constitutional arrangements. Large metropolitan areas have historically been the hub of minority settlement in the United States. Consequently, in cities such as New York, Chicago, Houston, and Dallas, each of the three main minority groups in America—black, Hispanic, and Asian—are highly represented. In Los Angeles and San Francisco, Hispanics and Asians represent large portions of the population, while Miami has particularly large Hispanic and black populations.[156] In 2016, 44% of the US urban population was white, compared to 68% in suburban

---

[154] Other pertinent concepts seem at least worth considering in this context. The federal "duty to consult" with indigenous communities before actions are taken that affect the interests of such communities; autonomous faith-based jurisdictional enclaves commonly deployed in multi-religious polities or with respect to international sports adjudication and arbitration are merely a few examples. As matters stand, sports governance bodies such FIFA, UEFA, or the IOC are considerably more autonomous than Chicago or Mumbai.

[155] Daniel Weinstock, "Cities and Federalism," in James E. Fleming and Jacob T. Levy, eds., *Federalism and Subsidiarity: NOMOS LV* (New York University Press, 2014), 269–270. *See also* Daniel Weinstock, "Pour une philosophie politique de la ville," *Rue Descartes* 63 (2009): 63–71 (discussing the neglect of spatiality as the basis for the distinct conceptual character of the city).

[156] William H. Frey, *Six Maps That Reveal America's Expanding Racial Diversity* (Brookings, 2019).

areas and 79% in rural areas.[157] In the same year, 22% of the urban population in the United States comprised of first-generation immigrants, compared to 4% in rural areas. In New York City and in Los Angeles—the two largest metropolitan areas in the United States—foreign-born residents make up 38% of the population while the percentage of foreign born in America's general population is merely 14%. The number of highly diverse communities in metropolitan areas saw a rise from 90 in 1980 to 542 in 2010 (compared to merely 74 in rural areas).[158] As we have seen earlier, large Canadian cities are distinctly more diverse than the countryside; no less than 48% of Toronto's population and 42% of Vancouver's population are first-generation immigrants (the nationwide percentage is 21%). The picture is similar in Australia's metropolitan centers. According to the most recent census (2016), 43% of Sydney's population was born overseas. Only a third of the city's population had both parents born in Australia. Meanwhile in the UK, recent data suggest that 37% of London's population is foreign born, nearly three times higher than in the country as a whole.[159] The most recent (2011) census indicates that London is home to 4.5 million non-white British residents, or 41% of all non-white British residents in the country, while London's population accounts for approximately 15% of the country's populace. All but 2 of the top 20 most diverse communities in the country are London boroughs.[160] Data from Continental Europe further suggests that large cities are super-diverse, and at any rate considerably more diverse than other regions in their respective polities.[161] Approximately one-third of Amsterdam's population, to pick one example, is foreign born, while merely 12% of the Netherlands' population is foreign born. In other major European cities (e.g., Frankfurt, Munich, and Zürich), the foreign-born population accounts for more than 25% of city populations, far higher than the countrywide average. In São Paulo—South America's largest city—there are more people of Italian descent than in Rome, alongside a large Afro-Brazilian population reflecting international migration to the city from Northeastern Brazil. The city has the largest Spanish, Arab, and Japanese population of the country. Sixteen major languages are spoken commonly in Mumbai, including Gujarati, Hindi, Marathi, and Bambaiya (a local, colloquial Hindi dialect). Twenty major languages are spoken commonly in Jakarta, including

---

[157] Kim Parker et al., "Pew Research Center Report: What Unites and Divides Urban, Suburban and Rural Communities" (Pew Research Center, May 2018), 24.

[158] Chad R. Farrell and Barrett A. Lee, "No-Majority Communities: Racial Diversity and Change at the Local Level, *Urban Affairs Review* 54 (2018): 866–897, 877.

[159] *See* Pew Research Center, *International Migrants by Country* (January 30, 2019) [data are drawn from the United Nations Population Division's bilateral matrix of international migrant stocks]; International Organization for Migration (IOM), *World Migration Report 2015*, 38.

[160] "2011 Census Snapshot: Ethnic Diversity Indices," Census Information Scheme, Greater London Authority Intelligence (December 2012).

[161] Fabrizio Natale, Marco Scipioni, and Alfredo Alessandrini, "Spatial Segregation of Migrants in EU Cities," *Divided Cities: Understanding Inter-urban Inequalities* (OECD, May 2018), 91–92.

Indonesian, Dutch, Portuguese, Betawi, Javanese, Sundanese, Malay, Madurese, Batak, Minangkabau, Chinese, Arabic, and Tamil. Similar ethnic and linguistic diversity patterns characterize megacities in Africa. A recent account of the right to the city in Johannesburg—the most populated city in South Africa, describes that city as "a place where trendy cosmopolitanism exists alongside squalor and desperation, and where radically different ways of life collide and interact in unpredictable, volatile and often violent ways."[162] Super-diversity abounds. Parts of that city have been "transformed into a unique melting pot of Middle Eastern, Indian, Pakistani and Bangladeshi cultures, an inner city Ethiopian quarter and a Somali enclave in Mayfair thrive and are expanding daily, a long-settled orthodox Jewish community remains around Glenhazel, a bustling 'Chinatown' sprawled in Cyrildene to the east, the working class suburbs of the 'old south' have retained their Portuguese character whilst largely swopping their European Portuguese residents for ones from Mozambique and Angola, Jabulani in Soweto has become a cosmopolitan and cultural node, and Bedfordview to the east ostentatiously flaunts 'new money' tainted by whispers of organised crime."[163] Lagos—the largest city in Africa with over 20 million residents—is home to many different ethnic groups, including the Yoruba, Hausa, Igbo, and Fulani, alongside many smaller ethnic groups, from Europeans to East Asians and Chinese. Other major cities in Africa, from Addis Ababa to Dar es Salaam are distinctly more diverse than any other region in Ethiopia or Tanzania, respectively. And the list goes on.

Management of diversity therefore constitutes a distinct and prominent feature of city governance. The bottom line is clear: what differentiates the metropolis is not its massive scale alone. Large cities are distinct because of their exceptionally diverse demographic composition and the unique policy challenges their makeup generates. Super-diversity is the reality of metropolis demographics and the essence of everyday urban life. No other parts of the polity present integration or accommodation challenges and opportunities similar in their scope and nature to those facing large urban centers. Taking this difference into account, enhanced constitutional standing for large urban centers seems justifiable.

The metropolis's super-diversity features centrally in contemporary urban/rural tensions. Much of the anti-city rhetoric associated with the current wave of ethno-nationalist populism (discussed at length in Chapter 1) is targeted at big cities' supposedly lenient, overly-accommodating, liberal approach toward expressions of "differences"—be they ethnic, religious, linguistic, cultural, sexual, and the like. According to this spatially focused narrative of political

---

[162] Marius Pieterse, *Rights-Based Litigation, Urban Governance and Social Justice in South Africa: The Right to Joburg* (Routledge, 2017), 15.
[163] *Id.*

division and strife, members of the polity who live outside the cosmopolitan metropolis tend not to share its permissive worldviews regarding diversity, and adhere instead to a more traditional, conservative or "authentic" set of values. In that dichotomous scenario, an across-the-board application of a single set of norms is destined to upset one side of the urban/rural rupture.[164] A creative application of the notion of "community standards"—essentially entailing contextualized, locality-specific criteria for applying constitutional principles in certain contested areas—may prove helpful in alleviating the one-rule-fits-all imposition of values, worldviews, and policy preferences on either side of the urban/rural divide.

The community standards doctrine was first introduced in the United States in the context of obscenity jurisprudence. In his opinion in in *Miller v. California* (1973),[165] Chief Justice Burger captured the essence of its rationale in stating that "it is neither realistic nor constitutionally sound to read the First Amendment as requiring that the people of Maine or Mississippi accept public depiction of conduct found tolerable in Las Vegas, or New York." "People in different States vary in their tastes and attitudes," he continued, "and this diversity is not to be strangled by the absolutism of imposed uniformity."[166] A similar rationale has also guided, in various ways, constitutional jurisprudence in other common law countries, from the UK to Australia and to Canada (e.g., *R v. Butler*, 1992).[167] The Supreme Court of Israel has expanded the concept to include local discretion in instances involving accommodation of religious communities' special needs.[168] The balancing of conflicting visions of rights in this context, the court held, "must be made of in view of the local character of the population in each neighborhood."

In recent years, the community standards concept has been invoked in debates in the United States concerning a range of issues, from religious freedoms to

---

[164] The study of the spatial foundations and manifestations of populist politics is a fascinating new field of inquiry. Such dichotomies inevitably oversimplify a complex reality, but there is undeniably an important set of questions to explore about the intersection of geographies of populism, the backlash against global constitutionalism, and the rural revolt against urban cosmopolitanism. *See, e.g.,* Christopher Lizotte, "Where Are the People? Refocusing Political Geography on Populism," *Political Geography* 77 (2019): 139–141. *See also* Ran Hirschl and Ayelet Shachar, "Foreword: Spatial Statism," *International Journal of Constitutional Law* 17 (2019): 387–438.

[165] *Miller v. California*, 413 U.S. 15 (1973).

[166] *Cited in* Mark D. Rosen, "Our Nonuniform Constitution: Variations of Constitutional Requirements in the Aid of Community," *Texas Law Review* 77 (1999): 1129–1194, 1150.

[167] *R v. Butler*, [1992] 1 S.C.R. 452. In *Brodie v. The Queen*, [1962] S.C.R. 681, Justice Judson held that an "undue exploitation" test should be used to consider "whether the exploitation of sexual themes served a genuine literary or artistic purpose" and that "undue exploitation" should in turn be interpreted based on the "standards of acceptance prevailing in the community." *See* Bret Boyce, "Obscenity and Community Standards," *Yale Journal of International Law* 33 (2008): 299–368, 326–327.

[168] *See, e.g.,* HCJ 953/01 *Solodkin v. Beit Shemesh Municipality*, IsrLR 232 (2004).

firearm control.[169] With respect to accommodation of religious freedoms, for example, Richard Schragger argued that "local regulations that burden or benefit religious belief, conduct, or exercise, have different institutional effects than do similar state or national regulations and that these differential effects should be taken into account when determining the contours of the Establishment and Free Exercise Clauses."[170] Others have argued that the community standards idea "provides a useful doctrinal analogue for how a court ought to analyze the notion that Alaskans' right to bear arms as distinct from those of New Yorkers, Chicagoans, and even the residents of the lower 48 states at large."[171] Such 'Firearm Localism' embraces the argument that courts "can and should incorporate the long-standing and sensible differences regarding guns and gun control in rural and urban areas, giving more protection to gun rights in rural areas and more leeway to gun regulation in cities."[172]

While not drawing an explicit comparison to the community standards doctrine, David Barron has further suggested that deference to municipal constitutional interpretation may be informed by similar principles of localism and geographic variation. Here, "a city should be entitled to assert its status as an independent, democratic polity that is capable of, and interested in, interpreting the state constitution or the Federal Constitution to enforce limits on central power."[173] In doing so, cities would provide a "special constitutional insight."[174] Overall, Barron argues, "a city's authority to engage in constitutional review would be expanded, but it would not be unlimited"; the city would be limited to its jurisdictional boundaries in questioning the enforcement of state law on constitutional grounds.[175]

The megacity's unique social and cultural fabric discussed in this chapter and throughout this book may well justify granting it such qualified powers to interpret pertinent constitutional provisions in a way befitting its cosmopolitanism and diverse demographics, as well as distinctive scale- and density-based challenges. Awarding similar contextualized interpretation powers to non-urban localities, may help ease the increasingly common tensions brought about by the unqualified, across-the-board imposition of norms and standards that may be welcomed by one side of the urban/rural divide but strike a nerve at the other.

---

[169] *See, e.g.,* Richard C. Schragger, "The Role of the Local in the Doctrine and Discourse of Religious Liberty," *Harvard Law Review* 116 (2004): 1810–1892; Joseph Blocher, "Firearm Localism," *Yale Law Journal* 123 (2013): 82–146; John Hill, "North to the Future of the Right to Bear Arms: Analyzing the Alaska Firearms Freedom Act and Applying Firearm Localism to Alaska," *Alaska Law Review* 33 (2016): 125–155; Mark D. Rosen, "The Radical Possibility of Limited Community-Based Interpretation of the Constitution," *William and Mary Law Review* 43 (2002): 927–1010.

[170] Schragger, "The Role of the Local in the Doctrine and Discourse of Religious Liberty," 1811.

[171] Hill, "North to the Future of the Right to Bear Arms," 146.

[172] *Id.*

[173] David J. Barron, "Why (and When) Cities Have a Stake in Enforcing the Constitution," *Yale Law Journal* 115 (2006): 2218–2253, 2252.

[174] *Id.* at 2238.

[175] *Id.* at 2252.

Taking seriously the uniqueness of large cities may also give rise to the possibility of recognizing distinct city-based identity and solidarity—often taken to be a defining attribute of a political community as such, and a supplemental argument for enhancing cities constitutional standing. Drawing on Federalist Paper No. 51, Jacob Levy argues that constituent units need to be sufficiently large to be able to generate citizen loyalty, independent of, perhaps even as an alternative to, their loyalty to the center.[176] To successfully serve as a check and balance on federal power, the constituent units must be able to compete for citizens' loyalty. As Loren King argues, cities may well qualify as a main source of identification by their residents and as "imagined communities" characterized by dense, spatial integration. and considerable interdependence among their residents.[177] If cities do "inspire durable loyalty," then they could be viable candidates "for recognized membership as distinct parties to a federal union."[178]

Daniel Bell and Avner de-Shalit argue that some cities have their own defining ethos or values.[179] These authors identify various cities by their main ethos, for example, Jerusalem as "the city of religion," Montréal as "the city of language(s)," Paris as "the city of romance," and New York as "the city of ambition." Idealist and somewhat cliché-ridden as their analyses may be, there seems to be at least a kernel of truth to their argument. As we have seen in earlier chapters, persistent city-based identities and loyalties are readily detectible, from Singapore's departure from the Malaysia Agreement or anti-China demonstrations in Hong Kong to the massive popular support by city residents for the transformation of Mexico City's constitutional status, and on to extensive city vs. state (e.g., Chicago) or city vs. province (e.g., Toronto) litigation. Less formal yet widely acknowledged are city-based identities such as *carioca* (a resident of Rio de Janiero), Hamburg German (a local dialect), or *"Medinat Tel Aviv,"* (Hebrew: "the state of Tel Aviv"), referring to the "city that never sleeps'" bustling and outgoing character in contrast with the rest of the country. (American readers will be familiar with city/sports team-related loyalty bases such as Red Socks Nation [Boston] or Steelers Country [Pittsburgh]). These instances of city identity bring us back full circle to the discussion in Chapter 1 of the near-exclusive treatment of states as the constituent territorial units of federalism. The modern nation-state has monopolized identity and solidarity bases. But the rise of large urban centers in what has been termed "the age of the city" may well challenge that hegemonic narrative.

---

[176] Jacob T. Levy, "Federalism, Liberalism, and the Separation of Loyalties," *American Political Science Review* 101 (2007): 459–477, 465.

[177] King, "Cities, Subsidiarity, and Federalism," 299–300.

[178] *Id.* at 316.

[179] Daniel A. Bell and Avner de-Shalit, *The Spirit of Cities: What the Identity of a City Matters in a Global Age* (Princeton University Press, 2011).

Conclusion

Several key arguments may be advanced for why the (non)constitutional status of cities and their dwellers no longer fits the bill of twenty-first-century urban realities. These may be divided schematically into: (i) *general arguments* (e.g., equal representation; anti-discrimination; multicultural accommodation; provision of minimum core of living conditions; immigrant and refugee rights) that are made especially applicable to urban settings given their demographic and socioeconomic realities; and (ii) *arguments that emanate from the urban condition itself*, and either refer to the city and its dwellers as core right holders (e.g., "the right to the city"), or see cities and their governments as more representative and more effective policy makers, owing to cities' relatively manageable size and the relative proximity of municipal government to its voting constituents.

In this chapter, I have advanced the claim that in addition to the consideration of general constitutional arguments, there are at least six additional arguments for extending constitutional status to cities, each emanating from the urban condition itself, that have not been given due attention in the pertinent literature. First, while the "one person, one vote" principle is commonly cited as the core tenet of political equality and democratic representation, constitutionally entrenched electoral rules may result in systemic underrepresentation and democratic deficits in large urban centers. In large cities as diverse as Toronto, Chicago, Zürich, Mumbai, and São Paulo, poorly apportioned electoral systems are structured in a manner that prevents increasingly large sections of a democratic polity's population from having equitable representation in a legislative body. In these instances, the voice of urban voters is worth less than that of others. As recent studies have further suggested, in nearly every single-member, first-past-the-post electoral system, urban vote is underrepresented. A move to proportional representation alongside the development of fresh ideas such as mixed rural-urban electoral districts may enhance urban voter representation and mitigate the incompatibility between extensive urbanization and rigid electoral systems that either unintentionally or by design underrepresent urban populations.

Second, there is a link between cities' constitutional weakness and their susceptibility to influence by the interests and policy preferences of big business. As cities are spatially anchored and constitutionally limited in their taxation capacity, private developer interests and corporate deep pockets sometimes become the most viable revenue option. Unlike cities, corporate capital is not spatially anchored, allowing corporations to engage in forum shopping or capital flight threats. Meanwhile, big business lacks neither the economic means nor the will to influence city-level decision-making. The result of the ever-increasing pressure on cities to deliver and compete, their lack of autonomously generated means of doing so, and the temptations of big business's deep pockets—accessible only at a political price—is to impel oversubscribed urban centers to cater to business interests, often at the expense of alternative, more broad-based and democratic if less lucrative, options.

Third, given that the vast majority of people live in cities, effective solutions to economic inequality and climate change should involve, emanate from, reside in, and apply to, the same. Constitutional empowerment of large cities bolsters their standing, representation, and taxation powers, and by corollary reduces their affinity with, perhaps even dependence on, corporate interests. This in turn may put cities in a better position to adopt more aggressive public housing and environmental protection schemes within their expanded jurisdiction.

Fourth, the massive concentration of people in cities, in particular in the Global South, means that the density factor should play a role in any serious conversation about the constitutional status of cities. At the very least, extreme density in urban poverty pockets impedes the realization of constitutionally entrenched economic and social rights, notably the right to housing and healthcare. It therefore accentuates the difference between de jure protection of these rights and their de facto delivery. As well, as more and more people cluster in cities, questions of spatially-based political underrepresentation of densely-populated urban agglomerations, and in particular of high-density slums, become acute. As the realities of politics and power unfold, the "one person, one vote" principle (itself too frequently compromised for urban dwellers) is not always sufficient in situations involving large populations who are involuntarily concentrated in extremely dense neighborhoods and uniquely impacted by certain issues over which they lack suitable political influence. In these instances, those living in extreme density areas may legitimately have a claim to augmenting their political voice in policy decisions pertaining to public housing, land development, education, healthcare, transit, and sanitation infrastructure, decisions that affect their interests most intensively as residents of extreme density areas.

Fifth, the severe socioeconomic inequality that exists among the districts of large cities, and the massive populations they contain, call for equalization of services and resources within the city. Intra-metropolis equalization would require a system of payments from better-off areas to support projects in areas that are worse off, akin to the systems of equalization payments between sub-national units in many countries, including Canada and Germany. Without meaningful constitutional status and robust taxation authority, cities lack the means of implementing this kind of redistribution scheme, while national and sub-national governments have little inclination or capacity to respond to the problem of inequality within cities.

Finally, as extensive urbanization marches on, megacities emerge, and spatial identity-bases shift, the continued consideration of province- and state-sized entities as the default constituent unit of federations ought to be revisited.

Similarly, large-scale demographic patterns and realities of diversity, integration, and social service provision put large urban centers in a substantively different position from any other form of "local government." This, I suggest, makes arguments from subsidiarity and stakeholding theory, commonly deployed with respect to the status of constituent units in transnational constitutional orders, highly relevant to discussions concerning constitutional dimensions of city power. It also opens the door for granting qualified autonomy to large urban centers in interpreting constitutional norms that are pertinent to the urban context, emphasizing a more pluralistic and spatially consciousness view of public law, and the relevance of concepts such as the margin of appreciation, non-territorial federalism, and community standards in the interpretation and application of constitutional norms. These different measures can be thought of as embryonic pathways toward a constitutional realization of the "right to the city."

Taken together, these various lines of argumentation form a strong and timely case in favor of extending enhanced constitutional standing to cities and their residents. In this "era of the city," the worldwide phenomenon of urbanization presents us with one of the main political and constitutional governance challenges of the twenty-first century. Unless and until cities achieve constitutional emancipation, they will continue to find themselves severely hampered in their ability to face the growing economic, social, spatial, political, and identity concerns and aspirations of city dwellers in the modern world. Widespread constitutional silence on the issue of city power thus exacerbates, rather than addresses, the challenges facing more than half of today's global population— and a larger share of humanity in tomorrow's world.

Acknowledgments

Over the past few years I have split my time between Toronto, whose metro area is home to a fifth of Canada's population; and Frankfurt, widely acknowledged to be one of Europe's most important business and transportation hubs. Academic engagements have taken me to countless other major metropoles, from Los Angeles, New York, and Chicago to Mexico City, São Paulo, Sydney, Tokyo, and Singapore. As one of the founding members and as former co-president of The International Society of Public Law (ICON-S), I have had the pleasure of contributing to the success of countless gatherings of public law scholars held in cities as diverse as Berlin, Copenhagen, Tel Aviv, Hong Kong, and Santiago de Chile. Yet, despite my own frequent encounters with the metropolis—and I would surmise this is true of the vast majority of my readers' own encounters with the same— our constitutional institutions, constitutional vocabulary, and constitutional imagination continue to operate under a Westphalian notion of the nation-state as the epicenter of the constitutional universe. This notion is challenged from above by a so-called post-Westphalian order, commonly construed as transnational, supranational, or global constitutionalism. Meanwhile cities are home to the majority of humanity, and are as omnipresent as they are crucial to today's society, culture, economics, and politics. Even so, cities seldom feature in constitutional texts, constitutional scholarship, or constitutional jurisprudence; oftentimes they do not make an appearance at all. This book begins to fill that gap.

Writing a book of this scope requires the invaluable contribution of many. Antoinette Handley, chair of the Department of Political Science at the University of Toronto, created a supportive and collegial work environment. Franziska Berg, Debbie Boswell, Valentin Büchi, Eileen Church Carson, Ryan Dorsman, Thoby King, Esther Lauer, Karlson Leung, Charis Lieberum, Michael Lutsky, Jan Mertens, Matthew Milne, Teraleigh Stevenson, Luis Sanchez Soto, Kerry Sun, Gabrielle Thompson, Janice To, Anju Xing, Jacob Webster, and Marinka Yossiffon provided excellent research assistance. Alex Hudson and Birgitt Sippel expertly helped with some of the graphics. Thoby King and Jen Rubio provided superb editorial assistance. Various colleagues, in particular Benjamin Boudou, Cora Chan, Chris Cochrane, Karol Czuba, Pierre de Vos, Theresa Enright, Moses Karanja, Madhav Khosla, Richard Schragger, Richard Stren, Anna Su, Steve Vertovec, and Arnold Weinrib, generously shared sources or helped with sage advice.

I presented various parts and chapters of this book in talks and conferences held at the National University of Singapore, the University of Göttingen, the University of Melbourne, the University of Milan, the University of Texas at

Austin, and at the University of Utrecht. I thank the organizers of these events, in particular Erika Arban, Antonia Baraggia, Gary Jacobsohn, Elaine Mak, Jaclyn Neo, and Alexander Thiele, for the opportunity to present my ideas, as well as the participants in these events for their insightful comments and suggestions.

I thank the series editors Richard Albert and Robert Schütze as well as Jamie Berezin at OUP, for their confidence in this project from its inception. Peter Olschinsky and Verena Weiss at Atelier Olschinsky's (Vienna) generously granted permission to use one of the striking images they created back in 2014 for the front cover of the book. Earlier versions of short parts of this book have been included in Ran Hirschl and Ayelet Shachar, "Foreword: Spatial Statism," *International Journal of Constitutional Law* 17 (2019): 387–438; Ran Hirschl, "Opting Out of 'Global Constitutionalism,'" *Law & Ethics of Human Rights* 12 (2018): 1–36; and Ran Hirschl, "Constitutional Renewal: Comparative Lessons for Canada," *Queen's Law Journal* 41 (2016): 1–10. I am grateful to these journals for permission to print in modified form several arguments originally published between their covers.

I gratefully acknowledge the generous research funding provided by the Alexander von Humboldt Foundation (through an Alexander von Humboldt International Research Award I was granted in 2016) and by the Max Planck Society (through a Max Planck Fellow Group in Comparative Constitutionalism). I thank Ulrike Beisiegel (former president of the University of Göttingen), and Matthias König (professor of sociology at that university), for their unflagging support of my nomination for the Humboldt Award.

Last, but certainly not least, three dear family members have shaped, each in her or his own distinct way, my thinking about the emerging urban challenge to constitutional thought. My late father-in-law Arie Shachar—a distinguished professor of geography and urban planning at the Hebrew University, Jerusalem— instilled the love for studying the megacity in everyone who knew him. My better half, Ayelet Shachar—a lifetime intellectual companion—offered tremendously valuable insights, theoretical and practical, from the inception of the project through to its conclusion. Her wisdom and our many hours of discussion together have made this book a considerably better one. Our son, Shai—currently an undergraduate student at Harvard—introduced me to the captivating world of cities, and in particular to the scientific thinking about complex transportation systems in an increasingly urbanized world. His fascination with and mastery of the urban scene, near and far, has given our extensive journeys together over the years a true sense of intellectual exploration. Finally, one of my favorite literary works of all time—Italo Calvino's *Invisible Cities*, a must-read novel for any aspiring comparativist—provided continuous poetic inspiration. In a deep, symbolic way, its title reflects the main theme of this book.

Ran Hirschl
March 2020

Table of Cases & Legislation Cited

For the benefit of digital users, indexed terms that span two pages (e.g., 52–53) may, on occasion, appear on only one of those pages.

ARGENTINA

Constitutional Provisions

Court Decisions

AUSTRALIA

Constitutional Provisions

Court Decisions

Legislation

AUSTRIA

Constitutional Provisions

BELARUS

Constitutional Provisions

BELGIUM

Constitutional Provisions

BRAZIL

Constitutional Provisions

Legislation

CANADA

Constitutional Provisions

Court Decisions

COUNCIL OF EUROPE

CZECH REPUBLIC

Constitutional Provisions

DENMARK

Court Decisions

Legislation

EGYPT

Constitutional Provisions

EUROPEAN UNION

Constitutional Provisions

Court Decisions

SOUTH AFRICA

SPAIN

SWITZERLAND

Constitutional Provisions

TURKEY

Constitutional Provisions

UKRAINE

Constitutional Provisions

UNITED KINGDOM

Legislation

UNITED STATES

Constitutional Provisions

Court Decisions

VENEZUELA

Constitutional Provisions

VIETNAM

Constitutional Provisions

Index

For the benefit of digital users, indexed terms that span two pages (e.g., 52–53) may, on occasion, appear on only one of those pages.

Tables and figures are indicated by *t* and *f* following the page number